The Vanishing Country

By the Same Author

The Betrayal of Canada

A New and Better Canada

At Twilight in the Country

*Pay the Rent or Feed the Kids: The Tragedy
and Disgrace of Poverty in Canada*

The Vanishing Country

IS IT TOO LATE

TO SAVE

CANADA?

MEL HURTIG

M&S

National Library of Canada Cataloguing in Publication Data

Hurtig, Mel
    The vanishing country: is it too late to save Canada? / Mel Hurtig.

Includes bibliographical references.
ISBN 0-7710-4215-9

1. Canada – Economic conditions – 1991-   2. Canada – Politics and government – 1993-   3. Canada – Social conditions – 1991-   4. Canada – Relations – United States.   5. United States – Relations – Canada.   I. Title.

FC635 H87 2002   971.064'8   C2002-903140-0
F1034.2.H86 2002

We acknowledge the financial support of the Government of Canada through the Book Publishing Industry Development Program for our publishing activities. We further acknowledge the support of the Canada Council for the Arts and the Ontario Arts Council for our publishing program.

Typeset in Minion by M&S, Toronto
Printed and bound in Canada

This book is printed on acid-free paper that is 100% ancient forest friendly (100% post-consumer recycled).

McClelland & Stewart Ltd.
The Canadian Publishers
481 University Avenue
Toronto, Ontario
M5G 2E9
www.mcclelland.com

1 2 3 4 5   06 05 04 03 02

This book is dedicated to our grandchildren,
Max, Jack, Benjamin and Paul,
Alanna, Katie, Arden, Georgia and Alia.
May their future be blessed.
May they live in times of peace.
May they share their good fortune with those in need.

CONTENTS

Part 4: The Differences Between Canada and the United States

Part 5: The Declining Country

Part 6: The Best Country

Canada Day, July 1, 2001.

Yesterday and today the papers have been full of stories claiming that one of Jean Chrétien's key policy advisors has suggested that Canada consider political union with the United States.

Now, Canada's two national newspapers are reporting a new public opinion poll showing that only 37 per cent of Canadians know the first line of our national anthem, almost half could not identify Canada's first prime minister, and overall 60 per cent failed a test asking simple questions about our country.

Today, after two years of research, I started writing The Vanishing Country.

Preface: A National Swan Song?

In my first book, *The Betrayal of Canada*, which was published in 1991, I warned that Canada was being destroyed by a powerful corporate elite and their representative, Brian Mulroney, "the least popular prime minister in the 124-year history of Canada."

I said that big business was now in control of our country's political agenda, and "They have little concern for the survival of Canada. Their goal is the rapid integration of Canada with the United States . . . the meshing of Canadian standards and policies with American policies, so that nothing stands in the way of their growing corporate power."

Those of us who fought the Free Trade Agreement during the 1980s and warned Canadians about the likely consequences of Brian Mulroney's plans and Ronald Reagan's "new economic constitution for North America" get little solace from the accuracy of our dire predictions.

Looking back, I can see now that I underestimated just how quickly Canada would change, and how rapidly our national sovereignty would dissolve.

Ultimately, this book is about only two questions. First, do you or do you not care about the survival of Canada?

And second if you *do* care, what *are* you going to do about the fact that our country is vanishing so rapidly?

The Vanishing Country will begin by reviewing where we've been as a country, and the often special, unique and successful policies proud Canadians developed over many generations.

Then we will look at the growing foreign ownership and foreign control of Canada and their impact on our sovereignty, our standard of living, and our quality of life. In this chapter we'll also look at the ominous likelihood of much greater foreign ownership and foreign control in the near future.

Next, we'll examine the Americanization of Canada, the important political, social, economic, and cultural changes that have followed the Free Trade Agreement (FTA) and the North American Free Trade Agreement (NAFTA). Then we'll again look at what we can expect in the future, a future that will, without question, bring even greater Americanization of our country.

Do Canadians want to become Americans? Do many Canadians think that we're going to become Americans, whether we like it or not? Are there important differences between Canadians and Americans, between Canada and the United States, and are these differences worth preserving? The chapters that will follow examine these questions.

Next, we'll come back to the question of standard of living and quality of life. Is it true, as we are told so often, that most Americans are much better off than most Canadians? Is it true that most Canadians still believe that we have a better quality of life?

The chapter that will follow will be all about why Canadians should fight to preserve their freedom to determine their own future, and why we should reject American standards and values before it's too late for us to do so.

One of the most important themes of this book looks at the huge differences between the goals of our political and corporate elites, and the wishes of the majority of Canadians. Exactly who are these people who are so quickly leading our country to oblivion, and what are their motives?

Two important questions follow. Why haven't our politicians done anything to stop the sellout of our country? And what role has the media played in the abandonment of long-standing Canadian values and policies?

Before we look at "The Best Country," the kind of egalitarian, just country I think most Canadians want, it's necessary to examine what has happened to our country since the election of Brian Mulroney in 1984 and the election of the Chrétien government in 1993. Has Canada changed for the worst? Are these changes important? What should our goals for the future be?

Lastly, in the conclusion of the book we'll examine the current political situation in Canada. If we have to make dramatic changes to save our country, where will these changes come from? Who will stand for Canada? Since we've gone from colony to nation, and are rapidly heading back to no better than a colony, is there anything we can do to save our country?

Towards the end of the book I discuss the four things that I believe *must* happen if Canada is to survive.

In 2000, Ekos Research Associates, the respected Ottawa-based polling firm, said, "it is our view that issues related to the themes of globalization and identity will emerge as the dominant national debate over the next five years." Moreover, most Canadians "harbour a strong commitment to preserving and enhancing a unique national identity" and "differences between Canada and the U.S. in the role of state and social policy have served as one of the touchstones of our national identity."

Author and columnist Lawrence Martin has written:

> How long can a country continue to integrate with a neighbour 10 times its population without eventually losing itself in the process?
>
> The most important debate is between the Canadian way and the American way. It's between corporate power and grassroots power, between democratization and corporate globalization, between North American union and no union.*

This book is about the tragic sellout of Canada. It's about a selfish, grasping, and greedy plutocracy abandoning the work of generations of Canadians, and the dreams of the vast majority of the people who live in this country, for American standards and values and priorities.

It's a book about avaricious and arrogant CEOs, cowardly public servants, and myopic academics who couldn't care less about national integrity, Canadian sovereignty and independence, or preserving the quality of life that has made Canada such a good country in the past.

While I have written on many of these subjects before, almost all of the research in the following pages is new and a great deal of it is important new material that is not available elsewhere.

And, while in the past few years I have presented a perspective about Canada that has been less than optimistic, never before have I encountered or heard from so many Canadians who are now answering "yes" to

---

* Southam News, June 4, 2001.

the question posed in the subtitle of this book. I think it's true that in recent years the degree of pessimism about the survival of Canada has reached levels never before seen in my lifetime.

I believe that it's not too late for us to save Canada, but for this to happen, important changes will have to be made very soon.

I hope readers of this book will consider the kind of country they want for their children and grandchildren and for future generations of Canadians.

A front-page *Washington Post* article by the paper's former Toronto correspondent argues that "many Canadians expect – even welcome – their nation's absorption into the United States."* The writer, one Steven Pearlstein, advises, "Economically, culturally, socially, demographically, even politically, Canadians say [Canada] is becoming indistinguishable from the U.S."† The title of the article was "O Canada! A National Swan Song?"

Andrew Cohen, then the *Globe and Mail*'s Washington correspondent, wrote of Mr. Pearlstein's piece:

> The report canvasses the views of Canada's leading industrialists, economists and thinkers. Unsparingly, they argue that the border between the two countries has vanished, that Canada has lost its distinctiveness, that Canada has become a satellite of the United States. In other words, Canada is through.
>
> As for any sense of civic nationalism holding the country together, well, that's gone too – particularly when it's defined largely in terms of social welfare programs.

Pretty bleak stuff. But is it necessarily true? Ultimately, I believe there is one key essential if we hope to save our country. I doubt that this solution will make sense to those who haven't read through the rest of this book. But I hope that those who do read the book will be convinced of the logic of my analysis.

And I hope they will then go to work to help save our country, before it's too late.

---

* *Globe and Mail*, September 11, 2000.
† Ibid.

Acknowledgements

My many thanks to all those who helped me with this book including my wife Kay Hurtig, my publisher Doug Gibson, and Julie Maloney, Marc Lévesque, Frank Graves, Michael Marzolini, Linda Grisley, Carole McCauley-Sinnett, Bruce Meyers, Gerald W. Boychuk, Andrew Sharpe, Kenneth Georgetti, Judy Webster, Dan Trefler, Joseph Martin, Barry Mersereau, Ross Finnie, David Perry, Harry W. Arthurs, Linda McQuaig, Stewart Taylor, Duncan Cameron, Doug Roche, Don Lowry, Daniel Dekoker, Peter C. Newman, Cathy Cotton, Dalton Camp, Paul Axelrod, Jane Stinton, Amanda Valpy, Michael Decter, Elizabeth May, Michael J. Prince, David Robinson, Paul Roberts, Mark Anielski, Andrew Jackson, Steven Shrybman, Jim Gillies, Giles Gherson, Richard Gwyn, Tom Kent, Eric Reguly, Isaiah Litvak, Scott Sinclair, Rod McQueen, Jim Travers, Paul Roberts, Tom Walkom, Desmond Morton, Paul Knox, Neil Brooks, Robert Hackett, Murray Dobbin, Jared Bernstein, Brian Murphy, Michael Wolfson, Gordon Laxer, Michael Adams, Jim Stanford, Tom Symons, Merrill Distad, Andrew Willis, Susan Riley, Jeff Simpson, Stephen Handelman, David Crane, Jennifer Zelmer, David Boyd, James Laxer, Mark Starowicz, Connie Connor and Duff Conacher.

BCNI Business Council on National Issues, now called the Canadian Council of Chief Executives. The powerful big business lobby group of 150 CEOs.

CAP Canada Assistance Plan. A program designed to transfer social money from Ottawa to other levels of government, mainly the provinces.

CCCE Canadian Council of Chief Executives (formerly BCNI).

CCPA Canadian Centre for Policy Alternatives.

CHST Canada Health and Social Transfer, the program which replaced the CAP.

CIBC Canadian Imperial Bank of Commerce.

COLLABORATORS term used in France for citizens who helped the Nazis during the German occupation in the Second World War.

COMMON MARKET A common market allows full circulation of goods, services, technology, capital, and people, with a common external tariff against imports from other countries.

COMPRADOR Agent of a foreign power.

CONTINENTALIST A term used to describe Canadians who believe in greater integration of Canada with the United States.

CRTC Canadian Radio-television and Telecommunications Commission.

CUSTOMS UNION The establishment of a comprehensive common tariff policy relating to imports and the free circulation of goods and services within the union.

DECILE A tenth of a quantity.

EI Employment Insurance.

EU European Union, presently composed of fifteen countries, but slated for expansion.

FIRA Foreign Investment Review Agency.

FDIIC Foreign direct investment in Canada. Direct investment represents significant ownership and control of a corporation.

FTA Free Trade Agreement between Canada and the U.S. which came into effect in 1989.

FTAA Free Trade Area of the Americas, a proposed agreement still under discussion.

G7 COUNTRIES Canada, France, Germany, Great Britain, Italy, Japan and the U.S.A. (Becomes G8 when Russia is included).

GATS General Agreement on Trade in Services, now being discussed in the WTO with a 2005 deadline for implementation.

GATT General Agreement on Tariffs and Trade. An international trade agreement that came into effect in 1948 and promoted liberalized world trade.

GDP Gross domestic product. The total output of goods and services for final use produced by both residents and non-residents in an economy.

GNP Gross national product equals GDP plus income from abroad, less payments to non-residents who participate in the domestic economy.

HMOs Health Maintenance Organizations (in the U.S.).

IMF International Monetary Fund.

IPO Initial public offering (of shares).

IRPP Institute for Research on Public Policy, founded in 1972, based in Montreal.

LICOs Low-income cut-offs are Statistics Canada thresholds, which are determined by analyzing family expenditure data, below which families will likely devote a larger share of income to food, shelter, and clothing than would the average family, adjusted for family size and community. Statistics Canada says LICOs are "A well-defined methodology that identifies those who are substantially worse off than the average" and those who are in "the most straitened circumstances."

LOW INCOME Low-income is broadly defined as incomes for families or individuals that are half or less of median income.

LOW INCOME GAP The amount that individuals or families fall below low-income or poverty lines.

MAI Multilateral Agreement on Investment, proposed by the OECD, the agreement met stiff opposition and foundered in 1998.

MARKET INCOME Market income is the total of earnings from employment, invested income, and retirement income. It is the same as total income less government transfers.

MEDIAN INCOME Median income is the point at which half of the population units have lower incomes and half have higher incomes.

MNCs Multinational corporations.

NAFTA North American Free Trade Agreement. The Canada–U.S.–Mexico agreement that came into effect in 1994.

NATO The nineteen-country North Atlantic Treaty Organization.

NEP National Energy Program.

OECD Organization for Economic Co-operation and Development. The organization of developed, industrial nations which has grown from twenty-seven to thirty countries in recent years.

POVERTY There is no official measurement of poverty in Canada. Social groups use the term to refer to those with incomes below the Statistics Canada LICO lines. Internationally, poverty is usually defined as living with an income less than 50 per cent of median disposable income. In common usage, poverty means deprived of the necessities of life, suffering, hunger, lack of proper shelter and clothing, and inability to take part in the community in a reasonable manner.

PLUTOCRACY Government by the wealthy elite.

PMO Prime Minister's Office.

PPP Purchasing power parity. The price in local currencies of the same goods and services. PPP rates provide a standard comparison of price levels between countries, whereas exchange rate comparisons may distort actual purchasing power.

QUINTILE A fifth of a quantity.

QUISLING A term originating in Norway referring to persons co-operating with the German invaders during the Second World War.

R & D Research and development.

TD Toronto Dominion Bank.

TRANSFER PAYMENTS Transfer payments generally refer to payments by Ottawa to the provinces or to individuals, or other payments made by the provinces. Transfer payments to individuals include old age security, Canada and Quebec pension plans, employment insurance, guaranteed income supplements, spouse's allowances, child benefit payments, welfare, workers' compensation benefits, GST credits, etc.

TSE Toronto Stock Exchange.

UNHDR *United Nations Human Development Report*, an annual UN publication.

UNHDI United Nations Human Development Index based on longevity, adult literacy, school enrolment, and real GDP per capita.

VICHY The puppet government in France that co-operated with the Germans in the Second World War.

WTO World Trade Organization, established in 1995 after final round of GATT negotiations. Headquartered in Geneva, the WTO has become increasingly interventionist and controversial, involving itself in matters far beyond trade. The WTO had 144 members in June 2002.

PART

1

The Good Country

How Fortunate We've Been to Live in Canada

Even when I was young, it always seemed to me that we were fortunate to live in Canada. My parents were in their teens and quite poor when they came to this country from Eastern Europe, but through hard work and determination they, and most of their friends, managed to work their way up out of poverty. By the time my parents were in late middle life, they lived in an attractive home and, while not wealthy, they were certainly comfortable and secure in their lives. They sent my two older brothers to university, where one became a doctor and the other a toxicologist.

One thing my parents and their friends had in common: they all thought Canada was a bountiful land of freedom and opportunity. And they had no hesitation in saying that they loved their country.

I was a child born in the Great Depression. I watched my two brothers go off to war, one of them serving overseas with the Canadian army for almost five years. I followed the war closely and when it was over, when my oldest brother finally came back to Canada and we heard his stories of heroism, terror, and sacrifice, I too began to count my blessings that I lived in such a fortunate country. I was, even beginning in my early teens, a proud Canadian.

I have always found it both amusing and perplexing when an interviewer asks me why I am "such a nationalist." Amusing, because I don't think that the ideas I have spoken and written about for the last forty years would be considered nationalistic in most other countries. Would, for example, the ideas of independence, self-determination, and freedom be considered nationalistic in the United States? Hardly. In fact they are the very cornerstones of proud American rhetoric about their own country.

By the time I was in my early thirties, I began to travel a great deal, mostly in Canada, but also in the United States, Europe, and Asia. The more I saw of our country, the more I marvelled at how huge and truly magnificent it is. The more I travelled elsewhere, while inevitably fascinated by what I saw, the more grateful I was to be a Canadian. I was not a chauvinist, not an aggressive flag-waver, but I was someone who recognized the good fortune of living in a very special and wonderful country, blessed by history, blessed with bountiful resources in an enormous area with a population density that was but a tiny fraction of that in the many crowded countries I visited around the world.

Without fail, on every trip anywhere between Cape Spear in Newfoundland and Long Beach on the west coast of Vancouver Island, between Windsor in the south and Tuktoyaktuk or Broughton Island in the north, I was constantly amazed at the beauty of our country.

The more I travelled, the more I read, the more of my fellow citizens I met, the more I realized how lucky I was, how very fortunate Canadians were.

Aside from our magnificent mountains, our spectacular three-ocean shorelines, our abundance of beautiful lakes, rivers, and waterfalls, with all their fresh water (and hydro power), plus our enormous forests, our mineral and petroleum reserves, and our bountiful agricultural land, aside from all these natural blessings, it wasn't too long before I realized there were many man-made reasons to increase my affection for my country.

It seemed to me that not only did we have a country with a relatively high standard of living and a promising, almost unlimited future, but it also seemed that over a period of generations we had managed to create a truly good country with a strong sense of shared values and for most Canadians, a good quality of life.

By and large, we had a caring, compassionate social philosophy. We were very much a free-enterprise economy, but we had a healthy mix of public and private ownership. We had government, but for the most part not too much government. Around the world we were invariably regarded as good people. Other people, by and large, liked and respected Canadians.

Without question, after the Second World War, a strong sense of Canadianism developed across most of the country. There was, more often then not, a feeling of a collective national purpose, of the development of a distinctive North American society where the ideas of the common good, of social responsibility, of pan-Canadian programs and values were taken for granted as reality or attainable desirable goals. There was pride in citizenship, not aggressive jingoism, but rather more a feeling of counting our blessings and acceptance of the concept of sharing our good fortune through programs such as equalization and publicly funded medicare.

As well, our population was relatively well-educated and our own Canadian culture, especially in painting, writing, and music, was much to be admired.

Journalist Richard Gwyn wrote about Canadianism:

> It means, essentially, the conviction that there is, on this side of the border, a distinctive and wholly valid way of being North American.
>
> In essence, this model amounts to a kinder and gentler way of being North American than the traditions and habits of Americans themselves. It is also more collectivist, with Canadians having a much stronger sense of reciprocal obligations – including the starkest cross-border difference of all, universal and publicly paid health care.
>
> A last strand of this model is the strong attachment to internationalism, and the pride that Canadians feel in our peace-keeping contributions and in our drive, by instruments such as the land-mines treaty, to promote global "human security."[*]

A utopia? Hardly. In the preface to *Betrayal*, I wrote:

> we did some things badly. Our treatment of the aboriginal people is a national and, more and more an international disgrace. Far too many Canadian men, women and especially children live in real, debilitating poverty. Our tax system, our laws relating to corporate concentration,

---

[*] *Toronto Star*, September 14, 2000.

and our laws governing the election and conduct of our politicians, are all desperately in need of radical reform.

Yes, there were lots of things wrong, lots of things that needed to be improved. But overall, after spending many years travelling across our country, there remained no doubt in my mind – Canadians were proud of their country and loved their country and they had good reasons for their pride and affection.

As we shall see in parts Two and Three in this book, all of this began to change with the election of Brian Mulroney in 1984.

I have asked an exceptional Canadian to write a few words about his vision of the kind of country we set out to create from the days of John A. Macdonald right up to the early Trudeau years. Tom Kent, journalist and distinguished public servant, has been, among other things, editor of the *Winnipeg Free Press*, deputy minister to two federal departments in Ottawa, head of a Royal Commission on the press, and a fellow-in-residence at the Institute for Research on Public Policy.

Late in his long experience of public affairs, L. B. Pearson remarked to me that he had usually felt closer to Scandinavians than to either the Americans or the British. His was a true reflection of the Canada that grew in the quarter century following the 1939–45 war.

Until then British traditions and styles had remained strong, uneasily mixed with the North American inheritance of a frontier society. After 1945, truly nothing could be the same again. With new ideas and a new economy came a distinct Canadian identity. The values were those of an equitable and equable society, its politics increasingly those of a liberal social democracy. The values endure. The politics have withered.

Equable means the tolerance of people secure in their equal rights, confident of justice and democracy. Equitable means a society where freedom is not only absence of restraint but opportunity open to all, where scope for economic entrepreneurship is married with public policies to protect the disadvantaged, to rectify abuses and limit inequalities.

Those values were expressed in economic policies that fostered steady growth and high employment; in increasingly accessible education and training; in extensive income supports; in universal health care and pensions. The effect, in combination with the moderately progressive taxation of the 1960s, was that the circumstances of life for people with average and lower incomes improved to an unprecedented extent. Canada became a significantly more equal society.

Postwar Canada had another distinction. Though small in numbers and modest in military force, Canadians were in the forefront of efforts for a just and peaceful world. We became respected moderators of disputes and keepers of peace; leaders in multilateral freeing of trade, in humanitarian relief, in development aid; identified not with one continent but with a distinct role in the diplomacy, security and betterment of nations.

There is little value in recalling those good days without considering how to correct what has gone wrong. It is not that the values of Canadians have changed. It is that politicians betrayed them.

One of the major themes in what follows is how our politicians and corporate elite have betrayed the values of generations of Canadians.

PART

2

The Sellout of Canada

Foreign Investment, Foreign Ownership, and Foreign Control

Three years ago, Peter C. Newman wrote:

> The trend has become a torrent . . . it's a fire sale resembling the liquidation of Eaton's . . . the Americanization of our economy is a disturbing new reality . . . we now control a smaller portion of our productive wealth than the citizens of any other country on earth. Instead of the proudly independent nation our founding fathers intended us to be, we are well on our way to becoming an economic colony of the Americans.
>
> Anything we attempt to do to assert our sovereignty – economic, cultural or political – will be brought to a standstill by the empire to the south of us. At this crucial juncture in our history we are led by a politician with only one priority: his government's re-election.[*]

Today, Peter Newman, one of the founders of the Committee for an Independent Canada, believes it's already too late, that we've forever lost our independence, the control of our destiny, and we've already, for all intents and purposes, lost our country.

---

[*] *Maclean's*, December 20, 1999.

In 1999, *Globe and Mail* columnist Eric Reguly, in a piece headlined "Americanization of Canada Inevitable," wrote: "The decline of Canada's economic sovereignty is actually much more extensive than the headlines suggest and the nationalists fear."[*] That was written not by some "rabid nationalist," but by a widely respected business journalist.

Note the word "inevitable." You'll see it often in what follows.

The levels of foreign ownership and control in Canada would not be tolerated by any developed country you can think of. For many good reasons.

Moreover, the foreign takeover of Canada has been accelerating. Every month more and more Canadian companies, of every description, are being taken over by non-residents, along with more and more land and resources. And, not only is Ottawa not concerned about the sellout of our country, incredibly they are actively encouraging it with sales agents around the world soliciting more of the same.

Not only are we selling our country, but much of the money foreigners use to buy up our industry, our resources, our wholesale and retail companies, our high-tech corporations – much of it is our own money. No other country, anywhere, would dream of allowing this to happen.

In the 1970s, a good majority of Canadians, and eventually even the Trudeau government in Ottawa, became very concerned about the rapidly growing levels of foreign ownership and foreign control in this country, which had reached 38 per cent of all non-financial-industry corporate revenue. The Foreign Investment Review Agency (FIRA) and other federal government action dropped this all the way back down to 27 per cent, a significant decline, but still well above the level for other developed countries.

After his election in 1984, one of the first things Brian Mulroney did was abolish FIRA and establish Investment Canada, an organization charged with soliciting even more foreign investment. The Chrétien government took the process a step further, establishing the toothless Industry Canada Investment Review Division, which has tracked foreign investment under the terms of Mulroney's obliging Investment Canada Act. Again, the goal was clear, to attract as much foreign investment as possible. By the time Brian Mulroney left office in 1993, there were thirty

---

[*] *Globe and Mail*, April 22, 1999.

industrial groups in Canada that were foreign-dominated in amounts ranging from 52 to 99 per cent.[*]

Since the Investment Review Division's records were first begun, June 30, 1985, until June 30, 2002, there have been a total of 10,052 foreign takeovers, of which only 1,394 were actually reviewed. Not one single takeover application has ever been rejected. Of the 10,052 takeovers, 6,437 were from the United States.

The following is most revealing and most important. The total of takeovers and new business investment tracked by the division during the 17 years since they were established amounted to more than $487 billion.

Stop for a moment and take a guess as to how much of that $487 billion was for takeovers, and how much was for foreign investment in new business in Canada. (Don't cheat by looking below!)

Okay, are you ready? A startling 96.6 per cent of the new foreign investment in Canada was for takeovers, and a paltry 3.4 per cent was for new business investment.

So the ramifications are clear. When Jean Chrétien, or our embassy in Washington, or John Manley, Paul Martin, or Tom d'Aquino, or our annual luncheons at Davos or in Manhattan solicit even more foreign investment in Canada, what they are doing is asking for more of the same, more of the sellout of their own country.

One has to ask – are these people stupid? Or is there some other explanation?

In front of me is a thick stack of pages from the Investment Review Division showing the monthly lists of takeovers. Here's the type of companies *taken over in one month*, randomly selected:

> producers of oil and gas, a paper roll manufacturer, a fabric and felt manufacturer, a data transfer services company, a wholesale fragrances and cosmetics firm, a distributor of aviation headsets, a pulp and paper equipment manufacturer, a distributor of petroleum products, a bottled water distributor, an alarm company, a manufacturer of electronic protection devices, an automobile auction business, a manufacturer of digital projection systems, a housewares and hardware distributor, a research firm developing hybrid seeds, a software developer, a consumer

---

[*] Readers should see *The Betrayal of Canada*, chart 16, for a more detailed look at percentages of foreign ownership in industries in Canada.

credit reporting firm, a computer hardware and software distributor, a manufacturer of detection and measuring systems, a golf retail chain, a wallpaper manufacturer, a distributor of plastic cups, a packaging material manufacturer, an education technology consulting firm, a fire protection sprinkler company, a wholesale clothing firm, a filter manufacturer, an insurance adjuster, a manufacturer of pressure valves, an internet software company, an industrial real estate firm, a natural gas pipeline company, a distributor and marketer of beef semen, a distributor of motorcycle parts and accessories, a home furnishing manufacturer, a construction equipment company, an automotive research and development company, a flooring manufacturer, a renter of construction equipment, a foundry, a vinyl products manufacturer, a moving company, a pest control firm. A shopping centre, a men's shirt manufacturer, a soil decontamination company, two inns, a market researcher, a catering company a carbonated beverage products firm, a career management firm, a distributor of golf equipment, a plastics manufacturer, a material handling equipment company a polymer bearings and seal company, a pharmaceutical research firm, an engine design firm, an advertising company, a laboratory testing and consulting company, a tool distributor, a kitchen manufacturer, a polar bear observation business, a teleconferencing firm, a seismic data services company, and a recycling company,

all in one single month!

And where were these companies located? In Calgary, Sherbrooke, Arnprior, Markham, Brossard, Mississauga, Gravenhurst, Vancouver, Saint John, Penticton, Winnipeg, Toronto, Les Cèdres, Kitchener, Saint-Laurent, Chatham, Burnaby, Brampton, Concord, Montreal, Moncton, Ottawa, Tilsonburg, Balzac, London, Magog, Waterloo, Thunder Bay, Burlington, Edmonton, Halifax, Hamilton, Niagara-on-the-Lake, Kelowna, Val d'Or, Richmond, Oakville, Etobicoke, Peterborough, Port Stanley, and Churchill.

All in one month!

Want to see the current or previous monthly lists of takeovers, even if it's guaranteed to make you depressed? If so, go to <investcan.ic.gc.ca>.

It would take pages and pages to list even a good sample of the prominent and important Canadian companies that have been taken over by non-residents in recent years, so it's difficult to decide which ones to select here as examples.

Let me mention only a diversified few. MacMillan Bloedel, Westcoast Energy, Club Monaco, Consolidated Bathurst, Tim Hortons, Canadian Hunter Exploration, Future Shop, John Labatt, Connaught Laboratories, Norcen Energy, Husky Oil, Canstar Sports, the Montreal Canadiens, Angus Reid, BioChem Pharma, Spar Aerospace, Beaver Lumber, Allelix Biopharmaceuticals, Moore Corp., Saville Systems, Vickers & Benson, Seagram Co. Ltd., Shoppers Drug Mart, and Highway 407 in Ontario, to name but a handful.

In the late 1970s, when an outside company tried to take over B.C.'s forestry giant MacMillan Bloedel, the province's largest company, the premier responded angrily, "B.C. is not for sale." But in 1999, when the American firm Weyerhaeuser gobbled up MacMillan Bloedel, there was hardly a protest.

But not to worry. For Canada's extraordinarily myopic former ambassador to the U.S., Raymond Chrétien, the process of "the devouring of corporate Canada" (as described by Eric Reguly) is but "part and parcel of the integration of North America." Mr. Chrétien is Jean Chrétien's nephew.

The takeover of MacMillan Bloedel Ltd. was a tragic case. *Toronto Star* economics and business columnist David Crane described the process well:

> Those Americans certainly have a lot of nerve.
>
> First, they pressured the White House and the U.S. Congress to compel Canada into limiting its exports of softwood lumber to the United States even though Canadian softwood lumber exports were traded fairly and without subsidy.
>
> The effect has been to reduce profits, employment and needed new investment in Canada's softwood lumber companies.
>
> Next, the Americans turn around and start buying up Canada's major softwood lumber producers, which are available at a cheap price – in part due to the constraints of the softwood lumber agreement.
>
> Weyerhaeuser could become one of the largest holders of forest lands in British Columbia:
>
> Is that what Canadians want?[*]

---

[*] *Toronto Star*, June 24, 1999.

I can't do better than Crane in describing the appalling $13 billion take-over of Westcoast Energy, a takeover no other developed country in the world would have allowed.

> There is no Canadian benefit from the takeover. But there is a great potential cost.
>
> Westcoast is an important Canadian enterprise, operating major pipelines that deliver natural gas to Canadian and U.S. companies. The company also owns Union Gas in Ontario, has been active in electricity generation and is a key shareholder in the Foothills Pipeline, the project to bring Alaska gas through Canada to U.S. markets.
>
> More recently, Westcoast joined Ballard Power Systems Inc. and Shell Hydrogen to form Chrysalix Energy LP to invest in early-stage companies with growth potential in the fuel-cell and hydrogen business.
>
> Westcoast is also highly profitable. It reported a record $340 million profit for common shareholders last year, 53 per cent more than the $222 million profit in 1999.
>
> In the takeover, corporate control and top jobs will migrate to the United States. Canada will be left with another branch plant.
>
> The big issue is that if we continue down this path of selling off major Canadian enterprises, Canada will become simply a derivative economy, lacking the scale to compete internationally.
>
> Under the takeover plan, almost all strategic head office functions of Westcoast would be transferred from Canada to the United States. Responsibility for Westcoast's Mexican, Chinese and other foreign operations would also go to the United States. Canadians who wanted these kinds of jobs would have to move to the United States.

So much for Paul Martin's and John Manley's concerns about the necessity of building strong Canadian multinational corporations based in this country. Crane continues:

> If the government of Prime Minister Jean Chrétien was really concerned about the hollowing out of Canada, Ottawa would block the sale of Westcoast. Unfortunately, this is highly unlikely because the federal government, like much of our business community, is terrified of doing anything that might upset the United States, and one U.S. goal is to gain greater control of our oil and gas industry.

The biggest issue is whether the Chrétien government even cares about the hollowing out of corporate Canada. There's no real evidence Ottawa does, which would mean that we are even farther along the road to becoming the 51st state of the United States, which would make Conrad Black, at least, happy.[*]

But what about the Investment Canada net benefit test for takeovers? Forget it. It's nothing more that a shameful, cruel joke. The takeover of hundreds of companies such as Westcoast clearly could not meet any intelligent net benefit to Canada qualifications.

But surely some of the press must be concerned. Here's a sample from a *Globe and Mail* editorial: "The news that Future Shop has become yet another Canadian retailer snapped up by a U.S. company will have been greeted with a collective shrug. And why not?"[†]

How much of Canada is Foreign-Owned and Foreign-Controlled? The Less the Public Knows, the Better

In what follows, please bear in mind two important points.

First, Statistics Canada is usually two to three years behind in reporting figures on the percentages of foreign ownership and foreign control. The percentage figures that follow will be for 1999, the latest available.

Second, in 2000 foreign direct investment (FDIIC) in Canada broke all previous records, by far. During the entire decade of the 1980s, FDIIC increased by a total of $66 billion. By comparison, in 1998, 1999, and 2000 alone, it increased by a total of $165 billion for the three years.[**]

In 1999, Jeff Rubin, chief economist at the CIBC, suggested that "Foreign control may now have reached, if not surpassed, the peak set in 1971."

---

[*] *Toronto Star*, November 6, 2001.
[†] *Globe and Mail*, August 16, 2001.
[**] Statistics Canada, *Canada's international investment position*, 2001.

About 69 per cent of all revenue from foreign direct investment in Canada goes to American firms.

Altogether in Canada there are now at least three dozen industries majority-foreign-owned and -controlled, including chemicals and chemical products, rubber, automobiles and trucks, the electrical apparatus industry, computers, non-metallic mineral products, mineral fuels, food processing and packaging, tobacco products, and machinery. The manufacturing industry in Canada is now over 50 per cent foreign.

By September 2001, there were 13,344 foreign-controlled corporations in Canada, and that number has been increasing every week since. About 7,000 were owned by Americans.

As bad as it is, foreign ownership in Canada is, for the most part, grossly understated. For example, if a Canadian company is taken over by a foreign firm, and the foreign firm's subsidiary in Canada finances the takeover with money it has obtained in Canada from a Canadian bank or another financial institution, or from any other source in Canada, Statistics Canada's balance of payments would not record the transaction in its foreign direct investment tables.

Another reason that foreign direct investment in Canada is badly understated relates to the fact that when Industry Canada calculates the amount of FDIIC, the calculations are based not on the actual market value of the corporation that has been taken over or even the price paid. Instead, the calculation of increased foreign ownership is based on the depreciated corporate book value, a figure that is invariably well below both the market value and the actual value of the transaction.

Yet another reason why the amount of foreign direct investment in Canada is often understated may be found in a trend that began to accelerate in 1997. This relates to when foreign corporations (mostly U.S.) began increasing their financing of takeovers of Canadian corporations by issuing large amounts of their own treasury shares, then exchanging them for the shares in the Canadian firms. Often, little or no cash is involved. As a result, business-page analysts who look only at dollar inflows frequently miss the boat in measuring the extent of FDIIC.

There's still another reason why foreign direct investment in Canada is understated. Even though responses to Statistics Canada's corporate surveys on the subject are mandatory, the actual response rates are below 80 per cent. Although Statistics Canada has the legal authority to compel responses, it doesn't do so.

Moreover, for all those who rely on the figures from the Investment Review Division, it's important to know that the agency does not keep track of the expansion of foreign corporations already in Canada.

How much does Ottawa want other Canadians to know about foreign ownership in Canada? The answer is, not very much at all, thank you. The excellent Petroleum Monitoring Agency, which once reported in detail on foreign ownership, assets, and sales in the industry, has been shut down. The once-splendid Statistics Canada annual report on foreign-owned corporations is now a truncated shadow of its former self and we can no longer learn what percentage of dozens of key industries are foreign-owned and foreign-controlled.

And, beyond any logical comprehension, John Manley abolished many of the public reporting requirements of foreign corporations in Canada, making it impossible to measure vitally important aspects of their operations.

The less the public knows the better. Where once it was possible to compare the sales and profit of foreign corporations in Canada with the number of their employees in this country, we can no longer do so. It had always been insightful to see how few Canadians were employed for every million dollars in foreign corporation sales. Since foreign corporations import far more parts and components and services from their parent companies, the contrast with Canadian-owned operations was invariably dramatic.

Now, such comparisons are no longer available. The information for companies such as Canada Safeway Ltd., IBM Canada Ltd., Daimler-Chrysler Canada Inc., Ford, and General Motors no longer has to be disclosed to the public.

So, General Motors of Canada Ltd. makes a huge profit in Canada in 1997 ($2 billion?) but since Ottawa changed the rules, the Canadian public is not privy to this information. But the CEO of General Motors warns Canadians, "Make no mistake . . . taxes in Canada are too high."

Manley's strange move was originally planned by bureaucrats in the Mulroney government. Somehow, they convinced the green new Industry Minister that it would be okay to wipe out the requirement that all federally incorporated private companies had to file annual statements that were available for public examination. They don't call him "Governor Manley" for nothing. Won't it be interesting to check the financial contributions to his leadership campaign.

Forgive me if I return to a point I have been making for years. No one in Ottawa, repeat, *no one*, has any idea as to how much of the takeover of Canada is being financed with our own money. Paul Martin and John Manley don't know, the people at the Department of Finance don't know; Bank of Canada Governor David Dodge and his economists and statisticians don't know; and no one in Industry Canada or Statistics Canada knows. And, why don't they know? The answer is simple. They don't care. Nor does there seem to be a Member of Parliament or a member of the press gallery in Ottawa who has figured out that the financing of foreign ownership is an important question that should be asked of the Prime Minister and the Minister of Finance.

Let's turn to the words of the Investment Review people:

> The source of funds used to establish or acquire a business is often unknown. It may be brought in from abroad, or obtained from a variety of sources within Canada. In some cases, very little capital may be brought into Canada by the foreign investor.

So, as but one of thousands of examples, the Caisse de dépot et placement du Québec supplies a cash-strapped American with $140 million so he can buy the Montreal Canadiens.

"In some cases, very little capital may be brought into Canada." No kidding. It should read "In most cases . . ."

Yet the assumption in both government and business in Canada has always been that Canada needs foreign investment and is dependant on increasing imported flows of foreign capital. Almost all of our newspaper financial columnists take this as a given. Little wonder. The Industry Canada document *A Primer on Foreign Direct Investment Trends* repeatedly refers to "inward" foreign investment, "inflows," "inward stock," etc. But if you ask some of the Ottawa Industry Canada experts on foreign investment if they or anyone else knows how much of the takeovers are financed in Canada, the answers are difficult or impossible to get.

Let me give you one recent example. A widely circulated government document refers to the large amount of foreign investment coming into Canada "from the U.S." But when I queried the government economist author, he admitted that he didn't have the faintest idea of how much of this foreign investment actually came in "from the U.S."

One last point about Investment Review. The threshold for reviews increases every year. In 2002 it amounted to $218 million. That means that any takeover below that amount is not screened for "significant benefit to Canada."

Not that it makes much difference. The review process is essentially a charade, a pretense. As indicated earlier, not one takeover has been rejected and there's no public record of any successful efforts to compel foreign corporations to keep the promises they made in their takeover applications.

Tom d'Aquino and his fellow patriots at the Business Council on National Issues (BCNI), since renamed the Canadian Council of Chief Executives, have been complaining for years that Canada isn't getting enough foreign investment. Let's turn to official Statistics Canada figures and look at the total amount of new foreign direct investment by decade:

1970s	$32 billion
1980s	$66 billion
1990s	$126 billion

In every year from 1994 to 1999, all previous records for foreign direct investment in Canada were broken. Then, in 2000 FDIIC exploded to another new record of over $44.7 billion, an amount that an official from Statistics Canada said was "Amazing. It just blew us away."[*]

Not enough new foreign direct investment? In 1999, as a percentage of GDP, new FDI in Canada was greater than that in the United States, France, Germany, Italy, or Japan. That is, in every G7 country except Britain. In 2000 it was greater than in all other countries.

In 2000 there was a new record of 509 Canadian firms taken over by foreign non-residents. The value of these takeovers, according to the Investment Review Division, was a startling $81.8 billion. The previous record, set the year before, was $18.1 billion.[†]

So, let's do a quick recap. Foreign direct investment in Canada in the 1990s far exceeded all previous records. By 2000 it was over two-and-a-half times as much as it was in 1990 and over four-and-a-half times as

---

[*] Telephone conversation, December 7, 2001.

[†] The Investment Review Division Figures and those of Statistics Canada don't match because to a certain extent they are "apples and oranges." The figures above are accurate per the Division's records.

much as it was in 1980. Now let's hear some more from some of our country's salesmen and women.

In July, 1998, Terence Corcoran, then of the *Globe and Mail*, told his readers "foreign investors are sharply curtailing their investments in Canada."[*]

A couple of months later, an article in *Canadian Business* told us "from a U.S. perspective, Canada has not been a great place to invest since 1991."[†]

Soon after, in 1999, the senior vice-president of the Alliance of Manufacturers and Exporters, under a headline that said "Foreign Direct Investment in Canada Is Drying Up," advised that in terms of foreign investment Canada is being left out, with three strikes against us.

In January 2000, Sherry Cooper, one of our most notorious continentalists, and Bank of Montreal executive vice-president, told her readers in the *National Post* that "Net foreign direct investment – investment in businesses and real estate – has been dampened, no doubt, by our punitive corporate tax rates."[**]

And while all foreign investment records continued to be shattered, a *Globe and Mail* columnist told his readers that "On foreign investment we simply don't rate as a destination of choice."[††]

A few days later another *Globe* columnist said that concerns about growing foreign ownership were "hysterical."[***]

Not to be outdone, the Conference Board stressed "the importance of boosting our ability to attract FDI," since "our record casts doubt on our relative attractiveness as a place to set up shop," which is a "cause for deep concern."

What can you make of all of these people? Have they been living in caves in Afghanistan? Or are they simply so blinded by their radical-right continentalist ideology that they consider it unnecessary to check with official regularly published records at Statistics Canada, Industry Canada, or the Bank of Canada, before they write their nonsense?

---

[*] *Globe and Mail*, July 14, 1998.
[†] *Canadian Business*, September 25, 1998.
[**] *National Post*, January 11, 2000.
[††] *Globe and Mail*, May 19, 2001.
[***] Janet McFarland, *Globe and Mail*, June 2, 2001.

On a CBC network morning radio show Tom d'Aquino tells listeners that the BCNI wants much more foreign investment in Canada. We're "missing the boat not attracting more. I see no danger in Americans, Japanese, and Germans owning Canadian companies . . . I have no problem with that; they're model citizens." Anyway, regarding the Americans, "we've bought up more of their economy than they have of ours."[*] And we could get even more foreign investment if Canada didn't have such an "unfriendly regulatory environment and anti-business bias."

On the same show, right-wing McGill economist and *National Post* columnist William Watson, when asked by me how much of the country he'd be prepared to sell, promptly responded that he'd be prepared to sell the whole country, depending on the price he could get. We should leave it to the market.

We'll come back to d'Aquino's misleading statement about Canadians buying up the U.S., but let's summarize what we've been hearing from the radical right in our country:

- We need not worry about the extent of foreign ownership and control in Canada.
- In fact we need even more, much more, and it's terrible that foreign investment has been drying up.

While d'Aquino and his sellout friends complain about not enough foreign investment and blame Canadian taxes, a report prepared for Industry Canada paints quite a different picture: "Canada enjoys relatively low costs of doing business compared to many other developed countries, including the United States." As to the question of Canadian taxes, the report goes on to say that the volume of inward FDI is not consistent with taxes being a major factor.[†]

Meanwhile, as Canadian pundits and our myopic business leaders were lamenting about what a rotten place Canada is to invest in, *The Economist* magazine studied twenty-five developed countries and

---

[*] CBC *This Morning*, December 13, 1999.
[†] *Assessing Recent Patterns of Foreign Direct Investment in Canada and the United States,* Steven Globerman and Daniel Shapiro, May 2001.

ranked Canada ahead of twenty-one of them in terms of an "attractive business environment" and said we were clearly one of the best places in the world to do business.

Has Canada been a bad place to invest? Here are the words of Morgan Stanley Dean Witter's vice-president and economist Jim Johnson:

> Canada has both the commodities and the good quality labour to cater to increased demand . . . You've got very well-educated people, plenty of them. You've got good urban centers with good infrastructure. High-tech industry needs intelligent, well-educated workers and good infra-structure, and Canada has that in abundance.

Is Canada a good place in which to do business? As I mentioned in my last book, KPMG has reported that of all the G7 countries, Canada has the lowest costs of doing business, almost 8 per cent lower than the U.S., and "costs in Canadian cities examined are consistently lower than in U.S. cities." And, in a more recent, more expansive ten-month KPMG study, "Internationally, Canada is again the most cost-competitive country in which to do business." Canadian cities finished on top in seven of twelve business categories studied in an examination of eighty-six cities.*

What does Canada offer investors? A well-educated workforce, sophisticated infrastructure, substantial R&D incentives, advanced technology, and an excellent quality of life. According to another recent study, four of the world's top ten best cities to live in are in Canada – Vancouver, Toronto, Ottawa, and Montreal.

Studies show that Canada is competitive compared to most other developed countries in terms of information-technology infrastructure, the abilities of our workers in knowledge industries, unit labour costs, transportation and distribution costs, manufacturing, electricity costs that are almost a third lower than in the U.S., construction costs, land costs, low crime levels, excellent leisure facilities, lower payroll taxes, lower health care costs, low inflation and interest rates, etc.

Now, stop for a moment and consider. Isn't all of this truly amazing? On the one hand, the Canadian government is almost down on its hands and knees going around the world begging for even more foreign owner-ship and foreign control; and at the same time its own government

---

* See *Comparative Alternatives*, G7, 2002 edition.

reports and advertising extol the multitude of reasons why Canada is such a good place to do business.[*]

If it's such a good place to do business with so many advantages, *why* should we be selling off our businesses to non-residents? If it's such a good place to do business, why sell off ownership and control when you know for certain that as a result profits will hemorrhage out of the country, tax revenue as a percentage of sales will be sharply reduced, good jobs will be fewer, and key decisions about your country will be made outside of Canada by people who don't give a damn about your country?

Meanwhile, as money managers and analysts in Toronto call for even greater relaxation of rules so that even more Canadian savings can be pumped out of the country, and as people like d'Aquino, Jack Mintz, President of the C. D. Howe Institute, and Conrad Black expound on the need for radical changes closer to American standards, isn't it remarkable that in recent years thousands of our companies have been taken over by foreigners who think that Canada – thank you very much – is a dandy place to do business?

How can we explain this? Is there any logical explanation? Before we look at foreign ownership in the United States and other countries, let's look at the hollowing-out of Canada to see if we can better understand why other countries that are buying up Canada would never allow so much of their country to be sold off to foreign control.

The Hollowing-Out of Canada: Don't Order Toilet Paper!

I have many favourite Brian Mulroney quotes. Let me mention only two.

> Free trade with the United States is like sleeping with an elephant. It's terrific until the elephant twitches, and if the elephant rolls over you are a dead man.[†]

---

[*] See for example the glossy material from Investment Partnerships Canada and <investiraucanada.ic.gc.ca>.
[†] Speech at Thunder Bay, 1983.

Here's the second:

> I've yet to see a takeover that has created a single job – except of course for lawyers and accountants.[*]

As we've seen, most foreign direct investment is for takeovers. And takeovers usually result in layoffs. We'll examine some of the economic downsides of foreign ownership shortly, but first let's look at how corporate Canada is being hollowed out.

By the mid-1980s, about half of the major U.S. corporations in Canada were 100-per-cent American-owned. Ten years later, some 85 per cent had no Canadian shareholders. And in the latest *Financial Post* list of the fifty largest foreign-controlled corporations in Canada, forty-six were 100-per-cent foreign-owned.[†]

As Canadian shareholders were eliminated, corporate boards were substantially reduced in size and more American directors were added, as were more U.S. CEOs and board chairmen. As external directors were eliminated, there was no longer a force to influence policy decisions which would be beneficial to Canada. Gone too was the ability to scrutinize the payment of dividends, management fees, and content costs paid to the parent company. Increasingly, local advertising, insurance, travel agencies, and many other companies are bypassed as head offices in the U.S. make purchasing decisions.

York University's President Emeritus, professor Harry W. Arthurs, has written eloquently on the impact of foreign ownership and the FTA and NAFTA agreements on Canada:

> For many Canadians, globalization, regional integration within NAFTA and continentalism are all more or less synonymous; all imply closer integration of Canada into the economic structures, idiosyncratic ideology and the powerful culture of American capitalism.[**]

Where in the past, foreign corporations operating in Canada

---

[*] *Where I Stand*, Toronto: McClelland & Stewart, 1983.

[†] *FP 500*, June 2002.

[**] "Globalization of the Mind: Canadian Elites and the Restructuring of Legal Fields," *Canadian Journal of Law and Society*, vol. 12, no. 2, 1999.

established subsidiaries which operated as "mini-replicas" of the parent firm, produced a relatively full line of goods for Canadian customers, raised capital in Canadian markets and were run by Canadian-based directors and managers who enjoyed a degree of autonomy from the parent firm [it was now] possible and profitable for transnational companies to alter these arrangements [often reducing] their operations in Canada to the point where they now do little more than distribute goods made elsewhere.

Foreign head office control has generally become more intrusive and extensive. Corporate functions once performed in Canada are assigned to absentee managers, service providers and professionals. These new arrangements increase the likelihood that deliberately, or by inadvertence, corporate decisions will be made without particular regard for Canadian law, conventions of business behaviour or the sensibilities of local communities or governments.

These outcomes are made more likely by the erosion of the formal channels through which Canadian perspectives were once transmitted to the transnational parent company: the senior management and board of directors of the Canadian subsidiary. . . . Canadian boards of directors survive, if at all, only in vestigial form; their managements are accountable not to Canadian directors but directly to the foreign head office . . . neither directors or managers are in a position to exert much influence. . . . These "hollowed out" Canadian subsidiaries are likely to be less willing or able to argue against plant closures or for extended product mandates or for a larger share of global R&D activities.

And they are very likely to contend that there is not much Canada can do to alter the mix.[*]

Moreover, in an effect now being felt across Canada, as foreign ownership and control continues to grow.

If the present trends continue, if the head offices of Canadian subsidiaries disappear or are confined to a narrow range of functions, if Canadian operations are increasingly managed by U.S.-centred regional

---

[*] IBM Canada Ltd. has a grand total of one director, Ford Motor Co. of Canada Ltd. and Canada Safeway Ltd., three each, Cargill, Toyota and General Electric Canada, five directors.

business units, we can expect some deterioration of the quality of Canadian metropolitan life.[*]

Of course, in the process of hollowing out, the impact falls on local restaurants, the clothing stores, the flower shops, the United Way, the local sports teams – you name it. In Arthurs's words, on "just about all elements of Canadian society."[†]

Gone too will be much of the tax revenue needed to pay for the "kinder, gentler society generations of Canadians developed as an alternative to the crueler, harsher American model," which we shall examine shortly.

Eric Reguly is direct and to the point, commenting on Arthurs's work:

> The hollowing-out trend has been in place for years and is the result of globalization, trade liberalization, economic integration and deregulation, all of which make it unnecessary for U.S. and multinational corporations to keep full-fledged, independent subsidiaries in Canada.
>
> Now the key functions have been transferred to head office, leaving the subsidiaries as branch plants that can't order toilet paper without getting approval from some pencil pusher in New York or Chicago or Atlanta.[**]

And more recently:

> The problem with the Great Canadian sellout is that it eliminates head offices, the lifeblood of any big city. Head offices provide the top-paying careers that can keep Canada's best and brightest from fleeing. They support and nurture other careers and jobs, from accountants and designers to chefs and cab drivers.[††]

And, if we keep selling off the country, "You will see a ghost town in downtown Toronto."[***]

---

[*] Ibid.
[†] Ibid.
[**] *Globe and Mail*, November 18, 1999.
[††] *Globe and Mail*, May 31, 2001.
[***] *Titans*, Global TV, April 30, 2001.

Is it not remarkable then that the very same men who complain so vociferously about the "brain drain" also are the most enthusiastic advocates of selling off even more of our country to foreign ownership?

One of the best discussions, and one of the most ominous, of the "hollowing out" of business in Canada is Isaiah Litvak's *The Marginalization of Corporate Canada*. Since the 1989 FTA and the 1994 NAFTA,

> Not only has Canada's direct power as a nation state been weakened, but its indirect power as well, namely, its ability to co-opt Canadian companies to serve Canadian national and global interests.[*]

Beginning with the election of the Mulroney government in 1984, such policies as restrictions on foreign ownership and any thoughts of industrial strategies

> gave way to pressures clamouring for privatization, deregulation, lower taxes and a hands-off, market-driven philosophy.
>
> Deregulation, privatization, free trade, and a welcoming policy towards multinational corporations became a Mulroney government mantra, largely adopted by its successor – the Liberal government elected in 1993.[†]

Once the FTA and NAFTA were in place, the agreements

> gave U.S. corporate management added scope and incentive for realizing increased economies of scale.[**]

This, along with the substantial increase in foreign ownership helped

> marginalize the Canadian business voice. The residual decision-making powers of Canadian subsidiaries of U.S. and other foreign multinationals have been substantially reduced, and a growing number of Canadian MNCs are more preoccupied with policy input in the United States than in Canada. The Canadian chemical industry is a case in

---

[*] Canadian Institute of International Affairs, Toronto, 2001.
[†] Ibid.
[**] Ibid.

point. Largely U.S. dominated, the Canadian subsidiary head offices of the major U.S. MNCs have virtually disappeared or have become mere shadows of what they used to be. The one major Canadian controlled chemical company, NOVA Chemicals, is now operationally headquartered in the United States.[*]

During the 1990s, "strategic elements and/or functions of Canadian MNC decision-making activities were transferred to U.S.-based subsidiaries." So now, "there is little economic justification for a Canadian headquarters. The free trade agreement accelerated the hollowing pace of U.S. subsidiary head offices in Canada and encouraged further rationalization and integration of Canadian operations with U.S. domestic operations." And, for Canadian corporations with assets in the U.S., it often meant a North American headquarters located in part or in whole in the United States" and "the political downgrading of the Canada–U.S. business borders." John Roth and Nortel were perfect examples. "By late 1999, only 28 of the company's top 400 executives were located in Canada." Yes, that's the same John Roth who in speech after speech warned Canadians about the "brain drain" while paying his employees in Canada significantly less than his similar employees were paid in the U.S. Meanwhile, IPSCO moved its executive offices from Saskatchewan to Illinois and the Thomson Corporation's operating head office was in Connecticut.

In industries such as petroleum, automotive, chemicals, pharmaceuticals, and information technology, the dominant foreign presence often inhibits the development of policy positions in the Canadian national interest. According to Isaiah Litvak:

> It is not merely Canadian corporate citizenship that is gradually eroded – it is also management's Canadian national sensitivities. In essence, the Canadian corporate decision-making platform is being marginalized by both Canadian MNCs and U.S. MNCs with Canadian subsidiaries.
>
> Canadian free trade critics were right to assume that the gravitational pull from the south would undermine the east-west forces, many of which were artificially created by successive national governments since Confederation.[†]

---

[*] Ibid., as are the quotations in the following paragraph.
[†] Ibid.

Perhaps some were artificial, but they were intentional and purposeful; they were designed to build an independent nation on the northern half of the North American continent.

David Crane nicely sums up what has been happening:

> The voice of Canadian business has been marginalized . . . decision-making powers have been substantially reduced. The Canadian companies now become "mere shadows of what they used to be."
>
> Canadian industry associations are becoming less important while membership in U.S. industry groups is becoming more important.[*]

Litvak spells out the result:

> Nominal "Canadian" CEOs of such companies no longer possess the clout or status of their pre-free-trade-era predecessors.

Even the conservative, big-business Conference Board of Canada warned about the hollowing-out process in a June 2001 report. High-paying jobs are disappearing, the tax base is being diminished, senior executives and other key officials are being forced to move to head offices in the U.S. if they want to keep their jobs. Key decisions about plant locations, R&D, product development, etc. are moved out of Canada, fewer goods and services are purchased in Canada, local charitable and community participation is diminished, Canadian offices become empty shells with a few figurehead regional executives. Or, apologies for saying so, pretty well everything I forecasted eleven years ago in *The Betrayal of Canada*.

Of course the main reason why so many large foreign corporations are 100-per-cent foreign-owned is so the parent company does not have to worry about Canadian shareholders complaining about low profits showing up in Canada. The Conference Board indicates that

> Stocks of foreign-owned subsidiaries are typically not traded on a Canadian stock exchange. Only a fraction of [survey] respondents – 11 per cent – reported that their stocks were publicly traded in Canada.

---

[*] *Toronto Star*, November 11, 2001.

Perhaps the most remarkable of all the expressions of concern about what has been happening came from Ray Protti, president of the Canadian Banker's Association, in the fall of 2001. Speaking to the Canadian Club in Chicago, Protti told his audience that

> An independent, self-confident nation requires a dynamic economy. And dynamism requires not just subsidiaries, but head offices.
>
> No country can resign itself to a national glass ceiling – one in which people are prevented from achieving their full potential, research and development is conducted elsewhere, spinoff industries are under-mined and the tax base is steadily diminished.

Strong words. But surely there are some obvious questions to be asked here. Perhaps Mr. Protti and Royal Bank CEO Gordon Nixon, who has made similar statements, would like to tell us if Canadian banks are prepared to stop funding so much of the sellout of Canada? As indicated before, much of the capital non-residents use to buy up our country comes not from outside Canada, but from our own friendly, obliging financial institutions. And would Canadian banks begin curtailing their headlong, burgeoning expansions outside of Canada and start making more Canadian savings available to Canadian entrepreneurs, large and small, in our own country? By the end of 2001, Canadian financial institutions had direct investment assets in other countries amounting to $148 billion, and were responsible for almost 40 per cent of all Canadian direct investment abroad.

As to the impact of takeovers on local communities, a *Globe and Mail* journalist has this wisdom to offer concerned Canadians regarding the takeover of Westcoast Energy:

> Duke's takeover of Westcoast is a blow to Vancouver's civic pride, but that's the stark reality of North American energy integration. Business takes precedence over pride.[*]

Setting aside the foggy reasoning behind such a statement, if business sense were indeed to be the determining factor, the takeover of Westcoast would never have been either considered or allowed.

As foreign ownership increases, more and more problems arise,

---

[*] *Globe and Mail*, September 22, 2000.

problems that other countries recognize but that Canadian governments are blind to. As always, David Crane puts it well:

> When our governments talk about working with Canadian business leaders to improve training or strengthen research, they are talking about a partnership with people, many or whom don't care about this country or whether it succeeds.
>
> Maybe that's why our standard of living has been falling behind countries in which business leaders have a vested interest and national pride.
>
> Maybe the question we should be asking is: Where can Canada get business leaders who value this country as much as the bottom line?[*]

Good question. For the Conference Board:

> When our best and brightest, or most entrepreneurial, leave to work elsewhere, they take their high incomes and their entrepreneurial drive with them. This is developed elsewhere and the jobs are created elsewhere.

For another perspective, let's return to Gordon Nixon, commenting on some $143 billion worth of foreign takeovers of major Canadian companies between January 1998 and early 2001. In David Crane's words:

> Mergers and acquisitions are a normal part of business activity, Nixon said, but there is a serious concern that, in the process, Canada is losing head offices. This is particularly the case when the foreign acquirer is American, because it's easy to run Canadian operations from the United States.
>
> "Over time, lost head offices will make a big difference in the kinds of careers that are available in Canada," Nixon warned. "Head offices not only buy paper clips and computers; they buy high-value services in law, accounting, consulting and financial services."
>
> "If your head office in the oil patch moves from Calgary to Houston, the odds are high that your principal law firm is no longer located in Calgary. So indirectly, other jobs migrate as well."[†]

---

[*] *Toronto Star*, June 25, 2001.
[†] *Toronto Star*, November 10, 2001.

Right, and by the way, as another bunch of the Toronto Stock Exchange corporations get sold off, Mr. Nixon's RBC Dominion Securities loses another big chunk of profitable future business.

The impact on the financial sector in Canada is crystal clear. As non-residents take over Canadian companies, Bay Street business goes elsewhere. Chuck Winograd of RBC Dominion told an audience of Toronto analysts that the firm's base of corporate clients is shrinking:

> This story is playing out in varying degrees in industry after industry. Canadian companies are being acquired by global firms who will not finance first in Canadian capital markets.[*]

And the result? Fewer IPOs in Canada, and even more pressure on Bay Street to move their resources down to New York and to pay big money for an even larger presence in the U.S. market.

How ironic it is that the big law and accounting firms that poured so much money into the big-business, free-trade "Alliance for Trade and Job Opportunities" will undoubtedly pay the consequences for their myopia. According to Harry Arthurs,

> While Canadian legal culture and professional practice still retain some distinctive features, as more and more Canadian lawyers learn to think and act like American lawyers, and as more and more of their clients expect them to do so, those distinctions will gradually fade away.

And, inevitably, the large American legal and accounting firms will take their place in Toronto, Montreal, Calgary, and Vancouver, gobbling up the long-established Canadian firms.

Bill Watson is the managing partner of the Chicago-based international legal firm Baker & Mackenzie, which is planning a large expansion of its firm in Canada. He says that "he believes Canada as a stand-alone entity is declining in importance . . . I think Canadian lawyers are going to find increasingly that large U.S. firms, large British firms are going to control that legal work."[†]

---

[*] Derek DeClot, *Financial Post*, October 24, 2001.

[†] *National Post*, February 27, 2002.

For some indication as to what we can expect much more of in the future, after the Enron debacle Arthur Andersen, then the fifth-largest accounting firm in Canada, was asked by the press to comment on the likely fate of the firm's almost 2,000 employees in Canada. But the Toronto spokesman for the company said that he was unable to talk to the press and suggested they call Andersen's head office in the U.S.

During the great free-trade debate, lawyers Donald Macdonald of Toronto (a former Liberal finance minister) and Peter Lougheed of Calgary (the former Conservative premier of Alberta) joined with Tom d'Aquino as principal front men for the big-business "alliance" that spent millions of dollars selling the free-trade deal to Canadians. There's little doubt that their massive cross-Canada advertising blitz played a major role in Brian Mulroney's re-election in 1988.

Today, there is also little doubt that both Macdonald and Lougheed have grave concerns about the increasing foreign takeover of Canada and the hollowing out of its corporate structure. And both now realize that due to the investment provisions in both the FTA and NAFTA, it is very difficult to halt or reverse what has been happening, without changing or revoking the agreements.

Comments by Peter Lougheed astounded Canadians late in 1999:

> I know people will fall from their chairs to hear me say this, but maybe right now we need to return to the Foreign Investment Review Agency. We need to be more interventionist. The passive approach isn't working. If (the present trend) continues, we are going to look at our country in about three years and say: What have we got left?[*]

The late Mr. Justice Willard Estey, who retired from the Supreme Court of Canada in 1988, was another free-trade supporter who has spoken out quite forcefully about "The Quiet Hi-jacking of Corporate Canada." In strong and articulate language, Estey criticized NOVA Chemicals for moving its top executives to Pittsburgh. One result will prove to be a "reduction in tax revenues which will be a real loss to the Canadian economy . . . at the end of the road Alberta will have empty gas wells and NOVA will have established a profitable enterprise . . . in the United States. . . . This type of corporate reorganization threatens the future of

---

[*] *Edmonton Journal*, November 13, 1999.

Canada . . . The effects of such transfers strip Canada of significant earning power, tax revenue and senior employment."[*]

"Bud" Estey went onto make an important point about the FTA and NAFTA:

> Most serious of all, under the several trade treaties to which Canada is now party, have we contracted away the right to require that our natural resources not be exported as raw material, but be processed in this country so as to produce end products for export and sale abroad with high labour content?

Well, yes in fact, we have done exactly that. In another interview, Estey was even forceful:

> I supported free trade a decade ago. Now I am starting to suspect that Canada may have contracted out our independence to those trade agreements. The problem is that we are letting corporations with no loyalty to this country strip it of its finite resources.

Former BCNI honorary chairman David O'Brien, of Canadian Pacific, has recently complained that "Canadian icons are falling like 10-pins."[†] Peter Lougheed now says that "What I anticipated is that we'd have government – plural – that would be sensitive to the issue of sovereignty." (Here Lougheed is taking as undeclared swipe at his successor, Ralph Klein, as well as the Chrétien government.)

Estey concludes:

> Put simply, the most serious issue now facing us in whether economic independence is drifting away from Canada.

Not so. The most serious issues are not *whether* this is happening, but whether enough Canadians understand that it *is* happening and will then decide that something must be done quickly before the country officially becomes an American colony.

For Donald Macdonald,

---

[*] This and all subsequent Estey quotations are from *Policy Options*, October 2000.
[†] Canadian Press, January 2, 2000.

Foreign investment remains a concern: the number of Canadian-headed enterprises is diminishing. I am worried. But I don't know what to do.[*]

Perhaps no corporation in Canada was more responsible for pushing the FTA than the Royal Bank. The bank's chief economists knew the wide-open, binding investment provisions of the agreement. Not to worry, said John McCallum, the bank's former chief economist and now a Liberal MP and Defence Minister.

Mr. McCallum said that the increased foreign control of the Canadian economy is healthy because it brings much needed investment, improves productivity and creates competition in the market place.[†]

Good grief. And this man is rumoured to be a future Minister of Finance!

One has to stop and reflect about these individuals, corporations, and organizations. Did they not ever actually read the two "trade" agreements? Did they not understand the investment provisions? Why did they so readily dismiss the warnings from the agreement's opponents?[**]

Or, is it possible, as seems to be the case, that some of them now well understand what a terrible mistake they made as their country is being sold out from under their children and grandchildren, but simply don't know what to do about it? And for the most part are afraid to admit it?

As for Tom d'Aquino and his friends, in a survey of BCNI members in 1999, 40 per cent of the CEOs said that there was at least a fifty-fifty chance that their own jobs would depart the country within ten years.

Even in the face of all the mounting available evidence, even if somehow his blindfold was lifted, I very much doubt if d'Aquino would ever admit that the so-called trade agreements he championed were putting the very survival of our country in jeopardy.

Instead, we will continue to hear from him the never ending and almost hysterical claims that Canadian taxes are discouraging more FDI.

---

[*] *Maclean's*, July 1, 2000.
[†] *Globe and Mail*, April 3, 2000.
[**] At least John Crosbie, Brian Mulroney's minister for international trade during the crucial FTA negotiations in 1988, admitted that *he* hadn't read the agreement.

(The reality is that corporate manufacturing and payroll taxes are lower in Canada than in the U.S., and Canada has the second-lowest manufacturing wages among the G7 countries.)

And, as I've asked several times in the recent past, if taxes are too high in this country for corporations, why are all these foreign corporations coming in and buying up the country?

Well, perhaps there is an answer.

No Radar on the Road

In *The Betrayal of Canada* I wrote at some length about how foreign companies load their Canadian operations up with expenses so that profits don't show up in Canada. This process is called transfer pricing. Sources in Ottawa tell me that there was hell to pay in the Department of Finance and Revenue Canada after my book appeared. Without question, Ottawa has been doing a better job lately, but there's also little doubt that the tightening-up that has occurred has been but a modest step in the right direction. Many billions of dollars in untaxed profits leave this country every year and of course it's you that has to make up the missing tax revenue.

Unfortunately, most of the hundreds of cases that Revenue Canada considers as problems are settled behind closed doors. The public rarely gets to learn about how Coca-Cola or Safeway or Ford or others have their Canadian costs inflated by head office in the U.S.

The Canada Customs and Revenue Agency pulled the veil aside a bit with their decision to take three major multinational drug companies to court. The companies were accused of avoiding over $157 million in taxes by overpaying their parent or related companies for drug ingredients. For example, Ottawa says that Glaxo paid $1,650 per kilogram for an ulcer medication ingredient, where it should have been paying $250 a kilogram.

It's not the first time that the foreign drug industry has been shown to be evading taxes in Canada. Back in 1983, Revenue Canada said that "a sample of 14 major drugs in Canada revealed that intrafirm prices were more than three times higher than the prices paid for the same drugs in the open market."

In one case reported by Colin Freeze of the *Globe and Mail*,

A company was paying its Panamanian parent $401 a gram for an anti-inflammatory; interchangeable versions were selling for $10.54.

Many of the contentious chemicals are manufactured in relatively tax-friendly countries such as the Bahamas and Ireland.[*]

Bear in mind that recent studies of health care costs in Canada show that drug prices are one of the major contributors to escalating medicare costs.

In one of the most interesting transfer pricing revelations, in February 1995, Ford Canada's former president sent a "blistering" letter to the new president saying its U.S. parent's transfer pricing policy was suppressing profits at the Canadian subsidiary. More recently it was reported that "The sales and marketing arm of Ford Motor Co. of Canada, Ltd., lost $6 billion between 1985 and 1995 because of an improper system of pricing parts and vehicles it purchased from its parent company."[†]

According to Lawrence Rosen, a Toronto forensic accountant, "Canada doesn't have a police force; everybody knows that. There's no radar on that road." For Ford's minority shareholders, "the effect of the transfer pricing system was to create huge losses in Ford Canada's sales division."[**] Soon after these complaints, Ford announced a buyout of its minority shareholders. They were asking too many questions.

Is transfer pricing a growing problem today? A past president of the Canadian Institute of Chartered Accountants told me that transfer pricing is the fastest growing taxation specialty in Canada. And of course the name of the game is to ensure that taxes paid in Canada are as low as possible and profits show up elsewhere. Today Rosen says, "There's no doubt about it; the government is not keeping pace with the big increase in transactions."[††]

In summer 2001 Colin Freeze revealed that Canadian tax collectors "have spent at least four years investigating Coca-Cola's Canadian

---

[*] *Globe and Mail*, July 7, 2001.

[†] *Globe and Mail*, April 30, 2002. The $6 billion figure comes from a lawsuit filed by minority shareholders in the Ontario Superior Court.

[**] *Globe and Mail*, June 20, 2001.

[††] Telephone conversation, January 27, 2002.

bottling operations in a probe that could involve more than $100 million in back taxes. The investigation is looking at whether Coke charged too much to its bottling operations in order to keep profits – and Canadian taxes – down."[*]

Excessive foreign ownership leads to diminished tax revenue. It's one of the main reasons why countries around the world would scoff at the idea of allowing as much foreign ownership as Canada.

Another major problem with excessive foreign ownership is the loss of jobs that results when foreign corporations buy parts and components and services offshore or from the U.S. when similar-quality goods and services are available in Canada at competitive prices. Sometimes this happens from force of habit, sometimes for tax reasons, and sometimes because the foreign company has a stake in the source located outside of Canada.[†] Most often the manipulated inter-corporate transactions involve the parent company selling to their subsidiary.

Foreign firms operating in Canada, on average, import three times as many parts, components, and services as similar-sized Canadian companies. In 1993 an OECD study showed that the ratio of foreign parts and components in manufacturing in the U.S. was 13 per cent. In Japan it was 7 per cent. In Canada it was over 50 per cent, and it is probably much higher today. This exceptionally high foreign content is one of the key reasons why Canada's unemployment rate has persistently been so much higher than it should have been, and it also distorts the much-repeated "dependency" on exports as a percentage of GDP. A very large percentage of our merchandise exports (67 per cent in 1999[**]) is manufactured goods, and much of this has already been imported. More about this later.

It's important to note that roughly 70 per cent of the foreign trade of U.S. corporations in Canada consists of sales to and purchases from their parent companies or affiliates, and of course these transactions are conducted on a non-arms-length basis with head office dictating the terms.

Services are a growing element of international trade. Again, it's important to note that almost 60 per cent of the services that Canada imports from the U.S. are imported by affiliates of U.S. companies in Canada.

---

[*] *Globe and Mail,* June 23, 2001.
[†] See for example "Oil Patch Jobs Go Offshore," *Edmonton Journal,* November 29, 2001.
[**] United Nations *Human Development Report,* 2001.

Overall, the result is a loss of jobs in Canada, for scientists, engineers, architects, accountants, lawyers, software designers, data processing and payroll staff, travel agents, and many, many others.

Like it or not, most imported services are purchased without Canadian sources being given an opportunity to bid. As foreign ownership in Canada grows, our commercial services deficit, billions of dollars every year, will continue to grow.

Over and over and over again, Canadians have been told that the globalized world is becoming more competitive and we have to do a much better job of increasing our innovation performance and our productivity: a small problem. Branch plant countries do very little R&D.

After years of increasing foreign ownership and after fourteen years of free trade, Canada is now in thirtieth place in a U.N. list of forty-eight high-development countries when it comes to high-technology exports as a percentage of total goods exports.[*]

Industry Canada reports that

> The total R&D propensity – defined as the ratio of R&D spending to sales – of foreign-controlled firms in the Canadian manufacturing sectors is significantly lower than that of their Canadian-controlled counterparts . . . foreign-controlled firms spend significantly less on R&D than Canadian-controlled firms.[†]

Well, of course. Economist Michael Porter writes:

> Typically a company's home base is where the best jobs reside, where core research and development is undertaken and where strategic control lies. Home bases are important to an economy because they support high productivity and productivity growth.[**]

Precisely. Meanwhile, the loudest complainers about productivity in Canada are exactly the same people who are demanding that remaining restrictions on foreign ownership in Canada be dropped.

---

[*] Ibid.

[†] Industry Canada, *Micro*, vol. 8, no. 1, Summer 2001.

[**] *Toronto Star*, September 25, 2001.

In the United Nations list of high human development countries, Canada is fifteenth in terms of R&D expenditures as a percentage of GNP (1987–97) and twentieth in business spending on R&D and a percentage of total R&D expenditures.[*]

And, when it comes to the number of scientists and engineers in R&D per hundred thousand people, Canada is in fourteenth place.[†]

In another study, Canada ranked thirty-fourth of fifty-eight countries in terms of their recognition of the importance of doing their own R&D. But how could it possibly be otherwise in a country where so many of our business leaders are focused on selling off their corporate assets to foreigners? And, anyway, IBM has told Canadians that all of this doesn't really matter. Borders are "like the equator, an imaginary line that doesn't mean very much."

What constantly amazes me is how the same corporate CEOs who have been leading the way in the accelerating sellout of our country are the same brains who constantly complain about Canada's so-called falling standard of living and lack of innovation. Both productivity guru Michael Porter and the Rotman School of Management's Roger Martin say that many Canadian business leaders have failed to understand the vital importance of innovation and productivity. And those who believe that a high degree of foreign-controlled industries will lead to greater competitiveness (try John McCallum) are so out of touch with reality that their arguments deserve the scorn of their fellow citizens.

So, given all of this, what can we expect in the future? Powerful lobbies now are demanding more foreign ownership in telecommunications, cable, and satellite broadcasting, banking, publishing, bookselling, newspapers, airlines . . . you name it. Perhaps a case might possibly be made for more foreign ownership in one or more of these industries – perhaps – but the cumulative impact of surrendering even more of our country to foreign ownership and control will be devastating.

In a country that for decades has had the highest foreign ownership and control of any major developed nation, in a country where foreign ownership and control have increased for thirteen consecutive years and

---

[*] Ibid.
[†] Ibid.

are already well beyond levels that would be acceptable in any OECD country you can think of, our business and political leaders want more, more, more, and then even more of the same.

What else can we see on the horizon?

> One of Canada's most successful mall developers yesterday forecast that most retail businesses in Canada will be owned outright or in part by U.S. or foreign interests within a few years.
>
> "Over the next five years I predict that all retailers serving Canada will be foreign owned," Mitch Goldhard said after a panel discussion.[*]

Then there are the railways. We've known for some time that the CNR is some 70-per-cent American-owned already and is officially classed as a foreign company by Statistics Canada. What about the Canadian Pacific? A *Globe* columnist says of probable complaints about a foreign takeover of CP:

> Much of the opposition to such a merger will be based on emotion, since the CPR has been a huge part of our national fabric in Canada almost since Confederation.

And anyway, "Why should anyone care who actually owns the railway?"[†]

Well, yes, by all means, let us not get emotional about the sellout of our country. Especially since BCNI and major free trade backer David O'Brien, the former CP CEO and president who broke Canadian Pacific into five companies, believes that each one of the five is a takeover target. Anyway, "In a free market there is little that Canadians can do to stop the disappearance of big companies through foreign takeovers."[**]

One *Globe* reporter wrote that Mr. O'Brien "has a reputation as a nationalist."

As for the future of the telecommunications industry in Canada, The *National Post* tells us that

---

[*] *National Post*, October 5, 2000.
[†] *Globe and Mail*, June 12, 2001.
[**] *Globe and Mail*, August 21, 2001.

A majority of Canada's business community expects U.S. or foreign-owned telephone companies to emerge as the dominant players in a consolidated Canadian telecommunications industry.

Rod McQueen, writing in the *Financial Post* under the headline "Even Rogers' patriotism is negotiable," had this to say:

He regularly wraps himself in the flag, passes himself off as the great defender of Canadian communications, all the while benefiting greatly from the monopolistic position thus endowed and hoping fervently that people have short memories about last year's speech.

So, Mr. Rogers, if you want to exchange your old friend, the Canadian flag, for the stars-and-stripes, that's fine. Just don't give us any more prattle about Canadian stories and national dreams.

Meanwhile, the British CEO of Telus suggests removal of foreign-ownership restrictions in the industry. Then there's John Tory, CEO of Rogers Cable Systems, and advisor to Brian Mulroney and Kim Campbell, who supports "aggressive lobbying efforts to lift Ottawa's ownership restrictions."[*]

Not to be outdone, A.T.&T. Canada Inc. tells Canadians that it is vital that the foreign-ownership limits for telecommunications companies be abolished, and Jean Monty, former chairman and CEO of BCE Inc., agreed (Bell Canada is already 20-per-cent owned by a Texas company).

Now, stop and consider for a minute. Why would giant Canadian corporations that have grown by leaps and bounds under Canada's regulatory system now want laws changed so that it would be easier for foreigners from outside of Canada to take them over? And why would a senior Bell vice-president say that foreign ownership is a non-issue? "There's a significant portion of the population that doesn't see nationality of a company as germane."[†] Well, the answer is really simple, isn't it? They will all make a big bundle selling off the ownership and control of their companies to foreign corporations.

For Shaw Communications, there's no time for debate. What they want is an "urgent review" of foreign-ownership restrictions.

---

[*] *Financial Post*, November 26, 2001.
[†] *Toronto Star*, June 23, 1999.

As for banking, in February 2001, the Chrétien government tabled a bill which will allow increased foreign ownership of Canadian banks.

In an extraordinary demonstration of patriotism, John Hunkin, chairman and chief executive of the CIBC, suggested that the federal government must relax its bank-ownership regulations. After all, "why would a foreign bank want to own 20 per cent unless they truly believed there would be a further change so that they could own – 100 per cent."

Never mind the fact that "Canadians have made very clear, at least in any polls I've seen, that they don't like the idea of a Canadian bank being owned by non-Canadians." What Hunkin and his colleagues are planning to do is to make certain that Canadians understand that foreign ownership of banks is "good for Canada."*

Canadians might want to consider such comments when they think about where they want to do their banking in the future. Not that there's that much choice. How about a good local co-op?

And consistent with its perpetual and enthusiastic right-wing continentalist position, the C. D. Howe Institute suggests that regulations relating to the foreign ownership of banks should be drastically cut back.

It should be noted, yet once again, that the C. D. Howe Institute, like the Fraser Institute, the IRPP, and the Conference Board, refuse to disclose the sources or the individual amounts of their funding. We do know that much of their funding comes from American corporations, while rumours persist that right-wing American foundations and other U.S. sources are major contributors.

In a telephone conversation in May of this year, the C. D. Howe's Jack Mintz made the astounding claim that "not even my board of directors knows where all our money comes from." Draw your own conclusions.

Public advocacy groups that wade into political topics are not supposed to be allowed to issue tax receipts for donations, but all of the above except the Conference Board do so.

---

* Southam Newspapers, June 30, 2001.

Everything's for Sale at a Price

Okay now, let's see what's left? How about the petroleum industry?

One of the most effective and well-organized industry lobbies in Canada has been that of the petroleum industry via the Canadian Petroleum Association and later the Canadian Association of Petroleum Producers, both with strong or even dominant foreign-controlled participants, including Imperial Oil, which has always done a masterful job of passing itself off as a Canadian company.

The name of the game for the foreign-owned segment of the petroleum industry has been and remains the same as it was thirty years ago: ship out of the country Canadian reserves of oil and gas as quickly as possible; make sure as much of the industry profits show up outside of Canada so they are not taxed in Canada; work to abolish Canadian priorities such as mandatory reserve requirements that guard against future vulnerability; and don't worry about declining reserves, while continuing to escalate export levels. Or, if the public begins to worry, demand more tax breaks to do more exploration and development.

What has been so remarkable about the renewed foreign domination of the petroleum industry in Canada is the nonsense out of Calgary, repeated across the land in our media, that no one is concerned about the issue and, after all, the level of foreign ownership in the industry is still below the level in the 1970s.

Is there anyone in Alberta concerned about the selloff of our energy resources? They are few and far between and virtually mute. "What would we be worried about?" an economist asks a *Globe and Mail* reporter. A Canadian Association of Petroleum Producers spokesman tells the same reporter that there's no reason for concern. After all, "U.S. producers [are] optimistic about Canada's industry and eager to invest here."[*]

A few lonely voices dissent. The former president of Economic Development Edmonton and former Conservative leadership candidate, Jim Edwards, said, after the takeovers of Canadian Hunter and Chieftain,

---

[*] *Globe and Mail*, October 10, 2001.

When we lose major head offices it affects us not only economically but also socially and psychologically.

Someone once said, if the 49th parallel didn't exist, Calgary would have been an agricultural center.

But, in Calgary, "the business community regards the trend as inevitable,"[*] even though Calgary has lost some 20 per cent of its head-office listings on the Toronto Stock Exchange and the number of Calgary head offices has dropped by a similar amount.

Eric Reguly writes about the impact on Calgary:

Head offices and job opportunities are vanishing. Dawn Mitchell, who until yesterday was head of communications at freshly dismantled Canadian Pacific, might be a typical example. She wants to stay in Calgary but might have to leave for a lack of career opportunities. "There are not a whole lot of head offices here now... I have to think about moving."[†]

How much of our oil and natural gas industry will we be selling off? "Everything's for sale at a price,"[**] says a Calgary petroleum industry analyst.

Should we be worried about the recent loss of Westcoast, Anderson Exploration, Canadian Hunter, Berkley, Chieftain, Gulfstream, Command, and $37 billion in takeovers in 2001?

Forget it. "Oilpatch plays down foreign ownership" says the headline on a Canadian Press story.[††] And, as a Calgary TD analyst tells us,

The concern that we're not maintaining control of our assets is really misleading because whether they're under U.S. ownership or Canadian ownership, they're still under the same rules and regulations.

And, so what if branch plant Imperial Oil "can't make a move without Exxon's approval"?[***]

---

[*] *Financial Post*, October 11, 2001.
[†] *Globe and Mail*, October 20, 2001.
[**] *Globe and Mail*, September 5, 2001.
[††] *Canadian Press*, May 31, 2001.
[***] Eric Reguly, *Globe and Mail*.

Brent Jang of the *Globe and Mail* puts it very well: "Being patriotic in Canada's oil patch means never having to say you're sorry about selling out to Americans."*

In the same paper, a headline tells readers that there is "No Need for Patriotic Alarm Yet: Observers."

True, no doubt. Surely we should wait until the oil and gas industry is 90-per-cent foreign-owned before we get too patriotic.†

Calgary is our most American city, by far. When one visits the city, one often feels that there are more American flags than in all the rest of Canada put together. As I've said elsewhere, asking "observers" in Calgary how they feel about the American takeover of the petroleum industry is like asking the Disney people how they feel about Mickey Mouse.

To be fair, not every single soul in Calgary is oblivious to the ramifications. "What happens if the U.S. owns everything and they ship it all to the States? What's left for us?" an anonymous analyst asked Claudio Cattaneo of the *National Post*.** Good question, since the National Energy Board is now a pale, castrated remnant of the regulatory agency that was once intended to protect the interests of Canadians. Oh yes, not to be left behind by any of this, the Liberal cabinet decided to relax Petro-Canada's foreign ownership limits.

Okay, before we go on to look at other countries' attitudes towards foreign ownership and then zero in on the United States, let's stop for a moment to consider public opinion in Canada. We already know that our patriotic political and corporate elite are prepared to sell anything to anyone. Let's see how most Canadians feel.

At the end of 1999, *Maclean's* asked Canadians whether they thought Canadian ownership of businesses operating in Canada was necessary "in order to maintain a strong Canadian identity in the next century." Eighty-three per cent agreed. Eighty-one per cent also agreed that "Canada can thrive in the new millennium by keeping its own values and not trying to become more like Americans."††

In another poll, 70 per cent said that they were opposed to more foreign control, and 61 per cent said they were angry that the government

---

* *Globe and Mail*, May 30, 2001.

† By 1999, even before the billions of dollars in takeovers that followed in 2000 and 2001, 53 per cent of all oil, natural gas, and coal revenues went to foreign firms.

** *National Post*, February 13, 2001.

†† *Maclean's*, December 20, 1999.

wasn't doing more to stop foreign takeovers.* And, a summer 2001 Decima poll showed that almost two-thirds of Canadians opposed foreign control of newspapers and almost 60 per cent were against foreign ownership of telephone and cable companies. More recently, in the spring of 2002, an Ipsos Reid poll showed that 80 per cent of Canadians said that they are concerned about the foreign ownership of Canadian energy resources.

Many of you will have read about the infamous Multilateral Agreement on Investment (MAI) that was brought down in flames by France and Maude Barlow and her colleagues around the world. There is not a tiny doubt in my mind that if the MAI had been adopted as law, it would have been the final nail in the Canadian coffin and the dream of Canada would have been over, forever. Now, who do you think was behind the MAI? Former University of Toronto economist Alan Rugman, a longtime advocate for more foreign ownership, revealed in 1998 that it was Canada that was boosting the Multinational Agreement on Investment. "The untold story is that *we're* the real heroes getting it going."

Some heroes!

Thank you Jean Chrétien, Paul Martin, and John Manley, the prominent prospective national pallbearers. And, thank you, cowardly, mute Liberal backbenchers.

Don't think for a moment that Ottawa has given up. Today, around the world, Industry Canada and Foreign Affairs and International Trade have staff soliciting more foreign direct investment. Investment Partnerships Canada has a staff of about fifty in Ottawa, and representatives in the U.S., Europe, and Asia. When I asked them if they were aware of the Investment Review Division's report showing that since 1985, over 96 per cent of the foreign direct investment that they monitored was for takeovers, they said they were unaware of this information. When I suggested that on this basis surely what they were doing was soliciting even more foreign takeover of our country, the response was evasive and defensive.

Meanwhile, Merrill Lynch, Inc., fined $100 million by the New York State Attorney for illegal activities in the U.S. in one of the most egregious examples of corporate immorality and deception on record, advises Canadians that takeovers of Canadian business helps Canada. Merrill Lynch fails to mention its lucrative role in facilitating the

---

* *Globe and Mail*, January 4, 2000.

takeovers of Westcoast Energy, Gulf Canada, C-MAC Industries, and other firms.

What's good for Merrill Lynch is good for Canada.

Foreign Ownership in the United States and Other Countries

No other major or middle-sized developed nation would dream of allowing the degree of foreign ownership and control that we have in Canada. Can anyone imagine for a moment the U.S. allowing its petroleum industry, its automobile industry, its computer industry, or a long list of dozens of other key industries, to be taken over by foreign owners? The possibility is laughable.

In April 2001, the Australian government blocked Royal Dutch Shell Group's takeover of a major Australian gas exporter, arguing that the foreign company's priorities might be very different and not in Australia's best interests. Imagine!

Elsewhere, a *New York Times* headline tells us the "The French Are Resisting American Funds and Investors," while in Italy, Telecom Italia is "off limits to foreign takeover bids" while the government is "putting the brakes on banking deals."[*] Non-EU ownership of French television is limited to 20 per cent and France has recently made it clear that they will not allow a foreign takeover of Vivendi.

Meanwhile, who is standing on guard for Canadian culture? Amazingly, Heritage Minister Sheila Copps advises that "Parliamentarians should feel free to consider lifting foreign ownership restrictions in the broadcasting industry." Moreover, the CBC should "enter into partnerships with private broadcasters such as CTV and Global,"[†] whose history of Canadian content is dismal.

Late in 1999, the French government rejected Coca-Cola's second bid to take over the French soft-drink brand Orangina. In the same year,

---

[*] *New York Times*, January 9, 2000.
[†] *Globe and Mail*, November 9, 2001.

Coke was forced to withdraw bids for the soft drink brands of Cadbury Schweppes. Meanwhile, in Germany, "the rare bid by a foreign firm for one of Germany's crown jewels has set off an uproar in a country where Anglo-American 'cowboy capitalism' is decried as a job killer." German law allows takeovers to be blocked by individual shareholders "with court challenges that can drag on for years."[*]

More recently, another *New York Times* headline proclaimed "Contempt in France for U.S. Funds and Investors."[†] And from Brussels:

> It is worth making the point that any foreigner making a bid for a major French company would certainly be blocked by the government.[**]

As well, in contrast to what we've just been reading about Canada, a recent headline tells us "Britain shuts down foreign TV ownership . . . Rules now limit a non-EU company from owning more than 20% of a British terrestrial broadcaster." A U.K. analyst indicated that firm British policies are intended "to stop large U.S. companies from taking over one of the U.K. broadcasters." The British Culture Secretary said that "In devising new rules, we must strike a balance between economic growth and our nation's democratic health."[††]

In Canada, apparently the only balance to be struck is between how much money can be made in selling out to the Americans, and how quickly this can be done.

In manufacturing, the comparative level of foreign control in Canada is over a third larger than in Britain, almost twice as high as in France, well over double the level in Sweden, and roughly five times the levels in the United States, Germany, and Italy. In Japan the foreign presence in manufacturing is less than 1 per cent.

In the European Union many mergers and takeovers are routinely blocked in the public interest. Recently, twelve years of efforts to make takeovers easier have foundered because of intense opposition.

And, how's this for an amazing idea?

---

[*] The Associated Press, November 19, 1999.
[†] *New York Times*, January 9, 2000.
[**] *Globe and Mail*, June 15, 2000.
[††] *Financial Post*, November 27, 2001.

We believe that it is appropriate to require merger applicants to bear a heavier burden to show that a major merger proposal is in the public interest.

So said a U.S. regulatory board that was proposing tough new rules to ensure that "corporate decisions won't hurt Americans."[*]

Now wasn't that *exactly* what the Foreign Investment Review Agency was all about?

Canada's Takeover of the United States

If one reads some of our political and economic newspaper columnists, or the regular widely published reports of the Toronto-based Crosbie and Co., Inc., the impression left is that Canadian companies are buying up the U.S. faster than American companies are buying up Canada. Here, for example, is one headline of many: "Canadian firms outpace Americans in foreign takeovers."[†] And according to a prominently featured article in the *National Post* headlined "Canada Leads U.S. on Takeovers," concerns that U.S. companies are buying up Canada "are misplaced."[**]

Okay, let's look at overall foreign ownership in the U.S. In the 1980s there was a wave of Japanese takeovers in the U.S. In New York, a businessman interviewed by *The Wall Street Journal* said "They were buying up everything. It was nuts! I think they got the Statue of Liberty."[††] Later it was German companies taking over Doubleday and Random House and the Chrysler Corporation, and British and Dutch companies rapidly adding to their own list of takeovers. So, with all of this activity, is there much foreign ownership in the U.S.? Well, not exactly.

There is not one single industry in the United States, not one, that is majority-foreign-owned and/or foreign-controlled, by anyone, let alone

---

[*] *Globe and Mail*, October 3, 2000.
[†] Southam Newspapers, July 13, 2001.
[**] *National Post*, November 16, 2001.
[††] *Globe and Mail*, December 15, 1998.

Canadians. Only two of scores of U.S. industries are remotely close, chemicals and book publishing, which are about one-third foreign.

Did anyone *really* think that it might be otherwise?

The latest available figures from the U.S. Department of Commerce are for 1999. At that time, majority-foreign-owned corporations accounted for only 6.4 per cent of U.S. industry GDP. Canadian ownership amounted to less than six-tenths of 1 per cent of industry GDP. In Canada in 1999, foreign firms took about 30 per cent of all corporate revenues, most of which went to American firms.

In terms of employment, only about 5.4 per cent of the U.S. labour force is employed by foreign corporations.

Are Canadians leading the way in foreign direct investment in the United States? Hardly. We're down in sixth place, with roughly 8 per cent of all FDI in the U.S. Has Canadian ownership in the U.S. led to large market penetration? Not exactly. Canadian exports to the U.S. amounts to only 1 per cent of the American market. Has there in fact been a large increase in Canadian investment in the U.S.? Yes there has, and we'll look at the causes and ramifications more closely when we come to review the economic results of the FTA and NAFTA.

But for now, and every time you read a story, as you undoubtedly will, about Canadians buying up the U.S., remember the following: The level of all foreign ownership in the U.S. is tiny; in Canada it is huge. Canadian ownership of the U.S. is minuscule, with little or no impact on what happens in the U.S. economy; American ownership of Canada is immense, has been increasing rapidly, and has a major negative impact on our overall standard of living.

Before we conclude our discussion of foreign investment in this section of the book, there are two important points to be made.

First, whenever the steadily increasing foreign ownership and control of Canada is raised, the continentalists counter with the fact that Canadian direct investment abroad now exceeds foreign direct investment in Canada. But is this oft-repeated statement true?

The answer is no, it is not. At least 30 and perhaps as much as 40 per cent of all so-called "Canadian" direct investment abroad isn't Canadian. In fact, it is investment made outside of Canada by foreign corporations operating in this country. Unfortunately, we can't quantify the amount precisely since Statistics Canada, for unknown reasons, discontinued tracking such foreign investments in 1995. The estimate of 30 to 40 per cent is based on historical data. (When we return to the question of Canadian investment abroad, we'll see one of the most unfortunate, and disheartening, results of the FTA and NAFTA.)

And secondly, more often than not, the information Canadians receive about foreign investment ranges from misleading to just plain nonsense. Let's take, as but one of many examples, two recent prominent articles by Barbara Stymiest, CEO of the Toronto Stock Exchange. Under the title "Corporate Myths" in the *Financial Post* and "Corporate Fears Ring Hollow" in the *Globe and Mail*, Stymiest downplays concerns about the hollowing-out of corporate Canada, since

> When you tote up the numbers for the last seven years . . . Canadian companies bought 384 more U.S. companies than the other way around. Somehow, this doesn't square with the hollowing out of Canadian corporate life. It looks more like the bulking up of corporate Canada.[*]

The only thing wrong with Stymiest's claim is that it isn't true. During the past seven years (1995–2001 inclusive), U.S. firms took over 3,008 companies in Canada, while Canadian companies bought 697 U.S. firms.

Quite a difference from what you've been told by someone who should have been in a position to know better.[†]

---

[*] *Financial Post* and *Globe and Mail*, May 10, 2002.
[†] The correct numbers are from the Investment Review Division of Industry Canada and the U.S. Department of Commerce.

The Americanization of Canada

An Unparalleled Seismic Shift

Today, as I write this, is Armistice Day, November 11, 2001, the eighty-third anniversary of the end of the First World War.

I have been away giving a few talks and now I am catching up on the newspapers that have accumulated on my desk.

In today's paper I read that 116,000 Canadians gave their lives fighting for their country in the two world wars and in Korea. I read about courage, sacrifice, bravery, and valour. I also read about horror, mutilation, devastation, death camps, massacres, the wounded bleeding to death in the mud, young farm boys being slaughtered in the trenches. I read about Vimy, Passchendaele, Ortona, Verdun, Ypres, and about young men from the Second Canadian Infantry Division being washed back to sea from the beaches of Dieppe.

I read about rotting corpses, shattered body parts, endless rows of white crosses, and unmarked graves.

I spent the morning reading, reminding myself of our proud history, of the heroes from across Canada who gave their lives for our country and the agony and suffering of those they left behind. The noon cannons from the legislature grounds interrupt my reading.

After lunch my reading takes a turn. One newspaper headline from earlier in the week proclaims that Canada must move much closer to the United States and a well-known columnist insists that we must harmonize our policies with those of the Americans. An editorial claims that we have no alternative but to adopt the American dollar, even though it would mean losing control of our monetary policy and the end of the Bank of Canada. A military historian demands that we abandon our long-standing support of the Anti-Ballistic Missile Treaty and side with American missile-defence policy.

Late in the afternoon I finish the pile of papers. Two more major Canadian oil and gas companies have been taken over and an important high-tech company is expected to go tomorrow. Then there is a multitude of stories about our business leaders and politicians suggesting more foreign control of our banks and our broadcasting and advocating moves towards Americanizing our health care system.

After a while I can't read any more. I am sickened by the avaricious sell-outs who are betraying our history, our heritage, and the men who lost their lives fighting for our freedom and for our country.

In the evening, after dinner I begin reading Pierre Berton's new book Marching as to War. *In the morning I call Pierre and ask him for his thoughts about what is happening to Canada. A few days later, he sends me this:*

> The money men, who care more about the bottom line than they do about national sovereignty, are destroying our country. They want us all to become Americans, with an American presidential system, an American commercial culture, and an American dollar. They do not understand that our history is unique because they do not read it; nor do they care that it is neglected in our schools. In their myopia and, indeed in their greed, they are blinded to the dissimilarity that exists on both sides of the border; we are a northern people, the creatures of a unique geography, as different from our neighbours as the Precambrian shield differs from the Florida everglades. They have suckered us into believing that "privatization" is the key to prosperity, by which they mean the commercialization of our natural resources and our national institutions. But it goes farther than that: what they really want is our national soul.

With the implementation of the Free Trade Agreement in 1989, there began an unparalleled seismic shift in our country. The Americanization that many of us had predicted and warned about proceeded much as we had anticipated, but at a far faster pace than any of us ever expected. Today, many Canadians believe there are grave doubts about whether our country can even survive.

Ten years after the FTA came into effect, a column supporting the adoption of even more American policies, standards and values, by former *Globe and Mail* editor William Thorsell, was headlined "It's time to think the unthinkable."[*]

A year later, another *Globe* op-ed piece advocating economic integration with the U.S. reported that "one-third of Canadians think Canada and the U.S. will merge by 2025."[†] The author, columnist Drew Fagan, told his readers that "Canadian citizenship has seldom been worth as little as it is now." (My own thought is that it would not be unthinkable if we were to expeditiously add Thorsell and Fagan to our exports to the U.S.).

By the summer of 2001, the then *Toronto Star* editorial-page editor Carol Goar was writing that

> Business leaders and their friends in Ottawa are urging the government to move swiftly to dismantle border controls, get Canadian oil and gas into the U.S. market and replace the loonie with the American greenback.

About the same time, an Ekos Research poll reported that almost half of those polled believed that Canada would become part of a North American union within ten years, and almost one in four thought that the nation-state of Canada would be gone within ten years.

That fall, Richard Gwyn, author and *Toronto Star* columnist, wrote:

> The moment of transition happened when we signed the Canada–U.S. free trade pact in 1989.
>
> Effectively, there is no longer a Canadian economy, but only a northern regional feeder of the U.S. economy.
>
> By ceding our economic sovereignty, we have made inevitable our having to cede sovereignty over our own borders.

---

[*] *Globe and Mail*, November 27, 1999.
[†] *Globe and Mail*, December 8, 2000.

Suddenly, a whole new form of continental integration is going to overtake us: political and military in nature, rather than the economic and commercial convergence we've come to take for granted, but that we also fear could overwhelm our sovereignty.[*]

If we're abandoning our sovereignty in economic, commercial, political, and military matters, what's left? And if anything at all *is* left, how long will it be before the American avalanche and the Canadian collaborators buries what remains as well?

One week after Gwyn's column appeared, the *Boston Globe* reported:

Notions once dismissed as the paranoid fantasies of Canadian ultra-nationalists – an end to border controls, the U.S. dollar as a common currency, the undercutting of Canada's tax codes and cherished social policies to align with those of the superpower next door – are now bandied about as the way of the future in corporate strategy sessions and policy thinkfests.

(I must apologetically confess that I was one of those misguided ultra-nationalists who had those paranoid fantasies). Boston continues:

Many U.S.–Canada watchers are convinced that formal divides between the two countries will vanish within a decade or two.

And, for all the talk of a "new partnership," no one doubts that Washington, not Ottawa, would call the important shots in such a union.

(Is there one single living human being, anywhere, who thought even for an instant that it might be Ottawa that would be calling the shots?) And finally, from Boston:

A new study by the Carnegie Endowment for International Peace, a think tank in Washington, flatly predicts that Canada will be swept into the U.S. economic embrace.[†]

---

[*] *Toronto Star*, October 18, 2001.
[†] *Edmonton Journal*, October 29, 2002.

Two months later, in December 2001, a front-page story in the *National Post* reported that:

> In an unusual admission of powerlessness, Jean Chrétien said yesterday that Canada has become so economically dependent on the United States that it must rely on the Americans to lift our economy out of recession.[*]

For the normally continentalist Conference Board of Canada, "the extent of economic integration in North American . . . has proceeded further than most Canadians would imagine." There must be "vigorous public debate and a coherent policy strategy if Canada is not simply to slip unawares and in an ad hoc fashion into mimicking the U.S. model."[†]

And, for David Zussman, president of Public Policy Forum, and frequently described as one of Jean Chrétien's key advisors, the issues are clear:

> Canadians in all parts of civil society should actively encourage a growing debate over new ideas which, until a few years ago, were completely taboo in respectable Canadian society . . . issues like dollarization, common perimeters and harmonization of standards.
>
> To many Canadians some of these questions might seem a bit threatening, that even thinking about them might seem unpatriotic.[**]

Much of what follows is in fact about threatening, unpatriotic ideas and the people who are betraying our country.

In the next chapters, we'll examine how Canada has rapidly become Americanized during the years since the election of Brian Mulroney and Jean Chrétien. Later, we'll ask if there's still a chance to do anything important about what has been happening to our country.

---

[*] *National Post*, December 22, 2001.
[†] *Performance and Potential*, 2001–2, October, 2001.
[**] *National Post*, June 29, 2001.

What's the Use of Even Having a Separate Country?

Aside from the ominous increases in the foreign ownership and control of Canada during the Mulroney and Chrétien years, harmonization, integration, deregulation, and privatization have been the dominant features of the Americanization of our country. Harry Arthurs writes:

> It is disconcerting . . . to reflect on the extent and rapidity with which Canadian policies, laws and practices were brought into line with those of the new global regimes. Particularly striking was the construction of new domestic and transnational institutions – new "constellations of legalities" – intended to ensure that policies, which reinforced globalization and regional integration, were well nigh irreversible.
>
> It is true that Canada, like other states, still holds the formal levers of power in its own hands. But the formal levers of power are not much use without a directing intelligence, a capacity to perceive where our interests lie and how they might best be defended. . . . Globalization of the mind has to some extent eroded that intelligence in the case of Canada, or more accurately, it has taught us how to think about those interests . . . in a particular way which is consonant with the views of elites across the global economy.

According to Isaiah Litvak,

> The heavy economic dependence on and interrelationship with the U.S. demand that when Canadian policy-makers develop initiatives in areas such as taxation, competition, technology, environment, exporting and so on, they test the potential efficacy of the policy in light of the interdependence.

But, if this is indeed true, then the logical question must immediately be: What's the use of even having a separate country? According to Litvak,

> The corporate power structure transcends the boundaries of nation states. . . . Setting a national policy agenda, including solutions to internal social and political problems, has been made more difficult. Political

leaders generally are now aware that the role of the state is to work more on behalf of common economic interests associated with regionalism and globalization and less exclusively with national economic interests.

But, isn't this precisely what many of us warned about during the 1980s free trade debates? The corporations are now in charge and the role of the elected representatives of the people is to serve the corporations.

Inexorably, long-standing Canadian policies, values, and standards have been and are being harmonized to match American policies, values, and standards. "Canada pushed on several fronts toward integration with U.S. Calls for tax harmonization and common currency gain support," reads a *Globe and Mail* headline.* The newspaper story went on to explain that Liberal cabinet ministers Sergio Marchi and John Manley were urging that Canada's tax policies be brought more into line with U.S. tax rates.

At about the same time, then Ontario premier Mike Harris told a Cleveland, Ohio, audience that neighbouring American states were more important to Ontario than most parts of Canada are, and that he had borrowed U.S. policy ideas to cut taxes, reduce welfare, and to impose workfare.

Not to be outdone, the federal government severely cut employment insurance payments to the lowest level since the program to assist the unemployed began. By 2000, payments were a fraction of what they had been historically, and were much closer to matching the low levels in the U.S.

Earlier, Ottawa amended its drug patent legislation to more closely match U.S. regulations, changes that have cost Canadians hundreds of millions of dollars and will go on costing millions more every week in the future.

As to any significant steps to curb global warming, when Brian Tobin was industry minister, he advised:

> There is a very strong consensus around the Cabinet table and in the caucus that Canada must do nothing in competitive terms that would handcuff our capacity to compete around the world and with the United States.†

---

* *Globe and Mail*, June 4, 1999.
† *National Post*, November 28, 2001.

Only a few days earlier, American Senators said signing the Kyoto climate-change treaty would inhibit the U.S.'s ability to compete with other countries.

For Alberta premier Ralph Klein, there's no doubt whatsoever about environmental concerns. After meeting with U.S. oilmen, he said,

> They feel it is inherently unfair for Canada to enter into the Kyoto protocol when in fact the United States has indicated it will not be a signatory . . .

Heavens forbid that we should move ahead of the United States on any environmental concerns!

Speaking of being competitive, only a few months after cutting Canadian taxes by a huge $100 billion in two budgets in 2000, then Finance Minister Paul Martin said that there were "enormous pressures" for even greater cuts to taxes and government spending. Dalton Camp responded:

> According to Martin, taxes must come down in tandem with George Bush's tax cuts so that we remain "competitive." He can't be serious: Canadians cannot possibly compete in its tax policy with a government where tax cutting is a fetish and where, to be plain about it, cutting taxes is a means to an end having little to do with the economy, but in order to fulfill ideological ends.
>
> What this country needs is not a finance minister who wants to keep up with the Bushes, but someone who wants to keep up with this country's unique and special promise.[*]

More recently, caucus sources reported that Paul Martin believed that taxes "must continue to come down" so that Canada's tax rates are competitive with the United States.

David Crane writes:

> The pressures for integration with the United States are unrelenting, and there is a sizeable body of opinion in this country that doesn't seem bothered by the fact that Canada's elbow room for pursuing

---

[*] *Toronto Star*, August 26, 2001.

a "Canadian Way" is steadily shrinking and that we will eventually become part of the United States.[*]

> The Conference Board of Canada suggests that economic integration with the U.S. means "Canada . . . will adopt U.S. standards. . . . The principal areas will include competition policy, product, health and safety regulations, as well as the economic regulation of networked sectors, such as transportation systems, communications, energy and financial services." Is that all? What's to worry?

To their credit, the Conference Board dares to speak words that other business groups furtively avoid:

> It is well understood that economic integration creates strong pressure to harmonize regulatory frameworks within North America.
>
> The critical question that arises is: to what extent will convergence of North American regulatory regimes also mean convergence in social systems?

That's not a difficult question to answer. If, as but one example, we follow the advice of some of our radical-right zealots and adopt American tax polices, our social programs, including medicare, go out the window. Won't it then be wonderful to have American-style health care, U.S. poverty rates, and the terrible violence in U.S. society that we will read about in the pages that follow?

As every week goes by, there are increased demands from our corporate elites that Canada harmonize even more of our policies with those of the U.S. The appeals come mainly from the same old, same old, who have shed their caution and now boldly proclaim as "inevitable" and "urgent" harmonization and integration policies that would have been unspeakable or derisively dismissed only a few years ago.

Brian Mulroney tells us that we must have a customs union with the U.S. Mulroney, by the way, has no qualms about us harmonizing our policies with those in the U.S. In a speech in September 2001, he ridiculed concerns about Canadian sovereignty, saying that Canada will need to have common defence, immigration, and tariff policies with the U.S.

---

[*] *Toronto Star*, September 30, 2001.

His former chief of staff and free trade negotiator, Stanley Hartt, who now works for a U.S. investment firm, tells us he and his company are overtaking the Canadian securities industry.

Mulroney's finance minister, Michael Wilson, becomes chairman and CEO of the Royal Bank's pension fund management division, RT Capital, and the company is sold off to a Swiss firm.

Alan Rugman says Canadians have to understand that

We're hooked into the U.S. system. We need an institutional framework that reflects that.

So, we should create a North American Competition Commission "to police mergers and anti-competitive behaviour."*

Then there's our immigration policies. The U.S. Ambassador, Paul Cellucci, a first-time, inexperienced, and outspoken ambassador with an inflated ego, warns that unless Canada harmonizes its immigration policies with those of the U.S., we will face a more restrictive border.

And Cellucci says because the U.S. is not going to ratify the 1997 Kyoto Protocol for the reduction of greenhouse gases, neither should Canada. Never mind the undeniable evidence that global warming is a terrible threat to life on this planet. If George W. Bush considers the agreement "fatally flawed," surely Canada won't hesitate to go along with American policy.

The *Globe and Mail* put it well in an editorial: "Close friends sometimes tread on the other's toes. Mr. Cellucci is stepping uncomfortably close."†

A government with anything other than a jelly spine would have firmly told Mr. Cellucci that, thank you very much, we're not interested in more of this kind of advice.

Then there's the question of how we should solve the softwood lumber dispute with the U.S. Weyerhaeuser, the giant American company that took over MacMillan Bloedel, says that it's clear there would be no problem if Canada simply moved to the U.S. system of calculating stumpage fees. So, all we have to do is shift Crown lands into the same sort of private, predatory auction system that exists in the U.S.

But surely we worry far too much about all this harmonization. Our

* *Financial Post*, June 20, 2001.
† *Globe and Mail*, January 29, 2002.

great Canadian patriot, Paul Tellier, who was Clerk of the Privy Council when Mulroney negotiated the FTA, isn't worried. Those who are concerned about Canada's sovereignty are raising a "red herring." Instead, what we need to do is "establish unified procedures and standards for processing people and freight coming to our shores." Anyway, "I think [sovereignty] is a very phony issue."[*]

For Tellier, the "Time has come . . . to think outside the box. All ideas are on the table" and "Integration is going on, it's inevitable, it's irreversible and it's happening faster than anyone expected."

How do CN workers feel about Mr. Tellier's Americanization of the railway? Not that great. They accuse him of importing American managers who are not familiar with Canadian regulatory standards and who want safety regulations softened.

Of course, not all harmonization is bad. Take, for example, the wages and benefits our CEOs now receive. Is there anything wrong with the fact that the heavy degree of U.S. ownership of key Canadian industries was reflected in the "stunning 42.9 per cent median pay increases" that chief executives in Canada received in 2000?

> Not surprising, one of the key forces behind the growth in CEO pay is the impact of rising compensation levels in the United States.
>
> Increasingly, with many of the companies [in the study], it's hard to find one that is still substantially Canadian, said Ken Hugessen, managing director of William M. Mercer Ltd.'s Canadian compensation practice.
>
> What it is doing is imposing the U.S. social order on good old Canada.[†]

Know any teachers, nurses, or social workers that have received a 42.9-per-cent pay increase?

As far as the Conference Board is concerned, there is no alternative but to concede that,

> In practice, Canada and Mexico will adopt U.S. standards wherever they effect trade. The principal areas will include competition policy,

---

[*] *National Post*, October 11, 2001.
[†] *Edmonton Journal*, May 23, 2001.

product, health and safety, regulations, as well as the economic regulation of networked sectors, such as transportation systems, communications, energy and financial services.

It's difficult to imagine that the people who write these words ever stop long enough to consider the implications of what they are suggesting. John McCallum, commenting on a Commons finance committee recommendation for massive harmonization with American policies, said, "It kind of sounds like there would be no country left." Well, yes, it kinda does sound that way, doesn't it?

Let's be clear; those Canadians who talk about harmonizing policies with the U.S. know well, although they never say so, that harmonizing means adopting U.S. policies. There are zero Canadian policies that Americans will adopt. Harmonizing long-standing Canadian policies and values to American policies and values essentially means capitulation. It means fear. It means buckling under to real or perceived intimidation. It means Canadians abandoning their county, its history, and its heritage. Those who believe that all these things are inevitable and that Canada has no choice are dead wrong. And, as we shall see, a strong majority of Canadians oppose those who are selling out our country.

The most important questions are clear. Are we going to continue to let the sellouts get away with it, or are we going to take actions to reverse what is happening before it's too late?

Turning the House of Commons into a Mausoleum

That's quite a little list we've just gone over. What a party the neo-liberals, the neo-conservatives, and our radical-right Americanizers are going to have! Let's see, we'll be able to abolish the departments of finance, environment, health, transportation, energy, communications, defence, trade, immigration, the competition bureau, customs and excise, forestry, and there's more to come. Think of the savings!

Come to think of it, won't we also be able to abolish elections as well? We could even turn the House of Commons into a museum. Or a mausoleum.

And, just imagine, maybe George Junior would appoint Brian as the new colony's first governor, and maybe even Lord Crossover to replace Adrienne Clarkson, with Barbara Amiel as Her Excellency.

Harmonization is the kissing cousin of integration. Let's return to the Conference Board of Canada. The integration of Canada with the U.S. "proceeded at a furious pace over the 1990s. Nor is there any reason to believe that this integration will be reversed in the years to come" says the Board. One only wonders exactly what this pro-big-business lobby expected would happen after they so enthusiastically lobbied for the FTA. Did they *really* not understand that "a furious pace" of integration would follow?

But now the Conference Board, if not worried, seems to be at last beginning to understand what it was that so many of us were predicting would happen:

> Integration in North America gives rise to a related question – can Canadians continue to compete in an even more integrated North American space without adopting U.S. regulations, U.S.-style education and health care, U.S. balance between private and public responsibilities and spending, or the U.S. currency without sacrificing the Canadian Way?

It's too bad that the Conference Board didn't think about asking this question *before* they jumped so enthusiastically on the free trade bandwagon. It's also too bad they don't appear to have the courage to provide the obvious answer to their own question. At least they admit that the extent of the integration "is not well understood by most Canadians."

For Anne Golden, the bright, ebullient, recently appointed president and CEO of the Conference Board, there's little doubt about what is now happening to Canada:

> We are gathering speed along the road to integration. Without vigorous public debate and proactive decision-making, Canada may soon run out of room to chart its own course within an integrated North America.

Meanwhile, Michael Hart, former Canadian trade official who is now at Carleton University, says, "the FTA has [brought about] a significant level of deepening cross border integration" and we can now see "accelerating integration" with "private-sector-led integration intensifying."[*]

Hart wants harmonization of standards, regulations, testing protocols, investment regulations, procurement policies, competition and subsidies policies, regulatory differences . . . "an initiative that is bold, broad, and deep."

Why not throw in the flag as well?

And how does Ottawa feel about this? George Haynal, then assistant deputy minister in the Department of Foreign Affairs and International Trade, advised:

> A process of policy convergence is already well in train. It is becoming more intense. It is building a level of integration that extends beyond the economy. . . . The question is less whether we need to negotiate new instruments to further the process, but whether the public realm is capable of keeping up with emerging forces pushing us into deeper integration.[†]

Get that? The question is not how we're going to put a stop to the intense, rapid integration that will destroy our country; the question is how will the Canadian public ever be able to keep up with what our political and economic elite have planned for us? Should one be surprised that Haynal has gone to work for Tom d'Aquino?

Most of us can remember a time when the Department of External Affairs was a strong, proud arm of government dedicated to Canadian independence and self-determination. Today the department is a mere adjunct to trade department salesmen whose major specialty is selling the country.

If you think Haynal's statement is shocking, how about that of Raymond Chrétien, who has little doubt about the future? According to Stephen Handelman, *Time* magazine's authority on Canada,

> Distilling his six years in Washington into a sort of valedictory address, Chrétien concluded that Canada's traditional defensiveness in dealing

---

[*] *Canada, the United States, and Deepening Integration: Next Steps,* June 12, 2001.
[†] Industry Canada, *North American Economic Integration Project,* 2001.

with the U.S. has been misdirected: cultural and economic protectiveness could disrupt the relationship most responsible for the country's prosperity. "We should not be afraid of economic integration."[*]

Is integration proceeding more rapidly than most Canadians realize? A year ago Eric Reguly wrote:

> What's on TV and in the newspapers and elsewhere . . . is evidence that integration, and not just the economic variety, is in reality happening so fast that it's becoming a blur.
>
> Energy integration is being led by the premiers and governors; . . . the feds have been shunted off to the side. Integration is happening in every industry. American dealers are moving north and are stealing Bay Street's business. The U.S. Securities and Exchange Commission's policies dictate the standard of Canadian regulation and disclosure.
>
> A study by the Carnegie Endowment for International Peace noted that Canada and the United States, in certain sectors, are becoming more integrated than the European Union.
>
> Integration on every level is happening quickly. It's time to start paying attention.[†]

Jim Travers, Ottawa correspondent for the *Toronto Star* and former editor of the *Ottawa Citizen*, sums it up:

> Call it traitorous, inevitable or simply necessary, but recognize that Canada is on track and moving fast toward greater integration with the United States.
>
> Canada is being drawn deeper into the economic, political, cultural and military sphere of the last superpower.
>
> The drums are beating for a forced march south.[**]

Why don't we call it what it is?
Traitorous.

---

[*] *Time*, July 10, 2000.
[†] *Globe and Mail*, September 1, 2001.
[**] *Toronto Star*, November 3, 2001.

No Cop on the Beat: Deregulation and Privatization

The Americanization of Canada means adopting political and economic policies such as deregulation and privatization.

A *New York Times* article describes power deregulation in California as "disastrous" and "an epic transfer of wealth."

> "People now realize that this was a monumental scam," said Gov. Gray Davis. Up to a third of the electricity that should have been available was taken off line, creating an artificial shortage that drove up prices ... "We had plenty of electric power available, but we didn't have a cop on the beat."
>
> The most egregious example of price gouging was when Duke Energy charged the state $3,880 for a single megawatt hour that had cost about $30 one year earlier.[*]

One month later, headlines proclaimed "Enron collapse sparks concern about future deregulation" as the gigantic collapse of the fraudulent energy firm shook Houston and Washington, and banks, accounting firms, investment dealers, and stock markets around the world.

"Enron was considered the leading voice for reducing government regulation to a minimum."[†] Many months after the fact we learned of how Enron masterminded artificial power shortages in California to boost prices.

Despite the debacles of power deregulation in the United States, Canada's radical right and the Ontario, Alberta, and British Columbia governments have plunged ahead down the road to higher costs, uncertainty, and possible chaos.

In California there's now a clear consensus that "Electricity is too essential to be left to the market. . . . It is a critical, life-giving resource, not a commodity."

---

[*] *New York Times*, November 4, 2001.
[†] *New York Times*, February 10, 2002.

Botched deregulation of the state's power sector led to soaring prices, near-bankrupt utilities, and black outs.[*]

The upshot of what has now happened in California is plain for all to see. Government took back control and now runs a huge state-owned electric utility in a public system similar to the one that existed prior to deregulation. In Governor Davis's words, deregulation and privatization were "a colossal failure."

Today, the power crisis in California is over, conservation has increased, and the state is exporting electricity.

The tragedy that occurred in Walkerton, Ontario, leaving seven people dead and causing some 2,300 people to become ill, is a sad example of what happens when radical-right ideology tramples common sense. In the words of the Hon. Dennis R. O'Connor's inquiry,

> I am satisfied that if the Ontario Ministry of Environment had adequately fulfilled its regulatory and oversight role, the tragedy of Walkerton would have been prevented or at least significantly reduced in scope.

But, if you have a government that, despite "numerous warnings" about increased risk, then proceeds to cut $200 million and 750 employees from its department budget, then should a disaster such as Walkerton come as a surprise? Yet, in Mr. Justice O'Connor's words, "There is no evidence that the risks were properly assessed or addressed."

Lockstep with deregulation comes privatization. Now, more than any other time in Canadian history, the radical right is successfully pushing an American-style, across-the-board privatization agenda: medicare, utilities, prisons, schools and universities, policing, Via Rail, every Crown corporation you can think of and Crown timber lands, airline terminals, and air traffic control; the list is endless.

Ottawa has even decided to hand over the administration and operation of its gun licensing and registration system to the private sector.

The far-right mantra is that civil servants on the public payroll are tenured, lazy, lacking in innovative skills and productivity, while corporate

---

[*] *The Economist*, July 21, 2001.

executives are energetic, imaginative, and, because they are driven by the profit motive, they work harder to succeed. (Think Enron and WorldCom, for example).

As journalist and author Linda McQuaig notes, the radical right believes

> that nobody ever gets involved in government or the political arena out of a desire to accomplish public goals, and that all the products of government – the building of schools, hospitals, roads, libraries, museums, public parks – happen only incidentally, as by-products of someone's desire to advance a personal career.

In fact, for many on the far right, for the most part the idea of the public good is an ill-considered concept far down any list of priorities, which always begins with profit. Government shouldn't be allowed to set priorities, unless of course the business round tables, the business-financed institutes, and the lobbyists have had a chance to successfully present their own priorities first.

In an excellent column about the proposed and now apparently aborted privatization of Ontario Hydro, *Ottawa Citizen* journalist Susan Riley writes:

> When are governments going to figure out that privatization isn't an economic cure-all, that while it may sound bracingly practical, it doesn't often do much for the ordinary citizen?

As the evidence accumulated, more and more it looked like the Ontario Hydro privatization would be a very costly mistake. Inevitably electricity costs would rise and Ontario's long-standing power price advantage over neighbouring U.S. states would disappear. So why was the Ontario government still considering proceeding with what would have been the largest and riskiest privatization in Canadian history? Riley has the answer; it simply boils down to right-wing ideology:

> The larger implication is clear: In public hands, utilities grow lazy and complacent and there is no motive to expand, improve or develop new markets.

Try telling that to the successful Hydro-Québec or Edmonton's popular and thriving Epcor. Epcor's CEO, Don Lowry, says:

> Epcor is 100 per cent owned by the City of Edmonton. In the last four years we set ourselves the goal of becoming one of the top integrated power utilities in Canada. Today our earnings have doubled the levels of 1998, hitting $300m before tax in 2001. We pay both federal and provincial tax and therefore compete on a level playing field with private sector companies. And we dividend back to the City of Edmonton over $100m per annum.
>
> Every day we pit our people against the best of the private sector and anyway you measure it, we're doing it right!

"No motive to expand, improve or develop new markets"? I suggest a newly privatized Ontario Hydro would quickly have to start looking over its shoulder.

Is there anyone anywhere willing to point to the privatization of Air Canada as a success story?

Surely there are countless examples of poorly run private corporations, and there are Crown corporations that deserve to be privatized. But the blinkered ideological rush to follow American philosophy and privatize the CBC and every other public entity in sight is not only a huge departure from Canada's long-standing tradition of mostly-private-but-some-public-where-warranted, but is also a terrible, costly mistake.

And surely the answer is that in some cases public utilities can provide economies of scale and efficiencies that the market cannot. Ask the people of California how they liked their electricity privatization, ask New Yorkers how they like privatized garbage collection, and ask the British how they like railway privatization. Dalton Camp wrote about what happened in Britain:

> A friend standing in line at a railway station washroom in Britain observed the following sign, erected by the management: "Due to service improvement, there are reduced toilet facilities on this floor."
>
> British Rail, once a wholly owned public railway, has been sacrificed to the gods of privatization. Instead of one publicly-owned

railway, privatization gave Britons 25 new railways. These, Britons were assured, would provide improved service, healthy competition, lower fares and further delights.

The result has been chaos . . . an awesome decline in the quality of passenger service, frequent delays and cancellations, not to mention the increased danger to life and limb now provided by a public service driven by the lust of private profit.

Meanwhile, the government is still shelling out millions of pounds in subsidy for maintenance and other infrastructure costs. The British experience speaks eloquently to the high public cost of free market capitalization.[*]

And what about the assertion that private companies are better-managed? *The Economist* tells us more about Britain's privately run railways:

Dreadful management made things worse. Top jobs went to executives with no knowledge of the industry; they called in consultants with no knowledge of the industry. Costs got out of control, tripling the total bill.

And, as for the future,

The government will, in effect, have to underwrite any future investment which means that the rail network has been renationalized in all but name.[†]

Let's see now. Did the privatized Air Canada (which helped drive two other private firms, Canadian Airlines and Canada 3000, out of business) lead to lower fares or better service? And given what has happened to Air Canada's share price, would private Canadian investors now like to invest in Robert Milton's private airline?[**]

Supposing I am invited to give a mid-week speech in St. John's, Newfoundland, as I was last year, but can't stay over on a Saturday night.

---

[*] *Toronto Star*, January 14, 2001.
[†] October 13, 2001.
[**] At this writing, Air Canada shares are $6.45. In May 2000 they were $20.90.

Want to take a guess as to what my *economy* Air Canada fare would be from Edmonton?

Try $4,054.23.

To Toronto? $2,819.45.

To London, England? $902.00.

How's that for helping out with national unity, and helping Canadians get to know their own country? But, then again, why would the last three heads of Air Canada, all Americans, care about national unity? In November, 1999, in reference to yet another American Air Canada appointment, Peter Lougheed said "This guy comes up from Boston – I bet he couldn't find Red Deer on the map."[*]

It's impossible to comprehend, given the U.S. experience with private jails, how the Ontario government could conceivably allow an American company to run the Penetanguishene superjail north of Toronto. What a colossal insult to Canadians, and what an absurd abandonment of Canadian standards and values. Not to be left behind, Alberta is now considering the privatization of its prisons. Ideology tramples common sense.

Shortly we'll look at the question of the Canada–U.S. border, and the pressure for its abolition. Not to worry though. Even if the border disappears and more drugs, guns, and criminals flow from south to north, we should be well-protected. The latest available figures show 85,000 private security personnel in Canada, while the number of police officers has dropped from over 59,000 in 1993 down to 56,000 in 2000.

There's another aspect to privatization. Frequently, in the past, when a Crown corporation has been privatized and the industry deregulated, the private Canadian company is then taken over by an American corporation. Just what we want.

Last year Ekos did a national public-opinion poll on the question of privatization. Only one in five Canadians said there was too little privatization. Once again it is clear that the will of most Canadians and the direction our political and corporate elites are taking us in are totally opposite.

The problem with letting "the invisible hand" rule is that, not that infrequently, as in the case of Enron, the invisible hand can't be seen stealing until well after the fact.

---

[*] *National Post*, November 26, 1999.

As the manuscript for this book goes off to the publisher, a *Toronto Star* editorial reads: "Private labs have failed to keep water safe" . . . "Drinking water not being properly tested."[*]

After what happened in Walkerton, it's hard to imagine.

Erasing the Border and Erasing the Country

Can you remember the dramatic Liberal television ads during the 1988 free trade election campaign, that showed a map and the Canada–U.S. border being erased as a warning to Canadians about what would happen if Brian Mulroney was re-elected? Since their election in 1993, the Chrétien government has had their erasers firmly in hand and have been hard at work.

During the free trade debates in the 1980s, big business sold the deal to Canadians as if it was essentially a trade deal which would get rid of tariffs and reduce the price of imported goods coming into Canada. The BCNI and friends rarely, if ever, mentioned all the other important aspects of the agreement relating to foreign investment, energy and resource sharing, and other clauses intended to permanently tie the hands of government, and many, many more unprecedented departures from previous Canada–U.S. arrangements. All of these new obligations were far more important then the mostly tiny tariffs which were still left after several rounds of international GATT negotiations.

Precisely the same sort of misleading tactics are now being employed in the corporate and political campaign to push us into an inescapable American embrace.

Not too long ago, if anyone seriously suggested abolishing the Canada–U.S. border, they would have been laughed out of the House of Commons, any provincial legislature, or even the Chamber of Commerce. Today, many of our leading radical-right collaborators are seriously talking about getting rid of the border. It's hard to believe that this is really happening.

---

[*] *Toronto Star*, June 14, 2002.

Who is it that is pushing us to consider making such a tragic mistake, which would surely be the modern Canadian Last Spike, the final nail in Canada's coffin?

Here's a short list: The Conference Board of Canada; B.C. premier Gordon Campbell; C.N. CEO Paul Tellier; Maurizio Bevilacqua, Liberal chairman of the Commons Finance Committee; Tony Valeri, chairman of the Liberal caucus Economic Development Committee; former Ontario premier Mike Harris; David O'Brien, former head of Canadian Pacific; The Canadian Manufacturers and Exporters Association; David Zussman, the prime minister's friend. And that's just a beginning.

So, what's the problem? Why not simply get rid of the border? Why not have a comprehensive customs union? Why not harmonize customs, immigration, and trade policies with the U.S.? Why not let the FBI and other American law-enforcement agencies share duties with Canadians in this country? Why not adopt a common currency with the U.S.? Why not welcome the National Rifle Association?

For TD chief economist Don Drummond, the border must be open and we should forget the "gibberish" that harmonizing our rules with those of the U.S. would hurt our sovereignty. "We don't have a choice here."*

No choice; no gibberish.

For Liberal strategist John Duffy, what would be required, "at a minimum," would be "harmonized immigration and security policies and systems to manage the flow of people at the continent's perimeter." But, wouldn't this create "big questions about sovereignty"?

No problem, says the overwhelmingly Canadian open-border crowd. While we're at it, let's go for a customs union, a common market and political union.

Anyway, what's to worry? According to Duffy,

Most of the people I speak for (mainly those under 45) don't agonize over Canadian identity.†

---

* *Edmonton Journal*, November 28, 2001.
† *Globe and Mail*, November 28, 2001.

With patriotic strategists like that, is it any wonder that the Liberals are continuing to sell out the country?

Then we must return to David Zussman, who

> argues that, in return for eliminating the border, the U.S. would undoubtedly demand changes to Canadian laws on drugs, immigration, refugees, terrorism – and even the Constitution's Charter of Rights and Freedoms.[*]

Well, if that's all . . .

For Peter C. Newman, since the events of September 11, 2001,

> Washington's pressure tactics threaten to define the limits of our citizenship by demoting Canada into a mongrel political entity known as "NAP" – the North American Perimeter.

Abandoning our previous control over our own border

> is too high a price to pay. Our border has defined us. It has been the symbolic barrier that delineates us as a people, separating us from the compatible but far from identical society to the south.
>
> Maintaining an effective border between us remains essential to Canada's survival.

Surely there isn't a single soul who seriously believe that in "a common perimeter" Canada would have any important say in key decisions that will be made about security or refugee and about immigration policy? And does anyone really believe that even if Canada agreed to a common perimeter, the U.S. would relax its own forty-ninth parallel rules?

And would becoming enveloped in a perimeter not automatically necessitate becoming deeply involved in George W. Bush's Son-of-Star-Wars plan?

Carol Goar puts it well:

> It has become fashionable in influential circles to ask why Canada and the United States need a border at all.

---

[*] *Toronto Star*, October 25, 2001.

But, if the question is essentially what can we do about a supposedly clogged border,

> No one, except frustrated truckers, seem to have examined the possibility that the border crossings are simply understaffed. It might be useful for the politicians and economists who are advocating wholesale changes in customs and immigration policy to go out and count how many lanes of traffic are closed on any given day.
>
> Borders have purposes that go far beyond regulating trade. They define where home is. They allow a nation to decide the laws and policies by which its citizens live. They give a people a territory within which their values hold sway. They create a sense of community.
>
> Now, according to business leaders and their advocates in Ottawa, such attitudes are obsolete. They brush aside concerns about sovereignty as knee-jerk anti-Americanism.
>
> It would be a mistake of historic proportions to assume that national independence is too much of a bother for Canadians.[*]

Mary Janigan of *Maclean's* has reported that, at a meeting between Canadian and U.S. corporate executives, "To everyone's surprise, the discussion constantly returned to U.S. security concerns about Canada."[†]

Never mind that there were more than 6 million illegal aliens in the U.S. at the time, and that thirteen of the nineteen September 11 hijackers entered the U.S. legally on student tourist or business visas. As far as many Americans were concerned, Canada had to assume some responsibility for what happened to the World Trade Center and change its policies pronto.

How Canada ever allowed itself to become such a scapegoat for the terrorists attacks in the U.S. is beyond my comprehension. As James Travers has written, "Despite compelling contrary evidence, this open but hardly careless society has been branded a soft touch for terrorists and bogus refugees."[**]

True, there has been activity by terrorists in this country, but can you name many countries where this has not been the case? True, we've made some security mistakes in the past, but do any even begin to rival

---

[*] *Toronto Star*, November 8, 2001.
[†] *Maclean's*, September 24, 2001.
[**] *Toronto Star*, December 13, 2001.

the colossal incompetence of the FBI, the CIA, and the U.S. National Security Agency with their combined $30 billion budgets?

We've done a great deal to beef up security in Canada since the September 11 attacks. But do we have to give away the country as well? Do we really have to accept serious new limitations on civil liberties, armed American law enforcement officials in our country, and harmonization with American immigration and refugee standards?

While it's true that Ahmed Ressam was arrested in December 1999 while attempting to enter the U.S. from Canada with a car full of explosives, it's also true that Canada played a role in his apprehension. Meanwhile, the U.S. was allowing terrorists to learn how to fly giant jets, nice innocent fellows who expressed no interest in how to take off or land the huge planes, but still somehow managed to get Americans to teach them to fly.

U.S. Ambassador Cellucci suggested that if Canada doesn't go along with American harmonization and perimeter requests, "The alternative to this might be that we would have to tighten up the border between the United States and Canada where we have all this commerce going back and forth."*

Oh dear! With a tightened border, how would we ever be able to ship the Americans all that oil, natural gas, and electricity they are so desperately dependent on us for? And what about the fact that for decades Canada has been the number-one destination, far ahead of all other countries, for U.S. exports? Millions of American jobs depend on exports to Canada. Is Mr. Cellucci suggesting that a tightened border would work only one way? (By the way, the security-conscious Cellucci promoted one of his drivers as head of security at Logan International Airport before the September 11 attacks.)

Paul Cellucci is gung-ho for a "NAFTA-plus" integration. Let's see now, exactly which of our Canadian standards, values, regulations, and customs would he like the U.S. to integrate with?

A couple of other points:

Anyone who visits California, Arizona, Texas, and other parts of the southern United States knows just how much of the U.S. economy is based on paying rock-bottom minimum wages to millions of illegal

---

* *Globe and Mail*, September 21, 2001.

Mexican immigrants. Now what would happen to workers' wages in Canada once we abolish the border? (Come to think of it, maybe that's what Tom d'Aquino and friends have had in mind all along).

And, how come no one seems to be talking about the other side of the security coin? Every one of those involved in the World Trade Center and Pentagon attacks on September 11 was a terrorist living in the United States, and many of them lived in the U.S. for years. If Canada agreed to abolish the border, what security would we have from other terrorists now living in the U.S.? Or, for that matter, from the insane disseminators of anthrax, or from the many weird U.S. militia members, racist Ku Klux Klan criminals, U.S. drug dealers, and American organized crime?

Not much, I would guess.

Would an open or non-existent border really bring greater risk of American criminal activity in Canada? The *Globe and Mail* tells us:

> A government study highlights a concern . . . that U.S. crime and guns will flow into Canada if the border is relaxed. Government documents indicate that 7,750 guns were confiscated at the border between 1994 and 1998.[*]

The suggestion that integration between Canada and the U.S. would be no different than the integration in The European Union is, at best, specious.

The European Union is profoundly different from any arrangements Canada might make with the U.S. In the EU there are fifteen countries with twelve more candidates hoping for entry. Germany, Britain, France, and Italy have an identical number of EU Council of Ministers votes, with Spain just slightly behind. All EU members have ceded some authority to the central council. No one country dominates. In contrast, the Canada–U.S. integration is the most asymmetrical of all industrialized countries.

Those who compare what is happening to Canada in relation to the U.S. with the European Union intentionally mislead. Not only are the comparisons illogical, but almost certainly most of those who make such claims know better. The Conference Board, in a brief paragraph, explains:

---

[*] *Globe and Mail*, November 8, 2001.

Issues of convergence are complicated by the current lack of governance institutions that match the North American–wide scope of business activities. Given the dominance of the United States in North America, it is difficult to see how such institutions could be set up in a fashion considered to be equitable by all. This situation contrasts sharply with the European experience, where the creation of governance institutions that are continent-wide in scope resulted in part from the existence of several major powers of roughly equal economic and political weight.

Anyone who now suggests that the U.S. will agree to establish new joint institutions that involve the U.S. surrendering even tiny amounts of power is hopelessly naive, ill-informed, or bent on deception.

Lastly, harmonizing our immigration policies with those of the U.S. would mean accepting many more immigrants from right-wing countries, even if they are run by oppressive, murderous, fascist military dictators, and few – if any – refugees fleeing from persecution in many other countries.

Canada has always been much more even-handed in its approach to those who seek asylum. Yes, we've made mistakes in the past, and yes, our system can be improved. But to adopt American immigration and refugee standards and policies would be a tragic injustice.

Ah, but you needn't really be too concerned. Three of every four of our "Canadian business leaders" say that "a common perimeter, including common rules for immigrants, refugees, and visitors, is essential."[*]

The Loonie and the Loony Tunes

Just as only a few years ago Canadians who advocated abolishing the border would have been treated with contempt and scorn, until recently proposals that we abandon our own currency would have been dismissed as loony.

---

[*] *National Post*, October 26, 2001.

While it is true that the Canadian dollar has dropped substantially against the U.S. dollar, other currencies have been sideswiped in an even worse way. Italy, New Zealand, and Australia, for example, saw their currencies plummet by about 60 per cent against the U.S. dollar.

Lower commodity prices, the large American current-account deficits requiring massive capital inflows into the U.S., stock market chaos and world instability have all hurt the Canadian dollar.

We all know the pro and con arguments about a low C$: travel in the U.S. has become terribly expensive, machinery and equipment imports from the U.S. are hurt. On the flip side, Canadian exports to the U.S. have exploded, not because of the FTA primarily, but because of the low C$. One study suggested that the declining C$ was responsible for 85 per cent of our increased exports.

But there's another very important point to be made, and Jeff Rubin makes it well:

Why hasn't the nearly 30 per cent devaluation of the Canadian dollar since 1990 blazed a trail of rising inflation? Particularly when the U.S. import content of the Canadian consumer price basket has risen almost 30 per cent?

The simple pass-through of rising import costs alone should have spelled steadily rising inflation and almost certainly higher inflation in Canada than stateside. Instead, Canada has had the lowest inflation in decades and has had lower inflation than in the United States in each and every year.

Now, why would that be? Haven't we been warned for years by the neo-conservative economists that the falling dollar would bring uncontrollable inflation? Rubin continues:

World firms charge different prices in different markets. The same Canali suit sells for $2,000 Canadian in Toronto and $2,000 U.S. in New York. The same holds true for a pair of Gap jeans that retail for $70 Canadian in Toronto, but sell for $70 in New York.

Multinational firms don't make Canadian consumers bear the true costs of exchange rate depreciation. If they did, they wouldn't have too much of a market up here.

Canadians aren't quite as poor as our beleaguered currency implies. We're able to buy many brand-name American goods at prices cheaper than American themselves pay in their own market.[*]

(Earlier this year, visiting family in Los Angeles, I bought a Bobby Jones golf sweater for $125 U.S. Two weeks later, I saw exactly the same sweater in an Edmonton store, priced at $125 Canadian). Economist Jim Stanford makes a similar point:

> Contrary to Bay Street mythology, the real standard of living of Canadians does not depend importantly on the value of the loonie. Like most Canadians, my standard of living depends exclusively on how much I earn in my job and the price of the things I buy. My salary is denominated in Canadian dollars. And most of the things I buy – my house, almost all private services, all public services (which I buy through my taxes), and about half of my manufactured products – are made right here in Canada, by Canadians, for Canadians. Even imported purchases reflect changes in the loonie only gradually and partially.
>
> To see this, go to a bookstore and pick out any volume that lists prices in both U.S. and Canadian dollars – like Stephen King's latest paperback, *Dreamcatcher*. The U.S. price is $7.99. At a 62-cent dollar, it should cost me $12.89 (Canadian). But the actual Canadian price is only $10.99. I am "saving" almost two dollars by buying it in Canada.
>
> The apparent savings are all the greater on big-ticket items, like cars. A new Impala LS sedan lists for about $24,000 (U.S.) in Boston. With a 62-cent dollar, it should cost me $38,000 in Canada. But I can buy one in Toronto for $29,500 (Canadian). Cars, like most other goods and services, are much cheaper in Canada than they should be given the apparent exchange rate.[†]

All things considered, the true purchasing power of the loonie in Canada is almost 20 per cent higher than its exchange rate value. The Canadian dollar can often buy in Canada what would likely cost at least eighty cents in the U.S.

A *Globe and Mail* editorial makes a couple of other strong points:

---

[*] *Globe and Mail*, November 24, 2001.
[†] *Globe and Mail*, November 2, 2001.

It certainly is difficult to follow the logic of those who say the new record low is proof that Canada should abandon national sovereignty and adopt the U.S. dollar – essentially converting our currency for U.S. dollars at its lowest value ever.

Canadians accept that a stable domestic economy matters far more than a weak international currency. We still enjoy a strong standard of living because we do not have crippling interest rates, soaring inflation and record levels of unemployment. It is not worth abandoning this stability for the sake of cross border shopping trips and our damaged national pride.[*]

(Remember when the same people who are now complaining about the low C$ were stridently complaining about too much Canadian cross-border shopping?)

Argentina gambled when in 1991 it strapped itself into a U.S.-dollar straitjacket.

As the dollar strengthened on international markets, Argentina's goods became too expensive to export and its prices for everything from wages to tango shows became too costly for either investors or tourists – ushering in a four-year slide with no end in sight. After 41 months of a steadily shrinking economy, one in every six workers is jobless. Each day an estimated 2,000 Argentines cross an invisible line from middle class to poverty.[†]

As Thomas Walkom explains:

When commodity prices fell, other commodity-exporting nations, like Canada, merely allowed their currencies to float downward against the U.S. dollar. In effect, these countries lowered the U.S. dollar prices of their goods, allowing them to compete in world markets.

With a fixed currency, Argentina could not make use of this safety valve. Instead, it began to go more into debt to bolster the peso. To pay for the increased debt charges, it slashed social spending.[**]

---

[*] *Globe and Mail*, January 28, 2001.
[†] *Wall Street Journal*, January 8, 2001.
[**] *Toronto Star*, January 8, 2002.

And then, in an inexorable downward spiral, things began to get even worse. At this writing, just under half of all Argentines are living in poverty, and much of what was once the country's middle class is now poor.

Blind to the terrible experience of Argentina, apparently indifferent to concerns about Canadian independence, continentalists like Sherry Cooper preach the demise of the Canadian dollar and push either for the adoption of a common North American currency or for the U.S. dollar.[*] For Cooper, the Canadian dollar is merely a "peripheral currency" and we shouldn't regard it as "an emotional symbol."[†]

Jeffery Rubin says of the Argentine experience:

> It's a huge lesson for Canada, It's a spectacular example of the failure of dollarization.

For Canadians, managing our own currency has effectively acted as a shock absorber in the past, and will do so when necessary in the future. But for Sherry Cooper, there's been enough talk already, "Let's dollarize and get it over with . . . while we are harmonizing immigration policy, border controls, airline security and trade policy, why not proceed to dollarize as well?"[**]

I have a better question. What keeps Sherry Cooper in Canada? Why doesn't she just move back to the U.S.? Almost every time I read one of her columns, I ask the same question.

Peter C. Newman sums it up nicely:

> How can a country claim to be independent when it has lost control of its monetary policy? What more appropriate symbol of American domination of Canada than to have their dollars in our pockets and purses as the currency of our lives?

Let's stop and reflect on of this for a moment. Do the advocates of adopting the U.S. dollar not understand what a colossal abandonment of Canadian sovereignty that would represent? Gone would be our ability to control interest rates and unemployment rates. Gone would be our

---

[*] *Financial Post*, December 7, 2001.

[†] *Canadian Press*, January 2, 2002.

[**] *Financial Post*, November 9, 2001.

own spending priorities. Do they understand this? Of course they do. Is that what they want? You bet.

The Department of Finance has it right: "Dollarization is unacceptable to us. It would mean zero influence over monetary policy, zero democratic accountability, and zero capacity to deal with crises."*

Monetary policy control is a fundamental requisite of government. Lose it and you also not only lose fiscal control, but inevitably political control as well.

Let's return to the question of why some Canadians are so aggressively pushing dollarization. Given all the obvious reasons why adopting the U.S. dollar would be a truly fatal move, why would these advocates of this abandonment be pushing the proposal so strenuously? We know that it's not always because they are not very bright, because some of them are clever. Linda McQuaig has the answer, and expresses it well:

> There would be another effect from adopting the U.S. dollar – it would put even more pressure on us to adopt U.S.-style tax and spending policies. The double whammy of labour discipline and convergence with U.S. policies certainly explains why some on the right are so keen about the idea. It's just a faster route to remaking Canada more strictly along market lines.†

Long-time continentalist Tom Courchene of Queen's University is another U.S.-dollarizer. I've read and listened to his reasoning and consider it to be not only flawed, but sometimes incomprehensible. Amazingly he says, "I'm quite nationalistic on this issue. I'm on the side of the angels." If Courchene is nationalistic, then I suppose we would also have to accept Conrad Black's bizarre statement that renouncing his Canadian citizenship was a patriotic act.

Courchene's solution is a currency union with the U.S. – creating a North American monetary union where we can keep the Bank of Canada.** He joins with the Fraser Institute's Herbert Grubel, Dale Orr of the U.S. forecasting firm WEFA, and B.C. economist Richard Harris in opting for a "common currency" or a "currency union."

---

* *National Post*, April 4, 2001.
† *National Post*, December 3, 2001.
** *Edmonton Journal*, May 7, 2001.

Anyone who believes that the U.S. would abandon its own currency for any kind of "common currency" is out of touch with reality. And anyone who believes that Canada would have any substantive say in decisions of the U.S. Federal Reserve Board is hopelessly naive. Monetary policy would be set in Washington and Canada would have no choice but to alter our fiscal and other policies accordingly. Goodbye social programs.

Once again, comparisons with the European Union are illusory, and those who do so either should know why or more likely *do* know why. In Europe many countries have decided to pool their sovereignty to create the euro. If Canada foolishly should wish to abandon its currency after almost 150 years the only alternative would be to adopt American money.

Okay, how do Canadians feel about all of this? In 2000, 70 per cent of Canadians said that maintaining a Canadian dollar is essential to economic sovereignty and national identity.[*] In another poll, 59 per cent said it would not be a good idea to adopt the U.S. dollar, 36 per cent said it would be a good idea.[†]

Once again, the gulf between overall Canadian public opinion and the opinions of our continentalist, corporate elite is apparent.

In the summer of 2001, almost half of Canadian CEOs polled approved of abandoning the Canadian dollar.

By November, when asked by the *National Post* if we should adopt the U.S. dollar, 54 per cent of Canadian CEOs said definitely or probably. Only 22 per cent said definitely not, while 78 per cent of big-business CEOs said Canada should consider adopting U.S. currency.[**]

Remember all those Canadians, whom I wrote about earlier, who died in the first and second world wars on behalf of our country? I wonder how they would feel about what follows.

---

[*] Ekos Research Associates, 2000.
[†] *Globe and Mail*, November 7, 2001.
[**] *National Post*, November 17, 2001.

"Ready, Aye, Ready" for the Lap Dog

In this morning's paper, there is news of secret talks proposing to merge the Canadian armed forces into a single North American Command. The proposal has come from the Pentagon, but has been enthusiastically received by some members of the government in Ottawa and by some of the leaders of our armed forces.

Only a few years ago such an abandonment of Canadian sovereignty would have been greeted with outrage. Today, the Liberals worry little about such mundane issues. At this writing, there now is talk of integrating "the Coast Guard, border police, customs and immigration [as well] as parallel Canadian organizations, including CSIS, the RCMP and the Canadian Customs and Revenue Agency could be included."[*]

Why stop there? Why not also integrate the House of Commons with the U.S. House of Representatives and Senate? And surely the White House would be able to find some basement space for the PMO.

Canadian historian Desmond Morton has written eloquently about defence. Where have attacks on Canada come from?

> Threats to our separate existence come across our southern border. Invaders from the south conquered New France in 1760. They tried again in 1775 and from 1812 to 1814. So did assorted Americans from 1838 to 1841, and Fenians from 1866 to 1871.

But that was long ago. In the twentieth century, Canadians seemed to love the idea of "the world's longest undefended border" with the U.S. At least it *was* "undefended" until, post-9/11, George W. Bush and colleagues decided to bring in the troops to patrol the border against all the hordes of dangerous terrorists from Canada.

Desmond Morton writes about the vitally important role Canadians played in the defence of freedom during the first and second world wars (while the U.S. sat back, eventually joining in years after the conflicts began, and in 1941 only after being attacked by Japan).

---

[*] Hugh Winsor, *Globe and Mail*, January 28, 2002.

In 1940, with the fall of France, William Lyon Mackenzie King abruptly realized Canada was now Britain's biggest ally in the war against Hitler.

In two world wars, Canada sent hundreds of thousands of fighting soldiers and up to a quarter of the flying personnel for the Royal Air Force. A hundred thousand Canadians stayed in European graves.

But, after the Second World War, Canada's defence relationship began a profound change:

In 1945, remembering that Washington had never accepted our Arctic claims, Ottawa paid for U.S. airfields in the North and for the then impassable Alaska Highway.

And Canada agreed to American requests to allow the placement of the Distant Earl Warning line of radar stations across the Arctic in 1955.

But, when Perrin Beatty, Brian Mulroney's defence minister, proposed 12 nuclear submarines for Canada's navy to patrol the High Arctic, the Pentagon nixed the plan as a nuisance for U.S. submarines under the polar ice cap.

So much for Canadian Arctic sovereignty. According to the University of Calgary's David Bercuson and Barry Cooper, we opened a new chapter in our relationship to the United States in Afghanistan:

Canadians have operated under American command before . . . but Canadian ground forces have never done so on a straight bilateral basis. In other words, all previous Canadian commitments of ground forces alongside Americans or under their command have been part of NATO operations or part of a coalition of countries formed for specific military objectives, such as the Gulf War of 1991.

Moreover,

Canada has been fully compliant in meeting the requests of the Americans in matters of border security, internal security and changes to refuge policy. In short, the government said "no" to a

North American security perimeter even as it was taking steps to put one in place.[*]

A letter-writer to the *Globe and Mail* comments:

> We entered the 20th century with Canadian troops serving under British officers. We enter the 21st century with Canadian troops serving under American officers. Are we addicted to colonialism?[†]

One measure of how far Canada has descended back down the colonial road is the attitude of our once-proud, independent armed forces. Jeffrey Simpson writes:

> the Canadian military believes Canada would be better served by integrating its forces within . . . U.S. structures, the hope being that Canadian officers might have some influence on U.S. decisions. The change would mean . . . full integration for all air, ground and sea forces involved in continental defence.
>
> The Canadian military says Canada must get inside whatever military tent the Americans are designing.[**]

Elsewhere, Simpson spells out what is happening very well:

> Canada used to have its own independent way of seeing the world. Three times in the last century Canada saw threats to world stability differently from the United States – in 1914, 1939 and during the Vietnam War. Now, however, we have become such defence and foreign policy lap dogs of the United States that – apart from inconsequential differences over irrelevancies, Canada just goes along with what the United States wants.[††]

Will there be any remnant of Canadian military sovereignty left if we sign on to George W. Bush's reckless and almost certainly unworkable missile defence system? Perhaps in some blinkered cabinet and PMO

---

[*] *National Post*, January 9, 2002.
[†] Bill Longstaff.
[**] *Globe and Mail*, December 5, 2001.
[††] *Globe and Mail*, May 23, 2001.

minds, or Alliance Party and C. D. Howe Institute headquarters, but certainly not in the foreign-affairs offices of nations around the world.

If we integrate with the U.S. military, will we also then join with the U.S. in renouncing the 1972 Anti-Ballistic Missile Treaty, one of the most important achievements in the history of nuclear de-escalation? And germ-warfare agreements? And the Geneva Conventions? How about the land mines treaty and the new International Criminal Court?

And if we did make the tragic mistake of becoming a part of Bush's mad multi-billion dollar scheme, will the Americans then promise that they won't shoot down nuclear missiles over Canada? You gotta be kidding. Once the world's buildup of nuclear weapons begins anew, as it assuredly will, will Canada be forced (or willingly agree) to deploy its own – or, more likely, American – nuclear weapons?

When the ABM treaty is shredded by the U.S., will not START 1 and START 2 be next? Will not Russia and China begin major buildups of their nuclear arsenals? Will they have any other choice? And will decades of arms control progress not evaporate?

Sooner or later, likely sooner, Washington is going to forcefully tell Ottawa that it expects Canada to become deeply involved in Bush's absurd missile-defence scheme.

And what will Ottawa's response be? Canada's Vice-Chief of Defence Staff, George Macdonald, says with respect to an "Americas Command": "We declared ourselves ready to consider an arrangement that could extend to land and sea."*

As for the future, historian Desmond Morton advises:

> Canadian wars will be American wars. Canadians will be loyal but subordinate auxiliaries. Like the Canadian Expeditionary Force at the Somme, or Northern Alliance fighters in Afghanistan, we will fight and die. Americans will give the orders, provide sophisticated hardware and announce victory.†

So much for Canadian sovereignty, so much for Canadian independence. From colony, to strong, proud nation, to a colony of "subordinate auxiliaries."

---

* *Globe and Mail,* January 2, 2002.
† *Globe and Mail,* December 31, 2001.

Paul Knox writes:

Canada worked hard throughout the cold war to balance its U.S. alliance with ties to Europe and the United Nations. Now, as Martin Shadwick of York University points out, the forces risk being seen as "an Office Overload for the Americans." If Ottawa doesn't make it clear that Canadian and U.S. military interests will at times, diverge "we could start getting invitations from Washington that we really don't want to get."[*]

And invitations that will likely prove to be impossible to refuse.

As we integrate our armed forces with the U.S. armed forces, and, mostly, under U.S. command, won't it be wonderful to see our young men and women flown off to the next American Vietnam, chanting "Ready, Aye, Ready" as they take off?

Richard Gwyn has it right:

A transformational change in Canadian foreign policy has just been enacted without public debate or even any sign there has been any debate about it within the government itself.

We're Americanizing ourselves without even asking whether that's what we want or whether we have any other choices.[†]

Senator Doug Roche, Canada's former Disarmament Ambassador to the U.N., writes:

Our values – integrity, compassion, equity, justice – are being shoved aside as Canada slides increasingly closer into a suffocating embrace with the United States.

United States' policies have become the driving force in the Canadian political system. Canada is being positioned to fight America's wars of the future.[**]

Is there really no alternative to serving on bended knee as a client state of the U.S.? Of course there is. We could return to our proud tradition of

---

[*] *Globe and Mail*, January 9, 2002.
[†] *Toronto Star*, January 9, 2002.
[**] Talk at the University of Winnipeg, January 25, 2002.

working with like-minded countries around the world to promote and enhance world peace.

Wouldn't a much better course of action for Canada be a continuation of our long-standing role as United Nations peacekeeper, while we keep our sovereignty and our role as an independent nation in the development of international treaties such as the important land mines treaty? But of course, we can't possibly be effective international peacekeepers and at the same time active combatants under U.S. military command.

Lloyd Axworthy, former foreign affairs minister, writes:

> Canada has built a reputation for promoting international responses to international problems. We have championed the efforts to eradicate land mines; we are an active proponent of arms control and disarmament treaties; we promote the creation and implementation of an International Criminal Court. These are all measures opposed by Washington, especially its Defence Department. The more we tie ourselves to U.S. military decision-making, the more we will inevitably compromise the ability of Canadian governments to pursue approaches that reflect our distinctive views of the world and Canada's role in it.[*]

People around the world are asking: What has happened to Canada? Where once we were regarded as a proud, independent country that was such a positive influence in multilateral forums around the world, today we're regarded as craven collaborators with American hegemony.

What a tragic betrayal to our war dead. What a tragic betrayal of future generations of Canadians.

The Downward Spiral of Canadian History – A Panama with Polar Bears

What should the objectives of Canadian cultural policies be? Daniel Schwanen, Senior Economist at the Institute for Research on Public Policy, puts it this way:

---

[*] *Globe and Mail*, February 4, 2002.

The objectives are to promote the availability of Canadian expression and storytelling to all Canadians, to foster excellence, to build capacity and infrastructure in cultural matters, to connect Canadians to one another, to promote Canadian interests and values abroad and to ensure that Canada is open to the world's diverse cultures.[*]

Surely the last objective must be regarded as redundant. Is there any developed country anywhere that is so open to and so swamped by foreign culture? Not to my knowledge.

Those who accuse Canada of being excessively nationalistic when it comes to cultural matters choose to ignore the long list of statistics that are published annually. For example, Canada imports more book titles every year than any other country in the world, including twice as many as the U.S. on a per capita basis. Well over half the books sold in Canada are produced outside of the country by foreign publishers. Over 80 per cent of consumer magazines on our newsstands are foreign. About 80 per cent of all tapes and CDs sold in Canada come from outside of the country, while over 94 per cent of film distribution revenue goes to non-Canadians, and about 95 per cent of screen time in Canadian theatres is devoted to foreign films.

Globe and Mail arts reporter James Adams writes:

> Some days, it seems you have a better chance of being struck by a Brinks armoured van than finding a Canadian film at your local multiplex.
>
> In Germany, the odds that a filmgoer will be able to see a German film are three in 20, in France for French films they are three in ten; in Canada it's been estimated that a filmgoer stands only a 1-in-20 chance that he or she will see a non-Hollywood production (from anywhere).[†]

It seems difficult to imagine that some of our outspoken continentalists want to break down the few remaining obstacles to the overwhelming American cultural inundation of the Canadian marketplace. For decades, movies, videos, CDs, books, magazines, and television content have been heavily dominated by U.S. product. Moreover, distribution, as in the

---

[*] *A Room of Our Own: Cultural Policies and Trade Agreements: Choices*, vol. 7, no. 4, IRPP, April 2001.

[†] *Globe and Mail*, February 2, 2002.

case of movies, is often controlled by American firms with little or no interest in Canadian content.

In the face of this long-standing reality, accusations of excessive Canadian cultural nationalism should be regarded as fanatical ravings. Yet, reading some of our nationally distributed columnists, or listening to Alliance politicians, you would think that Canadians are the world's leading cultural chauvinists.

Let's turn to television. Of the time that Canadian anglophones watch comedy or drama on television, 90 per cent is spent watching foreign programs.

Meanwhile, in appearance after appearance before the Canadian Radio-television and Telecommunications Commission (CRTC), Canada's private broadcasters promise more and better Canadian content that they then fail to deliver. Instead, in real terms, spending on Canadian content is declining. Even then, much of the Canadian drama material the private networks create is "fundamentally created by Americans for the American market," according to the Writers Guild.

Mark Starowicz, formerly of *As It Happens* and *Sunday Morning*, and the executive producer of the CBC's *Canada: A People's History*, describes what has been happening in Canada:

> Everything we believed in has been declared unfashionable. We are invited to lay aside our national culture, public broadcasting, accessible university funding (you should feel good about paying $20,000).
>
> Today the existence of Canada as a separate economic or cultural particularity, or even a legal jurisdiction, is not convenient to the modern global marketplace. It complicates the transnational pharmaceutical industry, the entertainment industry and the transportation industry, to name a few.[*]

Starowicz contrasts what is happening today with our history. In 1932, American radio stations threatened to swamp Canada, appropriating "every clear channel on the band, including those used by Canadian stations. The transmission power of the American stations virtually blotted out the weaker Canadian stations." But "a flood of determination swept Canada." Hundreds of groups – women, religious, farm, labour, veter-

---

[*] *Globe and Mail*, January 2, 2002.

ans, aboriginal, boards of trade – and numerous well-known public figures banded together. The result:

> The Canadian Radio Broadcasting Act of 1932 took control of the airwaves for the people. It is the constitution of this country's cultural sovereignty, the declaration that the population north of the 49th parallel was determined to have its own culture, and evolve its own agenda. The economic ripple nurtured generations of writers, singers and musicians who might never have been.

And it was the Conservative Prime Minister R. B. Bennett who introduced the Broadcasting Act to ensure that public broadcasting would bring the pleasures and benefits of our own culture to Canadians.

Starowicz points out that in 1971, the CRTC, under Pierre Juneau,

> created the Canadian music industry with one simple regulation requiring all AM radio stations in Canada to play at least 30-per-cent Canadian music. The private broadcasters reacted like scalded cats.
>
> I remember DJs contemptuously saying, "Now we have to reach into the Beaver Bin for some droppings" when they had to play a Canadian song. Now we have Celine Dion, Shania Twain, the Barenaked Ladies, Alanis Morissette, Sarah McLachlan and a list that could fill this entire page.

And today? Can you possibly imagine any potential Conservative, Alliance, or Liberal prime minister anywhere in the wings who would have the vision and courage to show similar leadership in defence of Canadian content? The chance of this happening is as remote as Ralph Klein becoming a member of Greenpeace. Besides, the ridiculous "trade" agreements that we have signed would now likely prevent them from doing so.

Starowicz says, "The lesson of Canadian history is unequivocal." We can "embark on the great project of linking a nation" and "if we need a new blueprint, reconvene [a new] Massey Commission."

Fine idea. But it probably wouldn't work unless we could renegotiate NAFTA and tell the WTO that we will not accept their jurisdiction over Canadian cultural matters. Period.

How can we explain the remarkable success of Mark Starowicz's landmark *Canada: A People's History*? Despite the fact that only one company – Sun Life – promised in advance to advertise on the series, and all kinds of corporate patriots rejected overtures, Starowicz and the CBC persevered and a television history about our country became a smashing success. Linda McQuaig writes:

> The utter failure of corporate Canada to sign on to this project reveals more than a surprising level of chintziness on the part of some major corporations – such as Nortel, the CPR and Bombardier – which have enjoyed the largesse of Canadian taxpayers over the years.
>
> Had it been left to the private sector, the history project would never have been more than a gleam in Mark Starowicz's eye.
>
> The private sector seems unable or unwilling to recognize that the public could want anything other than a steady diet of bland, sentimental consumerism.

Among the other companies that turned Starowicz down were Bell Canada, the Bank of Montreal, Air Canada, The Bank of Nova Scotia, Canadian National, PetroCan, Canadian Tire, and General Motors of Canada.

Almost all of the top ten advertising agencies in Canada are foreign-owned. One of them said "nobody will ever watch shows like this."

As far as the *National Post* is concerned,

> This newspaper has argued before and continues to believe that CBC-TV should be privatized. Public broadcasting . . . has been made redundant.

And, oh yes, the CBC produces "fare in which Canadians have little interest."[*]

Let's face it, if Izzy Asper owns the *National Post* and its pages advertise Mr. Asper's Global television shows, why would we ever need the CBC? According to Asper, "If there was no CBC, what would be missing?"[†]

Bill Templeman of Peterborough, writing of the remarkable outpouring of affection after the death of Peter Gzowski, said of those who want to close the CBC down or privatize it:

---

[*] *National Post*, February 2001.
[†] *National Post*, February 29, 2002.

If these critics . . . do not see the connection between a strong public broadcasting system and nation building as they scan all these tributes, they never will.[*]

What Brian Mulroney and Jean Chrétien have done to the CBC is tragic. With funding reduced by hundreds of millions of dollars a year, both radio and TV have had to institute debilitating cutbacks, which have resulted in declining quality and declining audiences. While CBC radio and TV both continue to produce some outstanding broadcasting, the reduced quality of some programming is often sad to hear and see. And, of course, the reduced quality and smaller audiences simply encourage the cultural Visigoths who apparently want even more *Temptation Island, Fear Factor, The Chamber, The Chair, Jenny Jones, Montel, Survivor, World Championship Wrestling, Celebrity Boxing, The Bachelor, The Osbournes,* or *Who Wants to Be a Millionaire?* There have been stories that Jean Chrétien hates the CBC because of some separatists in the French-language division. And other stories that he rarely listens to CBC English-language radio.

In any event, according to Chrétien,

> The power of communications, the American culture, it's not a problem as long as every nation finds a way to make sure the people know who they are, they know their roots and culture well . . .[†]

No kidding. Isn't that what we've been saying in Canada for at least the last thirty years?

As always, Dalton Camp was perceptive:

> The CBC today is not worth a damn to the Liberal government, the department of finance, and the parliament of Canada. This could be because the CBC belongs to the Canadian public, and the Liberal Party and the official opposition all belong to the corporations who have purchased their bland indifference.
>
> The present government has reduced the CBC to rubble [while their friend] Izzy Asper is an avid believer in the need to privatize the CBC. He has half of Parliament and all of Finance on his side.

---

[*] *Globe and Mail,* January 28, 2002.

[†] From a speech in Ottawa at the World Summit on the Arts and Culture, December 1, 2000.

It has been a shameful business and is becoming more so. Any responsible government would reinvest in the public's network to ensure that in both news and public affairs broadcasting, and national cultural activities, the CBC would have no equal.[*]

All too true. But then, any responsible government wouldn't betray its own people by selling out the ownership and control of the country. For Harry Arthurs,

> Culture – unlike cars or clothing – is not merely a consumer good: in its many manifestations it expresses the character and values of a nation, which is why culture is so often contested and controversial. That is why even countries with cultures more ancient, assertive and well-financed than Canada's – France for example – have been adamant in their resistance to the invasion of U.S. cultural goods.

Yet, in the face of all logic, the "enfeeblement of the CBC" is a clear indication of how blind, deaf, and dumb Ottawa is.

Despite the loud and oft-repeated claims of the Mulroney government that Canadian culture would not be affected by trade agreements, Canada's humiliating defeat in our attempts to ban split-run editions of U.S. magazines showed otherwise. When the Chrétien government gave in to pressure from Washington and the WTO and agreed to allow U.S. split-run magazines, Peter C. Newman called the decision

> a precedent of such magnitude that it will be pivotal in the downward spiral of Canadian history.
>
> Now that Ottawa has given in to the Time Warner–inspired lobby pushing the U.S. state department to defang Canadian magazine legislation, there is no longer any doubt about our status. We became just another client state of the American empire: a Panama with polar bears.
>
> Our new national incarnation is the scaredy-cats of the industrialized world.

The harm to Canadian magazines will be substantial. But, had Canada

---

[*] *Toronto Star*, August 18, 2000.

been unfair to U.S. magazine publishers before Ottawa's capitulation? According to Giles Gherson, Editor of the *Edmonton Journal,*

> Canada is the only place in the world where 50 per cent of all magazines sold are foreign. It's the only place where U.S. magazines are sold in any quantity with no change in content. Canada and the U.S. are the only two countries with a significant trade in magazines – they sell and we buy.[*]

While it is true that provisions in NAFTA contain some protection from trade rules, the agreement also allows the signatories to retaliate when cultural policies are thought to be inconsistent with the details of the agreement. Canada's experience with the WTO split-run magazines ruling is a clear indication of how meaningless the cultural exemptions really are. As in so many other cases arising from the FTA, NAFTA, and WTO agreements, Canada has been inundated with complex and often esoteric American legal arguments and threats of retaliation if Canada fails to alter policies which we deem to be in our national interest. At the same time, there is pressure from within Canada from the usual collaborators. Does anyone really doubt that not too far in the future, book publishing, bookselling, broadcasting, newspapers, and pretty well everything else will be opened up to foreign ownership and foreign control?

Back to broadcasting.

No one will ever doubt that the *National Post* is consistent in its pro-American advocacy. For the *Post*, the CRTC and its policies "are a relic of obsolete broadcast technologies."[†] As well, Canada's rule relating to foreign bookstores should be dumped.

Not to be outdone, the *Globe and Mail's* continentalist, Drew Fagan, writes, "Isn't it about time to end the nation's decades-long penchant for foreign ownership restrictions?"[**] A *Globe* editorial suggests that laws relating to foreign booksellers should be scrapped. Others want book publishing to be open to even more foreign ownership. Let's all just

---

[*] *National Post*, May 31, 1999.
[†] April 24, 2001.
[**] January 11, 2002.

ignore the fact that, while foreign books dominate the English-language Canadian market, 87 per cent of all Canadian books are published by Canadian publishers.

So, while the Aspers struggle with the enormous debt they incurred in buying up Lord Crossover's newspapers, the *National Post* and other papers across the country shrink their Canadian culture reviews. In Jeffrey Simpson's words,

> The Canadian publishing industry used to count on the country's print media to review and comment on books. In the past year, however, the amount of print media space devoted to books shrank dramatically. The smaller space for books diminishes a piece of the country's intellectual space to discuss ideas, to discover what others are writing and to debate the future. English-speaking Canada, which is largely a cultural extension of the United States, can ill afford this.[*]

While its true that Canadian cultural exports have increased, so have imports. In 2000, Canada's trade deficit in cultural materials was some $3 billion and about 83 per cent of our imports were from the U.S. Even though Canada is swamped by U.S. cultural products, I have yet to hear anyone suggest we keep out American or other foreign cultural material (although I'm sometimes tempted when it comes to "cultural" material of the kind Howard Stern has regularly delivered).

Exports are wonderful, but recently they have had their downsides. Canadian publishers of children's books say that cash-strapped schools and libraries have resulted in declining Canadian sales and,

> To offset the losses, publishers have turned more to exports with the frightening result that Canadian children's books are starting to be "de-Canadianized."
>
> U.S. spellings of words are becoming common. Vancouver is being dropped as one of the settings "to seek a more universal appeal."[†]

Well, of course, the best strategy of all would be to do what other countries around the world do – take significant steps to strengthen their own

---

[*] *Globe and Mail*, January 12, 2002.
[†] *Globe and Mail*, June 1, 2001.

cultural industries such as book and magazine publishing, broadcasting and films, and new-media firms.

Canadians like their culture, their authors, painters, musicians, and singers, and they regard their culture as an important part of their national identity.

For the United States, cultural products are commercial commodities, and there are powerful, well-financed lobbies to promote the sale of these products around the world. As Ray Conlogue of the *Globe and Mail* and others have pointed out, the U.S. makes more money selling movies than selling airplanes. And while countries around the world have taken meaningful steps to avoid being totally inundated by U.S. cultural exports, the U.S. government regards such actions as "protectionism." Conlogue tells us that

> In France, every movie ticket carries a surcharge that goes into domestic French film production. In effect, U.S. films subsidize French ones. In television, a $100 annual license fee on TV sets finances three public TV networks and thwarts U.S. broadcasters trying to enlarge their 55 per cent share of Europe's market.[*]

Of course nothing like this happens in Canada, where cowardly politicians and bureaucrats tremble in the presence of the American film industry's bully, Jack Valenti.

Conlogue, who is one of Canada's most astute writers on cultural matters, says:

> Some of us have been getting used to it for a while now. No scrap of control over our political or economic destiny, but tons of La La La Human steps.
>
> Problem though: The classic definition of nationalism is that you try to draw the cultural and political boundary in the same place. Cultural autonomy doesn't mean much in the long run if there's no policy in place to protect it.
>
> The argument that we have a new kind of nationalism amounts to admitting . . . we backed down again and again, and then we tried to forget how often.

---

[*] *Globe and Mail*, May 10, 2001.

So, we buckle under and abandon film industry legislation. Then we cave in on magazine dumping laws. And after we pour out our hearts and do what we can to show Americans how deeply we felt about the horrific events of September 11,

> Do you remember what Americans thought of that? Within a month the president imposed a brutal tariff on our softwood lumber exports. It was arguably illegal as usual, but a useful reminder about nationalism.
>
> That's what happens when your neighbour has real nationalism and you don't. Maybe telling ourselves fairy tales about a purely cultural nationalism will make us feel better.
>
> We're not much different from the hapless dog who keeps licking his master's hand while being beaten.[*]

Is there any sign that our political leaders believe Canadian culture is important? The answer is pretty clear if you examine total government expenditures on culture, which, in constant dollars, have declined by almost three-quarters of a billion dollars since 1990.[†]

The always interesting *Maclean's* magazine year-end poll, this one for December 25, 2000, had some good cultural questions. Only one-third of respondents wanted the CBC to be privatized. And three of every five Canadians approved of high Canadian-content requirements on both radio and television. Yet, the Americanization of Canada barrels ahead on all fronts. A friend's answering machine says I can leave a message for anyone, from ay to zee. CBC announcers refer to "kiyow-tees." A *Globe and Mail* movie review of *Black Hawk Down* is headlined "Us Against Them in Somalia." and Canada Post stamps celebrate the twenty-fifth anniversary of Disney World. And, true to form, Izzy Asper wants the CBC to stop broadcasting news and sports, a C. D. Howe Institute study says that professional sports and arts groups give little or no economic value back to their communities,[**] and Jack Valenti tells Ottawa that Canadian content regulations should be scrapped.

Oh, for a heritage minister who would stand up in the House of

---

[*] *Globe and Mail*, November 4, 2001.

[†] Statistics Canada, *The Daily*, May 27, 2002.

[**] *National Post*, March 6, 2002.

Commons and tell these people what to do with their advice and their biased "studies."

Instead, Sheila Copps is going in exactly the opposite direction. Here are the words of Todd Anderson, President of the Canadian Booksellers Association:

> In July, 2002, the Department of Heritage, in a bizarre decision, somehow ruled that the American on-line book distributor Amazon.com was not in contravention of long-standing cultural policy and the Investment Canada Act, and Amazon could establish itself in Canada even though the company will be foreign owned and controlled. To add insult to injury, Canada Post delivery trucks are acting as a shill for the American company as they deliver your mail.*

No doubt some Canadians will hail Sheila Copps's remarkable decision as a victory for Canadian readers. Perhaps it may be so, in the very short term. But it will be the hundreds of excellent independent bookstores across the country that will suffer; a great many will likely be forced to close down. And, inevitably, Amazon.com will bypass Canadian publishers and agents and import their books from the U.S., with a certain severe impact on Canadian publishing.

Sailing into Uncharted Waters and Achieving Leverage from a Prone Position

The one sector of the Canadian economy that has boomed since the FTA was signed has been the export of oil and natural gas to the U.S. From 1988 to the end of 1999, oil exports increased by over 76 per cent and natural gas exports jumped by a huge 165 per cent. In 2000, oil and gas exports set another new record, increasing by 77 per cent in the one year. In 1988, natural gas exports amounted to about 39 per cent of the total production, but by 2000, exports were at 59 per cent. In 1988,

---

* Personal communication to author.

exports of crude oil and equivalents were 33 per cent of production; by 1999 these had increased to 63 per cent.

Of course Ralph Klein and the residents of Calgary's office towers are delighted with these developments. But what about the rest of Canada? The question that has been totally missing from national public debate is whether we should be exporting so much of our conventional oil and our accessible gas reserves.

At one time, Canada's National Energy Board protected Canada's interests by insisting that no natural gas could be exported unless there was a reserve of at least twenty-five years of domestic supply. In short, the NEP was concerned about Canada's security of supply.

However, because of the FTA, NAFTA, and its own almost total abdication of responsibility, Ottawa's long-standing role of ensuring that supplies will be available for Canadians no longer exists.

Today, Canada's proven natural gas reserves, at current rates of production, are down to nine years, and conventional oil reserves have a life index of only eight years. While it's true that heavy oil production now exceeds that of conventional oil, natural gas drilling has not replaced production since 1982.

Nor does Ottawa care if Canadian oil and gas companies are bought up by foreign corporations. In contrast, most other petroleum-producing countries carefully guard the ownership of all their energy-producing companies. Despite great pressure from the U.S., Mexico has steadfastly resisted any other than minor changes to its entrenched policy of government control via state-run companies. In Mexico, the constitution restricts foreign participation in the petroleum industry and suggestions for greater foreign presence in the industry are quickly dismissed.

Mexico would never have agreed to the mandatory resource-sharing provisions that Canadians accepted in the FTA. Despite the fact that the U.S. bullied Mexico for similar concessions during the NAFTA negotiations, Mexico was firm in resisting the American pressure.

For Alberta Premier Ralph Klein, "foreign ownership is not an issue" in the petroleum industry. "There is a need for a co-ordinated and cohesive approach to North American energy supply. A continental energy policy."*

Note, "a *continental* energy policy."

---

* *National Post*, October 4, 2001.

One would have thought that when the U.S. feared an energy crisis in 2001, one reaction would have been to take urgent steps toward conservation, by reducing, for example, the number of giant SUVs and minivans being built. Legislation guaranteeing more fuel efficiency and more wind and solar power and other forms of renewable energy, and hikes in taxes to raise the low gasoline price in the U.S. closer to the levels in all other developed countries, have been long overdue.

No way. Instead, the Bush–Cheney strategy is straightforward: produce more so more can be consumed. Eric Reguly writes:

> The energy crisis showed Mr. Bush's true colours. He will pander to the right wing of the Republican Party, and he will pander most of all to the oil industry, which made the Bush family a fortune and financed the presidential campaign of father and son. It's payback time for fat boys in the Stetsons and cowboy boots.[*]

And the boys in Calgary finance the campaigns of Jean Chrétien, Paul Martin, John Manley, Anne McLellan, and other cabinet ministers, and, of course, their generous buddy Ralph Klein as well. With their low royalty and tax rates, the industry has been paid back many times over and will undoubtedly be the recipients of even more bountiful public largesse in the future.

As far as natural gas reserves are concerned, for the petroleum industry in Calgary, the key word is "relax." There's lots more gas to be found by pouring billions of dollars into new exploration and development. Never mind that the biggest reserves have been exploited and most established fields have declining rates of production. Never mind that finding rates have also declined while producers are selling everything in sight as quickly as they can. And never mind that while Canada has reached its production capacity, the needs of the U.S. have been expanding exponentially.

There's not much doubt about where Michael Phelps of Westcoast Energy stood before he sold his company to Americans.

> The energy story in Canada is a continental one. When it comes to energy, borders matter less and less.[†]

---

[*] *Globe and Mail*, August 7, 2001.
[†] *Globe and Mail*, February 27, 2001.

Got that?

The petroleum industry in Calgary complains that times are plenty tough and the sector could suffer because of a lack of cash flow. But it was less than a year ago at this writing that the Calgary bureau chief of the *National Post* reported:

> Behind the euphoria of billion-dollar profits is a new serious problem for Canadian oil and gas companies – too much cash and too few places to spend it wisely.
>
> The sector is expected to produce an unprecedented $8 billion in surplus cash flow this year – money it expects to generate from operations, but for which it has no spending plans.[*]

Is Ottawa at all concerned about our falling reserves?

No problem. Even if it means Canadians will have to rely on more expensive tar sands oil and high-cost natural gas in the future, the name of the game is to export as much of our relatively inexpensive, accessible oil and gas as quickly as possible. So, Jean Chrétien agrees that his former foreign-policy adviser Michael Kergin, who is now our Ambassador to Washington, will help arrange Ralph Klein's visit to Washington to meet with U.S. Vice-President Dick Cheney, so Klein can talk up even more exports in the future. "We want to work with him to facilitate moving energy across the border," said Cheney. "We consider Alberta a partner."

And what does our Ambassador Kergin think? "In the 21st century, in the case of Canada and the United States, the traditional concept of an international border has lost its relevance."[†]

Stephen Handelman asks:

> So who's making Canadian energy policy? Ottawa is taking more of a backseat than it cares to admit.
>
> David Taras, a University of Calgary political scientist, argues that the provinces have driven energy policy since U.S.–Canada free trade regionalized the North American market. "What few people have noticed is that we've now got a National Energy Policy in reverse."[**]

---

[*] *National Post*, February 22, 2001.
[†] *Globe and Mail*, October 15, 2001.
[**] *Time*, June 11, 2001.

Before he sold his Canadian Hunter Exploration Ltd. to the Americans, Calgary's Jim Gray said:

> Of course there's a crisis. For the first time ever, we are constrained in our ability to deliver natural gas. I have never experienced the circumstance we face today. We are truly sailing into uncharted waters.[*]

But, in any event, we actually don't have to worry about negotiating a new energy pact. Ralph Goodale, our former natural resources minister, tells it like it is:

> We aren't engaged in negotiating any sort of North American energy policy. We have one. It's the North American free-trade agreement, and it's working.[†]

Quite true. There are now no significant regulatory restrictions hampering exploitation of Canadian resources for export to the U.S. But what the Americans want is even faster development of Canada's reserves, quick construction of even more pipelines to the U.S., and swift approval for projects to siphon northern energy supplies into the U.S.

Listening to the repeated pleas of U.S. Ambassador Paul Cellucci for Canada and the U.S. to work together to assure the accelerated flow of energy to the U.S., any normal, non-servile government would make it clear that no such actions will be even contemplated until the Americans completely back off their grossly unfair, damaging, and illegal punitive actions (yet once again) related to Canada's softwood lumber exports to the U.S.

According to Cellucci, speaking at a meeting of energy executives in Toronto, energy is the basis for industrial growth and it is that growth that drives up demand for Canadian products.

No one seems to have thought to ask the ambassador if he meant products like softwood lumber.

Next on the agenda will almost certainly be a locked-in continental electricity agreement which will include a huge expansion of transmission lines to the south. With proper environmental consideration, new power

---

[*] *Edmonton Journal*, August 3, 2001.
[†] *Globe and Mail*, August 6, 2001.

production, based on renewable energy supplies, can be a bonus for Canada. But a mad rush to develop new sources of electricity for export will be destructive.

Not to worry. Jean Chrétien says, "We have a lot of energy, we are selling a lot of natural gas." And George W. Bush says he wants increased and reliable supplies.

All of this is a truly astonishing development, in a nation where the National Energy Program became a dreaded monster for many Canadians, including all those to the right of the political spectrum and most Western Canadians: it now appears that Bush's vision of a *continental* energy policy is somehow an acceptable reality.

The National Energy Program was poorly conceived, poorly explained, and poorly defended. The continental energy policy of George W. Bush, Dick Cheney, Ralph Klein, and Jean Chrétien has never been explained to Canadians.

Even today, well over a decade after the FTA was signed, most Canadians don't understand that, under the terms of the agreement, even if Canadians find themselves running short of oil or natural gas, or any other resource we sell to the U.S., or if we find that new supplies are going to be far too costly, we must still continue to sell relatively low-cost supplies to the U.S. on a pro rata basis based on our previous exports, and we cannot charge Americans more than we charge Canadians. No country I can think of would have signed such a stupid agreement.

And by the way, in this new continental bilateral arrangement, have you heard much about energy supplies flowing from the U.S. to Canada? Over 90 per cent of energy trade between the two countries is shipments from Canada to the U.S.

If all of this doesn't stretch the imagination, we have Jack Mintz telling Canadians that the prospect of a continental energy policy makes it important that Canada reduces taxes in the resource sector "to provide a more stable tax environment for the industry." Ignore the fact that the petroleum industry in Alberta pays a fraction of the tax and royalties paid in Alaska or Norway, for example, and never mind that a giveaway sweetheart deal for new oil sands development has already been arranged by Alberta and Ottawa, Mintz now wants even more tax cuts so we can ship even more oil and gas to the U.S.

Since natural gas is the preferred fuel for environmental reasons, most newly completed power plants in the U.S. and most of those being planned will use it. Yet many informed observers believe that it's going to be extremely difficult if not impossible to satisfy all the projected demand in the near future.

David Manning, former head of the Canadian Association of Petroleum Producers, says that Canadian natural gas is replacing coal or diesel in New York and Massachusetts power projects, with the result that undesirable emissions are falling, and "every bus on Long Island runs on Alberta natural gas."* Countering criticism from concerned environmentalists, John Manley suggests that increasing exports of Canadian natural gas will displace dirtier coal in the U.S. and be good for the environment.

Meanwhile, surprise, surprise, the Alberta government has agreed to new coal-burning power plants to supply electricity for export to the U.S., and while most Nova Scotia offshore natural gas flows to the U.S., the province imports expensive U.S. coal to power its electricity plants. So, we'll pollute here in Canada, making it possible for Americans to produce non-polluting electricity in the U.S.

"New coal-fired power plants bear huge risks," says an *Edmonton Journal* story, only six days after Manning told the paper's editorial board about how the U.S. was switching to Alberta natural gas because of environmental concerns. A few days later the Alberta government allowed a large cement plant near Edmonton to switch from using natural gas to coal. The prevailing wind will carry emissions from the plant over the city.

Don't worry about natural gas shortages in Canada, the industry tells us. We should export all we can; there's plenty more to be found. But a "blue-ribbon team of scientists" presented quite a different picture in fall 2001. New reserves are undoubtedly going to be more difficult to find and more expensive to produce. Reserves have dropped by ten years since an earlier study only four years ago. Many natural gas pools may well be considered unmarketable. And future supplies will increasingly mean short-lived pools of gas that will necessitate extensive and expensive drilling.

Ken Vollman, chairman of the National Energy Board, says that Canada's western gas basin is close to half-empty. Moreover, "new gas discoveries show a pronounced tendency to be smaller and to deplete

---

* *Edmonton Journal*, February 8, 2000.

more quickly than finds of just a few years ago," and the task of bringing on new production every year is getting harder and harder.[*]

Maurice Strong, in a 2001 speech, put Canada's energy policies in the proper perspective:

> We should not be carried away by the euphoria of expanding markets for our oil, gas, coal and electric power with the accompanying prospect of major new projects. . . . We must ask ourselves to what extent we want to become fully integrated into an energy economy that is the most wasteful, indulgent and harmful to the environment and the main contributor to the ominous risks to the future posed by climate change, and indeed the future of our civilization. . . . The fact that the United States is not only the world's only superpower but its super polluter is something that must evoke some profound soul-searching by Canadians before we find ourselves co-opted to the role of complicit junior partner in the process.[†]

Unfortunately, we're headed in exactly the direction Strong warns about. Jeffrey Simpson has it right:

> The ever-tightening energy links between Canada and the U.S. that will flow from September 11 will be a part of a pattern. Canada will be squeezed as never before to adopt U.S. models, copy U.S. laws and regulations or adapt Canadian ways to accommodate the U.S.
>
> Canada will be pressed to conform on border security, refugee determination, foreign and defence policy, energy, business practices, trade – anything that touches Americans' sense of self-interest and vulnerability.[**]

One would think that given the great American concern about its vulnerability with respect to oil supplies, and given the possibilities of future American confrontations with Iraq, Iran, and possibly even Saudi Arabia, the leverage Canada would have in our immense hundreds of

---

[*] *Edmonton Journal*, November 29, 2001.

[†] *Globe and Mail*, August 10, 2001.

[**] *Globe and Mail*, October 24, 2001.

billions of barrels of recoverable tar sands oil would be formidable. Total tar sands extractable oil is estimated to be more than ten times Saudi Arabia's reserves.

But it's difficult to apply leverage from a prone position, or from down on your knees. Listening to the Alberta and federal governments plead for more American money to develop new tar sands plants would be embarrassing if we hadn't been inured by three decades of the same mendicant behaviour.

Did any of these colonial-minded beggars ever hear of debt capital? Does anyone think the U.S. would delay the development of the tar sands by not providing all the debt capital that might be required, and at reasonable interest rates? And how about telling Canadian banks that the many billions of dollars that they're shipping out of the country every year are going to be needed here so our own Canadian companies can develop our own resources?

In short, why not develop these strategic resources ourselves, so that Canadians own the plants, purchases of equipment and services in Canada are maximized, and the profits stay in Canada, to be reinvested in Canada?

Let's see if we can put things in perspective. Many billions of dollars are needed to develop the tar sands, the Terra Nova field, the Hebron and White Rose fields off Canada's East Coast. Much of this development is being done and will be done by American firms. Even more billions will be required to develop petroleum resources and pipelines in and from the Arctic. Most of the profits in these resources developments will go to American firms, and most of the profits will leave Canada. Almost all of the new oil and gas production will be shipped to the U.S.

Now we're being told that even more tax and royalty breaks are required if the Americans are going to invest in these developments. Is this not quite bizarre? Only in Canada could this happen.

A crucial point relating to oil and natural gas. The prices for these commodities are now set in the U.S., not in Canada. What will happen if there's a major crisis in the Middle East or elsewhere, and supplies to the U.S. are curtailed or cut off? One thing for sure is that U.S. prices will go through the roof. Like it or not, because of our current locked-in arrangements, Canadian prices will do the same. How stupid of us to have left ourselves in such a vulnerable position.

Before we leave our discussion of oil and natural gas, let's briefly return to Ambassador Cellucci. There's not much doubt about where he stands. John Gray of the *Globe and Mail* tells us:

> As for energy, Cellucci seems baffled by the suggestion that Canadian oil and gas should, perhaps, be Canadian. He says that the United States wants to look on Canadian and Mexican energy as domestic, in effect as American. We're all the same; we're all in it together.[*]

A few days later, at an energy conference in Saint John, New Brunswick, Cellucci said governments shouldn't interfere with markets. (New Brunswick and Prince Edward Island are concerned that Sable Island natural gas will be sold off to the U.S. without a guarantee of adequate supply for their provinces.)

At about the same time, a public-opinion poll in the U.S. showed that 71 per cent of Americans say that they do not regard Canadian energy as foreign.

What is happening to the rest of corporate Canada is also happening to our stock trading firms. Slowly, but surely, foreign companies are playing a greater role in major share trades. Beginning in the 1990s, the TSE became more and more Americanized and more and more of what was its normal trading is now done in New York. In the process, the TSE becomes less relevant and some Canadian firms no longer trade on a Canadian exchange. A company like PMC Sierra is a good example. Its registered office is in the state of Delaware, and it no longer considers itself a Canadian company, even though much of its operations are in Burnaby, B.C.

"TECH TRADING FLIES SOUTH" is a headline from the *Financial Post*, with sub-heads "Bad News for the Loonie" and "U.S. Listings Rob Canada of Billions in Capital Inflows."[†]

> Almost half the trading volume of Canada's top 10 technology companies was executed in the U.S. over the past year.

---

[*] *Globe and Mail*, April 20, 2002.
[†] June 13, 2001.

And what can we expect in the future? An increasing number of cross-border financial deals are being handled by U.S. investment companies and increasing investment research with respect to Canadian firms in being handled not in Canada but in the U.S. Almost half the Bay Street IPO, merger, and bond underwriting fees are now going to American financial firms.

Three months before the Enron scandal, the Investment Dealers Association of Canada, with little fanfare, changed the rules for Canadian brokers to more closely conform to those in the U.S. The result was a substantial weakening of safeguards protecting Canadian investors. "Using U.S. Rules Sensible" proclaimed a *National Post* headline. "Ultimately, this is the first step toward most Canadian companies adopting U.S. accounting rules."* But the major impact of the changes to U.S. standards has been to lessen accountability and legal and financial investor protection.

Hurray. Bring on more Enrons!

Isaiah A. Litvak sums it up:

In 1999, approximately one quarter of the companies on the Toronto Stock Exchange (TSE) 100 index, a measure of the largest publicly traded businesses in Canada, reported their financial results in U.S. dollars. The numbers are growing, and a similar trend is apparent among smaller companies listed on the TSE. The reasons for the switch are pretty straightforward. For Canadian companies with significant U.S. operations, U.S. dollars make it easier for U.S. investors and financial institutions to evaluate their performance. Many of these companies are also listed on American exchanges. As of 1999, there were 223 interlisted stocks (that is TSE stocks that are also traded on the New York, NASDAQ, or American Stock Exchange). Seventy-five of those companies had half or more of their trading value executed on a U.S. exchange. As far as U.S. investors are concerned, these are de facto American stocks . . . If the TSE fades into irrelevancy, Canadian companies will have one less reason to stay in Canada. Is it not surprising that many Canadian business people are favourably disposed to a currency union between Canada and the United States.†

---

* February 14, 2001.

† *The Marginalization of Corporate Canada*, The Canadian Institute of International Affairs, October, 2001.

There's not much mystery about what has happened to transportation policy in Canada. For generations, east-west rail transportation was considered vital for Canada's survival, for national unity, and for economic reasons. But in recent years, with the downgrading of Transport Canada, the privatization of the CNR, the sale of Canadian short-line railways to American owners, the weakening of VIA Rail, and with people like Paul Tellier in charge of CN, north-south has replaced east-west as the cornerstone of Canadian rail policy.

Meanwhile, lobbyists are pushing for the entry of American airlines into Canada and allowing American firms cabotage in Canada, even if the U.S. fails to reciprocate. Moreover, they say, foreign companies should be allowed at least 49-per-cent ownership of airlines operating in Canada. And inevitably, the 49-per-cent rule would soon go out the window.

By now you're already totally depressed, good and angry, or justifiably quite overloaded with the details of the Americanization of Canada.

Let's move on to the question of how Canadians feel about what is happening to our country.

Who Wants to Become American?

As Canada rapidly proceeds towards integration with the Unites States, how do Canadians feel about what is happening?

There are two profoundly different answers to this question.

On the one hand, public-opinion polls show that strong majorities of Canadians oppose further integration with the U.S. and are very concerned about the repercussions for Canadian sovereignty and for the survival of Canada as an independent country.

On the other hand, Canada's corporate elite, for the most part, not only show no similar concerns, but are clearly in favour of even more integration with the U.S. and an accelerated pace of policy harmonization and the elimination of barriers to greater conformity with American standards, values, and policies.

Frank Graves and his Ekos Research Associates have done invaluable polling relating to Canadian attitudes towards Americanization and differences in Canadian and American values and attitudes.* One of the key Ekos findings from their detailed and extensive nationwide polling is that:

> Canadians reveal unusually high (and stable) attachment to country . . . that coexists with a belief that we are becoming increasingly Americanized, which most see as a negative force.

While a significant majority of Canadians say that Canada has become more like the U.S., at the same time, for every Canadian who would like us to become more like the U.S. in the future, there are four who would like to see Canada become less like the U.S.

While most Canadians agree that Canada is becoming more like the U.S. both economically and culturally, an overwhelming majority of Canadians are opposed to Canada joining the U.S. When asked which factors were responsible for the growing Americanization of Canada, strong majorities named U.S. takeovers of Canadian companies, American popular culture, NAFTA, and globalization. At the same time, large majorities believe that maintaining a Canadian dollar is essential to our economic sovereignty and national identity and a plurality oppose abolishing customs and duties at the U.S. border.

Three out of every four Canadians "feel that it is very important for Canada to preserve a distinctive identity as well as a unique system of values and national identity."

(Few would argue with the suggestion that Alberta has become the most Americanized province in Canada. Yet, the Ekos polls show that 80 per cent of Albertans said they would be concerned if Canada joined the U.S., a higher percentage than in any other province. Similarly, 81 per cent of Albertans said it was important for Canadians to maintain a unique system of values and national identity. How to explain these survey results given the heavy American presence and influence in Alberta? As someone who has lived in Alberta all of my life, there's little doubt in my mind that many Albertans have watched the impact of Americanization in their province, and are not too happy with what they see).

---

* See in particular *Exploring Perceived and Comparative Differences in Canadian and American Values and Attitudes: Continentalism or Divergence?* May 2000.

How do Canadians feel about Americans? Conventional oft-repeated wisdom suggests that most Canadians like Americans. But Ekos polling shows that "Canadians have more negative (36 per cent) than positive (24 per cent) views about Americans."

And, how do Canadians feel about their quality of life compared to the quality of life in the U.S.? Despite the constant barrage of right-wing propaganda from some of our newspaper columnists, and some of our "think tanks," by a two-to-one margin Canadians believe that average Canadians have a higher quality of life than average Americans and that quality of life is much more important than measuring well-being strictly in economic terms.

In fact, when asked "If you were Prime Minister for a day and had to pick an overall national goal for Canada to achieve by the year 2010, which of the following would you choose?" far more Canadians chose "Best quality of life in the world" or "Best health care system in the world" and "Lowest incidence of child poverty in the world" than those who opted for reduced taxes, elimination of public debt, or other right-wing favourites.

Despite (or perhaps because of) the extensive Americanization of Canada, the Ekos polls show that attachment to their country is more important to Canadians than it is in many other Western countries, and despite a growing provincialism, regionalism, and decentralization, the sense of belonging to Canada is far stronger than the sense of belonging mainly to a region, province, or city. "The proportion of Canadians who select a sub-national unit [i.e. town or region] as their primary source of belonging has decreased steadily." Moreover, "Canadian identity, although confused, is extremely important, particularly for English Canadians. It engenders powerful attachment."

Three of every four Canadians agree that "maintaining a unique system of values and national identity for Canada is important," but fewer than three in five now believe that is possible.

When asked in the *Maclean's* 2000 year-end poll whether Canada should "move closer to the United States in its laws and attitudes," 72 per cent of Canadians said no, while only 21 per cent thought we should.

In yet another poll, reported by Richard Gwyn, Praxicus Public Strategies Inc. asked Canadians if they thought they would be better off living in the U.S.

To the surprise of Praxicus pollster Dimitri Pantazopoulus, only 15 per cent of his respondents reckoned that things would be better for them south of the border. "Canadians generally feel comfortable in their home and native land," commented Pantazopoulus.

This, surely, is the nub of the matter. A distinctive style or spirit or sensibility has developed . . . (which) they would miss . . . in a society that lacks them.[*]

A year later, in late 2001, a Goldfarb poll showed that the percentage of Canadians (roughly one in five) who would move to the U.S. for more pay and lower taxes was down by almost half from an earlier poll. Similarly, polls asking Canadians whether they would like to become Americans show a large increase in the percentage saying no.

In their 2001 year-end poll, *Maclean's* asked Canadians how they would describe our relations with the U.S. One in three said like family or best friends, while 65 per cent said cordial but distant or openly hostile.

What about the poll which shows that as many as one in four Canadians would move to the U.S. and take a job there if given the opportunity? How can this be reconciled with the 85 per cent of Canadians who don't want Canada to join the U.S.? I asked Allan Gregg, the well-known pollster, that question. According to Gregg, some Canadians feel "I wouldn't mind for a time going to the U.S. to work, but I wouldn't think of doing it on a constant basis." Moreover, this one-in-four poll result, and many other polls over many years, reflect the pro-American bias of Quebec separatists, i.e. anything to get out of Confederation would be just fine.

It boggles the mind that these people could be so misguided. If Canada became part of the United States the separatists would quickly be utterly dismayed at just how fast French language and culture would be eroded. Can anyone imagine Washington agreeing to laws that required that all goods shipped into the state of Quebec had to have bilingual labels? Or that all Washington legislation had to be bilingual? Or that top military officers had to be bilingual? Given that under the U.S. constitution Washington has pervasive powers over education, social programs, resources, immigration, and culture, most

---

[*] *Toronto Star*, July 1, 2000.

Quebeckers would be appalled at their new federal government's intrusive and dominant role in their lives. In Canada, 78 per cent of Canadians agree that both the French and English languages should have equal status, rights, and privileges. Fat chance of anything remotely similar in the U.S.

(But Quebec polls regarding attitudes toward the U.S. come as no surprise. During the years of the free trade debates, the strongest support for the FTA came from Bay Street and the separatists in Quebec).

What's the bottom line for all these polls? Ekos reports that there is

Broad belief the Americanization of Canada is progressing and there is equally broad aversion to further convergency.

At the same time, there's an inescapable conclusion that Canada's corporate and political elite are resolutely taking the country in a direction that the overwhelming majority of Canadians oppose.

One more point about polls: 95 per cent of Canadians say they are proud to be Canadian.[*]

Veiled and Unveiled Treason

With my utmost effort, with my last breath, will I oppose the veiled treason which attempts by sordid means and mercenary proffers to lure our people from their allegiance.
– Sir John A. Macdonald, 1860

Just who are these people who are selling out our country and urging us to adopt more and more American standards and values, and to abandon the ideals and goals of independence and sovereignty we have valued for so many generations? And what should we call them?

I would call many of them, plain and simple and to the point, anti-Canadians. Of course they wouldn't like that at all; most of them profess to somehow be advancing policies in the best interests of Canada.

---

[*] Léger poll, March 2002.

Never mind that suggesting we open up the rest of the country to even more foreign ownership is like suggesting we drink more arsenic to calm our upset stomachs.

The idea that selling off even more of our manufacturing, our resources, our wholesale and retail firms, our airlines, banks and tele-communication companies, our book stores, and our publishers would somehow be good for us boggles the mind.

If they're not anti-Canadians, they certainly don't appear to care who owns and controls the country.

Okay, if we can't call them anti-Canadians, what can we call them?

Frequently those who advocate far-right policies are referred to as neo-conservatives (neo-cons) or neo-liberals. Based on their record, I buy the "con" part, but to suggest that these people have much to do with the traditions of Canadian conservatives or liberals would be doing a great disservice to the history and beliefs of tens of millions of Canadians over many generations. They certainly aren't conservatives in the tradition of Conservatives ranging from John A. Macdonald all the way to John Diefenbaker, Bill Davis, Robert Stanfield, and Dalton Camp. A true Canadian conservative opposes radical change, values established institutions, and supports the good of the community.

Nor do they have anything in common with American liberals.

So, then, what *do* we call them? In 1956 an important American book, *The Power Elite* by C. Wright Mills, was published. It described how the economic establishment and the political establishment had a combined stranglehold on the U.S. Will that description do for what's happening in Canada? Not quite, because even though it's accurate, it's not nearly strong enough. And, "the controlling plutocracy" is probably closer to the mark.

Still, there's something lacking, something that leaves us short of properly defining those who are selling out the country. While they might simply be called the ruling class or perhaps the corporate elite, or the establishment hierarchy (and they are, for the most part, all of those things), there's a better way to describe them.

Perhaps in Latin America some of them would simply be called compradors, in Norway quislings, and in France the Vichy.* But here in Canada one can't use such comparisons, even if they might be apt.

---

* See Glossary.

What then to term those who are turning us into colonial, dependant vassals? Are they the ones who will become the new colonial administrators? Probably.

In the European tradition of the word, can they properly be called collaborators? Surely that's what some of them have been, and are doing – collaborating with Americans in the abandonment of the last vestiges of our sovereignty, as Canada pursues policies very much in the U.S. interest.

Those who are selling out our country should best be called the *radical right*, for their policies are truly radical in the context of the history and the traditions of our country. They are radical because in many ways they have little or no precedence, they contradict long-standing Canadian values, and they advocate a far-reaching transformation of the character of our country, a transformation that is well outside the mainstream of Canadian public opinion.

And, who does the Canadian radical right most closely resemble? Clearly it is the far-right of the U.S. Republican Party, the Ronald Reagans and Barry Goldwaters, the Newt Gingriches and other American icons of laissez-faire, let-the-market-prevail ideology.

For the radical right, government by nature is bad, taxes are bad, legislation designed to protect and improve society is bad if it raises the cost of doing business and cuts into profits. For the Canadian radical right, taxes have to be cut even below the level of those paid in the United States. Of course that will mean enormous reductions in government spending, although the radical right rarely will spell out exactly *where* they would chop so many billions of dollars in government programs.

Would the cuts come from the pension payments and old-age security cheques that seniors receive? Or would they come from medicare? How about Canada's defence spending? Or the RCMP and local and provincial police forces? Or perhaps fire halls should be closed down and the firemen sent home? Should highways and bridges be built or repaired when necessary? And how about sewage-treatment and water-treatment plants? Or, for that matter, municipal sewer systems? The list is endless. We could chop the coast guard and forest-fire-fighting units, hospitals, libraries, public transit, the court system, the jails and penitentiaries. Why not send the judges, the prosecutors, and the prison guards home? We could save enormous amounts of money. And more of the well-to-do could live in gated communities with their own security forces, just as wealthy Americans do.

One other thing. There are lots of universities in the U.S. Do we really need our own universities across the country? And even if we do need some of these services, why not turn the universities and the prisons and the highways over to the private sector? The market will soon decide what is needed, and at what price.

There's an interesting pattern here shared by our bankers, communications people, oil company executives, and others who are so rapidly selling out our country and trying to have the rules changed so they can do so more quickly.

More often than not, these people made their ample fortunes in government-protected industries or in industries heavily subsidized by Canadian taxpayers. For example, our big five banks operate a hugely profitable oligopoly, thanks to Liberal and Conservative governments in Ottawa. Of course, the banks have been major financial contributors to both parties, their leadership campaigns, their election campaigns, and their annual operating expenses.

In the U.S., as *New York Times* columnist Paul Krugman has noted, "Republicans have shifted to the right . . . towards more conservative economic policies."[*] While this is undoubtedly true, it's also almost amusing. It's difficult to imagine how the party of Reagan, Goldwater, Nixon, and George Bush Sr. and his son might have room to move much further to the right. In most Western democracies American Republicans are justifiably thought to be from another age.

Then there are our own right-wingers who have shifted from traditional Canadian conservative policies in their mad rush to emulate the Americans. Our new radical conservatives are much like the regressive, wealthy politicians who now dominate the U.S. Congress. David Crane has it right:

> Basically right-wingers in Canada are living in a country they don't seem to like very much. They talk as though they would rather be Americans, which is why they want to make Canada as American as they can.[†]

---

[*] January 4, 2002.
[†] *Toronto Star*, June 18, 2000.

Let's be clear about what it is the radical right believes. First, integration is inevitable, like it or not (they like it), and "inevitable" is one of their favourite words. Second, that means we have no choice, we must adopt the U.S. dollar because the Americans will never agree to a new common currency. Third, we must enter into a customs union, which means harmonizing our trade policies with Washington's. We'll have to have the same monetary policy as the U.S., because that's an inevitable consequence of adopting the U.S. dollar. In addition, we'll have no choice but to harmonize labour and environmental policies. And the list goes on.

The standard repeated mantra of the radical right can be found every week in our newspapers, our magazines, and on our television and radio broadcasts. It goes like this:

- 86 per cent of our exports go to the U.S. and 45 per cent of our GDP is exports. So we must remember how dependant we are on the U.S.
- The difference between disposable income in Canada and the United States has widened dramatically.
- Canadian living standards are 30 to 40 per cent lower than in the U.S. and we're falling further behind.
- High Canadian taxes are largely to blame for our problems.
- Because of all of this, "We will have to reconsider our desire to retain independent social and cultural standards,"[*] and some of the first steps we will need to take will be to dollarize and get rid of the border.

We'll deal with these assertions in what follows, but first let's zero in on who the radical right in Canada is.

"A Hurricane Catching All in Its Path, and Nobody Controls It"

The place to start has to be Brian Mulroney and the remnants of his entourage, people such as Paul Tellier, Stanley Hartt, Peter White, Derek Burney, and the like.

---

[*] George Fleishmann, *Financial Post*, January 2, 2002.

There is no one in our 135-year history who comes close to Brian Mulroney as the all-time champion of the Americanization of Canada and the undisputed leader in the surrender of our sovereignty. Mulroney, whose popularity sank to an unprecedented 12 per cent, is not satisfied with the damage he has already done, and is now calling for "getting rid off all this stuff at the border, which inhibits the free movement of goods, services and people."*

Big business in Canada, Tom d'Aquino and his 150 large corporations who now call themselves The Canadian Council of Chief Executives (formerly the BCNI), co-chaired by Derek Burney and Paul Tellier, are the most powerful of the radical-right elite in Canada. They're the ones who helped get the free trade talks going. They're the ones who finance the politicians and the many right-wing think tanks whose biased studies show up so consistently and prominently in some of our right-wing newspapers.

Big business has amply rewarded Brian Mulroney, who now sits on the boards of international corporations, including Archer Daniels Midland; AOL Latin America, Inc.; Forbes Global; Hicks Muse Tate & Furst; and on the Advisory Councils of Chase International; J. P. Morgan Chase & Co., and others. And, what does big business think and want? If you love your country and the following doesn't make you ill, I don't know what will.

An October, 2000, *Background Report on the Views of Canadian Industry and Business Associations on Canada–United States Economic Integration*† pretty well tells you everything you need to know about who it is that is leading the sellout of Canada:

> We met with national industry and business association leaders and asked them to discuss . . . what challenges and opportunities lie ahead in an increasingly integrated North America.

Now, are you ready for this? Here is one of their major conclusions:

> We tend to overrate Canada's quality of life compared to the U.S. It should constitute one of Canada's competitive advantages, but has little effect to either attract firms or retain those who consider leaving.

---

* *Edmonton Journal*, October 29, 2000.
† Public Policy Forum.

So, forget all that stuff about quality of life. There are much more important things, like money. Then there are other recommendations arising out of our business leaders' forum:

> Some government policies and regulations, as well as personal and corporate taxation, should be harmonized with those of the U.S.
> Canada should remove the impediments to further integration with the U.S.

And here's a dandy that pretty well says it all:

> The areas in which Canada thinks it has the greatest strengths are not perceived as critical by global corporations – these include quality of life, health care and social programs.

Remember now, these are Canada's business leaders speaking (representing sixty national industry associations . . . "a well-informed group that constitute an excellent source of information").

When the question of the increasing foreign ownership in Canada was raised, not one single corporate executive participating in the forum thought it was a problem. How could this possibly be?

> A generation ago, most industry associations were composed of Canadian companies that operated primarily in Canada. In our survey, over half the associations consulted told us that the majority of their members (and frequently their most important members) are actually American companies – or at least multinational companies whose headquarters are based in the U.S. – operating in Canada.

As well, let's face it:

> Due to North American integration, more talented and ambitious executives have to go to the U.S. to advance their career, because the more important decisions are made south of the border.

Anyway, "The U.S. is simply more attractive." As well, "Industry association leaders are not, in general, preoccupied with social considerations."

And what are the policy implications for government arising from the report?

> Economic integration . . . is more like a hurricane, catching all in its path, and nobody controls it.

Moreover,

> For historical, cultural and social reasons, most Canadians look east and west rather than south. To maintain such an attitude would be a grave mistake.

And, in conclusion, once again for emphasis:

> The areas where Canada has the greatest strengths are not perceived as critical, such as quality of life, health care or social programs.

Who's selling out Canada? Big business is, and they don't give a damn about what most Canadians want or how they feel. To hell with democracy, to hell with public opinion, forget our history, our heritage, our values, and our past accomplishments. Quality of life isn't important. Only the corporate bottom line counts, and it doesn't matter who owns and controls the country.[*]

What's Good for Big Business Is Good for Canada

I can think of no group that has been even remotely as successful in selling out the country as the Business Council on National Issues (now the CCCE). Here's the way the BCNI described itself:

---

[*] It's interesting to note that a June 2002 Ekos poll showed that only 21 per cent of Canadians regarded themselves as "small-c conservatives" while 73 per cent of private-sector elites defined themselves in that way.

A non-partisan and not-for-profit organization, the BCNI is the voice of Canadian chief executives on public policy issues and globally. Its members head companies representing every major sector of the Canadian economy, and are responsible for a significant majority of Canada's private sector investment, exports, training and research and development. With about 1.3 million employees, member companies administer in excess of $2.1 trillion in assets and have an annual turnover of more than $500 billion.[*]

Just how effective have they been? Peter C. Newman's chapter on the BCNI in his 1998 book *Titans: How the New Canadian Establishment Seized Power*[†] is titled "Taking Over the National Agenda." Newman opens with a quote from Tom d'Aquino, CEO of the BCNI:

> If you ask yourself, in which period since 1900 has Canada's business community had the most influence on public policy, I would say it was in the last twenty years. Look at what we stand for and look at what all the governments, all the major parties . . . have done, and what they want to do. They have adopted the agenda we've been fighting for in the past two decades.

Newman says that Canada's business establishment took over the country's political and economic agenda and that d'Aquino "exerts an influence over Canadian public policy that C. D. Howe, even at the height of his wartime powers, would have envied."

When Jean Chrétien was minister of finance during the 1970s, "Chrétien publicly confessed, 'I don't do my budgets without consulting with de Business Council on National Issues.'"

Peter Newman sums up the Canada of today in one short sentence: "Whoever has the money has the power." And the BCNI has the money. Newman concludes:

> The members of Canada's business establishment have good reason to believe they are running the country's economy. Without ordinary

---

[*] BCNI, May 30, 2000.

[†] Viking/Penguin, 1998. This book is available in paperback. I urge all Canadians who care about their country to read it.

citizens becoming aware of it, Ottawa capitulated. The regimes of Brian Mulroney and Jean Chrétien came to agree that what was good for the BCNI was good for Canada.

Tom d'Aquino and the Business Council on National Issues . . . have become a coherent instrument of unprecedented power.

Here's d'Aquino on the subject of Canada's "think tanks":

While the BCNI chose to lead with flags flying high, we were not alone in advancing our concerns. Other business organizations were on side. Think tanks such as the C. D. Howe and Fraser Institutes and the Conference Board of Canada generated convincing analysis.[*]

But, wait a minute. These are all the same guys. The Fraser and C. D. Howe institutes and the Institute for Research on Public Policy are joined at the spine with big business, which finances them. It goes like this. Big business puts up the money, the institutes churn out the "studies" that reflect the policies big business supports, then the newspapers and magazines that also finance the institutes dutifully report the "studies" as newsworthy and reliable wisdom. And, members of the BCNI put up most of the institutes' money and much of the money politicians spend in leadership and election campaigns.

The Fraser Institute has an annual budget of about $5 million and a full-time staff of over forty. Michael Walker, its Executive Director, "was frequently dismissed as an extremist. Now his views seem much more mainstream," or so says the *National Post's Business* magazine.[†]

Dalton Camp described the institute as "a heavily bankrolled right-wing propaganda agency serving the interest of corporate Canada." As well,

For some time a number of people have been trying to find out what corporations are financing the Fraser Institute's "research" and publications budgeting. Fraser has refused to tell, although many of the contributions are tax deductible.[**]

---

[*] *Marching Towards Prosperity*, BCNI, November 1, 2000.
[†] December 2000.
[**] *Toronto Star*, July 8, 2001.

I must admit that over the years I have been one of those who has failed in attempts to find out where the institute gets its money, the most recent occasion being the week I am writing these words. Camp continued:

> The Fraser Institute is the love child of a lifelong affair between Big Tobacco and Libertarian Excess. The happy alliance has become nicotine's prime sponsor in Canada, the drug of choice of right-wing researchers seeking intellectual comfort in smoke-filled rooms, in the further interest of freedom and the killer weed.
>
> If Fraser's stuff must be published as news, why not a disclaimer: "The following findings are the product of the Fraser Institute, which believes second-hand smoke is harmless, a finding directly sponsored by tobacco interests. Readers may now light up and read on."

According to *Maclean's*, "These days, much of the Fraser Institute's economic policy outlook is accepted as conventional wisdom."[*] *Maclean's* didn't go on to tell us who was accepting this wisdom, but it would certainly be its BCNI members who fund the institute, and people like Conrad Black, and his right-hand man David Radler, who sits on the institute's board. Perfect fits. In November 2001, the Fraser Institute presented Black with an award at a luncheon in Vancouver, at which Black yet once again launched an attack on Canada and Canadian values.

Another Fraser Institute board member is David Asper of CanWest Global Communications.

On its 2000 income-tax statement, the Fraser Institute signifies that it qualifies as a tax-receipt-granting charity, since it does not attempt "to influence law, policy and public opinion" via conferences, speeches, lectures, publications, published or broadcast statements, etc. Can you believe that? Can you believe that the Canada Customs and Revenue Agency lets them get away with such blatant deception? In 2000, the Institute declared $3.34 million in "official donation receipts for income tax purposes."

According to the *National Post's Business* magazine "More than any other think tank in the country, the C. D. Howe Institute commands attention by mastering all the tools a think tank has at its disposal: academic credibility, the ability to generate media attention and the promise

---

[*] September 11, 2000.

of practical advice." For example, "Last year . . . the institute published a paper by well-known economists Tom Courchene and Richard Harris that argued for a North American currency union. It sparked a national debate that included Senate hearings."[*]

Martin Goldfarb, pollster and consultant, has put the situation well:

> Most CEOs have been out of sync with political and social attitudes of Canadians for a long time. Their perception of Canada is based on business principals, not the political and social ones that have become part of Canadian identity. Many CEOs have not been schooled in Canada. They cannot fully understand pride in "not being American."
>
> Canada has provided a way of life . . . that is the admiration of others around the world. So why do we want to align ourselves more with the United States? Canadian CEOs may forget that Canadians have many times rejected being Americans.
>
> Canada is more than a balance sheet. The CEOs in this country are out of touch with the hearts and minds of Canadians. Few of the CEOs promoting the adoption of the U.S. dollar have the charisma that would attract the political support necessary to implement such a policy in Canada.[†]

Well said, but with one flaw. Today's CEOs and the federal government have been as one since the election of the Mulroney government is 1984. So, more precisely, who are these people who are selling out our country?

Among others, they are most of the presidents and CEOs of our large banks and petroleum corporations, corporate media heads, the senior partners in many of the major law and accounting firms, and well-paid, influential lobbyists.

Then there's Paul Tellier, Canadian National Railway CEO and Brian Mulroney's former chief of staff, who says:

> Let's be perfectly blunt . . . our economy is increasingly integrated with the United States. This integration will continue. It is inevitable. It is irreversible.[**]

---

[*] December 2000.

[†] *Globe and Mail*, January 2, 2002.

[**] *National Post*, January 21, 2002.

Bear in mind that CN is no longer considered a Canadian company by Statistics Canada since it is majority-owned by Americans. Does that bother Tellier?

> I find this argument that you're no longer 100 per cent pure Canadian, this is horseshit, and you can quote me on that.[*]

Thank you. It tells us quite a bit about you. Note, what Mr. Tellier believes is both "inevitable" and "irreversible."

Then there's another great railway man, David O'Brien, who says whether we like it or not, Canada will have to adopt U.S.-style immigration policies. "We're going to lose increasingly our sovereignty, but necessarily so."[†]

For Pat Daniels, CEO of Enbridge in Calgary, Canadian policy should conform to U.S. expectations. Canada sometimes pushes its sovereignty "a little too far":

> I think it would be realistic for the U.S. to expect us to either get on side with U.S. foreign policy or expect some change in our relationship.[**]

Not to be forgotten is another Canadian patriot and business leader, John Roth, former Nortel Networks CEO. Roth has little concern and little doubt: "one by one foreign-practice and foreign-ownership restrictions are going to tumble."[††] None of these people have any doubt about their predictions of loss of sovereignty, and they all seem quite happy about it. And who else is gung-ho on the sellout of Canada? *Globe* columnist Jeffrey Simpson writes, "Bay Street lawyers and merchants bankers are in heaven. They grow fat on this business."[***]

Well, there are many, many more of the same. But let's now turn our attention to how the BCNI got started. It will give us a good indication of who else really runs the country.

Among those who recruited Tom d'Aquino in 1981 were Earle

---

[*] *National Post,* December 20, 1999.
[†] *Globe and Mail,* September 15, 2001.
[**] *Globe and Mail,* September 15, 2001.
[††] *Toronto Star,* May 23, 2001.
[***] October 27, 1999.

McLaughlin, champion continentalist CEO of the Royal Bank, and Imperial Oil CEO Bill Twaits. We've already talked about energy, now let's turn our attention again to Canada's chartered banks.

As if they weren't already powerful and profitable enough, somehow our wise politicians let the banks buy up most of the top brokerage firms and almost all of the biggest trust companies in the country. The result has been an obscene level of corporate concentration in Canada's financial sector.

Despite their perennial complaining, the banks have done very well indeed. In 1999, Canada's chartered banks racked up their sixth-straight year of record profits, $9.1 billion for the year. The following year, profits totalled $10.1 billion and in 2001, despite huge losses on their foreign loans and investments, the profits for the big six banks totalled $10.13 billion.

In 1999, the same banks closed over 300 branches and cut 7,000 jobs in Canada.

In his February 2000 budget, Paul Martin reduced bank taxes by over $500 million. (The previous year, over 3.4 million poor Canadians were forced to pay total income taxes of over $1.5 billion).

As their profits surged, ever anxious for more of the same, the banks quickly expanded outside of Canada. Probably more than any other industry, they campaigned for the FTA and NAFTA to ensure reduced barriers to their growing investments in the U.S. and Mexico.

By the end of the third quarter of 2001, Canadian banks had loans to non-residents outside of Canada amounting to $183.3 billion. Bear in mind, this represents only their loans *outside* of Canada. As indicated earlier, we have no idea how much they have lent to foreign corporations in Canada, but without question it amounts to many, many tens of billions of dollars. Most of these loans have been for the takeover of Canadian businesses.

Compared to the $183.3 billion in loans outside of Canada to non-residents, total bank business loans in Canada amounted to only $127 billion. Isn't that just great!

So, we know that, for example, the Bank of Montreal helped out with the $3.7 billion Union Pacific Resources (of Fort Worth, Texas) takeover of Calgary-based Norcen Energy Resources. And a thousand other takeovers are financed by Canadian banks without us ever hearing about it.

Globe and Mail financial writer Andrew Willis, writing about the takeover of Canadian Hunter, explained the process well by way of a conversation in a Calgary bar:

> Burlington pays cash for Hunter. Burlington borrows in Canada to pay that bill. Burlington can then deduct all its interest costs from its Canadian tax bill. Then our American friends take all those Canadian interest payments, and consolidates 'em on the parent company's financials back in good ol' Houston. And you can deduct all that interest from your income again.

And what happens to tax revenue in Canada?

> Ralph thinks it's all great. The guy's practically put "For Sale" signs at all the border crossings.
>
> Doesn't he see what's coming? Part of what paid off Alberta's debt was corporate taxes paid on oil company profits. Now you've got the Americans piling in. The moment the U.S. guys take control, they pile all their debts onto the Canadian sub's balance sheet.
>
> Presto: No more Canadian profits, no more Canadian taxes, and no more balanced budgets in Alberta.[*]

But so what? Our Canadian banks get well-paid for financing the sellout of Canada.

Between 1985 and 1996, some 65 per cent of foreign takeovers in Canada were financed in Canada. If and when more current figures ever become available, I suspect that the number will be closer to 80 per cent.

So, there it is. In a nation whose political and corporate leaders are perpetually down on their knees pleading for more foreign investment, foreigners readily oblige by buying up Canada with money supplied by our very own banks.

Bank of Nova Scotia CEO Peter Godsoe lamented in the fall of 1999 that "We're losing a large part of our country" to foreign takeovers. "Maybe that's a good thing, maybe that's a bad thing, but what is interesting is that there's no debate on it."[†]

---

[*] *Globe and Mail*, October 10, 2001.
[†] *Globe and Mail*, October 13, 1999.

Mr. Godsoe didn't tell us how the foreign takeover of so much of Canada might be a good thing, nor did he indicate that the Bank of Nova Scotia would stop funding foreign takeovers in Canada.

So let's do a wrap-up on our good old patriotic Canadian banks. The banks fund much of the foreign takeover of Canada. The banks close down branches and fire thousands of employees in Canada. The banks lend companies like Enron, Adelphia, Tyco, WorldCom, and other U.S. corporations billions of dollars and they lose many hundreds of millions of dollars in Argentina. The banks buy banks, share-option trading companies, investment dealers, discount brokers, insurance and mortgage companies, on-line brokers, and other financial companies in the U.S., Britain, Mexico, Chile, the Caribbean, Asia, Australia, and elsewhere around the world. Meanwhile, they also provide much of the funding for federal and provincial political parties and for objective "research" organizations such as the Fraser Institute. With this kind of record, who for a moment would not consider them to be good corporate citizens?

One other thing. In 2000, our poor bank and brokerage CEOs had to get by with earnings, not counting options, ranging between $3 million and $14 million.

In 2001, the Canadian Imperial Bank of Canada earned just under $1.7 billion and somehow managed to pay taxes at the effective rate of 5 per cent. How come? We can start with the fact that the CIBC has subsidiaries in West Indies tax havens like the Cayman Islands and Bahamas. Keith Kalawsky writes:

> One investor says he has asked the bank for details on why its tax rate is so low. "They provided us with an explanation that wasn't an explanation . . . But it's supposedly legal."[*]

Perhaps not so legal is the CIBC's relationship with the disgraced Enron. In April 2002, a U.S. District Court in Houston claimed that the Canadian bank helped Enron in a "Ponzi scheme," helping Enron to falsify financial statements and procure non-existent profits.[†] Worry not. The CIBC recently announced that it plans to double or triple its U.S. investment-banking business in the next few years.

---

[*] *Financial Post*, February 23, 2002.
[†] *Globe and Mail*, April 9, 2002.

The Name of the Game Is Money

We can have a democratic society, or we can have the concentration of
great wealth in the hands of the few. We cannot have both.
— Louis Brandeis

Just how did the people I've been writing about become powerful enough to take over the political and economic agendas of the Mulroney and Chrétien governments? While it's true that so far they haven't yet achieved every single one of their objectives, the list of their major successes is long and impressive. How did they get so powerful? There are three answers. First: Is Standard Oil, which owns and controls Imperial Oil, powerful? Is General Motors, which owns and controls General Motors of Canada Ltd., powerful? Giant foreign corporations are accustomed to getting their way in the U.S. In Canada, with our compliant, colonial-minded governments, it has been easy.

The second reason the BCNI became so powerful is the disgracefully high level of corporate concentration in Canada. I know of no other developed country anywhere, including the U.S., that would allow so few corporations to own so much of their country.

> The name of the game in the Free Trade Agreement is money. Not money for real investment in creating new and better goods and services, but money for takeovers, mergers . . . money for accumulation and concentration of wealth and power.

So said Eric Kierans in his appearance before a House of Commons committee in 1987.[*] I used this quotation in *The Betrayal of Canada*, and it's well worth using again, because Eric Kierans's words are an even more accurate summary today of what has been happening in our country than they were in 1987.

In *The Betrayal of Canada* I showed that in 1987 the top 1/100th of 1 per cent of all enterprises in Canada controlled a startling 56 per cent

---

[*] House of Commons Committee on External Affairs and International Trade, December 3, 1987.

of all corporate assets, and the top 1 per cent controlled 86 per cent of assets, and made 75 per cent of all profits. "When these shocking numbers were published by Statistics Canada in 1990, there were no front page headlines, even in the business sections of newspapers. There was no debate in parliament. There was hardly a stir in the nation."

Effectively, because of our tax laws and hopelessly weak competition laws, a small number of large corporations and powerful conglomerates not only owned and controlled much of the country, but also dominated in any discussion of tax and trade policies and "the workings of the political process, or public policy of any kind – and especially in discussions about the future of our country."

I went on to quote James Gillies, now professor emeritus of public policy at York University:

> The degree of concentration, or in other words the lack of competition, in many markets in Canada is the greatest in the world and the concentration of economic power is enormous.

Since 1987, there has been explosive growth in corporate concentration in Canada. Anyone who reads a daily newspaper is familiar with the long list of mergers and acquisitions recited regularly (with virtually no negative comment) on the business pages. Sadly, because of lack of funds, Statistics Canada no longer keeps track of corporate concentration the way it used to, so we can't compare what we knew in 1987 with what has happened since. But we do know that if we had a recognizably serious problem then, today it should probably be considered a likely critical contributor to our national destiny.

Today in Canada, monopolies, near monopolies, and oligopolies reign. The Competition Bureau has had few victories and penalties are rarely imposed. Since the bureau is also underfunded, it doesn't have adequate staff required to pursue cases. At the same time, the government attitude towards corporate concentration has been "don't bother us with unimportant issues." Worse still, informed speculation suggests that it was Tom d'Aquino and the BCNI who were instrumental in proposing Canada's weak corporate concentration laws.

In an international review of government competition and antitrust organizations, Canada's Bureau was criticized for having a "reputation, historically, for paying heed to political bodies." Even in the U.S., where big business funds the politicians as nowhere else, the corporate concentration laws are tougher than Canada's.

Some will point to Paul Martin's refusal to allow bank mergers back in 1998 as an indication that big business doesn't always get their way. Don't believe it. As sure as you're reading these words, the Liberals will give their blessing to major bank mergers but probably not until after the next election. As well, as if there weren't already far too few men owning far too much of the media, you can bet the situation is going to get even worse soon.

For those who are so fond of calming Canadian fears about submergence into the United States by referring to the European Union, it's instructive to note how the EU blocked the proposed merger between the two giant U.S. corporations, Honeywell and General Electric, and made two large French electrical companies rescind their mergers. In both cases, the European Commission felt that the level of corporate concentration would have been excessive and detrimental. No one seriously believes that the Chrétien government would take actions that were remotely similar.

Is it not amazing that the supposed champions of free enterprise, market economics, and competition not only never even utter the words "corporate concentration," but are directly responsible for market conditions that much more closely resemble monopolies and oligopolies then they do anything connected to true free enterprise?

Corporate Canada has managed to seize power because, as already mentioned, the companies themselves are enormously powerful and because that power is incredibly concentrated in this country. The third reason relates to the progressive Americanization of our politics, and the rapidly increasing role of big money in federal and provincial politics. In the Conclusion of this book, I'll review the role of corporate financing in politics in Canada and suggest changes we need to make to our election laws.

Imagine two strong rivers flowing across the continent to the sea. Periodically one or both of them rise up and flood the countryside. Excessive and growing levels of foreign ownership and corporate concentration are like two powerful overflowing rivers that converge and submerge everything in their path. The combination is devastating, and when it is out of control, little can be done about it.

From the Southams to Conrad Black to the Aspers: The Decline of Newspaper Democracy in Canada

Over the years I got to know quite a few Southam newspaper editors and publishers well. Some became good friends. While I often disagreed with their editorial perspectives, I admired the degree of editorial freedom that each paper enjoyed. Head office in Toronto rarely intervened and, for the most part, Southam publishers and editors were allowed to print what they pleased. The centre-left *Edmonton Journal* was as different from the ultra-conservative *Calgary Herald* as the *Montreal Gazette* was different from the *Vancouver Sun* on constitutional and language issues. The *Windsor Star* could endorse the NDP, the *Edmonton Journal* sometimes supported the Liberals, while other Southam papers were for the most part enthusiastic backers of the Progressive Conservatives. While there was some cross-ownership of television, radio, magazines, and newspapers, it was relatively modest and not considered to be a problem in most communities.

Today, all of this has changed.

In English-speaking Canada, almost all of the major newspapers now belong to a huge telecom or television firm. In Quebec, the giant printers Quebecor own *Le Journal de Montréal, Le Journal de Québec,* the big Vidéotron cable TV network, and elsewhere eight major-market Sun Media daily papers, and Bowes Publishers.

Meanwhile, Bell Canada Enterprises has purchased CTV and the *Globe and Mail,* while Izzy Asper's CanWest Global Communications Corp. bought up the Southam chain and other newspapers and the *National Post* from Conrad Black. The Asper family now owns the *Victoria Times-Colonist,* the *Vancouver Province* and the *Vancouver Sun,* the *Edmonton Journal* and the *Calgary Herald,* the *Saskatoon StarPhoenix* and *Regina Leader Post,* the *Ottawa Citizen,* the *Montreal Gazette,* the *Halifax Daily News,* and many other daily or weekly papers. The Aspers also own the Global Television Network and seven specialty TV channels.

And then there's Ted Rogers. Rogers owns *Maclean's, Chatelaine, Flare, Canadian Business,* and six other magazines, Rogers AT&T

Wireless, Rogers Cable and Rogers Media, and at least eight radio stations across Western Canada.

Together, BCE, the Aspers, Quebecor, and Rogers have combined annual revenues of about $35 billion.

Not to be forgotten is the Irving-family stranglehold on the New Brunswick print media, where it owns all three major English-language dailies and two weekly papers.

When Conrad Black bought up the Southam papers in 1992, there was great apprehension in newsrooms and editorial boards across the country. The pompous, autocratic Black had a reputation as an ideological bully and a condescending, pedantic proselytizer. If anything, the fears underestimated the reality that was to come.

A prominent former Southam editor-in-chief put it this way:

> Conrad Black made it very plain that he wanted all of his papers to reflect his ideology, and he made it plain in quite brutal ways. If not, goodbye.
>
> If he didn't like what was being produced, he wrote monstrous blasts in response as op-ed pieces. It didn't take long for everyone to understand. The papers began to shift to the right even without being told. But most editors hadn't quite realized just how far Black and Amiel were to the right.[*]

Stephen Kimber, formerly a columnist with the *Halifax Daily News*, says that when Conrad Black took over, "certain opinions about certain subjects became unwelcome."[†]

Across the country, dispirited journalists watched as their papers moved dramatically to the right of centre. Soon, both Black and his wife, Barbara Amiel, began appearing prominently on Southam editorial and page-ops across the country. And, at every paper, for the staff, "your politics began to matter in a very important way." New editorial staff from the Fraser Institute were hired. Syndicated columnists such as Dalton Camp and Richard Gwyn disappeared from Southam pages.

For Black, Canadians are "whining, politically conformist welfare addicts," and an "underachieving people." And, unless Canadian taxes

---

[*] Telephone conversation, November 15, 2001.
[†] *Globe and Mail*, January 7, 2002.

and social programs are bought down to U.S. levels, so many highly qualified people will leave Canada "that this process will eventually lead to Canada being resistless against a benign offer of federal union"[*] with the U.S. Note the "resistless" and the "benign."

Somehow, in contrast to all public opinion polls, Black concluded that most Canadians are simply frustrated people who deep down really want to be Americans.

Then there was Barbara Amiel, who had no reservations about supporting her husband's line:

> Canada . . . will probably go on jealously guarding its independence from the U.S. like someone jealously guarding independence from his own brain. One day, a Canadian Giscard [d'Estaing] will steer us into an American union.[†]

And who could ever accuse Amiel of not being objective when she can come up with a line like this: "In the *Globe and Mail* we had the hiss from the viper's den of Canada's mainstream left-wing media."[**]

Perhaps she was referring to "left-wingers" like former editor William Thorsell, columnists Peter Cook and Drew Fagan, and former columnist Terence Corcoran, for example?

Owning so many daily newspapers across the country (fifty-eight of 105) wasn't enough for Conrad Black. For years he had tried unsuccessfully to pry the *Globe and Mail* away from Ken Thomson. Not owning a paper in Canada's biggest and most influential city rankled him. Moreover, as far as Black was concerned, the *Globe and Mail*, *Toronto Star*, and *Toronto Sun*, "a back-scratching media cartel," had misinformed the country for decades."[††]

Calvin Trillin, writing in *The New Yorker*, described Black well:

> Black has always given the impression of being unafflicted with doubt about his political views, or about himself, although in his autobiography he mentions that in his mid-twenties he consulted a psychiatrist

---

[*] Letter from Black, *Globe and Mail*, January 5, 2001.
[†] *Maclean's*, December 31, 2001.
[**] *Maclean's*, August 13, 2001.
[††] *Toronto Star*, August 25, 2001.

because of symptoms that now sound similar to those that afflicted Tony Soprano.[*]

Rebuffed in Toronto, the pressing alternative for Black was to start a new daily newspaper, and at the same time it might just as well compete head-to-head across the country with the *Globe and Mail* as Canada's second national paper.

Black, with his usual reserved understatement, promised that the new *National Post* would "drive a silver stake through the heart" of the other Toronto newspapers and the nationally distributed *Globe and Mail*. It wasn't hard to guess what the new paper would be like. Ideologically, it often made Ronald Reagan and Margaret Thatcher look like socialists. Anyone in Canada not of the extreme right was likely a pinko, bleeding-heart, welfare-loving laggard.

There are some good things, some of them very good, about the paper. The design is impressive. And there were and are some first-rate journalists working for the paper, such as, to name a few, Roy MacGregor, Noah Richler, Cam Cole, Alan Toulin, Robert Fulford, Marina Jimenez, and John Geiger on the editorial board. Even some of the paper's right-wing columnists, such as economist William Watson or Andrew Coyne, for example, are good writers, though you might agree with very little of what they say. And, most important of all, the *Post* will quite often have important news that hasn't shown up elsewhere, especially out of their excellent Ottawa bureau.

One other big plus for the *Post*. The intense competition that faced the *Globe and Mail* helped turn that paper into a much better-designed, more accessible, and more readable paper. The *Globe* added some first-class journalists and, for the first time in many years, it moved away from the ultra-right, continentalist rigidity that was entrenched under editor William Thorsell.

But, these good points for the *National Post* often are drowned in a sea of far-right propaganda, manipulated headlines[†], and bilious

---

[*] *The New Yorker*, December 17, 2001.

[†] In June 2002, the paper reported an Ekos poll that showed that 83 per cent of Canadians either wanted things to remain the same between Canada and the U.S. or that Canada should become less like the States. The *National Post*'s headline for the story was "Canadians want closer U.S. ties: poll."

invective. A friend refers to the paper as "The American Post," and John MacLachlan Gray calls it

> The Tokyo Rose of American assimilation, inveigling the troops to bow to the inevitable . . . meaning "North American integration."[*]

Linda McQuaig encapsulates the *National Post* in three paragraphs:

> The strong right-wing voice of the *National Post* has continually emphasized the problems of medicare, suggesting that there is a crisis that can best be dealt with through privatization. Similarly, the *Post* has conducted a relentless campaign against the tax system – particularly its few remaining progressive features – in an attempt to convince Canadians that our overall tax and social-transfer system fails to serve their individual interests. To this end, the *Post* has attempted to destroy the connection in people's minds between paying taxes and receiving benefits and things of value. Instead, we are simply told our taxes are too high, particularly in comparison with the U.S., without any acknowledgement of any additional benefits we receive – which, of course, include full healthcare coverage and more public support for education . . . the *Post* seems willing – in fact, keen – to sacrifice the popular motivation towards social cohesiveness and replace it with an individualistic "tax rage."
>
> That a pro-market force like the *Post* would want to do this is perhaps not surprising; the goal of the publisher, the corporate mogul Conrad Black, is unabashedly to lower taxes and reduce the size of government.
>
> Certainly Conrad Black's *National Post* has done its best in the past few years to extinguish any notion that Canadians should want a separate identity or should in any way resist the market culture of America. The *Post*'s constant message has been that things are better in the U.S., and that any Canadian with any sort of ability would want to leave immediately for those greener American pastures.[†]

Without question, the *National Post* has had a major impact on politics in Canada. Despite the fact that its enthusiastic support for the Reform and

---

[*] *Globe and Mail*, November 7, 2001.

[†] *All You Can Eat: Greed, Lust and the New Capitalism*, Penguin/Viking, 2001.

Alliance parties produced dismal results, Ontario's "common sense revolution" and Ralph Klein's extreme right-wing policies could have been lifted directly from the *Post*'s editorial pages. Moreover, the *Post* is carefully read, page by page, by politicians and senior bureaucrats in Ottawa.

But the paper has also succeeded in offending great numbers of Canadians across the country with its stridency and never-ending advocacy of far-right political, social, and economic policies.

And the *Post* has lost buckets of money. After having defiantly announced in March 2000 that the *National Post* was not for sale at *any* price, sixteen months later Black sold half of it to the Aspers, along with the Southam papers, and the rest of the *Post* to the Aspers in August 2001. Speculation was that the paper had lost $200 million and was losing more every week.

One thing about Black: he constantly amazes. When asked by *Time* magazine why he sold his *National Post*, which was intended to transform Canada, Black advised that

A national newspaper in any country needs a resident proprietor, and I have not been a resident of Canada for 12 years.*

One wonders, then, if he had not been a resident of Canada for so long, why he would ever want to sink hundreds of millions of dollars of Hollinger money into the *Post* as a non-resident proprietor.

We know about Black's desire to become Lord Black and his amusing, acrimonious dispute with the Chrétien government over his aspirations. After he lost a final court battle, Black decided to pack it in. In one of the more memorable comedic lines in modern Canadian history, a bitter Black termed his renunciation of his Canadian citizenship and flight into exile "an act of patriotism."

There was at least one bit of very good news when Black abandoned his country and his citizenship. In an interview with Linda Frum, he announced that, "in terms of involvement, activity and interest, my Canadian life is almost comatose.... I've gone on to other things.... No one should shed any tears for me."† As to the widespread disdain that so many Canadians have for him, Black writes that, "If I have earned their

---

* *Time*, September 3, 2001.
† *National Post*, November 10, 2001.

paroxysmal dislike, my years in Canada were not only a financial but a moral and cultural success."[*]

Or so he says.

As to the matter of his eagerly pursued title, in a brief letter to *Maclean's*, a British member of parliament, Rob Marris, skewers Black nicely:

> I am delighted to say that I have been able both to retain my Canadian citizenship and to sit in the British parliament. So could have Conrad Black, if he had stood (successfully) for election and democracy, instead of for the aristocracy and feudal privilege.[†]

When the Fraser Institute gave Conrad Black their Founder's Award in 2001, they described him as a person who exemplifies "the mission and philosophy of the institute."

Allan Fotheringham describes the Fraser Institute this way:

> Funded with lots of cash, the Fraser Institute is a collection of pointy-headed right-wingers who would do right-wing polling and issue right-wing "studies" and generally worship at the shrine of Barry Goldwater and other such intellectuals.
>
> For some strange reason, newspapers still print the periodic nonsense put out by this supposed think tank.

But the reason isn't really strange at all. People like Conrad Black and the Aspers are enthusiastic supporters of the work of the Fraser Institute, and probably, over the years, have been among their major financial supporters.

In case anyone might have heaved a big sigh of relief when Conrad Black sold the *National Post* to Izzy Asper, the Winnipeg television mogul quickly set them straight. There would be no important editorial changes for the paper, or in its approach to the news.

Soon after Asper bought the first half of the *Post*, from Black, Asper enthusiastically proclaimed, "I can think of no greater miracle in the 20th century than the *National Post*." And, let's be clear about this, the *Post*

---

[*] *National Post*, December 19, 2001.
[†] December 24, 2001.

represented "a common-sense point of view" which Asper supported.

Asper's two sons, Leonard and David, were quick to dispel any doubts about where the family stood on matters of public policy. In a January 2001 speech to the Canadian Club in Winnipeg, Leonard Asper made Conrad Black seem almost moderate. For example,

> Canada is a failure. . . . No rational economic being would want to earn profits in Canada. . . . The entrepreneurs and risk takers are on a train south. . . . It is folly to have signed a free trade agreement and then not have brought our fiscal policies in line with the United States.[*]

For the other son, David Asper, the family's critics are "bleeding hearts" and "leftists." Editorials attacking the Aspers' unprecedented suppression of editorial freedom appearing in the *Toronto Star*, the *Globe*, or the *Sun* are "irrational tirades," and criticism about editorial freedom is nothing more than "nonsense uttered by our competitors."

The astute Dalton Camp, one of the finest political writers Canada ever produced, put it this way:

> The corporate culture, swollen by greed and nourished by material lust, is slowly destroying the nation's social values and family values, including the family newspaper.
>
> David Asper has come to my attention because of his remarkably abusive oratorical style, which is striking for its bullying tone. The most common kind of bully is the bullying son of a rich man. The world, alas, is full of them.[†]

Among other things, David Asper described some of their newspaper employees as "riff-raff."

Who does David Asper remind you of? Well, of course, it's none other than Lord Crossover himself, who frequently insulted his own employees and other journalists across the land.

Political scientist David Taras, in his excellent book *Power and Betrayal in the Canadian Media*,[**] notes that Conrad Black hired right-wing

---

[*] *National Post*, January 18, 2001.
[†] *Toronto Star*, December 26, 2001.
[**] Peterborough, Broadview Press, 2001.

editors and columnists and that his papers feature right-wing political and economic commentators, all promoting the corporate and continentalist agenda.

In what has to be regarded as an astonishingly heavy-handed and arrogant suppression of editorial freedom, the Aspers decided to supply their newspapers with editorials from Winnipeg, which their fourteen largest papers across the country are obliged to run. Worse, "In order to be consistent within the publisher's space on editorial pages, local editorials won't contradict Southam's core positions."

Michael Cobden of the University of King's College in Halifax writes about the impact on journalists across the country:

> If you're working for someone who tells you that "on some issues, Southam will speak with one voice across Canada," and that "local editorials won't contradict Southam's core positions" you will probably make bloody sure that Southam's positions are not undermined in your paper in any way.

Cobden, former Toronto and Kingston editorial writer and editorial-page editor, pins down the Aspers' motivations:

> CanWest's purpose is to mould Canadians' thinking. "Southam believes that exploring issues from a Canada-wide perspective, rather than only regionally, is good for the country."[*]

What a contrast with the Southam papers before Conrad Black got his hands on them! *Ottawa Citizen* columnist Charles Gordon writes of a standard Southam annual report paragraph, this one from 1992:

> A major strength of Southam publications is that each is absolutely independent in setting its own policy on all matters involving news and public opinion. This has been Southam policy for more than a century. It is a policy we are proud of; publishers and editors make their own editorial decisions, free from interference.[†]

---

[*] *Globe and Mail*, January 30, 2002.
[†] *Ottawa Citizen*, January 31, 2002.

Peter Desbarats, former dean of journalism at the University of Western Ontario, was also a senior consultant to the 1981 Royal Commission on Newspapers. On the last day of 2001, Desbarats capsulized what has been happening in Canada:

> By 1981, Canada had a higher degree of newspaper concentration than most other developed countries and, according to the report that year of the Royal Commission on Newspapers, had done less than any other country to preserve a diversified and pluralistic press. But the Rubicon was crossed in 2001 when the Canadian Radio-television and Tele-communications Commission approved the takeover of the Southam chain, Canada's largest, and half-ownership of the *National Post* by CanWest Global Communications, owner of one of two private national TV networks. This degree of cross-ownership of major print and broadcast media was unprecedented in North America and perhaps without parallel anywhere.

While the CRTC expressed some concern about the potential for unprecedented editorial control,

> In 1981, a national poll by the Royal Commission on Newspapers revealed that 79 per cent of Canadians would be concerned if one owner controlled major television and newspaper enterprises in their communities. The same concern exists today, leading some to call for another public enquiry. This would probably be as futile as the last one, considering the Aspers' Liberal Party sympathies.[*]

By now there have been millions of words devoted to the Aspers' extraordinary, unprecedented behaviour. I think best of all is this paragraph from a *Globe and Mail* editorial:

> As editorial after editorial from head office seals off important national issues from future consideration by local boards – the editorial line will have been set in stone – the flavour of arguments arrived at by people living in the community and informed by that community is lost. What does that tell each newspaper's readers about how much stock

---

[*] *Globe and Mail*, December 31, 2001

Southam, and CanWest, put in the people who produce the paper they have been buying?*

Three former Montreal *Gazette* editors, Joan Fraser, Norman Webster, and Mark Harrison, write:

> Over time, as the corporate editorials cover more and more public issues, the range of topics on which local papers may express their own views will diminish dramatically. The imposition of a single corporate editorial line in a majority of Canada's metropolitan newspapers can only serve to curtail the vigorous public debate on which democracy depends.†

And what about what's actually in the Asper's not-to-be-argued-with editorials? An editorial on Canada's health care system tells readers (and staff) that "the debate about the role of private health care providers and private facilities is phoney," people are trying "to turn 'private' into a dirty word," and "the debate about whether private clinics should be allowed overnight patient stays is bogus." As well, "Water [is] worth exporting," and income taxes should be flat. I could go on, but you get the picture. "We should have one, not 14 official editorial policies"** says Izzy Asper, who, despite all the articulate criticism from across Canada, somehow still doesn't get it. Or perhaps he does, but doesn't care.

So now that the Aspers are supplying their papers with must-run editorials from which there is to be no divergence, how likely will it be that Global TV producers, reporters, and commentators will be unaware of the Aspers' mandated lines? Of course, they can certainly ignore the Winnipeg edicts, just as they certainly can begin looking for a job elsewhere.

And what about the inner workings of the Asper empire itself? Let's see now. Would a Southam paper reveal blatant manipulation of news at Global? Would a Global public-affairs show investigate the cutbacks and loss of editorial freedom at the Southam newspapers? Would anyone criticize the radical-right rants of David Asper?

---

* *Globe and Mail*, December 10, 2001.
† Montreal *Gazette*, December 5, 2001.
** *Globe and Mail*, February 13, 2002.

Then again, if Bell Canada comes out in favour of more harmonization with the U.S., or in favour of opening the door to foreign ownership of newspapers and television in Canada, will a *Globe and Mail* editorial criticize BCE? And will *Maclean's* chastise Ted Rogers if he wants to sell the Blue Jays to an American who wants to move the team to Fort Lauderdale?

One has to sympathize with the many excellent journalists who are on Southam editorial boards across the country, now subjected to censorship unparalleled in modern Canadian history. And, of course, it's not just the editors. What Southam columnist or reporter is going to write about the Aspers' brutal squashing of journalistic freedom?

Fifty-five journalists at the Montreal *Gazette* protested the egregious behaviour of the Aspers, whom they accused of centralizing opinion, vacating the power of the Southam editorial boards, and reducing the diversity of opinions and the breadth of debate offered to readers across the country. They wrote a strong, condemnatory open letter that was published in the *Globe and Mail*. David Asper responded to the protest by calling it, "childish . . . with all the usual self-righteousness . . . part of the ongoing pathetic politics of the Canadian left." And, "To them I say if you don't like working for us, exercise your freedoms to work elsewhere."[*] Few other Asper employees followed the courageous example set by the *Gazette* staff. It's not difficult to figure out why. Given the terrible concentration of media ownership in this country (most of it by extreme right-wingers), where would they find jobs after the Aspers fired them? There's only so many jobs at the *Globe and Mail* and *Toronto Star*, and a long list of talented men and women waiting in line for them.

Today, increasingly, the Southam papers feature the big-business, ultra-conservative corporate line, far distant from the priorities of most Canadians. Frequently, editorial pages seem to have been written by the Fraser Institute or the CCCE.

As for "the greatest miracle in the 20th century," it didn't take the Aspers very long, after gaining full control of the *National Post*, to downsize the miracle. About 130 staff were let go and sections of the paper were either cut or reduced in size. Since the Aspers made much of their fortune

---

[*] David Asper, speech in Oakville, Ontario, December 14, 2001.

"by importing U.S. schlock for our TV screens, barely meeting CRTC standards," in the words of Allan Fotheringham,[*] you can expect even more homogenized news, reduced "news holes," and more American wire-service content in their newspapers.

Southam must-be-published editorials are written by or under the direction of Southam News Editor-in-Chief Murdoch Davis. To best understand the quality of his objectivity, you may wish to know that he believes that concerns about media concentration are "a red herring." (Want to guess what Winnipeg head-office instructions might be with respect to reviews of this book?)

There are those who say there really isn't that much interest in the growing foreign ownership in Canada anymore. In the highly dubious event that that is true, why might it be so?

Every year Statistics Canada updates figures on foreign ownership. They are published in the annual report of the Corporations Returns Act, and more recently in the *Canadian Economic Observer* and in the Statistics Canada *Daily* on the Statistics Canada Web site.

In June 2001, when the data for 1998 showed that foreign control had jumped to 32 per cent, and that there was yet another new record of foreign direct investment, there were no calls to Statistics Canada from the press, and nothing in our two national daily newspapers, or in six other daily papers that I checked. I asked the people at StatsCan in Ottawa why this would be so. "Simple," came the answer. "The press gallery just isn't interested." When the report for 1999 was published one year later, once again there were no calls to Statistics Canada, and nothing in the papers.

The headline on a story by a *Globe and Mail* columnist is indicative of many similar headlines and stories over the years: "Foreign capital flow a blessing, not a curse." The writer didn't bother to take the time to check whether or not the blessed capital actually was a "flow" from outside the country, or how much of the "flow" (almost all of it) was for buying up Canada.

For the *National Post*, Canada's foreign-ownership rules have "no defensible rationale."[†] In a 1999 editorial, the *Post* suggested that we

---

[*] *Globe and Mail*, November 24, 2001.
[†] *National Post*, May 28, 2001.

should "get rid of remaining controls on inward foreign investment," including publishing, broadcasting, telecommunications, banks, trust and insurance companies, fisheries, airlines, uranium mining, real estate etc." In fact, it's okay to sell the whole country. What we need in Canada is "A truly open-door investment policy."*

The *Post* has regularly published reports by a Toronto investment firm that downgrade the foreign takeover of Canada using statistics that vary wildly from the official numbers assembled by the Investment Review Division in Ottawa. It just so happens that the Toronto firm is in the business of facilitating foreign takeovers in Canada.

In June 2000, a headline in the *National Post* told readers: "U.S. takeover of economy fails to occur." In the body of the story we learn that eleven of the top fifty corporations, ranked by revenue, are more than 50-per-cent foreign-owned. What the article did not reveal is that of the top 500 companies, 32 per cent were foreign-owned. By June 2002, the number had increased to 35 per cent. And what about owner-ship of the media in Canada? The *Post* asks, "Would it really matter if the New York Times Co. owned the *Globe and Mail*? If AOL Time Warner owned *Maclean's*? If Tribune Co. owned Torstar Corp.? If Disney/ABC owned CTV Inc.?"†

Well, yes, it would matter and it would matter a great deal. Is it possible that the people who overpaid Conrad Black for his papers are losing a great deal of money every month at the *Post*, and who are three to four billion dollars in debt, would love to be able to sell out to a foreign firm? Ask Izzy.

Anne Golden of the Conference Board brought down the wrath of the *National Post*'s Peter Foster when she suggested in a *Globe and Mail* page-op that if present trends continue, "Canada may soon run out of room to chart its own course." Typically, Foster advised: "This is assumed to be a bad thing."** Foster believes that concerns about foreign control are "misguided," and we should "be thankful for U.S. acquirers."

Then there's Brian Mulroney's free-trade buddy, Stanlet Hartt. No foolish sentimentality for Stanley:

---

* *National Post*, June 1, 1999.
† Matthew Fraser, *National Post*, November 12, 2001.
** *National Post*, October 11, 2001.

Mr. Hartt said foreign takeovers of the odd national icon, like the Montreal Canadiens, will also continue. "People are always lamenting these things either out of sheer ignorance or out of some misplaced national pride.*

Heaven protect us from misplaced national pride.

In sum, most of the media – newspapers, magazines, television, and radio – are controlled by right-wing continentalists who either expect their views to be reflected in the media that they own, or who are upset if views they do not agree with somehow mysteriously and unexpectedly appear too often. Since these same people are major contributors to the right and radical-right "think tanks," the media soaks up the "think tank" propaganda, presenting it as if it was actually objective research.

Because of the heavy degree of foreign ownership of corporations in Canada, much of the newspaper and television advertising in Canada is placed by foreign-owned advertising agencies (most of the top ten) on behalf of foreign corporations. So, newspapers and television either ignore or downplay the growing levels of foreign ownership in Canada. Out of sight, out of mind.

Dalton Camp summed it up nicely:

> It is possible to judge the vitality of a democracy by the vitality of its newspapers. The newspaper industry in Canada has been enfeebled by accountancy, ridden by debt acquired by the impudence of an excessive private egocentricity. Convergence has elevated old boilerplate to new eminence. It soon will be possible to travel the country and read a dozen newspapers, each with the same news, features, columns, and opinions under a dozen different titles.†

And, since media concentration in Canada has reached levels that would not be tolerated elsewhere, it follows that corporate concentration is not a problem for the media in Canada. Can anyone remember the last time there was an editorial in a Southam paper criticizing corporate

---

* March 1, 2001.
† *Toronto Star*, December 16, 2001.

concentration in Canada? Does anyone want to bet that there will be one any time in the foreseeable future?

Robert Hackett, co-author of *The Missing News* and a professor of communications, writing about a small number of wealthy, far-right conservatives, asks:

> How can progressive social movements succeed when they are demonized, trivialized or ignored by the media on which they generally depend to reach broader publics?
>
> It is going to be more and more difficult for popular-democratic movements to influence public discourse on the environment, globalization, or other vital issues.[*]

Is Ottawa at all concerned?

According to a Canadian Press story, Heritage Minister Sheila Copps has told a House of Commons committee "that concentration of media ownership in Canada was necessary to place Canada at a competitive advantage on an world scale" and "the government must take care not to hamstring investors."[†]

Can you believe it?

And this woman wants to be prime minister.

It's just possible that by the time this book is published, the Aspers will have moderated their appalling repression of journalistic democracy. There has been so much outrage since the disgusting firing of Russell Mills, publisher of the *Ottawa Citizen*, that even Izzy Asper must be concerned by the intense animosity across the country, not to mention cancelled subscriptions and declining ad revenue.

Many people are now aware that when Izzy Asper appeared before the Heritage Committee last September, he promised that his newspapers would be "fiercely independent in editorial policy." And a great many people are bitter about this broken promise and what has happened to their newspapers.

Too bad that we don't have a government in Ottawa that cares about such things as the freedom of the press and concentration of ownership in the media.

---

[*] CCPA *Monitor*, Fall, 2001.
[†] *Edmonton Journal*, November 9, 2001.

But, then again, should we really expect more from Izzy Asper's close friend, Jean Chrétien?

The Brain Drain and Walking the Streets Safely; Or, He Who Has the Most Pays the Least

For people like Conrad Black, Jack Mintz, Tom d'Aquino, and the like, high taxes have created a serious "brain drain" that has been bringing harm to Canada. Former Nortel president John Roth told us that "Over the past year I have spoken out over the brain drain . . . I don't think Ottawa fully realizes the extent to which Canada's talent is under attack . . . We have suffered the loss of almost an entire generation."[*] (This from the man who long ago located most of his top employees in the U.S.).

Of course the objective is clear. We must drastically lower taxes in Canada even below the tax rates in the U.S. Paul Martin's $100 billion in tax cuts in 2000 are not nearly enough. Personal and corporate taxes have to be slashed to levels never before contemplated in modern Canada or in most other developed countries. And, of course, that means social benefits will have to be guillotined as well, although that is mostly left unsaid.

Having talked Paul Martin into cutting corporate taxes by tens of billions of dollars, despite the burgeoning corporate profits of the last half of the 1990s, big business now not only wants even greater tax cuts, but it also is demanding that tax rates be *lower* than those in the U.S., "at least" 10 per cent lower than corporate rates in the U.S., pleads the CCCE in a letter to finance minister John Manley. Here's Jack Mintz: "If we're just a level playing field with the United States, it's not going to do it."[†]

The constant barrage of editorials, newspaper columns, and chamber-of-commerce speeches about the supposed brain drain leave no doubt that Canada's "best and brightest" are fleeing the country in droves, driven out by punishing high taxes. Even Industry Minister Allan Rock has joined the chorus, warning that Canada must stem the "outflow

---

[*] *Globe and Mail*, December 19, 2000.
[†] *Globe and Mail*, February 13, 2002.

of talent and capital." (Someone should ask him how he will vote when the issue of lifting the caps on foreign RRSP investment next comes before cabinet).

Fortunately, two well-known and widely respected Canadian economists make a shambles of the brain drain hysteria. Ross Finnie of the School of Policy Studies at Queen's University has produced one of the most valuable studies.[*]

> The data will show that the brain drain is in fact not very significant in terms of the total numbers involved, but there is reason for concern regarding certain types of individuals.

However, quite contrary to the chorus of complaints and demands from the Canadian radical right, to address the brain drain to the extent that it is indeed a problem with the loss of doctors, nurses, and some high-tech workers, Finnie's careful study concludes that "tax cuts would comprise a very blunt and inefficient instrument" for dealing with the problem.

Doctors and nurses left Canada in large numbers during a time of major cutbacks in the funding of health care, to the point where "practising medicine in Canada [became] a much less attractive proposition."

Despite problems in some sectors, Finnie concludes that "levels of permanent out-migration are currently near an all-time low." In fact, they are *far* below the historical levels of records kept all the way back to 1851!

Finnie makes another important point. Almost a third of all those who leave Canada for the U.S. return to Canada. As well, inflated "brain drain" figures include large numbers of Asian, European, and other foreign students who leave Canada to return to their country of origin.

Another important revelation is that, contrary to what we've most often been told, the overwhelming majority of people who leave Canada earn *less* that $50,000 a year (according to tax data), and the number who earn less than $20,000 far exceeds the total number earning over $50,000! (Compare this reality with Brian Mulroney's claim that "Canadians making $150,000 a year or more are eight times more likely to leave than the average."[†])

---

[*] "The Brain Drain: Myth and Reality – What It Is and What Should Be Done," *Choices*, vol. 7, no. 6, IRPP, November 2001.

[†] *Globe and Mail*, May 30, 2002.

A major Finnie conclusion is that

> Moving to the U.S. has not ... gained any special attraction over these recent periods, and this challenges the notion that Canada necessarily needs to become more like the U.S.

But, if we believe Conrad Black and the *National Post*, Canada is rapidly losing our "best and brightest" and our high-income earners.

Finnie shows that fewer than .009 per cent of taxpayers leaving Canada earned $150,000 or more in the year preceding their departure, and some of these will return to Canada. "These outflows are, furthermore, offset by individuals of a similar type moving into the country."

(While writing this book I had the great pleasure of swearing in as Canadian citizens seventy-seven new immigrants from thirty-three different countries, people of almost every colour and religion. Among them were a U.S. oncologist, an Irish psychiatrist, a Chinese software specialist, an English accountant, and many other talented, professional people, all of whom expressed great joy on receiving their Canadian citizenship. As I have written elsewhere,[*] and as others have conclusively shown, the number of highly qualified immigrants who arrive in Canada every year *far* exceeds the number leaving Canada).

No one will deny for a moment that talented individuals leave Canada for the U.S. They always have, and they will in the future, just as citizens from many countries around the world gravitate to larger countries.

But the hysterical cries of emigration disaster coming from the far right in Canada are as distorting as suggestions that high Canadian taxes are the principal cause, and that sharply reduced Canadian taxes will solve the problem. Finnie argues, on the contrary, that the impact of such tax reductions could be exactly the *reverse* of what was intended.

> The effects of the reductions in public spending necessitated by a tax-cut policy would presumably have various emigration-*increasing* effects through their impact on the quality of life available in this country, which is a countervailing appeal for many who currently choose *not* to leave. These certainly include public health care (and other social

---

[*] See Part Six in *Pay the Rent Or Feed the Kids*, McClelland & Stewart, 1999.

programs). But the benefits also include the various public goods which *cannot* be purchased such as the ability to safely walk the streets almost anywhere at any time, the more generous safety net and other such advantages.

Finnie puts the big tax-cut to (or below) U.S. levels in the right perspective:

> Any significant cuts in social spending would further diminish the deep satisfaction many Canadians feel by being part of a society where equality of opportunity, compassion for the disadvantaged, cultural identity and other goals related to common purpose and social justice are given a more central place.

(As I have written before, Conrad Black believes that caring and compassion is socialism.)

Finnie warns that,

> If Canada simply became more like the U.S. (due to a set of deep tax cuts), those who value this country precisely for the ways it differs from its southern neighbour would not find it as attractive to remain here, and some of those individuals would leave.
>
> A final consideration of the tax-cut strategy is that Canada's public social spending also has a productive element. The nation's public education and health systems, more generous welfare plans and other tax-financed programs not only have important social insurance and redistributional functions and in some cases, notably health care, important efficiency properties, but also contribute to our more favourable records regarding infant mortality, literacy, incarceration and other social indicators.

(We will be looking at these indicators more closely shortly).

In sum, Finnie's research suggests that the tax-cut scenario would at best yield "puny" results and would likely be damaging to the kind of Canada most citizens value. Moreover, the emigration problem has been greatly exaggerated. Simply "following the American lead in a race to the bottom" is entirely opposite to the long-term best interest of our country.

A few further points about physicians who move abroad. Dr. Peter Barrett, a past president of the Canadian Medical Association, has shown that the net loss (the number of doctors who emigrated compared to the number who returned) decreased sharply during the last half of the 1990s. By 2000, the net loss was only about one-third the level of earlier peak years.

In *Pay the Rent Or Feed the Kids* I looked at U.B.C. economist John Helliwell's excellent work relating to the brain drain. More recently, Helliwell has written:

> In the 1990s, even at their highest level during the decade, the flows (out of Canada) were small relative to earlier times.

Helliwell believes there has been "a widespread misinterpretation of brain drain data. For example, examination of data for Ph.D. students at the University of British Columbia shows that fewer than half who left Canada are Canadian citizens, the rest coming from more than 100 different countries." Helliwell goes on to point out that many U.B.C. Ph.D. students come from the United States, and more than a few end up staying in Canada.

Helliwell echoes Finnie's comments:

> Many of these proposals are explicitly intended to make Canada more like the United States in terms of public spending and taxation levels and structures. The well-being results suggest these would involve lowering the standards of those aspects of life individuals regard as the most important . . .[*]

Finnie's conclusion is clear. He says that given the abundant evidence, why would we focus on "being more like the U.S. in order to stem the brain drain?" Yes, we do pay higher taxes here, but

> Our higher taxes buy various goods and services that individuals have to pay for in the U.S. (health care and education being two important examples). So lower post-tax income can still result in more truly disposable income.
>
> Canada is simply a better place to live, an obviously sweeping judgement, but one with which I think most Canadians would agree.

---

[*] Ibid.

And, repeating a vitally important point,

> Canadian post-tax incomes can be lower than those in the U.S. and still leave people better off here.

Finnie quite destroys the radical-right reasoning respecting big tax cuts and the brain drain:

> general income tax cuts should not play a central role in the brain drain debate because the (net) effects of smaller cuts on the number of persons leaving would not likely be very great, while the "spillover" effects of any larger cuts in terms of reduced government revenues and associated reductions in public spending and other effects would be so large as to render any resulting brain drain effects relatively puny by comparison.[*]

Returning to John Helliwell, in a superb paper,[†] the noted British Columbia economist showed that in the year 2000 there were actually 175,000 *fewer* Canadian-born persons living in the U.S. than there were in 1980, and that Canadians living in the U.S. as a percentage of the Canadian population fell steadily throughout the 1980s and 1990s from some 23 per cent all the way down to 2 per cent.

In 1980, there were some 843,000 Canadians living in the U.S., but twenty years later that number had dropped to about 675,000, and this despite the provisions of the Free Trade Agreement and NAFTA that make it much easier for Canadians to work in the U.S. Emigration from Canada to the U.S. as a percentage of the Canadian population during the 1990s was at the lowest level since Confederation. Helliwell goes on to make a number of other important points.

In relation to the flow of science and engineering workers, both Canada and the U.S. are increasing their stocks, but "the Canadian stock is increasing twice as fast as that of the United States." Estimates are that Canada has an annual net gain of university-educated Ph.D.s and other

---

[*] *Choices*, vol. 7, no. 6, IRPP, November 2001.
[†] *Globalization: Myth, Facts and Consequences*, Benefactors Lecture 2000 (published privately), 2000.

postgraduates who are highly-skilled immigrants representing a brain *gain* of some $5 billion a year in education costs.

John Helliwell has produced a dramatic chart that shows the number of Canadian-born individuals living in the U.S. as a percentage of the Canadian population. The line bisecting the chart goes from top left in 1900 (about 22 per cent) down to the bottom right in 2000 (about 2 per cent). Helliwell writes:

> The most striking feature of these data, however, is the extent to which migration flows have shrunk. . . . From the Canadian perspective, at least, the body drain has been steadily declining over the century.*

In another study, Don Wagner of the University of British Columbia concludes:

> On the whole, what is remarkable . . . is how few people move despite substantial economic incentives to do so.
>
> At bottom, the brain drain is too small to justify substantial tax cuts on its own. Moreover, large tax cuts would not eliminate it.
>
> . . .
>
> The brain drain is small relative to the brain drain in the late 1950s and early 1960s.
>
> In most knowledge occupations, the drain is small relative to the total number of individuals working in those occupations.
>
> The drain is small relative to the supply of individuals entering the highly-skilled professions and it is substantially smaller than the brain gain from the rest of the world.

And lastly,

> Very few interviewees cited lower taxes as a reason for moving.†

Do quality of life and Canada's social programs make a difference? According to Roger Martin, dean of the Rotman School, "Parents of young

---

* Ibid.
† *Policy Options*, IRPP, December 2000.

children and retirees are often drawn back to Canada from the United States by social programs, health care and relatively low crime levels."[*]

Another reason that so many senior Canadians return to Canada is that "The estate tax in the U.S. is extremely high."

It's interesting to note that in 2000, 420 doctors left Canada, far below earlier levels, but 265 doctors returned to Canada. Why? Most were totally fed up with the U.S. health care system, HMOs, and private-insurance-company interference with the conscientious and ethical practice of medicine.

Keith McArthur of the *Globe and Mail* writes about comments by Roger Martin:

> Businesses looking for a culprit behind the so-called brain drain should look to themselves before attacking tax rates, Martin said yesterday.
>
> Employees in Canada are significantly underpaid for the work they do compared with their counterparts in the United States.
>
> Using salary figures obtained from Nortel Networks Corp., Mr. Martin showed that Nortel pays its employees significantly less in Canada despite the fact that "These same engineers are working on exactly the same things for the same markets."[†]

Journalist Rod McQueen picks up on the same theme:

> Business at its worst is when honchos become convinced that they are public-policy gurus, stuffed to the gills with great ideas. In fact, the most predictably pompous topic for any chief executive is a diatribe against government failings. High taxes à la John Roth are a perennial favourite.
>
> Why are these people always kvetching? Almost two-thirds of all business in Canada with annual revenues of less than $15 million paid no tax at all in any of the four years ending in 1998, according to Customs and Revenue.
>
> Subsidiaries of big companies fare particularly well. More than 2,600 – or 40% of all subsidiaries – were tax free.

---

[*] *National Post*, December 30, 2000.
[†] *Globe and Mail*, December 2, 1999

Maybe when Mr. Roth gives his farewell speech, he'll dispense with his usual doggerel about high tax rates and talk about the real issues: how is it that he who has the most, somehow pays the least?[*]

Roth was "the same guy who in 2000 was paid $71 million while presiding over a $100 drop in the Nortel share price, a catastrophic collapse that wiped out $300 billion in shareholder values."

In 2001, while Nortel stock was on its way down to junk-bond status, Roth pulled in $123 million in stock options.

Corporate Greed and Tax Hysteria

We've already heard from Leonard Asper that "No rational economic being would want to earn profits in Canada," and "The entrepreneurs and risk takers are on a train south." (One must assume, then, that Asper is not a "rational economic being").

According to Jack Mintz, unless we reduce corporate taxes, "There would be no advantage to investing in Canada. Instead, there would be a significant disadvantage." Now, note this from Mintz, in fact, please read it twice:

> Public policies that subsidize education, infrastructure, health care and social services are swamped by tax disadvantages.[†]

Can't be much clearer than that, can it? Reduce tax rates to or preferably below U.S. levels, then get rid of all those costly social programs that Canadians have developed over the years, because there are "tax disadvantages."

Do corporations in Canada really pay too much tax, as we hear from our corporate elite every week, if not every hour of every day? Canadians are bombarded with shrill demands for lower taxes on corporations so we can be "more competitive" or so our business can be on "a level

---

[*] *Financial Post*, May 23, 2001.
[†] *National Post*, October 26, 2001.

playing field" with American business, since, after all, they are our largest trading partner.

For the moment, let's set aside the fact that business in Canada has consistently had a better return on capital than in the U.S., or in any other G7 country. And let's ignore the fact that despite our "punitive tax burden" Canada has had a merchandise trade surplus with the U.S. for the past twenty-six consecutive years.

A good way to measure corporate income tax is to compare it with GDP. Let's look at how federal corporate tax has compared to GDP in Canada for the past four decades.

1960s	3.0 per cent of GDP
1970s	2.4 " " "
1980s	2.0 " " "
1990s	1.8 " " "

So, we can see that despite record profits in recent years, corporations have been paying federal income taxes at a much lower effective rate than in previous decades.

Bear in mind that in his two budgets in 2000, Paul Martin sharply reduced corporate taxes, despite a record-breaking string of corporate after-tax profits which reached all-time highs in the 1990s and set another new record in 2000.

Corporate tax revenue can also be measured as a percentage of total federal government revenues:

1960s	19.0 per cent
1970s	16.0 per cent
1980s	12.4 per cent
1990s	10.8 per cent

A similar comparison of personal income tax revenue as a percentage of all federal income is most revealing:

1960s	32.2 per cent
1970s	41.3 per cent
1980s	43.0 per cent
1990s	46.9 per cent

So, while the corporate tax share in the 1990s was only 57 per cent of what it was in the 1960s, personal income tax was 55 per cent higher. And while the corporate share has declined in every decade, the personal tax share has increased in every decade.

I don't know about you, but I didn't ever hear any of Canada's finance ministers talk about such a huge shift in taxes away from corporations onto the shoulders of individuals and families. Can anyone remember Michael Wilson or Paul Martin telling Canadians about this remarkable change in government policy? For that matter, can anyone remember an editorial in the *Globe and Mail* or the *National Post* questioning such enormous changes?

Poor corporations. In 1999, they had their highest profits relative to GDP in twenty years, an increase of 25 per cent over the previous year. In 2000, net profits increased by another 29 per cent. While profits were down in 2001, they were still above historical levels.

Are Canadian corporations overtaxed? During the 1990s, corporate tax revenue as a percentage of GDP was in the middle of the OECD pack with thirteen countries having higher rates, and fourteen lower rates. Setting aside income taxes for a moment, in 1998 twenty-three OECD countries had higher rates of social security taxes than Canada.

Statistics Canada tells us that from 1980 to 1997, among twenty-three OECD nations that were studied, the corporate-tax-to-GDP-ratio increases in Canada were lower than in nineteen other countries.

In 1998, fourteen OECD countries had higher total tax-revenue-to-GDP ratio than Canada, and fourteen were lower. Canada's rate of 37.4 per cent was well below the average for the OECD in Europe (39.8 per cent) and for the EU nations (41.3 per cent).

If tax revenues in OECD countries in 1998 are measured in U.S. dollars on a per capita basis, sixteen countries had higher tax revenue than Canada.

The OECD's 2001 projections for general government tax and non-tax receipts, as a percentage of GDP, forecast Canada at 41.2 per cent, compared to the European average of 44.1 per cent. Overall, Canada was once again in the middle of OECD countries.

Soon after Paul Martin's huge corporate tax cuts, a survey of 400 senior business executives showed that they considered further tax reductions the most important issue facing the country.

Just how much is enough? In 2002, combined federal and provincial corporate tax rates were already lower than rates in most major U.S.

states. In Ontario, for example, at 38.6 per cent, they were far lower than the 43 per cent in neighbouring New York. Canadian corporate tax rates were also lower than in countries such as Germany and Japan. Moreover, Canadian federal corporate tax rates are scheduled to drop from 27 per cent down to 21 per cent by 2005.

Let's go back to the assertion that Canada is a poor place to do business. Forgive me if I repeat a point I made in *Pay the Rent Or Feed the Kids*:

> Contrary to the plaintive cry so often presented on the business pages of our newspapers and in our business magazines, corporate Canada has been doing very well indeed. Year after year after year, Canadians have been told just how very tough it is for business to make a buck in this country. Too-high taxes, too much red tape, and so on. Year after year after year, Canadians have not been told the truth.

And the truth is that for every single year of the 1980s, Canadian business had a better return on capital that the average of the G7, the European Union, *and* the United States. From 1990 to 1998, the return on capital in Canada was better than in the U.S. for six years, and better than in the G7, OECD, and European Union every single year.

Poor corporate Canada. As is the case with so much of their shrill propaganda, the reality is quite different. Here's a perfect example. In August 2000, *The Economist* magazine published the results of a survey, based on seventy different factors, which concluded that Canada was going to be one of the top countries in the world to invest in over the following five years ("Canada comes out extremely high on all counts"). The very next day, the *National Post* headlined a story "Canadian Industry Faces Extinction." The thrust of the article was that big tax cuts for corporations were an urgent priority.[*]

Is Canada a good place to invest in? In 1999, in an OECD study of 21 countries, 16 were deemed to have greater "state control" than Canada, 19 (including the U.S.) had greater "barriers to entrepreneurship" than Canada, 17 had greater "economic regulation," and 19 (including the U.S.) had greater "administrative regulation" than Canada.

Is Canada a good place to do business? The KPMG study released

---

[*] *National Post*, August 16, 2001.

early in 2002 showed that Canada has a huge 14.5 per cent cost advantage for business over the U.S.

Now let's hear again from the C. D. Howe Institute's Jack Mintz, corporate Canada's field marshal in their war against taxes:

> Why do I focus on the cost of doing business as a way of measuring the impact of public policy on a country's potential for earning income and improving prospects for economic growth? The cost of doing business is central to understanding how public policies can affect an economy's standard of living.[*]

Someone should send Mintz the last three KPMG annual reports and an OECD publications catalogue.

Big business tells Canadians that high taxes are killing the country and depressing our standard of living. But OECD studies show that low tax rates and high economic growth are not necessarily linked. Bruce Little, the *Globe and Mail*'s excellent economics columnist, comments on an OECD document and work by economist Andrew Jackson:

> It is almost an article of faith in some quarters that the surest route to faster economic growth lies on a path strewn with lower taxes. Sometimes, however, articles of faith don't quite match the evidence supplied by the real world.
>
> The OECD compared growth rates and tax burdens in 22 countries. Countries with similar growth rates had wildly different tax burdens; countries with similar tax burdens had wildly different growth rates.
>
> The highest tax country was Denmark, at 50 per cent, but its GDP per person grew by 2.3 per cent annually compared to the United States tax load of 28 per cent and 1.7 per cent a year GDP growth per person.

And there were numerous other examples. France, Finland, Germany, Italy, the Netherlands, Norway, Denmark, and Sweden all have much higher tax rates than the U.S., but in recent years all have higher productivity growth rates. In 2000, the Netherlands had under 3 per cent unemployment, with some 50 per cent of workers working only 36 hours a week. Netherlands' total tax-revenue-to-GDP has consistently been well

---

[*] *Most Favored Nation*, C. D. Howe Institute, October 2001.

above Canada's during every year in the 1990s, and among the highest in the OECD. In a list of all the twenty-nine OECD countries, the Netherlands had one of the highest effective corporate tax rates; only two of these countries, Norway and Luxembourg, were higher. Only Austria and France had higher payroll taxes than the Netherlands.[*]

Given all of this, it's interesting to note that in early 2002, *The Economist* projected that the Netherlands would be the best place to do business over the next five years. Moreover, the Dutch model "demonstrates that economies can grow and jobs can be created without dismantling the rigid and overly generous European social-welfare system."[†]

Often the information we receive in our press presents a distorted picture of taxes in Canada. For example, a *Globe and Mail* columnist told readers that "In Canada, governments collected an average of 41.3% of individuals' income in taxes last year . . ." Let's compare this statement with information contained in Statistics Canada's publication *Income in Canada*. In 1998, the average implicit effective income tax rate for Canadian families was 20.1 per cent, and for individuals it was 18.3 per cent.

Now let's do another comparison with other countries to see how Canadians compare when it comes to personal income taxes as a percentage of GDP. The answer is: not very well. Taxes on personal income as a percentage of GDP in Canada are well above the OECD and EU averages. In 1998, twenty-one OECD countries had lower levels of personal income tax than Canada, and only five were higher.

Mind you, looking only at taxes while ignoring benefits received gives a very misleading picture. Economist Pierre Fortin points out that from 1980 to 1998, the overall tax rate in Canada rose from 30 per cent to 38 per cent of GDP, but the overall transfer rate rose from 9 to 17 per cent, leaving the net of the two unchanged at 21 per cent of GDP.

To be underlined here is that both taxes paid and government transfer payments to persons need to be considered when gauging the tax "burden."

While everyone knows that nominal tax rates are higher in Canada than in the U.S., Canada has many generous write-offs that effectively lower taxes that are actually paid. Moreover, when health care costs are factored into consideration, a great many Canadians are better off than

---

[*] Statistics Canada, *Perspectives*, Autumn 2001.

[†] *The Economist*, May 4, 2002.

Americans with similar incomes. For example, Canadians in the lowest income quintile had after-tax income shares in 1997 far higher than Americans in the lowest income quintile.

In 2000, Michael Wolfson, Assistant Chief Statistician at Statistics Canada, and Brian Murphy, who is with the Social and Economic Studies Division, produced an important study, *Income Taxes in Canada and the United States.** The authors point out the important and often substantial differences between tax rates, and taxes actually paid. A major conclusion was that for "almost one-third of families with incomes of less than $25,000, American families paid the same proportion or more of their income in taxes." And what about the big difference in taxes for the highest income group? Wolfson and Murphy show that in the U.S. they effectively paid only 5 per cent less of their total incomes than comparable Canadian families.

All this aside, increasingly, the Canadian tax system is being shaped to resemble the less-progressive U.S. system. Large tax cuts in British Columbia, Alberta, and Ontario provide five-figure tax reductions for the well-to-do, and minor reductions for the bottom 60 per cent of taxpayers. These three provinces are also the ones that have had to make severe cuts to social services and have increased post-secondary tuition costs, and constantly complained that they don't have enough money to pay health care costs or to pay for smaller classrooms in their schools.

Murray Dobbin, the B.C. writer and broadcaster, says it as well as anyone.

> The anti-tax campaign is designed to permanently lower government revenues and thus further weaken the ability to deliver social programs, redistribute income, and manage the economy in a way that benefits all of us and not just a privileged few.
>
> For over 15 years, Canada's business elite have been attacking the very idea of government as a positive force in society. This attack has been relentless in its intensity, and multi-faceted.

A result has been that "Many Canadians came to accept the proposition that 'we could no longer afford' good government." Are wealthy Canadians overtaxed? Taxable income figures can present a misleading picture.

---

* Statistics Canada, *Perspectives*, Summer 2000.

Many wealthy Canadians have income from sources not taxed, such as inheritance and gifts. In fact, Canada eliminated its inheritance tax in 1970. When you include these other sources of income and wealth, then wealthy Canadians are clearly *undertaxed* compared to other groups.

Overall, for Canadian families:

The OECD records that the disposable income of families earning the average industrial wage, expressed as a per cent of gross pay, is actually higher in Canada than in the United States.

In 1995, the median family in Canada had $30,200 to spend after taxes, compared with $29,500 for the median U.S. family (both in Canadian dollars). The Canadian family is even better off than the $700 difference, because it has already paid for health care in its taxes, while the American family may have to pay private premiums or bear the costs of sizeable medical bills if it is among the 43 million Americans without health insurance.

In terms of average disposable income as a percentage of gross pay, Canadians are slightly better off than Americans because, even though governments in Canada collect a higher potion of GDP than they do in the U.S., Canadians receive much more back in government services and transfers.

It's interesting to compare the radical right's tax hysteria with the much more balanced KPMG research. According to Dobbin:

Surveys of CEOs making actual decisions on where to invest and locate, show that taxes rank from 5th to 7th place in terms of priority, behind things like an educated labour force, access to resources and markets, electricity costs, labour costs, borrowing costs and social infrastructure and quality of life.

KPMG reveals that taxes affecting corporations in Canada are extremely competitive with those in other developed countries. The 1997 KPMG study, "The Competitive Alternative," compared the costs of doing business in Canada, the U.S., and U.K., France, Germany, Italy and Sweden. It showed that Canada had the lowest effective corporate income tax rate – i.e., the tax rate actually paid after all the tax breaks and credits were deducted. Canada's rate (which included federal and provincial taxes) was 27.4 per cent.

Germany and France had high rates of corporate taxation (60.5% and 54% respectively) But neither of these countries is considered "uncompetitive" with Canada or the U.S. in attracting investment. This demonstrates the point argued earlier: that corporate income tax levels are well down the list of factors considered by corporations when they are deciding whether or not to invest.[*]

We're constantly reading and hearing about tax rates of 40 per cent, 50 per cent, 55 per cent, or even more. Forget statutory tax *rates*. Let's look instead at the taxes actually paid.

In 1998, the top quintile of Canadians earned, on average, $113,374. On this income, they paid tax amounting to 24.5 per cent. While the average Canadian family paid $12,489 in income taxes, they received back from government an average of $6,892 in government transfers. In fact, in 1998 the average Canadian family kept 89.9 per cent of its market income. That's quite a different picture than you will get from the tax-rage rants of our corporate elite.

About two-thirds of all capital gains in Canada are made by the top 1 to 2 per cent of Canadian income earners. By 2001, the capital gains changes made by Paul Martin will have cost almost $6 billion in lost tax revenue. For higher-income Canadians, the effective combined federal and provincial tax rate on capital gains will be only 22 per cent.

You might want to compare that with your own tax rate.

Have things been getting better or worse for high-income Canadians? We've already seen that the number of high-income men and women leaving the country is at a historical low level. Here's one of several good reasons why that might be the case. For a married earner with two children under the age of sixteen, the combined federal and provincial tax on an income of $200,000 has dropped by more than $50,000 over the past thirty years. Meanwhile, a family earning $20,000 is paying about the same tax as it paid in 1971.

Not to be forgotten is the fact that Canada is one of only three developed countries that has no death taxes.

---

[*] *10 Tax Myths*, CCPA *Monitor*, October 1999.

Jack Mintz and other perpetual bellyachers about high Canadian taxes use Ireland as an example of how low tax rates attract foreign direct investment. In 2000, Ireland received $8.4 billion in foreign direct investment, while "high-tax" Canada received net foreign direct investment of $44.7 billion. And, while foreign direct investment in Canada broke all previous records in 2000 for the sixth consecutive year, a *National Post* headline told readers "Tax policies keep capital out of Canada."[*]

With a friend like Industry Minister Allan Rock, corporate Canada has no fears. For Rock, personal tax rates are not a priority, but corporate taxes are at the top of his list, and U.S. rates will have to be "the benchmark." Does anyone suspect that perhaps Rock's leadership-campaign fundraising from big business has been below expectations?

The Ottawa economic consulting firm Infometrica has calculated that a tax cut of $1 billion a year would likely create about 9,000 jobs, but $1 billion spent on roads and hospitals would create 25,000 jobs. Someone should send Allan Rock a copy of the study.

In the words of noted Economist Lester Thurow:

> Look at it this way. If the economic race was simply to go to those who had the lowest taxes in the world, Canada would never be a winner. It is never going to have the world's lowest tax rates.

Instead,

> Building and financing a stronger education system would have a much bigger payoff in the long run than simply cutting taxes.

There's one thing that is pretty consistent in our most vocal advocates of tax cuts; the more money you have made in Canada, the greater your accumulated wealth, the louder and more insistent are your claims that taxes in Canada are too high.

The same day that I am writing these words, a new Statistics Canada document shows that the top 40 per cent of Canadian families own 88 per cent of family wealth in Canada, while the bottom 40 per cent own the grand total of 2 per cent. Once again, we can see the steadily widening

[*] *National Post*, September 19, 2000.

gulf between the wealthy and the rest of Canadians, and the priorities of the majority of Canadians and the very different goals of our corporate elite. In poll after poll after poll, year after year, public opinion clearly demonstrates that heavy majorities of Canadians put social programs such as health care and education far ahead of tax cuts in their list of important priorities.

Academics to Be Ignored

Before we go on to look at differences between Canada and the United States, and between Canadians and Americans, there's one last group in the continentalists' pantheon that deserves special mention, a small band of high-profile academics.

At the top of the list, two economists, Tom Courchene of Queen's University and Richard Harris of Simon Fraser University, seem determined to advocate policies that would end Canada as we know it. Courchene says Canada no longer has a national economy and we had better agree to a North American monetary union. While he recognizes that these moves would severely curtail the federal government's policy-making prerogatives, Courchene seems to think this would be a very good idea. In any event, in a few years "while a political entity called Canada will exist, practically speaking it won't matter."

Richard Harris says that "we are in fact more integrated with the United States than any pair of countries in the European Union." The implication seems to be that since this is so, why worry about our dollar and other foolish matters? Why not proceed to integrate even further? Why not a customs union and a common market with the U.S.? Why not harmonize our taxes, get rid of foreign ownership restrictions, and agree with the U.S. on environmental policies?

For Courchene and Harris, there's no time to waste: "delay on Canada's part . . . could prove costly," and we must "make haste in investigating the possibility of establishing a monetary union," even if this "would mean the end of sovereignty in Canadian monetary policy."[*]

---

[*] From *Fixing to Monetary Union*, C. D. Howe Institute, June 1999.

Then we have the prolific and ubiquitous right-wing historian Michael Bliss who says that Canada is simply "a northern suburb of the United States."[*] As far as Bliss is concerned, Canada has "already chosen the road of continental integration" and there is no turning back, since we have "effectively abandoned the vision of being an economic and military power separate from the United States." And we are "no longer obviously healthier than the United States . . . in social policies." As well, "The southward drift of Canadian talent has resumed."

The *National Post* loves Michael Bliss and they publish him frequently. It's hard to know if Bliss writes Conrad Black's speeches, or vice-versa, but the similarity is remarkable. Try this from Bliss, for example: "The Americans will not mind if we babble on soppily about being kinder or gentler . . ." And it's time we stopped "living on a sense of high moral superiority." Moreover, "Since 1776, the essential Canadian question has always been what kind of Americans we would become. We were wrong to think we would evolve into a radically distinct people . . . The differences between our rights-based pluralistic democracies survive mostly at the margins of daily life."[†] As well, "We still mouth platitudes about our achievements and importance and sovereignty, but do we really believe them?"[**] And, "Increasingly, it's a waste of time letting your Member of Parliament know what you think. Do you ever find yourself wishing you had a Congressman you could call up or write to?"[††]

Dalton Camp said it all: "Michael Bliss, the historian, impresses me as a man on the edge of joining the United States Marines."[***]

We can't leave the list of academics to be ignored without paying tribute to the resolute Canadian Queen of continentalism, Wendy Dobson, former C. D. Howe Institute president and now professor at the University of Toronto's Rotman School of Management. Dobson wants "deep integration" with the U.S. and proposes what in her mind is a deadly serious "Big Idea," which

---

[*] *National Post*, January 29, 2002.
[†] *National Post*, September 29, 2001.
[**] *National Post*, November 30, 2001.
[††] *National Post*, September 21, 2001
[***] *Toronto Star*, October 31, 2001.

is needed to wrap what we want and need – customs-union-like and common-market-like arrangements . . . in exchange for what a wide swath of what U.S. political interest want: joint continental defence, closely aligned immigration policies toward third-country migrants, border security and energy security.

Moreover, we should be "eliminating the border . . . in trade and investment decisions."[*]

So there we have it again: conform, integrate, harmonize, capitulate, and why not sell the entire country? Besides, everything is inevitable and there are many Canadian values that aren't worth preserving.

We've already seen that the vast majority of Canadians strongly disagree with people like Courchene, Harris, Bliss, and Dobson. In the next chapters we'll explore why.

Before we do, it's most interesting to note that both Tom Courchene and Richard Harris have been invited down to Washington to attend conferences with the CIA. Harris did not accept, but Courchene took part in extensive discussions about dollarization.

A key conference participant was Gary Hufbauer of the Institute for International Economics in Washington. Hufbauer admitted to me that he is "associated with the CIA" and has worked with, among others, Wendy Dobson, who is "down in Washington all the time."[†] And CIA "associate" Hufbauer is up in Canada from time to time, where, among other things, he has done work for Industry Canada and more recently has been asked to advise the C. D. Howe Institute on their "Border Papers" examining Canadian–American relations. Wendy Dobson chairs the Border Papers advisory group, and says that while she is aware of Hufbauer's connection with the CIA and has known him for "many years," she is not concerned about him acting in an advisory capacity for the Howe Institute. Besides, the CIA comes to the Institute for International Economics in Washington frequently for seminars and it would be very difficult to discourage their attendance, even if one wanted to.[**]

---

[*] C. D. Howe Foundation, April, 2002.
[†] Telephone conversation, June 6, 2002.
[**] Telephone conversation, June 21, 2002.

Also of great interest is the fact that it was Hufbauer who "put the stake in the heart" of Canada's sectoral free trade ambitions and who advocated the "broader kind of FTA" we now have.[*]

As I said earlier regarding the C. D. Howe Institute, draw your own conclusions.

A Breathtaking Gap and Standing the Public's Choices on Their Head

These academics, and their corporate counterparts, all have things in common.

First, the policies they advocate represent a continuing and accelerating adoption of American standards and values.

Secondly, most of them seem to believe that there are few important differences between Canada and the United States that are worth preserving.

Third, few if any of them seem to care a whit about Canadian sovereignty, and they consider the further Americanization of Canada to be inevitable.

Given that the Americanization of Canada is quickening, the obvious questions must then be: Are there important differences between Canada and the U.S., between Canadians and Americans, and are these differences worth preserving?

The suggestion that Canadians and Americans are not similar in many respects is as nonsensical as the idea that there are few significant differences.

What is certain is that Canada's radical right and many of our political commentators regard the differences between the two countries as insignificant ("They pale beside what we share" or "Our similarities greatly outweigh our differences," in the words of two prominent Canadian journalists[†]).

---

[*] Telephone conversation with political scientist Gilbert Winham (Dalhousie University), June 24, 2002, relating to Hufbauer's participation in the Macdonald Royal Commission.

[†] Jeffrey Simpson, September 10, 2001, and Edward Greenspon, October 2, 2001.

For Conrad Black, Canadians are "indistinguishable" from their U.S. neighbours and we are Canadians "almost by historical accident," and we would likely be hospitable to "a friendly American takeover bid." While this is simply more Black nonsense, it is indicative of the mindset of much of the Canadian corporate elite, i.e. there are few differences of importance between Canadians and Americans ("indistinguishable") and as a result Canadians would look kindly upon a U.S. takeover of our country.

There are so many errors in fact and logic in Black's comments, that they support one thing that more than a few of us have long proclaimed: there was no brain drain when Conrad Black left Canada.

Those who advocate the further Americanization of Canada not only downplay the difference between the two countries, but they also strongly criticize Canadian practices that differ from those in the U.S., while praising American policies. Some of these people are stridently anti-Canadian.

Before we have a close look at the differences between the two countries, differences most of the radical right would like to see disappear, we need to again return to the important question of how most Canadians feel about what has been happening to Canada.

We know that the vast majority of Canadians not only do not wish to become Americans, but they wouldn't move to the U.S. even if the opportunity presented itself. Moreover, they are clearly concerned about the degree of integration between Canada and the U.S. that has occurred in recent years, and they are opposed to further integration.* As well, Canadians strongly value the idea of belonging to Canada. In the words of pollster Frank L. Graves and colleagues, "We find that sense of belonging to Canada is quite high. Comparatively, Canada has the highest levels of belonging to country of all areas tested in the World Values Survey . . . Canadians believe that there is a national identity, and that it is a source of pride and belonging."†

However, the wishes, feelings, and values of the vast majority of Canadians are quite opposite to those of the political and corporate elite

---

* A *Globe and Mail* April 2002 Ipsos-Reid poll showed that 72 per cent wanted Canada to remain as an independent country, compared to 23 per cent that wanted closer ties to the U.S. Somehow, the *Globe* managed to publish the story about this poll under the title "Canadians Support Closer Ties with U.S."

† *Identity and National Attachments in Contemporary Canada*, Frank Graves with Tim Dugas and Patrick Beauchamp.

who are selling out our country. Ekos reports "a striking gap and pro-found differences between private sector leaders and the general public."

Another important point is obvious. Though Canadians love their country, though they don't want to become Americans, though they do wish to maintain their identity and values, increasingly they believe that they're going to become Americans, whether they like it or not.

> Moving to compare the public and senior decision-makers, the gap in vision across elites and the general public is breathtaking – particu-larly when we look at private sector elites. Private sector leaders essen-tially stand the public's ordering of choices on its head and then dramatically widen the gap. The public's first choice is the last choice for private sector leaders and the widened margin is dramatic. This widening rupture is troubling.[*]

In all the following areas, the vast majority of Canadians support our overall policies in contrast to American policies: health care, social programs, education, the justice system, our cultural institutions, and multiculturalism. When Canadians are asked what distinguishes Canada from the U.S.A., Ekos reports the following responses: our health system is better; our health system is universal; our culture and multicultural-ism are different from the U.S.; we are more peaceful/compassionate and easygoing; our social programs are better; our political system is better; our quality of life is better; we have less crime in Canada, and it's much safer here.

It's interesting to note that when Americans are asked which goals and values should be most important in shaping government policy, safety and security were near the top of the list, well below health, the environment, integrity, and ethics, and other topics on the Canadian priority list. Little wonder: 60 per cent more Americans than Canadians feel unsafe walking alone on their streets, and for good reason.

There are public-opinion polls, and then there are public-opinion polls. Many people realize that the wording in a poll can easily be manip-ulated to achieve the desired outcome. Even a small word change can predetermine the poll results. The polls that need to be treated with scepticism are those initiated by corporations, lobby groups, so-called

---

[*] Frank L. Graves, Ekos, address to Canadian Club luncheon, January 2001.

"think tanks," and by a newspaper that sets out to prove public support for its editorial positions. Often, in such cases, the results are headlined, but the exact questions asked are not revealed. Many such polls, through receiving little or no close scrutiny, are widely reported in the Canadian media. Inevitably, once they are published, newspaper columns and editorials comment on and repeat the results.

One poll, published in the summer of 2001 and reported prominently in virtually every major newspaper in Canada, said that 85 per cent of Canadians support closer economic ties with Americans, and 75 per cent want closer social and cultural connections. These supposed public-opinion results can only be described as nonsense. They fly in the face of years of polling that show exactly the opposite. One prominent and highly thought-of Canadian pollster described the poll as "fact creation" and "patently untrue."

Yet, the press in Canada accepted the poll without question.

In 2001, I asked that two national public-opinion polls ask a simple, direct, right-to-the-point question. The first poll asked "Should Canada join the U.S.?" Eighty-five per cent of Canadians said "No," while 12 per cent said "Yes" (3 per cent had no opinion). Of those who had some university education, only 8 per cent said "Yes."[*]

The second poll was conducted a month later, after the September 11 terrorist attacks in the U.S. This time Canadians were asked if they wanted Canada "to be admitted to the United States and elect politicians in Washington." And this time, the results were almost identical: 85 per cent opposed the idea and only 10 per cent were in support.[†]

How do Canadians feel about a strong national government? Is there a Canadian identity worth preserving? The polls show 76 per cent of Canadians believe that "Canada cannot survive without a strong national government to provide shared goals and values" and they also show most Canadians believe that there is a national identity, and "that it is a source of pride and belonging" and "the state has played a crucial role in constructing national identity."

---

[*] Telephone interviews conducted on a random sample of 1,663 Canadians, eighteen years of age and over.

[†] 1,004 adults, the Vector Poll.

PART

4

The Differences Between Canada and the United States

The Schizophrenic Country

In what follows I will look at differences between Canada and the United States, but first I must make two points.

Virtually all of the criticism of the U.S. that follows comes from American sources. No doubt these criticisms and descriptions will be labelled anti-American. And, for the most part they are indeed that. But they are mostly anti-American criticisms originating from respected American sources, people who love their country, but despair over what has been happening to it, just as many Canadians despair over the Americanization of Canada for similar reasons. I suspect that the following pages will properly describe *why* the overwhelming majority of Canadians don't want to become Americans.

Secondly, almost all Canadians recognize that there are many good things about the U.S. and millions of wonderful Americans in all parts of the country. Without question, Canadians like Americans more than they like the U.S.A.

If a friend of mine from overseas was travelling to the United States for a first-time visit, and wanted an introduction to the country, here are the things I would tell them to do.

For a wonderful variety of the "best and the brightest," the most interesting and most innovative, the most fascinating and dynamic men and women in the country, they should listen to National Public Radio, an amazingly good daily collection of news, commentary, public affairs, music, art, and literature.

For exactly the opposite experience, they should click through the scores of U.S. television channels. Here they will find some very good TV, but for the most part, a repetitive mass of banal, violent, often vulgar or even pornographic, ultra-nationalist boredom.

I would suggest that they read the *New York Times*, one of the world's greatest newspapers, every day they are in the U.S. They should look through the *Times* Sunday Book Review section, the Arts and Leisure section, the political columns and reports. Some of the best writers in the country cover international events, poetry, music, dance, the wonderful and awful U.S. movies, theatre, painting, sculpture, and architecture. The abundant, vibrant American artistic genius is there to see and enjoy.

And they should read *Harper's* magazine, especially its brilliant editor, Lewis H. Lapham, one of the finest political, social, and economic commentators anywhere. Also, if they haven't already done so, they should read some of the many brilliant contemporary American novels such as Joseph Heller's *Catch 22*, Kurt Vonnegut's *Slaughterhouse Five*, or Cormac McCarthy's *All the Pretty Horses*.

If they can, they should visit the marvellous New York art galleries, the Smithsonian in Washington, and the Getty Museum in Los Angeles. For a taste of American cinema, if the tourist has not already been inundated with U.S. films in their own country, they might watch the Academy Award winner *A Beautiful Mind*, and then one of the awful summer blockbusters for a sense of the good, the bad, and the ugly. The ugly could be any one of the many dismal, violent, chauvinistic Hollywood movies, that are, for the most part, according to the director Robert Altman – and I agree – aimed at fourteen-year-old male minds in forty-eight-year-old bodies.

As in all large countries, including Canada, there are enormous regional differences. The differences between Massachusetts and Arkansas are as wide as the differences between Rosedale and the Bridle Path in Toronto on the one hand, and Vancouver's East Hastings Street on the other.

If they can, the new tourist should visit a superb American university such as Harvard, and one of the excellent U.S. hospitals that rival those anywhere in the world. Worth noting are the many fine community colleges and public universities such as Berkeley or the City University of New York, although a considerable number of these are now becoming unaffordable for many families as government financing and student aid have been cut back.

When they are in the U.S., they will discover the abundant energy, the dynamic, vibrant, garish, kooky, noisy, and sometimes decrepit cities.

If they spend any time at all in New York, they will discover one of the world's most exciting cities. They should do what most tourists do and visit Fifth Avenue, Park Avenue, and Broadway, the department stores, the theatre, and the fine restaurants and delis. But, to get a different sense of the city, they should also visit First and Second Avenue, and walk through the communities to see how people live. They should walk in New York as much as possible, within the limits of safety.

If my tourists friend were fortunate, they might visit gorgeous, tranquil New England, and the magnificent Monterey coast in California, and some of the beautiful U.S. national parks. Everywhere they will find kind, enthusiastic, energetic, and hospitable people. For the most part.

Americans are an amazingly industrious people. The United States didn't become the world's wealthiest and most powerful nation without the dynamic energy and innovation that has long been so characteristic of its citizens.

Murder and Principles

When George W. Bush addressed the U.S. Congress on September 20, 2001, he said "We're in a fight for our principles."

In a press conference on October 11, he said, "The United States is a nation that understands the value of life." And, "I know how good we are."

58,000 Americans died in Vietnam.

Since 1979, about 85,000 American children have been killed by firearms in the U.S.

A gun will take the life of an American child at the rate of a classroom every two days.

Nearly three times as many children under ten die from gunfire as the number of law enforcement officers killed in the line of duty.

Here are the number of children killed by firearms in 1996:

Japan	0
Britain	19
Germany	57
France	109
Canada	153
U.S.A.	5,285

According to the U.S. Center for Disease Control and Prevention, compared to children in other developed countries, U.S. children under the age of fifteen are:

- 16 times more likely to be murdered with a gun
- 11 times more likely to commit suicide with a gun
- 9 times more likely to die in a firearms accident.

American children under the age of fifteen are twelve times more likely to die from guns than children in twenty-five other industrialized nations *combined*!

This year, on average, a U.S. child or youth under the age of twenty will be shot to death by a gun every 2½ hours. In Canada, fewer than two a month will be killed by guns.

Every week in the U.S. there are headlines such as "Failing law student guns down professors" or "Four-year-old brings loaded gun to school" or "Another high school shooting" or "Fired employee kills former fellow workers. Five dead, four wounded."

In a recent poll, 43 per cent of American parents said that they feared for their child's safety at school. One in three believes that it is "very likely" that a Columbine-type shooting could happen in their community.

According to the marvellous Washington, D.C., Children's Defense Fund,

More American children died in 1998 from gunfire than from cancer, pneumonia, influenza and HIV/AIDS combined.

The United States has the highest homicide rate of any of the world's top thirty developed nations.

With two exceptions (D'Arcy McGee and Pierre Laporte), Canadians do not assassinate their political leaders, and relatively few prominent citizens are murdered. There has never been an attempted killing of a Canadian prime minister or premier. U.S. presidents Abraham Lincoln, James Garfield, William McKinley, and John F. Kennedy were assassinated, as were other prominent U.S. political figures including a mayor of Chicago, Anton Cermack, Robert Kennedy, Martin Luther King, and Malcolm X. Both Teddy Roosevelt and Ronald Reagan were wounded in assassination attempts. Among the many other well-known personalities who have been murdered in the U.S. was Beatle John Lennon.

In the United States there have been dozens of school shootings in recent years. Metal detectors in U.S. schools are now common.

In 1999, 15,333 Americans were murdered, about one every thirty-four minutes. There was one robbery every minute and a rape every six minutes.

The same year, there were 536 murders in Canada. Throughout the 1990s, the homicide rate per one hundred thousand was three to four times higher in the U.S. than in Canada.

In 2000, there were 15,517 murders in the U.S. and 542 in Canada. The Canadian rate per hundred thousand was less than one-third of the U.S. rate.

In Canada, firearms accounted for 34 per cent of all homicides. In the U.S., the percentage was twice as high.

In Ottawa-Carleton in 2000, there were 8 homicides. In Washington, D.C., there were 123. In Toronto there were 81 homicides; in Chicago there were 644.

In the U.S., there are about 240 million guns. Handguns are everywhere. In most American states it's even legal to carry a concealed gun. In Canada it's illegal for civilians to transport a handgun without a permit. Meanwhile, more than half of the firearms recovered from crimes in Canada have come into the country illegally from the U.S.

Despite horrific incidents of gun violence, attempts to toughen U.S. legislation in any meaningful way have been met by the National Rifle Association's Washington lobby, one of the best-financed and most successful lobbies in U.S. history. Even after the Columbine High School massacre when thirteen were killed and twenty-six wounded, almost nothing has changed in the U.S.

Even though the polls show broad support for tougher gun control legislation, U.S. politicians are both terrified of the well-organized and aggressive pro-gun lobby, and grateful for the large financial donations it provides.[*]

Meanwhile, handguns sales in the U.S. have escalated dramatically. In one recent month alone, over 1 million handguns were sold. As for the tragic loss of lives among children in the U.S., have no fear. *The Economist* headlines an article "The American gun lobby thinks children should be taught to use guns."

> Gun magazines in the United States delight to show the young, kitted out with mufflers and eye protectors or casual in camouflage caps squinting through the sights of a rifle while braced in their father's arms. They are sometimes very young indeed: four or five. Such images repel Europeans and the anti-gun lobby, but America's gun enthusiasts see them quite differently: as symbols of freedom, tradition and delight in fatherly instruction. "Those sure were the good times," reads one advertisement. "Just you, Dad, and his Smith & Wesson."[†]

Such images also repel most Canadians.

The Economist reports that

> The suicide rate for Americans aged 15 to 24 tripled between 1950 and 1994, from 4.5 to 13.7 per 100,000.
>
> Guns matter. A study has compared suicide rates in Seattle, in Washington state, with those across the Canadian border in demographically similar but less well-armed Vancouver, British Columbia. Among 15- to 24-year-olds in Seattle, the total suicide rate was 40 per cent higher, mainly because more youngsters killed themselves with guns.[**]

---

[*] In May 2002, the Bush government sent two briefs to the U.S. Supreme Court supporting individual gun ownership. According to the Brady Center to Prevent Gun Violence, "It's a terrible setback for people concerned about gun violence in the United States. Eighty people a day die from gun violence and to have an administration that is so pro-gun is just tragic" (*Globe and Mail*, May 2002).

[†] *The Economist*, December 23, 2000.

[**] December 8, 2001.

In 2000, firearms were involved in 41 per cent of U.S. robberies, while in Canada the rate was 16 per cent. The same year U.S. police arrested 561 persons per hundred thousand for drug offences; in Canada the equivalent rate was 177.

In the United States, there are almost 6.5 million men and women in prison, on parole, or on probation, one out of every thirty-two adults in 2000. The U.S. incarceration rate per hundred thousand is over five times Canada's. Building new prisons is one of the fastest growing industries in the U.S.; over the past decade new prisons cost over $25 billion and total annual prison costs now exceed $31 billion. Far more is spent building prisons than universities.

By 2000 there were over 2 million inmates in U.S. jails and prisons. The U.S. now has the highest incarceration rate of any developed country, about 700 per hundred thousand people. In Canada, the rate is about 115.

In January 2002, the *Globe and Mail* carried a story titled "Every winter, thousands of bald eagles gather to eat salmon, bringing Americans along with them."

> More Americans come to Brackendale each year, anxious for a glimpse of their country's best-known wilderness icon. The irony is that many U.S. visitors had never seen a bald eagle until they came to B.C.

How come? Not too difficult to explain. Americans have shot almost all of their feathered icons in the U.S.

The United States, born in violence, is one of the developed world's most violent countries. Canadians and people around the world are appalled and repelled by the wanton violence in the U.S., whether it's road rage or the slaughter of children. Most of us find it incomprehensible that any affluent society would permit the virtually uncontrolled proliferation of firearms and would be unable to learn from the brutal, devastating carnage that occurs every year in every part of the United States.

One of the many reasons that most Canadians have no desire to become Americans is our abhorrence of the violence we see across the border. If George W. Bush really "understands the value of life," he would do something significant about guns in the U.S. But why would we expect Bush to be any different than all of his predecessors? And why would we ever expect Congress to be different?

Canadians *are* different. And thank God for that.

Poverty and "Compassionate Conservatives"

In the 1960s, American president Lyndon Johnson declared a "War on Poverty" in the United States. According to economist John Kenneth Galbraith, "In the United States, the war against the poor has been won."[*]

Year in, year out, decade after decade, the world's wealthiest nation has poverty rates that far exceed those in virtually all other developed countries.

In 2000, UNICEF produced "the most comprehensive estimates so far of child poverty across the industrialized world. The document, *A League Table of Child Poverty in Rich Nations*,[†] studied child poverty in twenty-three OECD countries. Before I give you the comparative results for Canada and the United States, it's worth quoting briefly from the editorial at the front of the document:

> The following statistics represent unnecessary suffering and deprivation . . . They also represent a failure to hold faith with the developed world's ideal of equality of opportunity.
>
> Whether measured by physical and mental development, health and survival rates, educational achievement or job prospects, incomes or life expectancies, those who spend their childhood in poverty of income and expectation are at a marked and measurable disadvantage.
>
> Those who grow up in poverty are more likely to have learning difficulties, to drop out of school, to resort to drugs, to commit crimes, to be out of work, to become pregnant at too early an age, and to live lives that perpetuate poverty and disadvantage into succeeding generations.
>
> No one would argue that being born into poverty is the fault of the child. It is merely the lottery of birth. And it is fundamental to shared concepts of progress and civilization that an accident of birth should not be allowed to circumscribe the quality of life.

Let's look at the differences between Canada and the United States in some of the topics mentioned above.

---

[*] Speech in Toronto honouring Senator Keith Davey, January 1997.
[†] *Innocenti Report Card No. 1.*, UNICEF Research Centre, Florence, Italy, June 2000.

First, child poverty. Using the OECD definition of poverty, in the list of twenty-three OECD countries, the U.S. was second from the bottom with a child poverty rate of 22.4 per cent. Only Mexico was worse. Canada's rate was a dismal 15.5 per cent, but still well below that of the U.S. The U.S. child poverty rate was over *five times* the rates for Sweden, Norway, Finland, Belgium, and Luxembourg, and two or three times the rates for Denmark, the Czech Republic, the Netherlands, France, Hungary, and Germany.

Of the twenty-three countries, the U.S. and Mexico had by far the highest percentages of working poor. In terms of the impact of social policies, Canada's policies reduced the child poverty rate from 24.6 per cent down to 15.5 per cent. But meagre U.S. social assistance dropped the American child poverty rate only 4.3 points, down to 22.4 per cent.

In terms of the population as a whole, adults and children, the United Nations reports that Canada has one of the worst records among developed nations, way down in sixteenth place. The United States is a shocking twenty-seventh, keeping company with Russia and Mexico.[*]

Even employing the most conservative international estimates of poverty, between 1987 and 1997 the U.S. poverty rate was 17.3 per cent. For comparison, here is a list of some other countries using the same conservative method of calculations for the same years:

Finland	3.9 per cent
Luxembourg	4.1 per cent
Belgium	5.5 per cent
Norway	5.8 per cent
Germany	5.9 per cent
Netherlands	6.2 per cent
Denmark	6.9 per cent
France	8.4 per cent
Sweden	8.7 per cent
Ireland	9.1 per cent
Spain	9.1 per cent
New Zealand	9.2 per cent
Canada	10.6 per cent[†]

[*] *State of the World's Children*, 2000.
[†] United Nations *Human Development Report*, June 2000.

From time to time you will read reports citing the official American poverty rate. If it wasn't so pathetically sad, the *official* U.S. rate would be considered a joke. Official U.S. poverty lines were drawn almost forty years ago. Since then there has been almost no significant change in the American definition of poverty and what constitutes an acceptable American standard of living. The Washington-based Economic Policy Institute says that "most researchers now agree that the U.S. 'poverty line' income is not sufficient to support most working families." The poverty line for a two-parent, two-child family is $17,463. When a more realistic budget of basic family needs is calculated, 29 per cent of all U.S. families with one to three children fell below the basic needs level, about two-and-a-half times the official poverty numbers.[*]

About half of these families include a parent who worked full-time. Aside from the to-be-expected problems the poor face, such as hunger, being evicted from their housing, having their utilities disconnected, etc., access to medical care is of growing concern.

While "Policy makers in the United States have moved towards the conclusion that work is the solution to poverty," large numbers of American families simply cannot earn enough working to make ends meet. And while official poverty lines badly understate the true level of poverty, hence alleviating public and congressional guilt, all comparisons using internationally accepted guidelines show how misleading the commonly employed official U.S. poverty figures are.

Families without health insurance face "dire financial consequences. A medical emergency can be a devastating financial blow and require families to choose between buying food or seeing the doctor." Roughly 37 per cent of U.S. workers do not have health insurance through their employers; only 30 per cent of workers in the lowest wage quintile have health insurance. "Even if low-wage workers are offered employer-sponsored health insurance, their plans are more likely to require sizable employee contributions."[†]

Even using the absurdly low official U.S. poverty rates, all of the following U.S. states have child poverty rates between 20 and 30 per cent:

---

[*] Heather Boushey, Chauna Brocht, Bethney Gundersen, Jared Bernstein, *Hardships in America, The Real Story of Working Families*, Economic Policy Institute, Washington, D.C., 2001.
[†] Ibid.

Alabama, Arizona, Arkansas, California, Kentucky, Louisiana, Mississippi, New Mexico, South Carolina, Tennessee, Texas, and West Virginia. In the nation's capital, Washington, D.C., the official child poverty rate is over 30 per cent, but the real rate is far higher.

In Canada, the highest after-tax provincial child low-income rate (1999) was in Newfoundland at 19.3 per cent, following by Manitoba at 18.6 per cent, Quebec at 16.1 per cent, and Nova Scotia at 13.7 per cent.

In 2002, there are now more homeless in New York than there were twenty years ago, and the shelters are "crammed with children."[*]

According to the Children's Defense Fund, in a list of twenty-six industrialized countries, the U.S. is sixteenth in efforts to lift children up out of poverty, eighteenth in the gap between rich and poor children, and last in protecting children against gun violence. Moreover,

> An American child is more likely to be poor now than in any years between 1966 and 1980, and the gap between rich and poor is the greatest ever.

In the United States,

> Rampant child hunger, homelessness, insecurity and suffering persist.
> Seventy-four per cent of poor children today live in working poor families who cannot make enough to escape poverty.
> In a list of 24 major industrialized countries, the United States is the only country without universal health care insurance, the only country without paid maternal/parental leave at child birth, and the only country without family allowance/child dependency grants.
> Only 49 per cent of poor children who are eligible for food stamps (which stave off hunger) get them.
> Between 1976 and 1998, there was a 91 per cent increase in the number of American children who lived in a family with an income *below half* the poverty line.

And, in contrast to existing stereotypes, most poor children in the U.S. are white; about one-third are Black or Hispanic.

---

[*] *New York Times Magazine*, March 24, 2002.

As well, "The U.S. spends more in one week on the military than we spend in an entire year on Head Start to get poor children ready for school."

This despite the fact that extensive empirical research has clearly shown that in the U.S. Head Start programs improve IQ scores and result in: less need for special education programs, better grades, less likelihood of conflict with the law, and a host of other benefits. In one respected study, for every $1 spent on children at the preschool levels, the savings resulting from grades that did not have to be repeated, increased tax revenues due to better job opportunities, less involvement in crime, and welfare savings produced a net benefit of over $7.

Are things getting better or worse?

> The chance of an American child being poor in an average year was 15.7 per cent in the 1970s, 20.5 per cent in the 1980s, and 21 per cent in the 1990s.[*]

Every day in the United States about 800 low-birth-weight babies are born. Most are from poor families. Every day over 1,500 babies are born without health insurance. The Children's Defense Fund tells us that:

- Every 44 seconds an American baby is born into poverty.
- Every 20 seconds a child is arrested.
- Every 4 minutes a child is arrested for drug abuse.
- Every 8 minutes a child is arrested for a violent crime.

The State of America's Children (2000) says it all in a single sentence. "In the United States, rampant child hunger, homelessness, insecurity and suffering persists."

In 2001, the Washington-based Economic Policy Institute published an important new book, which examined the standard of living of the working poor in the U.S.[†]

The book shows the failure of the Clinton–Bush policies of kicking

---

[*] *The State of American's Children*, yearbooks for 2000 and 2001. Children's Defense Fund, Washington, D.C.

[†] Boushey, Brocht, et al., *Hardships in America: The Real Story of Working Families.*

people out of welfare into poor-paying jobs. A shocking 29 per cent of U.S. families with one to three children under twelve had incomes below basic-needs levels for their communities. Most of these families included at least one parent who worked full-time.

Common among these families was hunger, inadequate child and health care, eviction from housing, and other serious hardships. Simply put, in the U.S., "the market has priced basic items such as health care, child care and housing above what many families can afford . . . safe transportation is also out of reach for many families." As well, insufficient food leading to frequently missed meals or utilities and telephones being disconnected were other frequent problems among the working poor. "For a great many, child care means the child ending up caring for itself."

Canadian economists Andrew Sharpe and Lars Osberg have calculated the U.S. poverty rate for the elderly at 24.4 per cent, while in Canada it is 4.4 per cent for men and 11.1 per cent for women, and Statistics Canada reports that it is only 2.2 per cent for elderly families.[*] For the elderly, the poverty gap (how far persons fall below the poverty line) is roughly twice as much in the U.S. as it is in Canada.

In the United States, a two-parent family with two children earning $1,420 a month is not considered to be or counted as being poor. That said, the poorest fifth of all U.S. families have average monthly incomes of only $1,186.00

About 40 per cent of the poor in the U.S. live in abject poverty, with total incomes less than half the official poverty line. About 1.1 million U.S. families have total incomes of less than $10,000 a year.

Using the OECD definition of poverty throughout the entire decade of the 1990s, the child poverty rate in Canada averaged 13.9 per cent; in the U.S., it was 22.7 per cent. By comparison, in the Netherlands it was 4.1 per cent, and in Denmark 4 per cent.

In August 2001, the *Globe and Mail* headlined a story from Washington, D.C., "Census reflects good life in U.S."

Americans have never been wealthier, better educated or better housed, according to a major new release by the U.S. Census Bureau.[†]

---

[*] *Income in Canada*, Statistics Canada, 1999.
[†] August 7, 2001.

About the same time as this story appeared, *The Economist* reported that

> Annual wages for the bottom fifth of single-mother households rose from $1,350 in 1993 to $2,400 in 1999.

In New York City, between the late 1970s and the late 1990s, the incomes of the poorest fifth of New Yorkers fell by 33 per cent in real terms.[*]

What about welfare payments to the poor in the U.S.? Here's an example. In New York State a poor family of three gets a monthly rent subsidy of the grand total of $286 a month, a small fraction of the rental cost of a two-bedroom apartment. Meanwhile, homeless-rights lawyers say the number of families trying to find a spot in homeless shelters is the largest since New York City began keeping records twenty years ago. One in five shelter residents has a full-time or a part-time job.

In September 2000, the *New York Times* reported that millions of Americans "grappled with hunger." According to Lynn Parker, Director of Child Nutrition, The Food Research and Action Centre in Washington, D.C., "There are millions of children starving in the United States."

In the U.S., the minimum wage of $5.15 hasn't changed in five years. "The average family must earn at least $13.87 an hour, a wage few hope to attain, to pay for a two-bedroom apartment."[†]

As for homelessness, "This is off the charts," says New York's chief assistant corporation counsel, who has been defending the city's homeless policies in court. "This is completely careening out of control," says the executive director of the Coalition for the Homeless. "How shocking to have an all-time high in the number of homeless . . . at the end of an economic boom."[**]

And what a boom it was. The longest, biggest economic expansion in modern U.S. history. But, it doesn't matter if it's Richard Nixon or John F. Kennedy in power. It doesn't matter if it's Bill Clinton or George W. Bush. As a society, Americans have decided to accept unconscionable poverty levels that are *far* worse than most other countries have allowed, even in their worst economic downturns.

You decide for yourself if the following has any relevance. At this

---

[*] *New York Times Magazine*, March 24, 2002.

[†] *Time*, January 7, 2002.

[**] *New York Times*, August 1, 2001.

writing, there are 189 members of the United Nations. The United States and Somalia are the only two countries that have failed to ratify the UN Convention on the Rights of the Child.

Note that many or most of the countries with very low poverty rates have per capita incomes well below U.S. per capita incomes. All of these countries care about their underprivileged far more than Americans do. All of them have developed common sense policies that substantially reduce and alleviate poverty. Generation after generation of "compassionate" American conservatives have shown that they are willing to abandon their poor and accept the crime, violence, and poor health that poverty breeds.[*]

In *Pay the Rent Or Feed the Kids,* I describe the terrible tragedy and disgrace of poverty in Canada. As the Americanization of Canada proceeds, the likelihood or ability of Canadians to take meaningful steps to relieve poverty in Canada is diminishing.

This said, it's important to understand that those who want to turn us into Americans are asking for far worse levels of hunger, homelessness, crime, violence, child and family suffering, and deprivation in Canada.

Should we be concerned? The aforementioned Drew Fagan tells us that

> The Canadian government . . . is finally coming around to the obvious conclusion that the United States is the benchmark against which this country must be judged in a myriad of public policy areas, especially economic.[†]

Some benchmark!

"The Secession of the Successful"

Why is there so much violence in the United States compared to other developed countries? Might it have a great deal to do with the high level

---

[*] According to Barbara Amiel, "Conservatism is by definition 'compassionate'" and "America has never been so well" (*Maclean's,* December 25, 2000).

[†] *Globe and Mail,* February 22, 2002.

of poverty? And why is there so much poverty compared to other developed countries? Could much of it relate to grossly unfair distribution of income in the U.S.?

The United Nations studied the distribution of income in thirty-two countries between 1987 and 1998. They compared the incomes of the richest 20 per cent with the incomes of the poorest 20 per cent. Canada came in a poor number sixteen in terms of the fairness of income distribution. The United States was second-last, in thirty-first place!*

The 2001 edition of the United Nation's *Human Development Report* showed that all of the following countries had a more equitable distribution of income than the United States: Australia, Austria, Belgium, Canada, Czech Republic, Denmark, Estonia, Finland, France, Germany, Great Britain, Greece, Hungary, Iceland, Ireland, Israel, Italy, Japan, Luxembourg, Malta, Netherlands, Norway, Poland, Portugal, Slovakia, Slovenia, Spain, Sweden, and Switzerland.

During the past twenty years, the poorest fifth of Americans lost about 5 per cent of their already pathetic real income, while the top 20 per cent gained on average $246,500, an increase of 64 per cent.

And how has the average full-time American worker managed during the past two decades of unprecedented wealth creation? In 1979, the average male worker earned $678 a week. By 2000 (in constant dollars), they earned $646 a week.

Late in 2001, the U.S. Congressional Budget Office found that in inflation-adjusted dollars,

> the income of American families in the middle of U.S. income distribution rose from $41,400 in 1979 to $45,100 in 1997, a 9 per cent income increase. Meanwhile, the income of families in the top 1 per cent of families rose from $420,600 to $1.016 million, a 140 per cent increase. Or, to put it another way, the income of families in the top 1 per cent was 10 times that of typical American families in 1979, and 23 times and rising in 1997.

Economist Paul Krugman asks, "Why has the response to rising inequality been a drive to reduce taxes on the rich? Good question. To understand political trends in the United States we probably need to

---

* United Nations *Human Development Report*, 2000.

think about campaign finance, lobbying, and the general power of money to shape political debate."*

Probably?

Like you'll probably get into an accident if you fall asleep at the wheel. In 1999, the *New York Times* reported that

> The gap between rich and poor has grown into an economic chasm . . . The top 1 per cent of Americans will have as many after-tax dollars as the bottom 100 million.†

By the end of the year, the gap between rich and poor in the U.S. was greater than at any time during the previous fifty-five years.

According to *The Economist*,

> In America, between 1979 and 1997, the average income of the richest fifth of the population jumped from nine times the income of the poorest fifth to around 15 times.**

By 1997, the average income *increase* of the top 1 per cent of Americans was almost triple the *total* average income of the bottom 90 per cent of Americans.

In 2000, the *New York Times* reported:

> From 1986 through 1997, the average income of the richest 1 per cent of [individual] Americans soared 89 per cent to $517,713, from $273,562.
>
> In 1997, the average income for the bottom 90 per cent was $23,815, up a scant $364, or 1.6 per cent from 1986.††

Looking at income distribution in the U.S. over a longer period, 1947 to 1999, the Economic Policy Institute reports that the bottom 80 per cent of Americans lost ground in terms of their real incomes, while only the top 20 per cent gained.

---

* *New York Times*, January 4, 2001.
† September 5, 1999.
** June 16, 2001.
†† September 17, 2000.

Comparing all the countries listed in the 2000 *Human Development Report*, when the U.N. measured the share of total income of the poorest 10 per cent, Canada came in a terrible forty-fifth. The U.S. was an appalling eighty-third.

When the poorest 10 per cent was compared to the richest 10 per cent, or when the poorest 20 per cent was compared to the richest 20 per cent, the U.S. income distribution was near the bottom of the lists, far behind any other G7 or EU country.

And how did the big bosses do? During the 1980s, the average U.S. CEO was paid about forty times as much as the average U.S. worker. In the 1990s, it was about ninety times as much. By 1999, the average CEO received about 480 times what the average worker earned.[*]

How do most Americans feel about what has been happening? Ekos polls reveal "Stark and growing levels of social class polarization in American Society." When asked by Angus Reid if "it is the responsibility of government to reduce the differences in income between people with high income and low incomes," 51 per cent of Canadians agreed, but only 28 per cent of Americans.

Robert Frank of Cornell University spoke at an IRPP conference in January 2000:

> One of the things I admire most about Canada is its commitment to equality as a social value. You simply couldn't have a meeting like this one in the United States. Oh, perhaps you could assemble 30 people at a liberal think tank like the Brookings Institute for a discussion of inequality. But the idea that hundreds of high-level government officials might take time out to listen to professors talk about this subject – that would be unthinkable in the current climate.
>
> Nor does that climate promise to change soon. Concern about income and wealth inequity in the U.S., never high to begin with, has diminished sharply in recent months. A *New Yorker* cartoon sums up the prevailing mood.
>
> "I know we live in troubled times . . ." a husband remarks to his wife as the two lie comfortably sunning themselves on a lushly landscaped terrace next to their Olympic swimming pool, ". . . but I don't feel troubled." Like that couple many who came to Washington in the wake of

---

[*] *The Economist*, May 5, 2001, and Standard & Poors.

the 2000 presidential election don't seem to regard inequality as a serious social problem. And many influential members of the American economics profession share this view.[*]

Since those words we have had President George W. Bush's plans for a $1.6 trillion tax cut. The top 1 per cent of U.S. families will receive 40 per cent of the tax benefits, the bottom 20 per cent will get .8 per cent.

In terms of state taxes, Paul Krugman has pointed out that a family earning $30,000 per year now pays considerably more tax than they did in 1990, while a family earning $600,000 per year pays considerably less.[†]

Meanwhile, the *New York Times* reports:

> Even as Congress finances a crackdown on tax cheating by the working poor, it is appropriating little money to detect abuses by people usually among the wealthiest Americans, who do not rely entirely on wages for their income.[**]

And one more point about wages in the U.S. An Economics Policy Institute study showed that, by 2001,

> The median wage in the U.S. remains substantially below the level reached in 1973. There are a growing number of jobs paying poverty-level wages.[††]

As the distribution of income in the U.S. widened, a clear, continuing, accelerating process has been underway, a process that the former U.S. Labor Secretary Robert Reich called "the secession of the successful."

Canada's levels of income and wealth distribution are shameful. Most of those who want to turn us into Americans think that the even worse income and wealth distribution figures in the U.S. are not only to be admired, but to be emulated. They will never admit this, but the policies that they advocate are clear as clear can be: more for the rich and let the rest fend for themselves.

---

[*] IRPP, *Policy Options*, March 2001.
[†] *New York Times*, January 11, 2002.
[**] April 7, 2002.
[††] *Wage and Income Trends – Up the Down Escalator.*

Health Care in the United States:
"United in Fear and Loathing"

In 2002, preliminary estimates suggest that health care spending will be over 14 per cent of GDP in the U.S., while Canadian costs were expected to be 9.3 per cent of GDP.

If Canada had to spend as much of its GDP on health care as the U.S., the additional costs in 2002 would have been about $53 billion.

Moreover, while health care spending as a percentage of GDP is expected to rise to close to 16 per cent in the U.S. within the next few years, in Canada health care spending relative to GDP has been fairly stable for much of the last decade.

While there is little question that American doctors and hospitals, for the most part, have better average access to CAT scans, MRI units, lithotripters, and up-to-date radiation therapy, Canada is beginning to catch up. Meanwhile, the horrible built-in problems in U.S. health care each year could fill volumes. Yes, there are serious problems in Canada that need to be solved, but they are nowhere near the severity of the problems that exist in the U.S., especially for the lowest 40 per cent of earners, the poor and unemployed. And these problems are getting worse, not better.

The 2001 edition of the U.N.'s *Human Development Report* says that in a list of 102 countries, only Thailand and the United Arab Emirates had a higher percentage of GDP devoted to private health care costs than the U.S. In terms of per capita total health expenditures, the United States led all other countries.

In a U.N. list of thirty-three "high human development" countries, when the percentage of low-birth-weight babies is measured, ten countries have a better record than Canada. Only three countries have a worse record than the United States. Even a number of "medium development" countries have a better record than the U.S.

In terms of the infant mortality rate (per 1,000 live births), Canada has one of the best records, while the U.S. is tied for twenty-ninth place. A similar comparison can be found in under-five mortality rates.

In 2000, the United Nations reported that in terms of life expectancy at birth (1999) Canadians would average 79.1 years, Americans 76.8 years. Among developed countries, the U.S. was down in twenty-fifth place in life expectancy in a list of thirty-eight countries.[*] Canada and Iceland were tied for second, just behind Japan. The average Canadian will likely live 2.3 years longer than the average American.

In 1999, the number of poor children in the U.S. without health insurance increased by more than 350,000 to over 12 million, while some 50,000 Americans lost their life savings because of medical bills. Approximately half of all the hundreds of thousands of bankruptcies in the U.S. are caused by medical bills that can't be paid.

All told, there are 44 million Americans with no health insurance, and another 39 million with poor quality or inadequate insurance. At the same time, health care premiums in the U.S. continue to climb and corporations have begun to cut benefits. Many middle-class families saw their annual premium increase to over $ $6,000. In California, full coverage for two parents and two children costs almost $7,400 a year.

In the U.S., well-to-do Americans by and large receive good-to-excellent-quality medical care. There is an abundance of superb medical research and there are many top-quality hospitals across the country.

But in Canada we don't bankrupt the sick or kick them out of hospital if they can't pay their bills. In an average year, tens of thousands of American families lose their homes because they can't pay their medical bills.

It's true, waiting times tend to be longer in Canada, but in the U.S., millions of Americans never even get to be on a waiting list because they have no medical insurance.

Some 37 per cent of unemployed Americans are uninsured, and 14 per cent of the general population.[†] Meanwhile, as premiums continue to rise, more and more Americans can no longer afford health insurance. When Americans lose their jobs, most of them lose their health insurance.

The number of Americans without insurance or with inadequate insurance is equivalent to twice the entire population of Canada and another 21 million additional men, women, and children as well.

According to the Economic Policy Institute,

> Multiple studies show that the most efficient way to provide health insurance to everyone is through a national health insurance program

---

[*] United Nations *Human Development Report*, 2000.

[†] *New York Times*, November 18, 2001.

which would provide health insurance to every American. This plan would save at least $150 billion annually, which would fully offset the costs of expanded and improved coverage for the uninsured and under-insured.

One burgeoning cost in the U.S. system is administrative charges. Allan Rock pointed out that,

If you look at a Toronto hospital and a hospital of equal size in Boston, the one in Boston has 317 people in the Billing and Collections Department while the Toronto hospital has 17. We don't have to worry about assessing personal risks, because everybody's in.[*]

In any comparisons of standard of living between Canada and the U.S., there's a lot more than taxes to consider. For example, Lars Osberg and Andrew Sharpe have calculated that in 1999, medical expenses as a proportion of disposable income amounted to a high of almost 9 per cent in the U.S., compared to 1.3 per cent in the United Kingdom, 3.3 per cent in Australia, 1.7 per cent in Sweden, 1.6 per cent in Norway, 3.2 per cent in Germany. In Canada, in 2001, they were 3.1 per cent.

While private medical care expenses in Canada over the past forty years have ranged from a low of 2 per cent of disposable income to a high of 4.7 per cent, in the U.S. they have steadily escalated from 3.7 per cent in 1960 to 4.6 per cent in 1970 to 5.6 per cent in 1980 to 8.3 per cent in 1990 and are likely to reach well over 10 per cent in the very near future.[†]

In January 2002, *The Economist* reported:

In America, paying for health care is like having a nasty recurring fever. Just when it seems that harsh medicine has brought costs under control, the temperature rises and spending shoots up once again. Among those hardest hit are employers, who have long offered health insurance as a way of attracting and retaining workers, and now pay the lion's share of $440 billion in private health insurance, covering 160m Americans aged under 65. This year American businesses can expect to

---

[*] CCPA *Monitor*, March 2002.
[†] OECD *Health Data* CD-ROM.

spend roughly 13% more on health benefits than in 2001, the largest annual increase for more than a decade.[*]

Is health care spending in Canada out of control, as so many right-wingers charge? According to an OECD study, in recent years, except for Finland, Canada outperformed every one of twenty-eight other OECD countries in keeping costs in line with GDP. And in terms of overall health attainment results, the World Health Organization Report 2000 ranked Canada number seven, the U.S. number fifteen.

McGill political scientist Ted Schrecker writes:

> By the mid-1990s, it was estimated that 10 million American families were spending at least 20% of their incomes on medical care. Sometimes, medical insurance payments per month rival mortgage payments per month. Indeed, Americans pay more than half again as much per person, per year, for health care than do Canadians.[†]

In the U.S., health care costs in 2001 were expected to rise by more than 10 per cent. The 44 million uninsured were expected to increase in numbers because of the 2001 downturn in the U.S. economy. Meanwhile, many more workers are being asked to pay much more for their health insurance, and prescription drug costs increased by some 18 per cent during the past year. U.S. Senator Byron L. Dorgan of North Dakota "plans a new push to allow imports of cheaper prescription drugs from Canada," but "The pharmaceutical industry, renowned for its ability to protect its interests on Capitol Hill, is preparing to ride out any political storm" with a vastly increased lobbying team.[**]

Now, almost 40 per cent of U.S. workers do not have health insurance through their employers. Only 30 per cent of low-wage workers are provided insurance, and even if they are, the employee share of premiums is often unaffordable and the coverage limited.

But what about U.S. government Medicaid coverage for the poor? In the typical U.S. state, a parent in a family of three earning over $7,992 a year (59 per cent of the poverty line) is not eligible for Medicaid coverage.

---

[*] January 19, 2002.

[†] CCPA *Monitor*, December 2001/January 2002.

[**] *New York Times*, April 1, 2002.

Even the elderly with U.S. Medicaid coverage are in big trouble. A recent report indicates that an increasing number of U.S. doctors are refusing to see Medicaid patients because the government pays them too little to cover their costs. In many U.S. communities, the poor and elderly have great difficulties finding a doctor who will see them.[*]

According to the U.S. Department of Health and Human Services, health costs will likely rise even faster this year than in the past, and consumers will be forced to spend even more of their own money on health care in the future, since employers are going to be less likely to offer coverage because of the rapidly growing expenses.

How would you like to be poor and sick and live in the U.S.? Poor American children are eight times less likely to visit a doctor than other American children. As for the 12 million American children under the age of eighteen who lack health coverage, The Children's Defense Fund minces no words:

> When children lack insurance coverage, they are more likely to suffer from preventable health problems and from delays in receiving appropriate health care. Studies show that low-income, uninsured children are more likely to have eye and ear infections, lead poisoning, serious dental problems and chronic conditions such as asthma and diabetes.

According to *The New York Times*, millions of Americans, "many chronically ill . . . buy stripped down [medical] coverage at exorbitant prices because they can't buy coverage through an employer."[†]

A writer in the *Toronto Star* relates an oft-repeated story:

> Even those who were lucky enough to have health insurance [in the U.S.] do not walk away without debt. The insurance policies usually required a co-payment of 20 per cent. This payment structure encouraged people from the working class (or lower) to delay seeking treatment in the hope that the symptoms would subside.
>
> This was a gamble that my father once played and lost. Instead of rushing me to a hospital when I became stricken with meningitis, my

---

[*] *New York Times*, March 17, 2002.
[†] June 24, 2001.

parents waited almost three days before we made the trip. I became deafened for life.

After living under the American system, accessing medical treatment here in Canada is liberating. When I feel ill, I call my doctor and get help.[*]

In George W. Bush's 2002 budget, plans were to reduce Medicaid payments by $9 billion. That's money that would have gone to public hospitals and the poor. In Missouri alone, the cuts will "jeopardize health care for more than 850,000 people who are poor or disabled," according to the state's Department of Social Services.[†]

In the U.S., for-profit hospitals "dump" patients who show up without insurance over to public institutions such as county hospitals. But this is becoming increasingly difficult, since about 10 per cent of community hospitals have closed over the past decade, and many of the rest are badly underfunded.

In another UN study, in terms of the percentage of people who were not expected to survive to age sixty, nine countries in a list of forty-four "high human development" countries had better longevity rates than Canada, while twenty-nine had better expectations than the U.S.

Canada has a consistently higher rate of immunized children than the U.S.

Dalton Camp wrote that

America is drifting inexorably toward a plutocracy, to a sadly diminished democracy. Consider, as evidence, the American people's dislike and fear of their private health-care system, managed by the HMOs. There is a patients rights bill coming before Congress. The agents of private self-interest are united against it: the Health Insurance Association of America, the American Association of Health Plans, the United States Chamber of Commerce, the Business Roundtable, the National Federation of Independent Business, the Centre for Responsive Politics, and Haley Barbour, former chair of the Republican National Committee, now a maximum lobbyist. And if all these means and methods fail, the president has promised he will

---

[*] Miguel Aguayo, February 13, 2001.
[†] *New York Times*, February 2, 2002.

veto the bill, a measure sponsored by Edward Kennedy, Democrat, and John McCain, Republican . . .[*]

Most Americans despise and mistrust their private health care plans. The outrage against the health insurance bureaucracy has grown each year [into] a universal cry for patients' rights – freedom from the oppression and bullying of their health insurance firms.

Canadians would have the same loathing of a system so fundamentally rigged for profit and against the provision of services.

In a national poll, only 18 per cent of [Americans] sampled believed they were properly served by their health-insurance provider.[†]

HMOs in the U.S. are increasingly despised. According to the *New York Times*:

Elderly and disabled members of Medicare HMOs used nearly 50 per cent more of their own money, on average, for medical care in 2001 than they did three years ago . . . The increase was even steeper for those in poor health.

Out-of-pocket costs rose 62 per cent to $3,578 for people in poor health.

The increases were "stunning" said Marilyn Moon, a Medicare policy expert at the Urban Institute in Washington.[**]

The Economist comments on the widespread hatred of HMOs in the U.S.:

In the early 1990s, only a handful of Americans were subjected to managed care. Now four out of every five workers have been herded into health plans, and managed care has taken over from communism as the bogeyman that unites the country in fear and loathing.

These are the organizations that torture thousands of Americans every day with incomprehensible forms, unanswered phones and unpaid claims.

---

[*] *Toronto Star*, June 24, 2001.
[†] June 27, 2001.
[**] February 14, 2002.

Only 15% of Americans say they have a great deal of confidence in HMOs.[*]

Is there some explanation for so many Canadian doctors returning from the U.S.? The *New York Times* quotes a Manhattan cardiologist:

> The inability to control the way we practice medicine and deliver care to patients is the reason physicians are leaving medicine in record numbers . . . I can tell you that on an ordinary working day, if I didn't have a single patient to see, I would still be busy for eight or nine hours doing nothing but paperwork and phone calls that are directly related to managed-care issues.[†]

The same *Times* story continues:

> Patients often had something quite different to say. "I doubt that a single doctor I have seen over the last 10 years would know me if he or she fell over me on the street, including my current 'primary care physician' whom I have probably seen six or seven times over the past two years," one reader said in an e-mail message to me. "The feeling I get is that I am just another widget coming down the medical care assembly line."
>
> She added: "I don't get the feeling the doctors care one whit about me as an individual. This particularly struck me when I recently was seeking a specialized type of medical care and I telephoned some providers trying to locate the right one for me. The first question with which one was invariably assaulted on the phone was not 'What could we do for you?' or 'What problem[s] are you having' but rather 'What insurance do you have?'"

David Burgess, an American living in France, became seriously ill. He was in and out of hospitals for operations but eventually returned to work full-time.

> Last summer, I asked a friend of mine, a dean at a medical school in New England, what the cost of my care would have been in the United States.

---

[*] June 23, 2001.
[†] December 15, 2001.

"About $700,000," she said.

I did get a bill for 43 francs (about $6.50). I'm not sure what it was for, but I paid it.[*]

In the U.S., "uncomplicated" open-heart surgery can cost $50,000 to $70,000. A more complicated case can run up costs of half a million dollars.

The father of a friend of mine was in hospital in Phoenix. When he was checking out his dad, the nurse asked "Aren't you going to take the box of Kleenex?" My friend said "No thanks, we have Kleenex at home." The nurse said, "You should take it. It cost you $9."

While it is true that some Canadians have been forced to seek health care in the U.S., in 1998/99 they amounted to less than 1 per cent of the Canadian population, and most were "snowbirds" vacationing in the U.S. who required emergency treatment. The vast majority of Canadians who become ill in the U.S. return to Canada for treatment because of the terrible health care costs they would incur in the U.S. Health insurance companies frequently hire private jets to fly Canadians patients back to Canada because they save a great deal of money doing so.

Is it any wonder that Canadians rush home from the U.S. as soon as they can if they become ill or are injured? Anyone who has had even a single experience with U.S. medical costs comes away in a state of shock. Even a minor procedure can cost thousands of dollars.[†] A few days in a U.S. hospital can mean costs in the four- and five-figure range.

According to a study by Dr. Murray Finkelstein of the Mount Sinai Hospital in Toronto,

There is no relation between consumption of services and income [in Canada] which is in great contrast with our neighbours to the south where, if you're poor and sick, you're likely to report that you couldn't see a doctor because you couldn't afford it.[**]

Paul Krugman writes in The *New York Times*:

---

[*] *The International Herald Tribune*, reported in the CCPA *Monitor*, June 2001.

[†] *The New York Times Magazine* (May 4, 2002) detailed a bunion operation costing the patient $8,439.24.

[**] *National Post*, September 1, 2001.

> A society, in which rich people get their medical problems solved, while ordinary people die from them, is too harsh even for us.

And what about poor mothers? In Alberta, the total costs of having a baby, including anaesthesia and prenatal sessions, runs to about $3,400, paid by medicare. In California, a normal vaginal birth runs about $9,500 plus anaesthesia costs, a Caesarean birth about $14,300, plus anaesthesia.

What would happen to you if you lived in the United States and got cancer, or any other serious illness, and didn't have health insurance? Or, if you did have insurance and were told which doctor you had to see? Or, if your doctor was told by the HMO that the X-rays you needed wouldn't be paid for? Or, if the doctor you were assigned to was indifferent or incompetent? Or, if you qualify for Medicaid but you can't find a doctor who will take you because Medicaid pays such low fees?

Or, supposing your insurance company will only pay for a limited stay in hospital? In 2002, despite the fact that she was clearly severely disturbed, Andrea Yates was released from hospital because her insurers had only approved a fourteen-day stay. Yates went home and drowned her five children, ages five years to six months.

Linda McQuaig writes:

> While those without insurance are theoretically entitled to treatment (for a fee) at public hospitals, gaining access to that treatment can be extremely difficult, and many simply go without. Or, as in the case of 57-year old Larry Causey, they find other innovative ways to be treated. As reported in the *Post* last month, Mr. Causey went to a Louisiana post office, slipped the teller a robbery note and then went outside and waited for police to arrive. He was taken to jail where he was able to get treatment, otherwise unavailable to him, for his colon cancer.[*]

There are many other points that need to be made about health care in the U.S. to counter the distorted nonsense of the Ralph Kleins, the Mike Harrises, the Fraser Institute, and some of our troglodyte newspaper columnists. Briefly:

---

[*] *National Post*, May 7, 2001.

- Numerous studies show that private hospitals are substantially more expensive than public hospitals, and that patients in for-profit hospitals have a significantly higher risk of dying than in not-for-profit hospitals.
- Projections suggest that health care costs for employers in the U.S. will double within the next five years and employees will see their costs go up by at least 50 per cent during the same period.
- While drug costs in Canada have been rising far too fast, they are well below costs in the U.S. Many American prescription drugs cost twice as much as they do in Canada. Thousands of Americans are buying drugs illegally from Canadian sources to save money.
- Every country that has a national health insurance plan spends *far* less per capita and as a percentage of its GDP on health care than the U.S. The U.S. is not an example to be copied, but an aberration to be shunned.

By any chance, is the U.S. health care system related to distribution of income? Here's the *British Medical Journal*:

> What matters in determining morality and health in society is less the overall wealth of that society but more how evenly wealth is distributed. The more equally wealth is distributed the better the health of that society.*

Tom Koch, adjunct professor of gerontology at Simon Fraser University, puts it this way:

> This isn't simply only about health care . . . In countries like the U.S., where the general range between rich and poor is vast, people at the low end of the scale don't really participate in the general public life. They don't have the energy, education or money. They're *too* poor and *too* sick.†

In 2000, Ekos Research Associates asked people in eight countries about their satisfaction with their health care system. The highest level of

---

* See Dennis Raphael in *Policy Options*, October 2000, IRPP.
† The CCPA *Monitor*, March 2001.

satisfaction was in Canada, at 58 per cent, followed by the Netherlands, Germany, France, Austria, Sweden, and Britain. The lowest level of satisfaction was in the U.S., at 10 per cent.

Let's turn some of the U.S. numbers into equivalent Canadian numbers. Do we really want 4.5 million Canadians left with no health insurance, including 1.2 million children? Do we really want to spend an extra $53 billion a year on health care? If so, where will the money come from? And do we really want a system where before you are admitted to a hospital your credit has to be checked, and if you don't have proper insurance you are shunted off to a poorer-quality hospital? And do we really want scores of Canadian families to lose their homes every week because of their medical bills?

In any event, whatever you do, when you're sick in the U.S., don't forget to take the Kleenex.

Education and Social Consciousness

In 1983, a report commissioned by the Reagan administration warned of "a rising tide of mediocrity" in U.S. schools.

Almost ten years later, even the normally conservative *Economist* was referring to "American's lousy public school system" while describing the university system as "the best in the world." Perhaps the worst in the world, among developed countries, are inner-city U.S. public schools.

> Overall, American schoolchildren do frighteningly badly in international tests. Teachers tend to blame the poor results on lack of money. This is rubbish. Countries who spend less on education achieve far more. America's problems are structural: too much money spent on bureaucracy, too few politicians directly accountable for schools, bad teachers hard to get rid of, good ones rewarded little.

And "too many poor children receive a wretched education."[*]

---

[*] February 23, 2002.

In contrast, Statistics Canada reports that international tests indicate that

> These results suggest that the Canadian education system has, by improving reading skills among the economically or socially disadvantaged, helped overcome the educational disadvantage associated with low socio-economic status.[*]

The Economist says that "American high school students are among the worst in the industrialized world . . . America tolerates educational inequalities that would make the Old World blush." Among developed countries, the U.S. is twenty-third in their rate of high school graduation, and about a third of college freshmen have to enroll in remedial reading, writing, and math classes before they can attend regular courses.

According to *Business Week* magazine, only a third of U.S. Grade 8 students were proficient in reading, and fewer still were proficient in writing and math. In 1998, the U.S. ranked nineteenth among developed countries in math results, sixteenth in science, and seventeenth in school graduation rates.[†]

Over the past decade, Canada has improved from the middle of the pack in international test results to become almost the very best. In reading, math, and science, Canadian fifteen-year-olds now do exceptionally well in comparison with thirty-one other countries, ranking second in reading, sixth in mathematics (the U.S. was nineteenth), and fifth in science, for second overall. Canada is one of the very few countries with high scores in all three areas. Even students from the "25% of families with the lowest socio-economic status scored above the average for all students in OECD member countries."[**]

Without question, some American universities are among the very best in the world, but some are "shocking in their mediocrity and poverty," in the words of Canadian historian Desmond Morton. Tuition fees at most private U.S. universities are multiples of average tuition fees in Canada. While it's true that the great American universities are superb, it's also true that most American students can't afford to go to them.

---

[*] Statistics Canada, *The Daily*, December 4, 2001.
[†] March 19, 2001.
[**] Statistics Canada, *The Daily*.

According to John F. Helliwell, in 1998, total public and private education spending in Canada (7.2 per cent of GDP) was behind only Sweden (9 per cent), Denmark (8.4 per cent), and Finland (8 per cent), but ahead of the United States (6.8 per cent) and the OECD average (6.3 per cent). Helliwell goes on to advise that the share in Canada of total costs paid privately is lower than in most countries (.5 per cent of GDP). For the average OECD country, private education expenditures were 1.1 per cent; for the U.S., they were almost four times higher.

The 2000 edition of the United Nations *Human Development Report* says that, in terms of public education expenditure as a percentage of GDP (1995–97), among a list of forty-three "high human development" countries, Canada ranked ninth and the U.S. fourteenth.

What does all of this mean? Certainly, when it comes to public policy in health and education, most Canadians are social democrats, with policies much closer to those of the West European countries than those in the U.S. In Canada, by and large, we've created a good, equal-access system in primary and secondary education. Unfortunately, as we shall see, this has been changing at the post-secondary level as we move closer to American policies in some universities and in some provinces.

Bob Gustafson, formerly a Director of Education in Manitoba and now an education professor in Florida, writes:

> As a Canadian now living in the United States, I often reflect on what exactly gives Canadians their unique identity. What is it that separates us from our American neighbours? In social services, including education, I believe it has been our desire to care for all students and to ensure that all benefit from the wealth of the community, the province and the nation. This social consciousness has been a foundational aspect of Canada.
>
> The United States, on the other hand, is characterized by an intense individualism, the sense that the individual's concerns outweigh those of the community and especially those of the marginalized, for in the meritocratic philosophy, they have chosen to be less deserving. There is an infatuation with the business model; social services are to be concerned primarily with the bottom line and their contribution to business growth. There is a growing view that all social services are ripe for privatization and that profits can be made by turning over public enterprises to private entrepreneurs.

Hopefully, the Canadian public school system will escape the political and economic clutches of those who see public systems and students as exploitable objects. Hopefully, Canadian public education will retain its own identity and not become a mirror image of its American neighbour.[*]

Hopefully. For the most part, the public education system in Canada is superior to that in the U.S. We don't have nearly as many run-down schools that are short of qualified teachers. We don't have the proliferating voucher system that sees 96 per cent of the recipients ending up in religious schools, where, like it or not, they are expected to take part in religious ceremonies. And, for the most part, we don't have the common problem described in the following letter from Dallas, Texas:

> You must either be very rich or very poor to raise a family in most large American cities. Middle-class parents such as my wife and I can send our children to a decent public school only by moving to a larger house in the distant suburbs ...[†]

"The Border Still Matters"

One of the most important differences between Canada and the United States lies in the area of social spending. While Canada's record in this respect is very poor compared to that of most Western developed countries, year after year the United States ends up at the bottom or near the bottom of any OECD comparisons when social spending is calculated as a percentage of GDP.

Social programs in the U.S. tend to reflect a general social antipathy towards the poor. Poverty is regarded as "moral failure" by many in the U.S., while most Canadians (but certainly not most of our corporate elite) regard poverty as largely a product of a malfunctioning economic and social system.

---

[*] Canadian Educational Association, *Education Canada*, vol. 42, no. 1.

[†] Letter from Mark Agee to *The Economist*, March 9, 2002.

Ekos spells it out succinctly:

> It is almost unarguable that a key distinguishing feature . . . is that social policy in Canada plays a more positive and constructive social role in terms of achieving higher equality . . . A series of social indicators confirms this interpretation.
>
> Beyond all, Canada differs in the role the state and social policy have served as one of the foundation stones of national identity.[*]

Michael Adams of market researcher Environics says:

> Canadians desire a sustained welfare state, perhaps not the socio-democratic paradise envisioned by the Canadian left, but certainly not the almost unfettered free market that exists to the south.[†]

And Richard Gwyn writes about an Environics poll:[**]

> A couple of years back, the polling company surveyed Canadians and Americans in comparable cities – Winnipeg and Kansas City – to measure national attitudes on major social questions.
>
> The differences were pretty stunning. Canadians came across quite clearly more liberal-minded and less violent . . . Two of three Canadians compared to fewer than half of Americans said those who couldn't get jobs should be entitled to welfare.

After major "reforms" in 1996, welfare benefits in the U.S. became more limited and parents were required to work for their benefits within two years or less. While the welfare "case load" has dropped, many of those who no longer qualify live in abject poverty.

In 1996, Bill Clinton clamped down on food stamps for poor children, a program that had been in effect for over half a century. The rules are now so strict that many of the poor don't even bother applying. Most Canadians have found the concept of food stamps offensive in the past, and still do today.

---

[*] Ekos Research Associates Inc., 2000.
[†] *Globe and Mail*, July 3, 2000.
[**] *Toronto Star*, July 1, 2000.

In February 2002, President Bush proudly proclaimed "the pathway to independence and self-respect" in announcing more "workfare" requirement for the poor and proposals to encourage marriage, but no meaningful programs to assist the poor. According to the Children's Defense Fund,

> The President says his welfare reform plan is all about getting more parents working but his plan doesn't invest in the supports low-income families need to get and keep a job, such as child care, education, training, and transportation. He says it is important for families to work yet his budget proposal and his welfare proposal would deny child care to tens of thousands of children over the next five years. He requires more hours of work but not one dime more for childcare. Right now only one in seven children eligible for federal child care assistance gets it. It has been proven that in order to keep a job, families coming off welfare need child care.
>
> We think the President's plan misses the opportunity to provide real help for families struggling to get off welfare and into the workforce.
>
> The President's plan does not take into account:
> - how many new workers are losing jobs because of the recession.
> - that half of the families who have left welfare for work earn below poverty wages.
> - that the lack of affordable child care and accessible transportation are still major stumbling blocks for millions of families trying to make the welfare-to-work transition.[*]

The American constitution calls for the separation of church and state. Despite this, George W. Bush wants "faith-based organizations" to use taxpayers' money to run much of the U.S. social welfare programs. According to Bush, religious charities will do a better job than state governments in helping the poor. Needless to say, despite the fact that many Americans are very religious, the idea has appalled and frightened many who work with the underprivileged in the U.S.

In Canada, even more would be frightened and appalled. Considerably more.

---

[*] Press release, February 26, 2002.

And, no matter who delivers social assistance, the *New York Times* says that many believe that

> Mr. Bush has squandered the surplus, endangered the pillars of the social welfare system, and blew an opportunity to address a host of pressing national problems – all in order to pay for a tax cut for the rich. [*]

Despite the erosion of Canada's social programs brought on by Brian Mulroney, Jean Chrétien, Mike Harris, and Ralph Klein, political scientist Keith Banting, at the School of Policy Studies, Queen's University, writes:

> As the century drew to a close, the Canadian and American welfare states were as different as they were in the mid-1970s . . . The two systems have changed, and they are different in different ways than they were in the 1970s. But convergence is not the big story. In social policy at least, the conclusion seems clear. The border still matters. Distinctive cultures and politics still matter. [†]

While Canada's social spending pales in comparison with most European countries, U.S. rates of social assistance are scandalously inadequate. Social expenditures in Canada through the 1990s ran at about 12.5 per cent of GDP, well above the American rate of 8 per cent.

For years Canadians have been told by our right-wingers that we spend far too much on social programs. The Fraser Institute, that beacon of darkness in the night, says that Canada's "social safety net is incredibly generous." A *Globe and Mail* editorial advises that "Canada spends generously on programs for the disadvantaged."

Nonsense and double nonsense.

A study of twenty-six OECD countries showed that nineteen spend more on social programs as a percentage of GDP than Canada. Only Mexico, Korea, Turkey, Japan, Australia, and the United States spend less. Overall, how does social spending in the U.S. compare with spending to GDP in other developed countries? A 2001 OECD study placed the U.S.

---

[*] August 12, 2001.
[†] Working paper, School of Policy Studies, Queen's University.

third-last in gross public social expenditure and second-last in the public share of gross social expenditure.[*]

In 2002, if Canada's social spending was only the average of the European Union countries, we'd be spending an additional $47 billion on health, post-secondary education, child care, job training, disability allowances, and other programs designed to assist poor families, children, and individuals. No one is suggesting that we increase social spending by such a large amount, but Canada could do much, much better than it has been doing since the Mulroney and Chrétien governments came to power.

A UNICEF document put it this way in the summer of 2000:

> Countries with good unemployment benefits, family allowances and services, disability and sickness benefits, and other forms of social assistance have low poverty rates.
>
> Clearly ... no country with a high rate of social expenditure has a high rate of child poverty.[†]

To underline a point I've made already in a slightly different way, many if not most of the countries that have poverty rates that are lower than the U.S. also have both higher tax rates and higher GDP growth rates than the U.S.

Canadians should be ashamed of our high poverty rates, but in comparison with the U.S. our social programs are infinitely superior.

While our own Americanizers aren't happy about this, a Pollara Omnibus survey showed that 88 per cent of Canadians said that they thought it was important for Canadians to retain our distinctiveness from the U.S. in health care and 77 per cent in other social programs.

What do you think the chances will be of our doing so if we become Americans?

---

[*] *Labour Market and Social Policy*, Willem Adema, OECD, 2001.
[†] *Innocenti*, vol. 1, Summer 2000.

"The Ultimate Imperative for Canadians"

Just before Christmas, a friend from Ottawa, his sister from Toronto, and their mother, who lives here in Edmonton, came for a visit. We sat in front of the fire with a glass of wine, talking politics, golf, the economy, books, and many other things.

The sister, a banker, had been living in New York for the past thirteen years, but had recently moved back to Canada. I asked her what it was like living in New York. Her response was exuberant: "It was fabulous, exciting, amazing, and enormous fun." After she provided some details, I asked her why she had decided to return to Canada. She answered in four words: "The quality of life."

The United States is the world's wealthiest nation, the world's economic superpower, the world's strongest military power, far ahead of all other countries.

Do Canadians aspire to be any of these? The answer is: We never have and we never will.

But we have something else that's very important, an excellent quality of life, although it has been eroded since the Mulroney and Chrétien governments began Americanizing our policies, programs, and values.

In a speech to the Canadian Club, Frank Graves put it this way:

> Quality of life is seen as the ultimate imperative for Canadians ... There is a desire to maintain a unique Canadian identity.
>
> Human capital is key: health and health care, education, kids and skills ... a path to quality of life.
>
> Auctioning tax rates is not a durable competitive strategy since the next country can always try and cut taxes further still.[*]

In 2000, Ekos Research Associates asked Canadians if they agreed that "The average Canadian has a higher quality of life than the average American." 63 per cent agreed, 33 per cent disagreed.

---

[*] January 2001.

When asked, "If you were Prime Minister for a day and had to pick an overall national goal for Canada to achieve by the year 2010, which of the following would you choose?" here are the results:

Best quality of life in the world	66%
Best health care system in the world	64%
Lowest incidence of child poverty in the world	62%
Lowest crime rates, safest communities in the world	61%
World's smartest developer/user of natural resources	54%

All the other choices relating to taxes, the debt, etc. were below 50 per cent. "Highest standard of living of industrialized nations" came in last at 30 per cent.

Ekos comments that

> Canadians don't want to define their society or themselves in narrow economic terms. [Rather] the emphasis is on issues surrounding human well-being and human outcomes.

Nevertheless, our radical-right CEOs, plus some of our editorialists and newspaper columnists, seize every opportunity to tell us how far and how fast Canadians are falling behind due to too-high taxes, too much government, too-high social spending, and so on. There's one major problem in what they all say: much of it is grossly distorted baloney.

Canadians are constantly bombarded with reports that our standard of living is far behind that of the U.S. and we're falling even further behind every year so that it's now 75 per cent or less than U.S. levels. In an editorial, the *National Post* puts us "as much as 40 per cent behind."[*] When I read this quote to an expert in comparative incomes at Statistics Canada, he described it as "utter nonsense." In another *National Post* headline, readers were informed that a study found "American standards of living 10% to 50% higher" than those in Canada.[†] And a Southam columnist told his readers that "The average American's income is now 40 per cent higher than the average Canadians."[**]

---

[*] December 29, 2001.

[†] August 2, 2000.

[**] *Edmonton Journal*, December 28, 2001.

Objective studies relating to income and disposable income present quite a different picture. And studies relating to quality of life are even more revealing.

Brian Murphy and Michael Wolfson of Statistics Canada produced an excellent, detailed paper in 2000, *Income Inequality in North America: Does the 49th Parallel Still Matter?*[*] They conclude that the forty-ninth parallel matters a great deal and that despite the more open border and the convergence of Canadian and American policies, socially distinct Canadian policies have resulted in "substantial differences in overall income distribution patterns."

Contrary to right-wing reports about how poorly Canadians do compared to Americans, the two authors present a different perspective. For example,

- At least one-quarter of all Canadian families are absolutely better off than their U.S. counterparts in terms of purchasing power.
- Family disposable incomes in the lower third of the distribution in Canada are actually the same or higher in terms of purchasing power than in the U.S.
- From 1985 to 1997 most of the increase in U.S. family incomes was concentrated at the top of the income distribution.
- In terms of overall comparative economic well-being, 40% of Canadian families were absolutely better off or not appreciably worse off than their U.S. counterparts.

While it was true that many Americans, particularly the wealthy, were financially better off than Canadians, the differences are much smaller than those claimed by Canada's plutocracy and by much of our media. The median in earnings distribution, measured in purchasing power, showed Canadians 13 per cent behind their American counterparts. Wolfson and Murphy point out that the frequently used currency exchange rate comparisons are very misleading when comparing the actual purchasing power of families in each country and as distribution of income in the U.S. becomes even more polarized, average figures become even more misleading. Moreover, even when figures show that disposable income is higher for some in the U.S., U.S. residents must

---

[*] Statistics Canada, *Canadian Economic Observer*, August 2000.

allocate almost three times as much of their personal spending to health care as Canadians.

In conclusion, "these data do not support any impressions of a dramatic widening of income gaps between the two countries." Moreover, in recent years, "transfer programs in Canada have generally been more redistributive than the U.S. and have responded more strongly to increasing market income inequality." All things considered, at the median point, U.S. families had about 7 per cent higher purchasing power than similar Canadian families, and in terms of market income residents of Ontario, Alberta, and B.C. were, on average, better off than residents of most American states.

As indicated earlier, income distribution inequality has been rising much faster in the U.S. than in Canada. In any measurement of comparative national living standards, that inequality becomes an important consideration. Worth noting is that the lowest 80 per cent of Canadian families received a higher per cent of total family income than do the lowest 80 per cent of U.S. families.

Wolfson and Murphy carefully studied incomes in Canada and the U.S. in 1997, and found that 7.3 per cent of U.S. families had incomes of less than $10,000, but only 1 per cent of Canadian families did. More Canadian families had incomes between $10,000 and $24,999 (24.8 per cent to 21.1 per cent) and more in the $25,000 to $49,999 range as well (29.9 per cent to 26.5 per cent). All measures are adjusted to Canadian dollars.

It's important to note that these three groups make up 62.5 per cent of all Canadian families and 60.3 per cent of all U.S. families.

So, it's safe to say that as many as three out of every five Canadian families had a higher income than three out of five American families.*

A far too common and highly misleading measurement is to equate standard of living with GDP per capita. This calculation is reasonable only if the distribution of income was equitable. But, for now, let's consider only how Canada stacks up compared to other countries when we calculate GDP per capita. For many years, after the Second World War, Canadians, based on the calculation of GDP per capita, prided themselves as having the second-highest "standard of living" in the world,

---

* Statistics Canada, *Perspectives*, Summer 2000.

just behind the United States. But, by 2000, Canada had fallen to seventh place.*

Despite the fact that experts commonly regard it as misleading, the media constantly employs GDP per capita as a supposedly reliable indicator of a county's comparative standard of living. A much more reliable measure of how the general population is faring is median income. But, to oversimplify in a nevertheless accurate way, suppose there are eleven people in a room and one earned a million dollars last year, and all the others earned only $10,000. The average income of the eleven would be $100,000. Sounds pretty good, but the reality would of course be that one person would be wealthy and the other ten would be living below the poverty line.

The second problem with simply measuring standard of living based on GDP per capita is that "it leaves out a host of considerations such as crime, pollution, transportation difficulties and a whole range of problems that detract from the quality of life."† For example, a serious car accident boosts the GDP. Ambulance, police, hospital, doctors and nurses, insurance, auto body, towing, and many other workers are involved and their activities add to the GDP.

U.S. Senator Robert F. Kennedy put it this way:

> The Gross National Product includes air pollution and advertising for cigarettes, and ambulances to clear our highways of carnage. It counts special locks for our doors, and jails for the people who break them. GNP includes the destruction of redwoods and the death of Lake Superior. It grows with the production of napalm and missiles and nuclear warheads. And if GNP includes all this, there is much that it does not comprehend. It does not allow for the health of our families, the quality of their education, or the joy of their play. It is indifferent to the decency of our factories and the safety of our streets alike. It does not include the beauty of our poetry or the strength of our marriages, or the intelligence of our public debate or the integrity of our public officials. GNP measures neither our wit nor our courage, neither our

---

* GDP per capita (PPPUS$). United Nations *Human Development Report*, 2002.
† See *Reality Check: The Canadian Review of Wellbeing* published by the Atkinson Foundation in Toronto.

wisdom nor our learning, neither our compassion nor our devotion to our country. It measures everything, in short, except that which makes life worthwhile.

In an earlier study, using the widely employed Penn World Table purchasing-power method of calculation, Wolfson and Murphy concluded that "about 60 per cent of Canadians (ranked in terms of their family disposable incomes, adjusted for family structure) have higher incomes than their similarly defined U.S. counterparts."[*]

Journalists and politicians who use average income and exchange-rate comparisons in any straight-out quality-of-life comparisons are either economically unfamiliar with statistical analysis techniques or they intentionally set out to deceive. Sometimes it's a combination of the two. The best comparisons are always those that employ median income and disposable income adjusted for actual purchasing power. By this method of calculation, the median Canadian in recent years has been close to or better off than the median American.

Then, when benefits received from government are considered, and health care, education, and other social costs in the U.S. are factored in, there's little doubt that most Canadians are better off than most Americans.

Looking only at average incomes and forgetting the rest, it is true that there has been a growing gap between Canadian and American incomes. But, almost all of this gap can be attributed to the extremely high incomes of men in the top 5 per cent of earners in the U.S.

Another factor to be considered relates to the cost of living, which is much higher in most American cities than it is in Canadian cities, and far lower in Canada than it is in a long list of cities such as Tokyo, Hong Kong, London, Zurich, Paris, Singapore, Copenhagen, Buenos Aires, Brussels, Milan, Sydney, Frankfurt, and Amsterdam.[†]

And as for all those panic-stricken Americanizers, such as Sherry Cooper, who want us to abandon the Canadian dollar, in January 2002, the TD Bank said:

---

[*] *New Views of Inequality Trends in Canada and the United States*, Monthly Labor Review, U.S. Department of Labor, April 1998.
[†] *The Economist*, July 22, 2000.

The falling loonie does not, in itself, drag down the purchasing power of Canadian households. . . . The purchasing power of the Canadian dollar does not depend directly on the exchange rate. It depends on domestic consumer prices . . .[*]

Since Canada's annual inflation rate has been at very low historical levels, and since imports have grown dramatically while the loonie's value has dropped, it's clear that the dollar's purchasing power is actually far higher compared to the significantly undervalued exchange rate. In May of this year, Statistics Canada, in a new study, reported that for most products measured in actual purchasing power, prices in the U.S. were only 1 per cent lower than prices in Canada, and prices for services in the U.S. were on average 4 per cent higher.[†]

Of great interest is the fact that the low loonie has been the key contributing factor in our increased exports, yet, while some imports have been more expensive, they have had a minuscule inflationary impact, since, as indicated earlier, many imports are priced to sell in the Canadian marketplace.

In any consideration of quality of life, the average number of hours worked is an important factor. By 1996, the average weekly hours of all Canadian workers had fallen to just under 38. But Sharpe and Osberg have shown that by 1997, per-adult working hours in the U.S. were 204 hours *above* their 1980 level. That would be the equivalent of working more than five extra 40-hour weeks in a year! During the same years, workers' leisure time *increased* by 234 hours in Finland, 187 hours in France, 182 hours in Spain, and by large amounts in many other countries as well. Average American workers now work 3½ more weeks in a year than Japanese workers, 6½ more weeks than British workers, and 12½ more weeks than German workers.

In Canada, on a comparative basis, while American workers were working the equivalent of five extra weeks, on average, Canadian workers were working only one more week.

Sharpe and Osberg say that the large changes in hours worked "represent substantial changes in well-being that should be reflected in a rea-

---

[*] Southam columnist Eric Beauchesne, January 31, 2002.
[†] Statistics Canada, *The Daily*, May 30, 2002.

sonable measure of economic progress. However, since leisure hours receive zero valuation in GDP accounting, neither the declines nor the increases are reflected in GDP per capita."[*]

The evidence is clear that Canadians have a quite different attitude towards long hours of work than Americans. But then, so do men and women who value their leisure hours in almost all developed countries.

Six Statistics Canada researchers studied the relation between income inequality and mortality in Canada and the United States:

> Another major difference between the two countries is the way in which resources such as health care and high quality education are distributed by the marketplace so their utilisation tends to be associated with ability to pay; in Canada they are publicly funded and universally available. As a consequence, in the United States an individual's income, in both a relative and absolute sense, is a much stronger determinant of life chances and in turn, "health chances" than in Canada.[†]

In plain English, this is one good explanation why Canadians live longer than Americans.

Of course, everything is relative. The average Canadian middle-class family is much better off than over 95 per cent of the world's population. Almost half the world's population live on $3 or less a day. And many, many more have incomes that are but a small fraction of those in Canada.

As we have seen, year after year, Canada places ahead of the United States in the UN's annual Human Development Index which measures life expectancy, adult literacy, combined education enrolment, and GDP per person.

The book *The Wellbeing of Nations*, published in 2001, is a detailed country-by-country analysis of quality of life.[**] Overall, in a list of thirty-seven countries, Canada is ranked seventh, the United States is ranked twenty-seventh. In terms of health, quality of community and equality, Canada also ranks well ahead of the U.S.

The Economist publishes the *Pocket World in Figures* every year. In its

---

[*] The Index of Economic Wellbeing Indicators: *The Journal of Social Health*, Spring 2002.

[†] Michael Wolfson et al., April 2000.

[**] By Robert Prescott-Allen, Island Press, Washington, 2001.

2001 edition, in a table titled "Highest quality-of-life index," Vancouver is rated the number-one city. There is no American city in the top fifteen.

In his book, *Most Favored Nation*, C. D. Howe president Jack Mintz, after again arguing for much lower taxes in Canada, asks, "Can governments sustain a high standard of living if they account for more than a third of the economy?"

> Social services, particularly labour market programs such as employment insurance and social welfare, have a limited, sometimes negative, impact on productivity in the economy. Community and environmental programs that include regional and industrial assistance have questionable impacts on productivity.

If there were ever succinct examples of how greedy and selfish Canada's radical-right corporate elite are, and how terribly out-of-touch they are with the goals of average Canadians, the above quotation and Mintz's quote on pages 161-62 would be very hard to beat.

According to Isiah Litvak,

> business lobby groups and many "think tank" supporters such as the Fraser and C. D. Howe Institutes have advised the government that matching the current U.S. [tax] benchmark is not good enough; Canada must do better.

And if we did do this, how exactly could we possibly pay for medicare and Canada's other social programs? Yet, incredibly, as indicated earlier, according to our business leaders,

> We tend to overrate Canada's better quality of life compared to the U.S. It has little effect to either attract firms or retain those who consider leaving . . . personal and corporate taxes should be harmonized with the U.S.[*]

So, by all means, let's not make the mistake of overrating the value of the quality of life!

---

[*] Public Policy Forum, *The Views of Canadian Industry and Business Associations on Canada–United States Economic Integration*, October 2000.

Sadly, the way we're going, quality of life will increasingly continue to take second place to corporate profits in our national priorities.

John McCallum put it this way:

> The risk is that we will wake up one morning to discover that, for all practical purposes, Canada and Canadian values have disappeared from the planet. Or, more likely, with the drift of Americanization so gradual, Canadians wouldn't even notice the effective disappearance of their country. In either case, wouldn't that be a pity?[*]

A pity indeed. The above words were written when McCallum was a Liberal backbencher. Now that he's in the cabinet, and a possible future finance minister, is he likely to speak out against the growing foreign ownership and foreign control of Canada and the Americanization of our country, or will he be like Herb Gray was, silent, lips sealed, somehow forgetting every word in the excellent Gray Report,[†] because he didn't dare to offend the boss and those who finance the Liberal Party?

The day that these words were being written, an Asper editorial from Winnipeg told readers across Canada that the Canadian standard of living had fallen to only 60 per cent of that in the U.S. The very same day, the authoritative and widely respected Luxembourg Income Study[**] reported that the average Canadian is about 89 per cent as well-off as the average American and the real incomes of poor families with children were 26 per cent higher in Canada.

Of course, had median income been measured instead of average income, the comparative results for Canada would have been even better.

---

[*] *Globe and Mail*, August 30, 2001.
[†] *Foreign Direct Investment in Canada*, Information Canada, 1972.
[**] Paper No. 266, *Comparing Living Standards Across Nations*, Timothy Smeeding and Lee Rainwater, 2002.

America as a Rogue State

As in other matters already described, the U.S. is a schizophrenic nation. It refused to join the League of Nations, established after the First World War to promote international peace and security. Current U.S. support for the United Nations varies all the way from moderate, to tepid, to an even hostile attitude of confrontation and the non-payment of hundreds of millions of dollars in arrears UN dues. Conversely, the U.S. leadership in the Marshall Plan's remarkable rehabilitation of war-torn Europe after the Second World War was exemplary, and it was Franklin Delano Roosevelt who was instrumental in setting up the plans for the UN.

From time to time, the U.S. goes through periods of introversion and isolationism. Since the election of George W. Bush, many commentators have suggested that the U.S. has entered a new period of isolationism, but they are wrong. Rather than isolationism, the U.S. is now vigorously practising almost unparalleled, arrogant, activist unilateralism.

In the words of Moises Naim, editor of the Washington, D.C., *Foreign Policy* magazine, no country "is doing more to undermine the multilateral approach to issues of global concern than the United States today."[*] In an editorial, the *Globe and Mail* said:

> The United States is pursing an aggressive strategy that can only erode international co-operation on future issues. International agreements have been the foundation of peace and prosperity for 50 years, and it is alarming to see them abandoned ...[†]

While 143 countries, including Canada, signed the 1966 International Covenant on Economic, Social and Cultural Rights, the United States did not.

While 167 countries, including Canada, signed the 1979 Convention on the Elimination of All Forms of Discrimination Against Women, the United States refused to do so.

---

[*] *Globe and Mail*, July 25, 2001.
[†] Ibid.

While 191 countries, including Canada, signed the 1989 Convention on the Rights of the Child, the United States once again declined.

While 178 countries have approved the first-ever rules aimed at reducing global warming – the Kyoto Protocol – the United States, the world's biggest polluter producing about a quarter of the world's greenhouse gas, wants no part of it. In the spring of 2001, George W. Bush confirmed that the U.S. was withdrawing support for the Kyoto agreement. Never mind that some fifteen hundred scientists had released a report that made it clear, beyond doubt, that horrendous problems relating to sea levels, flooding, crop production, fresh water supplies, violent storms, drought, and other ominous results were certain unless significant steps were taken to reduce global warming.

Canada strongly supports international agreements to limit world trade in small arms and the milestone Land Mines Treaty, and the new International Criminal Court for the prosecution of war criminals which has been signed by 139 countries and already ratified by close to 80.

The U.S. opposes all of these.

The U.S. has not ratified the 1996 Comprehensive Test-Ban Treaty. Canada and 160 other nations have signed the agreement. When a proposal to send the treaty for ratification came up, 140 countries voted in favour; only the U.S. voted against.

Currently, 143 nations support a new international protocol for a biological-weapons monitoring agreement, but as far as the U.S. is concerned, "It's dead."

In 2001, the U.S. Treasury Secretary announced that the U.S. was pulling out of an OECD agreement to take long-awaited action against international tax havens.

The United States wants to put nuclear and laser weapons into space. Most Canadians, and the Canadian government (at least for now), are strongly opposed.

Jeffrey Simpson of the *Globe* writes:

Canada has resolutely opposed the militarization of space, signing international treaties to that effect and speaking against militarization in multilateral forums.

If Canada were to become mixed up in antiballistic missile defense, it would most inevitably lead to being party to the long-term U.S.

ambition to militarize space. The move would, in turn, require Canada to change basic policy of many decades' standing.*

So, given all of this, given the terrible dangers of nuclear proliferation and weapons buildups, what is Canada likely to do? In December 2001, Richard Gwyn suggested:

> Our signing on to the controversial U.S. National Missile Defense plan is now a done deal but for the formality of Washington winging its request northward.†

Nevertheless, at least at this writing, Canada was working to support the multilateral Conference on Disarmament and negotiations for a Convention for Non-Weaponization of Outer Space.

Perhaps one of the greatest differences between Canada and the United States, between Canadians and Americans, is their attitude towards war. Most Canadians prefer our long-standing Canadian history in support of peacekeeping and agencies such as the United Nations and multilateral international agreements. On the other hand, the United States is becoming increasingly unilateralist, increasingly arrogant, with little regard for many international rules and regulations, especially those relating to foreign and defence policy. Recently, the U.S. backed away from a joint agreement with Russia to destroy significant parts of their stockpiles of nuclear weapons; instead, the weapons will be put in storage or in "operational reserve," and the U.S. plans to spend billions of dollars to develop new plutonium "pits" or nuclear bomb triggers.

The *Economist* summed up George W. Bush's nuclear missile plans well in a single sentence: "What folly for America to spend billions on missile defences, while unravelling the rules which limit the weapons that may some day get through or around them."** The important thing to remember is that in almost all of this, Canada stands together with almost all other Western democracies, while the U.S. stands almost alone. Historically, Canadian attitudes towards defence and foreign

---

* *Globe and Mail.*
† *Toronto Star*, December 9, 2001.
** September 8, 2001.

policy have differed profoundly from those in the U.S. and, at least for now, they do so today.

Whereas Canada rushed to Britain's assistance when the First World War began in 1914, it wasn't until 1917 that the U.S. finally became involved. And when Adolf Hitler was overrunning Western, Central, and Southern Europe and slaughtering millions of Jews, and others; while London was being bombed every night, killing many thousands; in an egregious display of indifferent isolationism, the U.S. waited over two years to declare war, and did so only after being attacked by Japan at Pearl Harbor in 1941. As Peter C. Newman wrote about both world wars, "Canadians wanted to step up to be counted. Canada went to war because the politicians followed the will of the people, not the other way around."*

Nevertheless, more recently Canadians have displayed ambivalence towards war. Few Canadians, very few, supported the Vietnam War. The vast majority were strongly opposed. With respect to Afghanistan, in the words of Richard Gwyn, the message to pollsters is of our "underlying unease that this war's effect upon us has been almost entirely negative."

What Canadians prefer is "The 'soft' power of humanitarian aid, rather than the hard power of guns and bombs . . . Humanitarianism *is* our thing."

In contrast, Gwyn writes, "Today's America is Rome, pure and undiluted."

> But being Rome is more than just having power and cruise missiles . . . It's a matter of attitude, or psychology, of self-perception.
>
> It's knowing that you are Rome and not caring what anyone else thinks or really caring about anyone else at all. It's also about being prepared to kick ass, any ass, anywhere – without apology or self-doubt and, if need be, without explanation.[†]

Americans keep telling us that we don't spend enough on the military, and every time they do, the *National Post* and their Alliance comrades repeat the accusation like puppets with megaphones. Every American ambassador to Canada calls for Ottawa to spend much more on the mil-

---

* *Maclean's*, October 22, 2001.
† *Toronto Star*, November 18, 2001.

itary. And so do some Canadian senators, with a close eye on our defence contractors, who export millions of dollars in arms every year, and who would be dismayed if we failed to back Bush's Star Wars plan.

And, why not spend more? Forget child poverty. Forget buying more MRIs. Forget more R&D. Forget lower university tuition and smaller classroom sizes. Why not spend at least $4 billion to $6 billion more on the military every year on top of our current $12.3 billion? Historian Jack Granatstein wants us to spend $8 billion more by 2008 to "keep the elephant fed and happy." In a paper for the C. D. Howe Institute, Granatstein says that Canada has no choice but to support American military and foreign policy.[*]

There is, of course, the small question of money. How remarkable it is that the very same voices in Canada who are constantly demanding even more big tax cuts are the exact same people who want to spend billions more for defence. And shouldn't our priority be to feed our own poor kids before we worry about the poor elephant?

In total funding, Canada has the seventh-largest NATO military budget. But we're constantly being urged to be more like the United States in defence spending and policy. Yet, when asked, 60 per cent of Canadians oppose such a suggestion, while only 38 per cent support it.

Far more Canadians are worried about American foreign and defence policies than are Americans. In particular, George W. Bush's illogical, potentially disastrous, not to mention hopelessly expensive National Missile Defense Plan is widely regarded with great apprehension in Canada, and pretty well everywhere else.

To proceed, Bush has withdrawn from the 1972 Anti-Ballistic Missile Treaty, the successful cornerstone of international arms control and strategic stability. What will the result be? China, Russia, and Europe have all forcefully warned about the consequences. Without question, China will add to its nuclear arsenal and further develop its delivery capability. Other countries will have few if any reservations about returning to or commencing nuclear testing. Weapons of mass destruction will proliferate around the world. The Nuclear Non-Proliferation Treaty will become meaningless.

As David Crane put it so aptly,

---

[*] *A Friendly Agreement in Advance*, June 2002.

The proposed National Missile Defence, a $500 billion (U.S.) high-tech system to shoot down foreign missiles and a centre-piece of the Bush administration's military strategy, now appears to be nothing more than a costly, high-tech Maginot line.[*]

And how do Canadians feel about the proposed Bush defence shield? By almost a two to one margin, they oppose it.

As John Turner once pointed out, and as George W. Bush has affirmed, in America it's "my country right or wrong," and "you're either with us or you're against us." Consistently, and virtually without reservation, the U.S. believes that its political and international views are superior to all others, and that it has the right to act accordingly. In the words of Lewis H. Lapham, within the hierarchies of American business and government are people "incapable of imagining, or unwilling to acknowledge a world other than the one they had inherited from John Wayne and Ronald Reagan."[†] Few would deny that the United States is a highly militaristic superpower that from time to time has exhibited aggressive, imperialistic behaviour in their own self-interest or in support of their version of defending democracy. While Canada has many faults, to suggest that Canada is militaristic, imperialistic, or aggressive would surely provoke derision.

Perhaps one of the greatest of all differences between Canada and the U.S. has been the long-term aggressive American direct intervention into the affairs of other countries.

In the last half of the twentieth century, the U.S. supported murderous dictators, funded death squads in several countries, planted "misinformation" to thwart elections that might not go the American way, funded and trained terrorists, and supplied weapons to help overthrow elected governments. The United States helped arrange the overthrow of democratically elected governments in Brazil, Guatemala, Dominican Republic, and Chile, and supported brutal dictatorships in many countries in Central and South America, including El Salvador, Panama, Ecuador, and Colombia, as well as in Iran, Indonesia, and the Philippines. During the 1960s, the CIA plotted the assassination of Patrice Lumumba, the head of the Belgian Congo, and the Dominican Republic's leader,

---

[*] *Toronto Star*, September 13, 2001.
[†] *Harper's Magazine*, November 2001.

Raphael Trujillo. At about the same time, the agency attempted to do away with Fidel Castro, with, among other things, an exploding cigar.

These actions followed the 1953 coup in Iran, which overthrew what was then one of the region's rare democracies, ousting a populist, elected prime minister. It was the CIA's intervention in the political life of Iran that earned the U.S. the title of the "Great Satan" in the growing world of Islamic activism.

In the 1970s, the CIA successfully engineered the overthrow of the democratically elected governments of Guatemala and Chile. Over the years,

> The agency quietly evolved into what some said was an "invisible government" a kind of amalgam of the State Department and the Pentagon. In many foreign lands, the CIA station chief had more clout than the U.S. ambassador, plus more money, a bigger and brighter staff, and far fewer restrictions.
>
> "The CIA had its own political desks and military staffs," noted Arthur Schlesinger Jr., a close advisor to J.F.K. "It had in effect its own foreign service, its own air force, even, on occasion, its own combat troops." Overseas, "case-officers" – spies – lived like well-heeled expatriates, operating under "cover for status," that is posing as diplomats or economic advisors.[*]

In *The Trial of Henry Kissinger*, by Christopher Hitchens, the American author paints a detailed portrait of U.S.-planned murder and torture in Chile, East Timor, and Bangladesh. According to Hitchens, Henry Kissinger, national security advisor and secretary of state in the Nixon and Ford administrations, personally took charge of the massive bombing campaigns in Cambodia and Laos that took the lives of 1,350,000 men, women, and children, almost all of them civilians.

As for Chile, Kissinger was directly involved in the murder of General René Schneider in 1970, the year that Salvador Allende was elected president. After American mining companies complained to Richard Nixon about Allende, Kissinger helped organize plans to destabilize the government and helped fund a military coup, providing money, machine guns, and grenades. On September 11, 1973, General Augusto Pinochet

---

[*] Sam Tanenhaus, *Vanity Fair*, January 2002.

overthrew the Allende government. Allende died in the final battle, and subsequently Pinochet and his generals murdered thousands of Chileans who had supported the democratically elected Allende government.

In December 1975, Henry Kissinger personally approved the Indonesian army's invasion of East Timor, which cost the lives of almost a quarter of a million people.

According to Lewis Lapham,

> Robert McNamara, the American secretary of defense in the summer of 1965, explicitly defined the bombing raids that eventually murdered upwards of two million civilians north of Saigon.
>
> In 1991, Madeleine Albright, then the American secretary of state, was asked in an interview on *60 Minutes* whether she had considered the death of 500,000 Iraqi children (of malnutrition and disease). She said, "We think the price is worth it."[*]

During the Iran–Iraq war in the 1980s, the U.S. supplied Saddam Hussein with large quantities of weapons and encouraged Pakistan and Saudi Arabia to support the Taliban. John Pilger writes in *The Mirror*:

> Zbigniew Brezinski, who was President Carter's National Security Advisor, revealed that on July 3, 1979, unknown to the American public and Congress, president Carter authorized $500 million to create an international terrorist movement that would spread Islamic fundamentalism in central Asia and "destabilise" the Soviet Union.
>
> The CIA called this Operation Cyclone and in the following years poured $4 billion into setting up Islamic training schools in Pakistan. (Taliban means "Student".)
>
> Young zealots were sent to the CIA's spy training camp in Virginia, where future members of al-Qaeda were taught "sabotage skills" – terrorism.
>
> Others were recruited at an Islamic school in Brooklyn, New York, within sight of the fated Twin Towers.
>
> At the time, the late 1970s, the American goal was to overthrow Afghanistan's first progressive secular government, which had granted

---

[*] *Harper's Magazine*, November 2001.

equal rights to women, established health care and literacy programmes, and set out to break feudalism.

When the Taliban seized power in 1996, they hanged the former president from a lamp-post in Kabul.

His body was still a spectacle when Clinton administration officials and oil company executives were entertaining Taliban leaders in Washington and Houston, Texas.[*]

Even today, most Americans have no idea that Bin Laden and his muja-hedeen were trained and armed by the CIA in the 1980s. Many of the future terrorists were trained in Virginia.

Canadians are very different from Americans in foreign and defence polices, in our support for international agreements and organizations, and in the fact that we rarely believe that we have the right to intervene in the affairs of other democratic countries. Let's hope that our weak-kneed federal government doesn't change all of this in a cowardly reaction to U.S. pressure following the events of September 11, 2001.

Canada should take steps to improve security, do a better job screening and tracing those who enter the country on visas, and work with Americans on intelligence matters. And we should beef up our military presence in the Arctic. But we should do so in accordance with our own national priorities, our traditions as an independent country, while working with other countries around the world to promote peace and disarmament and effective international agreements that do so.

One last point about defence and foreign policy. Do our radical right Americanizers not have children or grandchildren? Have they not ever stopped to think that after we formally become an American colony or American states, our boys and girls will be drafted to fight in new American wars, new Vietnams, new Gulf Wars? Most Canadians abhor the idea. A great many American political leaders appear to be ardent supporters of military conflict, despite all their rhetoric to the contrary.

---

[*] *The Mirror*, January 29, 2002.

Beer and Other Weighty Matters

M any huge books have been written about the differences between Canada and the United States. In the past nine chapters I've mentioned some of the most important. Let me briefly touch on a few others.

Our countries started out very differently. In the West, Canada was opened up by the Hudson's Bay Company, the North West Company, the Canadian Pacific Railway, the North West Mounted Police, and waves of immigrants who, for the most part, came to a place of relatively well-established order and institutions.

In the United States, the American Revolution was followed by a terrible Civil War between the Union and Confederate states that tore the country apart and resulted in the death of over 617,000 Americans.

The opening of the American West was violent and was characterized by a gunslinger mentality. The opening of Western Canada was comparatively peaceful and orderly.

About 40,000 Loyalists left the U.S. for Canada and they played an important role in the development of Nova Scotia, New Brunswick, Ontario, and parts of Quebec.

In short, Canada's history has been far less violent than the history of the United States. We've already seen how that difference persists today.

Of course it's wrong to generalize on all of our differences. Parts of the U.S., notably Massachusetts, Oregon, Wisconsin, and parts of California, are very much more liberal than, as one example, southern and south-central Alberta.

While it's certainly true Canadians have had our share of bigoted rednecks, we've never had anything like the extent of the prolonged murderous racial violence of the Ku Klux Klan that has existed in the U.S.

Before we turn to some other important differences between the two countries, let's return to the words of polling expert Frank Graves:

> Canadians remain truly different from Americans. Canadians are considered more liberal in their social and political values . . . more consensual, secular and pluralistic.

And most Canadians would be proud of these characteristics and values.

(Too bad that they are quite opposite to the values of the corporate elite who are running and selling our country.)

Another major difference between the two countries can be found in attitudes towards immigrants. Only about 30 per cent of Canadians believe we have too many immigrants; in the U.S. well over half think there are too many. In another poll, 45 per cent of Canadians said that they would not be unhappy if a family member married someone of a different race. In a startling comparison, only 4 per cent of Americans said they would not object. Most Canadians believe that Canada is a better country because of multiculturalism; fewer than half of Americans hold the same view about the U.S. More than twice as many Americans as Canadians would restrict immigration to whites.

Of OECD member countries, in recent years Canada has had the fourth-highest immigrant inflow as a percentage of population. Canada needs immigrants; they already make up more than 70 per cent of our net workforce increases and informed projections show that within one generation our natural population increase will be down to zero and net immigration growth will have to make up 100 per cent of our national population growth.

Meanwhile, in the U.S., immigration statistics show the level of immigration in 1999, per 1,000 inhabitants, was only one-third the Canadian level.

Edward Greenspon of the *Globe and Mail* comments about multiculturalism:

> Let's start with our splendid diversity. Isolated pockets of resistance should not obscure the fact that Canadians have nurtured within our geographic space a truly global community, a role model for the 21st century. Remarkably, our increased diversity has been accompanied by growing tolerance.
>
> Canadians repeatedly cite diversity as one of the greatest aspects of their national identity. It is more important to them than the French-English fact. In the 30 years since the passage of the first Multiculturalism Act, we've overcome our parochial past and gone from official multiculturalism to genuine multiculturalism. It's not just a policy any more, but a way of life.

The United States is a much more patriotic, nationalistic, chauvinistic, and aggressive country than Canada. Visit the U.S. and you will find American flags everywhere, on cars and trucks, on buildings and billboards, and red, white, and blue decals proclaiming God Bless America, United We Stand, In God We Trust, Pride and Power, and similar slogans overprinted on the stars and stripes.

How absurd it is for some Americans to accuse Canadians of being too nationalistic. Canadians are proud of our flag and it was wonderful to see the outpouring of emotion during and after the Salt Lake City Olympic games. I suspect most Canadians would like to see more of the same. I also suspect most Canadians cannot understand why so many American flags fly across our country.

There are so many differences between the Canadian and American political systems that entire books have been devoted to the subject.[*] Both systems have their advantages and their serious defects. The U.S. system of checks and balances between the power of the president and Congress is appealing, but it also can result in prolonged legislative gridlock. The Canadian system has more democratic features, but the dominant power of the prime minister in a majority government is a serious defect.

Allan Fotheringham has put it well:

In our benighted system, one man alone sitting at 24 Sussex Drive appoints, with no one knowing or questioning, nor only our Chief Justice of the Supreme Court but all the justices, the Governor General, 10 Lieutenant Governors, the Chief of Staff of the Armed Forces, the head of the CBC, the head of CRTC and everybody including Bob's Your Uncle.[†]

Few Canadians would agree that the excessive concentration of power in the Prime Minister's Office is desirable. In the U.S. House of Representatives and in the Senate, U.S. legislators frequently speak out against their own party's policies and their own President. In Canada, the government MPs are, for the most part, puppets terrified of the conse-

---

[*] See *Canada and the United States: Differences That Count*, edited by David M. Thomas, Broadview Press, 2000.

[†] *Globe and Mail*, August 14, 2001.

quences of offending the prime minister. In the U.S., good congressmen and senators can develop national reputations and followings through their committee system. In Canada, the House of Commons committees are almost always dominated by acquiescent government members.

Gordon Laxer, the University of Alberta's political economist and Director of the Parkland Institute, writes about another important political and economic difference, and quotes George Grant:

> Until recently Canadians have been much more willing than Americans to use governmental control over economic life to protect the public good . . . Ontario Hydro, the CNR, and the CBC were all established by Conservative Governments.

This Conservative state-nationalism left important legacies and helped "spawn a political culture that was very distinct from the American." Moreover,

> Canadians were eager to find positive features to distinguish themselves from the United States. This was not hard in the 1960s and 1970s when the U.S. was torn apart by racism, ghetto riots, violent crime, aggression in Vietnam, political assassination and a president caught lying. Canadians became proud of Canada's public services that evoked a more "caring, sharing" philosophy.

In short,

> Canada's distinctiveness has been built around a broader public life and a more activist state than its powerful neighbour.[*]

There is little question that one of the main differences between Canadians and Americans lies in their attitude towards government and the role of the state. According to Ekos, commenting on the work of Seymour Lipset,

> Americans are supposedly more wary of government, more individualistic and less supportive of strong government intervention in their lives.

---

[*] *Canadian Review of Sociology and Anthropology* vol. 37, no. 1, 2000.

But they don't mind strong intervention in the lives of other people in other countries.

Are there other fundamental philosophic political differences between Canadian and Americans? When asked by Ekos if their political persuasion was more small-*l* liberal or small-*c* conservative, many more Canadians described themselves as liberal, while more than twice as many Americans said they were more conservative. Moreover, "As Canadians get older they become more and more liberal. For Americans, the support of liberal values declines with age."*

With the exception of a rare appointment from the Senate, all Canadian federal cabinet ministers are elected members of parliament. In Washington, cabinet members are selected by the President and often come to office with little or no political experience. For the most part, Canadian cabinets have much better regional representation and are less likely to be dominated by white, male millionaires.

Another major political difference is that effectively the U.S. has only two political parties, whereas in Canada, at this writing, we have six parties represented in the House of Commons, and for decades at least three or four parties have had seats in the House. The United States is one of the few democratic countries with only two major parties, and many people claim that they are remarkably similar once in power. Of course the same may be said for the Liberals and Conservatives in Ottawa: witness the Chrétien government's continuation and extension of Brian Mulroney's policies. But at least in Canada voters have the choice of other parties and elect MPs from the left and the far right as well as from the two parties that have always governed the country.

Some political commentators believe that the traditionally low voter turnout in U.S. elections is caused, at least in part, by the limited choices.

An important difference between Canada and the United States, and one that is quite contrary to the image presented by our radical right, is that Washington controls a much greater percentage of all government policies and spending in the U.S. than Ottawa does in Canada. The constant attacks on the supposed over-centralization of government in Canada frequently come from exactly the same people who want us to become Americans. How Bizarre. Washington has far greater control of health, education, social policy, and resources in the U.S. than Ottawa has

---

* Ekos Research Associates, 2000.

in the same areas in Canada. What a shock it would be for Quebec separatists or the few Western separatists if Canada became part of the United States. Almost all the powers that the provinces now have would be eroded. Any American governor who visits Canada for the first time is invariably astounded by how much more power a provincial premier has.

One has to be careful about how voter turnout is measured as a percentage of eligible votes. But it is safe to say that in modern times the national voter turnout in Canada has been significantly higher than it is in the U.S. While it is true the voter turnout in Canada has been declining, in every recent election the Canadian turnout is better than the U.S. In one international comparison, the U.S. placed 139th in a list of 167 democracies when the percentage of eligible voters who actually voted was measured. Another difference is that, for the most part, there are more elected women in Canadian governments than in the U.S. Canada has had a woman prime minister, while countries such as India, Pakistan, New Zealand, Norway, the Philippines, Israel, Indonesia, Finland, Latvia, Lithuania, and Sri Lanka have had women presidents or prime ministers. The United States has never had a female president or vice-president. Measuring the overall percentages of elected women in government in advanced nations, Canada is in 13th place, while the U.S. is way down the list in 26th place.[*]

Writing about his most recent book, *Better Happy Than Rich? Canadians, Money and the Meaning of Life*, Michael Adams notes that:

> There are still many differences between the social values of Americans and Canadians.

And, contrary to conventional wisdom on the subject,

> Today, there is evidence that Canadians, in fact, place greater emphasis on personal freedom and harbour less deference to traditional institutions such as the state, the family, and religious organizations than do their American neighbours.
>
> For example, Canadians have greatly reduced their commitment to traditional religious institutions. When surveyed, almost half of all Americans say they strongly believe their children should receive a

---

[*] United Nations *Human Development Report*, 2001.

religious education. By contrast, less than a third of Canadians feel the same. These Canadian proportions are in sharp decline from earlier in the century; as are the Canadian numbers for church attendance and for identifying with a particular faith. American commitment to religious belief and practices has remained much more constant.

Without question, one of the biggest differences between Canadians and Americans can be found in their attitude towards religion. When asked by Ekos if religious values and beliefs should be kept out of politics and government, 70 per cent of Canadians, but only 50 per cent of Americans, agreed. When asked if political leaders should reflect stronger religious beliefs and values, almost twice as many Americans agreed compared to Canadians.

Ekos tells us that Americans are almost twice as likely (42 per cent) as Canadians (22 per cent) to attend religious services at least once a week. Today, only about one-third of Canadians over the age of fifteen attend a religious service at least once a month. In the U.S., the rate is about 60 per cent. While 73 per cent of Americans say that they believe in hell, only 43 per cent of Canadians claim to. More Americans believe in extrasensory perception (60 per cent) than in evolution (53 per cent)!

Globe and Mail columnist Jeffrey Simpson writes:

> *God Bless America* is a national hymn; that God has blessed America is an article of faith among Americans. Republican presidential candidate George W. Bush, asked which world figure had influenced him the most, said Jesus Christ. No disrespect to Christ or his teachings, but if a Canadian politician gave that answer, most of the country would get squeamish.[*]

While Americans are much more religious than Canadians, it remains for some highly perplexing that they are also much more violent and more racist.

A great many Americans believe that "AIDS may well be God's punishment for immoral sexual behaviour."[†]

---

[*] *Globe and Mail*, March 31, 2000.
[†] *Atlantic Monthly*, December 2001.

While there are a considerable number of religious fundamentalists in Canada, the percentage pales in comparison with the U.S. About 40 per cent of Americans describe themselves as "born-again" Christians, including President George W. Bush, who was born again with the help of Billy Graham.

Michael Adams writes that "48 per cent of Americans said that the father of the family must be master in his own home." Only 5 per cent of Canadians strongly support such patriarchal authority. Adams calls the sharp decline in Canadian public opinion on this subject "an authentic social revolution," and says he and his colleagues were stunned by the equivalent polls in the United States. He also found that "College or university educated Americans are three times as likely as their Canadian peers to believe that the man should be boss."[*]

While most of the Canadian political and corporate establishment is fixated on the United States, relatively few Americans know much or care much about Canada. Richard Nixon and Ronald Reagan both believed that Japan was the United States' biggest trading partner. Only 14 per cent of Americans know that their biggest trading partner is Canada; more than half guessed it was China or Japan.[†]

At his first state dinner in September 2001, President George W. Bush said: "The United States has no more important relationship in the world than the one we have with Mexico." After the September 11 attacks on the World Trade Center and Pentagon, Bush thanked a long list of countries for their support, and somehow failed to mention Canada. Besides, "America has no truer friend than Great Britain."

Did it help to have the extreme right-winger and Canadian expatriate David Frum on the White House staff? Obviously not. The *Globe and Mail*'s Washington correspondent writes, "David Frum regards his homeland as sort of a pathetic lost cause."[**] More than a few Canadians regard David Frum in the same way.

While Canadian newspapers and television are packed with news, reviews, and commentary from the U.S., in that country Canada is barely over the horizon and rarely on the radar screen. Even in major

---

[*] *Globe and Mail*, July 4, 2001.
[†] *Globe and Mail*, May 7, 2002.
[**] *Globe and Mail*, December 31, 2001.

U.S. newspapers such as the *New York Times* and *Los Angeles Times*, news from Canada or articles about Canada are scarce, at best, but mostly non-existent. Almost one in three Americans believe that Canada is "just another state like Michigan or Oregon."[*]

As far as the American administration in Washington is concerned, Canada is taken for granted and Canadian governments are generally regarded as a bunch of compliant wimps. Meanwhile, U.S. congressional and state politicians have no concerns about offending Canada with their egregious, chauvinistic trade actions, such as their perpetual harassment of Canadian softwood lumber exports.

There are a thousand other differences, some of them important, some amusing and some of them quite insignificant. In no particular order:

- Americans are *far* more litigious. A friend reports a licence plate spotted in California that says HIT ME – I NEED THE MONEY.
- We use the metric system and most of us use English spellings. Many Canadians speak French, many Americans speak Spanish.
- Americans are rabid about basketball and football. Canadians love their hockey and curling.
- Americans elect judges, sheriffs, and district attorneys. Few Canadians would cast a vote for any politician who recommended that we elect police chiefs or crown prosecutors.
- Americans think it is a compliment when they say we're just like them. Many Canadians are not amused. As a Washington lobbyist put it, "Most Americans think most Canadians are just like them. They just wear more clothes."

A letter to the *Globe and Mail* in 2001 from an American living in New Jersey is similar to letters often received from the U.S. by Canadian newspapers and magazines:

> Canada and Canadians represent a vibrant community with a degree of civility unfortunately lost in too much of the United States.
>
> Then there was the cleanliness of so many of your major cities. I worked in Mayor Ed Koch's office in New York for more than a decade and I observe cities as a professional urbanist. The typical Canadian city

---

[*] Ipsos-Reid poll, May 2002.

has well cared for infrastructure, and a populace that seems to really care for "their city."

Your country is bountiful in the traits of civility and respect.[*]

In April 2002, the Associated Press reported that

An overwhelming majority of Americans agreed that an overwhelming majority of Americans are increasingly rude. Seventy-nine per cent of those surveyed said a lack of respect and courtesy in U.S. society is a serious problem.

There's one other thing that I feel obliged to mention: Canadian beer is a helluva lot better than American beer.

---

[*] John W. Wolfe, Highland Park, N.J.

PART

5

The Declining Country

Fighting Poverty Among the Wealthy

In 2001, Carol Goar wrote:

> Fifteen years ago, when Ottawa embarked on free trade negotiations with the United States, Canadians were told that there would be no effect on their culture, social programs, health-care or sovereignty. It was purely a commercial arrangement, former prime minister Brian Mulroney said.
>
> Today, Canada resembles the U.S. in ways that go far beyond commerce. Social benefits from unemployment insurance to welfare have been chopped. Executive salaries have soared. The gap between rich and poor has widened dramatically. A much larger share of health care is delivered by the private sector.[*]

Canada had far too much poverty, an unfair distribution of income, and a shockingly unbalanced distribution of wealth before the FTA came into effect. But since then, there have been two important changes.

First, no matter how awful the figures were in 1989, they are *much* worse today.

---

[*] *Toronto Star*, November 8, 2001.

Secondly, throughout much of the last couple of decades, there had been evidence that Canadians were unhappy with the growing gap between rich and poor, and at a very minimum, there was at least the pretense that Ottawa and some of the provincial governments cared about our growing disparities in living standards, income, and wealth.

Today, even the pretense and rhetoric from government are almost totally absent, or totally unconvincing.

To be blunt, Canada's political and corporate elite don't give a damn about the poor, and are completely unfamiliar with the concept of, or the desirability of, an egalitarian society. Since the Free Trade Agreement came into effect in 1989, contrary to everything we were repeatedly and so earnestly promised, Canada has not only become heavily Americanized, but in more than a few ways it has become a declining country, and certainly a vastly different country than most of us have aspired to.

The same year the FTA began dominating much of the public policy decision-making process in Canada, the House of Commons, in a unanimous all-party resolution, promised to abolish child poverty by the year 2000. Today, there are over 300,000 more poor children in Canada than in 1989, about 300,000 more poor families, and about 430,000 more poor individuals. While poverty rates in this country are far below those in the U.S., they are much higher than in most other developed countries.

Meanwhile, despite endless promises from Paul Martin and Jean Chrétien, not only are more Canadians now living in poverty, but the number who are living in abject poverty, with incomes less than half the poverty line, has increased substantially.

So, under the circumstances, what is Ottawa planning to do about our high levels of poverty in the future? No problem; they're going to redefine the low-income cutoffs so that, in the words of the Canadian Council on Social Development, "With one computer key stroke, poverty is significantly reduced."*

At the same time, thanks mainly to the Fraser Institute and the *National Post*, persistent efforts are made to downplay "the poverty business," which is "not concerned with the poor, but is concerned with taking money away from the wealthy."

Thirty-four years ago, way back in 1968, the Economic Council of Canada warned:

---

* Letter from David P. Ross to Maryanne Webber, Statistics Canada, April 10, 2000.

> Poverty in Canada is real. . . . Its persistence at a time when the bulk of Canadians enjoy one of the highest standards of living in the world, is a disgrace.

In his Senate report on poverty in 1971, David Croll said that it was urgent that important steps be taken to alleviate the heavy degree of poverty in Canada.

Urgent, thirty-one years ago!

When the House of Commons declared its war on poverty in 1989, 3.8 million Canadians were poor. By 1999, almost 4.9 million Canadians were poor. In 1989, about 14 per cent of all Canadians were poor; by 1999, it was 16.2 per cent.

During these same years, the number of children living in working-poor families increased substantially, as did the number living in squalid or very substandard accommodation.

In 1989, when the House of Commons passed its resolution, 15.2 per cent of all Canadian children were poor. In 1999, 18.5 per cent were poor. When the House of Commons passed their resolution, there were 1,016,000 Canadian children who fell below the Statistics Canada low-income cutoff lines (LICOs). By 1999, over 1.3 million Canadian children were living in low income. In 1989, about one in every seven Canadian children was poor; by 1999, it was about one in every five. While Statistics Canada says that there were 1.3 million low-income children in Canada in 1999, Ottawa admits that there are as many as "2.5 million children in low-income families in Canada."*

Almost every Canadian knows that the United Nations Human Development Report has for years ranked Canada the number-one country in the world; more recently we fell to number three. During these years, was Canada number one or even number three for our children?

Hardly.

The United Nations Children's Fund report, *The State of the World's Children, 2000*, says that when child poverty in industrialized nations is measured, sixteen countries have a better record than Canada, and only six developed countries (including Russia, Mexico, and the United States) have a worse record. So according to the UN we're seventeenth in our treatment of children. And a more recent report from the

---

* *The National Child Benefit: Progress Report 2000*, March 2001.

Luxembourg Income Study says that we've slipped all the way down to twenty-third place![*]

All of the following countries have child poverty rates below Canada's: Australia, Denmark, Germany, Greece, Hungary, Ireland, Israel, Japan, Poland, Spain, and Switzerland. Furthermore, all of the following countries have child poverty rates that are *less than half* of Canada's rate: Austria, Belgium, the Czech Republic, Finland, France, Luxembourg, the Netherlands, Norway, Slovakia, Sweden, and Taiwan.

In these and the following international comparisons, it's important to note that many of the countries with a better record than Canada in terms of child poverty and overall poverty are countries that are not as well-to-do as Canada. Some have per capita national incomes well below our own.

How can this possibly be?

The answer is simple. Most developed countries have governments that care a great deal more about underprivileged men, women, and children than our own government does.

It's interesting and revealing to look at distribution of income in Canada and compare it with other developed countries. Of the leading twenty-three developed nations, when the income of the richest 20 per cent of the population is compared to the income of the poorest 20 per cent, fifteen countries have a more balanced distribution of income than Canada. Only seven have greater disparities between rich and poor, including such great egalitarian beacons as Turkey, South Korea, Mexico, and the United States.

So, Canada isn't number one or even number three in this respect. We're number sixteen. All of the following countries have a more equitable distribution of income than Canada: Austria, Belgium, the Czech Republic, Denmark, Finland, France, Germany, Hungary, Italy, Japan, Luxembourg, Norway, Slovakia, Slovenia, and Sweden.[†]

In 1998, Paul Martin promised at a meeting with the National Council of Welfare that children were one of his top priorities and that families with children would have first call on the government's resources, which included the largest surplus since Confederation.

In 2000, Martin met with the Campaign Against Child Poverty in

---

[*] *Poverty Rates for Children*, http://www.lisproject.org/keyfigures/childpovrates.htm.
[†] United Nations *Human Development Report*, June 2000.

Toronto and led them to believe that he and the government planned important initiatives which would reduce child poverty.

Despite the fact that three different polls commissioned by his own Department of Finance showed that child poverty and child care were both a much higher public priority than the debt or tax cuts, Martin ignored the polls and proceeded with his whopping tax cuts, while continuing to reduce the debt.

In the words of Steve Kerstetter, former National Director of the National Council of Welfare,

> My own views are that social policy people at finance have proven themselves collectively to be unsympathetic to the plight of the poor, and that the department as a whole has gone out of its way to pander to rich people.

Today, even after five years of sizeable federal budgetary surpluses, the child poverty rate is much higher than it was twenty years ago.[*]

Increasingly in Canada our political and corporate elites are characterized by a widespread denial of need, the scapegoating of, indifference to, and outright hostility to the poor. If they're on the streets, the trend is to fine them, ship them out, or lock them up. Somehow, those who deny the terrible poverty in Canada are able to ignore the increased demand at food banks, the packed shelters, the sad reports from schools, churches, and social workers across the country. Today, with almost 5 million Canadians living in poverty, we should be ashamed.

What does poverty in Canada mean? It means being hungry, it means going without meals, not having warm clothing, living in dilapidated accommodation. It means children not having school supplies and not being able to participate in extracurricular activities, not being able to afford lessons and not being able to continue their education.[†] It means poorer health and lack of hope and very often it means deep despair.

The Ottawa-based Caledon Institute on Social Policy says that much of the responsibility for our high rates of poverty must rest with

---

[*] The most recent Canadian poverty figures at this writing were for 1999. Projections suggest a modest decrease in 2000 and an increase in 2001.

[†] Young people from high-income families are two-and-a-half times as likely as those from low-income families to attend university.

typically neoconservative bureaucrats, especially in the federal finance department, which has dominated social policy over the past two decades. Both corporate and political elites in Canada have proved more conservative than the general population, and are more supportive of cuts to social spending.[*]

Caledon is dead-on about the bureaucrats at finance, one of whom is now the Governor of the Bank of Canada, but the real blame must go to their bosses, Jean Chrétien and Paul Martin.

The word abject is defined as miserable, wretched, degraded. Do many Canadians live in abject poverty? In a UN list of twenty-four "high human development" countries, eighteen have a smaller percentage of their population living *below half* of half the median income. The U.S. is last on the list, with abject poverty rates far higher than all others.[†] In 1998, in Canada, almost half a million men and women under sixty-five had total incomes less than half of the poverty line.

How poor is poor? In 1999, on average, the lowest 20 per cent of Canadians, including families, after all their income from all sources was taken into consideration, had to get by with the grand total of $941 a month. Average unattached men and women in the lowest quintile had to somehow survive on $555 a month.

How poor is poor? In 1999, 83,000 single mothers had total incomes of less than half the poverty line.

The same year, over 260,000 individuals were poor even though they had full-time jobs, and 94,000 families were poor even though *both* husband and wife had full-time jobs.

In 1984, the poorest fifth of Canadians had an average annual market income of a paltry $7,814. By 1999, the market income of the lowest 20 per cent of Canadians had fallen all the way down to $4,590. That's $382.50 a month!

In the ten years following the House of Commons resolution pledging to wipe out child poverty in Canada, the average market income for all Canadian families fell by $3,300.

Aside from Ottawa, how have other Canadian governments responded

---

[*] *Relentless Incrementalism*, September 2001.
[†] United Nations *Human Development Report*, 2002.

to the high levels of poverty in Canada? Here's the National Council of Welfare:

> There has been a sharp increase in the ranks of the poorest of the poor since 1989 as governments at all levels cut back services and income supports for poor people. Cuts in welfare by provincial and territorial governments and cuts in employment insurance by the federal government go a long way to explaining the appalling situation.
>
> These figures provide the definitive rebuttal to people who believe that poverty is not a problem in Canada. It is tragic to think of so many people living in abject poverty, and it is appalling to see these figures remain at high levels.[*]

In the last half of the 1990s, amid growing affluence, the number of Canadians forced to live on incomes less than half the poverty line doubled.

Over 40 per cent of all food bank recipients in Canada are children. One wonders if Jean Chrétien, Paul Martin, Mike Harris, Gordon Campbell, and Ralph Klein ever gave these children even a moment's thought when they so drastically cut social spending, transfer payments, and welfare.

Food banks in Canada were intended as a temporary stop-gap measure; instead, they have become firmly entrenched in our society. Governments welcome them, because, in their minds, it gets them off the hook.

An annual report of the Canadian Association of Food Banks reminded Canadians that, at the 1996 World Food Summit,

> Canada recommitted to the right of everyone to have access to safe and nutritious food, adequate food, and the fundamental right of everyone to be free of hunger.

Between 1989 and 1998, food bank usage in Canada more than doubled. More and more seniors are now forced to depend on food banks. There are now more and more better-educated, hungry adults, more families

---

[*] *Poverty Profile*, 1998.

with children, more students, and more men and women employed in low-pay jobs who are reliant on food banks.

Most food banks in Canada provide only a few days' supply of groceries, and many restrict assistance to once a month. Some food banks are open only a few hours a month. In February 2000, a church food bank in Winnipeg decided to close "because it is attracting too many people."

Meanwhile, studies in Toronto and Edmonton show that

> many adults and children continue to go hungry and miss meals despite the assistance of a food bank. In our study almost half of the food banks reported that they ran out or were running out of food. Many rationed limited supplies and some turned people away empty-handed. Nutritional studies of food bank recipients have demonstrated the inadequacy of diets reliant on donated food.

Even the federal government admits that some 3 million Canadians face "food insecurity."

More than half of all welfare families in Canada, and more than one-third of single-parent mothers do not have enough to eat.

According to Dr. Henry Haddad, past-president of the Canadian Medical Association, "About 1.5 million Canadian children go to school with their stomachs empty every morning. That's awful and it's not acceptable."

Apartment vacancy rates across Canada have been shrinking steadily, down from 2.6 per cent in 1999 to 1.3 per cent, late in 2001. In Toronto, at this writing, the vacancy rate for two-bedroom apartments was .6 per cent and average rents were well over $1,000.

Compare the total incomes of poor families with the cost of two-bedroom apartments in Canada's major cities. If rent in Toronto is over $1,000 a month, and if average family food expenditures are about $500 a month, where does the money come from for such things as clothing, personal and household care, utilities, transportation, education costs, and everything else that people need?

From 1980 to 1992, between 150,000 and 240,000 affordable-housing units were produced every year. Between 1995 and 2000, on average, fewer than 1,000 a year were constructed. Ottawa ended its national housing program in 1993 and Ontario stopped funding social housing in 1995. Despite study after study and report after report, the housing needs of Canada's poor have been largely ignored, or, at best, met with a token response.

According to the Federation of Canadian Municipalities, Canada desperately needs at least 450,000 new low-cost rental units over ten years. But adequate social housing is simply not a priority for Ottawa or for most provinces. While the Federation says that a minimum of $1.6 billion a year is necessary to solve Canada's low-income housing problem, Ottawa brags about its five-year, $680 million federal-provincial shared-cost program. Across the country, shelters and hostels have been running at capacity for years. In wealthy Calgary, Canada's largest shelter opened this year and was quickly packed. Toronto has a 62,000-person waiting list for low-rent units. And across the country 800,000 households are forced to pay more than half of their total incomes for shelter.

In 1993, soon after he became prime minister, Jean Chrétien said that "The place of aboriginal people in the growth and development of Canada is a litmus test of our beliefs in fairness, justice and equality."

And he was right. Indeed, it is an accurate litmus test of how Jean Chrétien and Paul Martin really care about poor, underprivileged Canadians. For reasons that seem unfathomable, the 261,000 "persons registered under the Indian Act" living on reserves are *not* included when poverty rates in Canada are calculated. Canada's Indians living on reserves have appalling levels of poverty. Over half the population aged fifteen and over has less than $10,000 in income from all sources. Off reserves, almost half of the aboriginal urban population suffers from low income, as do 60 per cent of aboriginal children.

Winnipeg, Regina, and Saskatoon have aboriginal poverty rates above 60 per cent. In London and Edmonton the rate is over 50 per cent. In Montreal, Thunder Bay, Calgary, Vancouver, and Victoria, the poverty rates are between 42 and 49 per cent. Altogether, of a total of some 375,000 urban aboriginals, some 49 per cent or 184,000 are poor. On reserves, 36 per cent have annual incomes under $5,000, and 55 per cent have incomes under $10,000.

As a percentage of the population, about a third as many aboriginal men compared to non-aboriginal men get a university degree in Canada and about a fifth as many women.

In Canada, the top fifth of Canadians, those with the highest incomes, lives much longer than the poor, on average eleven years longer for men and almost eight years longer for women. Poor Canadians are much more likely to be in poor health, have chronic health conditions, suffer from mental stress, and live in substandard housing in high-crime neighbourhoods.

Unemployment insurance, or what is now ridiculously titled employment insurance, is a prime example of the move towards Americanizing social spending in Canada. While it's true that unemployment levels moderated during the last years of the 1990s, they dropped by only some 20 per cent, while the number of EI recipients dropped by almost 50 per cent.

And what about the much-trumpeted child benefit program? According to social policy expert Richard Shillington,

> The Child Tax Benefit [CTB] has meant reduced support for most poor children.
>
> Support for kids on welfare has actually declined, after adjusting for inflation, since 1985; the CTB has lowered support for 90 per cent of children in Canada.
>
> What is even more surprising for an anti-poverty program, is that support is lower for the majority of poor children!
>
> Incredibly, the CTB excluded most welfare families from increased support. Welfare families have seen their support levels continue to decline.
>
> While welfare is now the program of last resort (to receive it families must have exhausted their financial assets) welfare families are excluded from receiving much of the CTB assistance despite much opposition from municipal governments, the UN committee on economic, social and cultural rights, and almost every social policy and advocacy group in the country.
>
> Support payments per child on welfare peaked in 1989. By 2000 they had declined by some $200 or about 20%. [*]

Meanwhile, the top 40 per cent of Canadian families receive 40 per cent of government transfers while millions of needy Canadians live in conditions of miserable poverty.

In 1989, a shocking 52.9 per cent of all single-mother families lived in poverty. Have no fear, though. Thanks to the bountiful generosity of

---

[*] IRPP *Policy Options*, November 2000.

Brian Mulroney, Jean Chrétien ("Children must remain at the top of our agenda"), and Paul Martin ("The level of child poverty in this country is a disgrace and there has to be a great national effort to deal with that"), the average income of these families increased by – wait for it – 10.5 cents a day over the next ten years.

Today, in Ontario, single-parent families live 60 per cent below the poverty line, and in wealthy Alberta and in Manitoba they average 50 per cent below the poverty line. About 37 per cent of lone mothers who are working earn less than $10 an hour, and 26.5 per cent of all workers in Canada earn less than $10 an hour. 61 per cent of all children living with lone mothers who worked full time are poor.

During the 1990s, wages in Canada barely kept up with inflation, but minimum wages suffered substantial real erosion. In Ontario, minimum-wage workers make only $274 for a forty-hour week. While welfare payments, especially in Ontario, British Columbia, and Alberta, have been substantially reduced, hundreds of thousands of men and women across the country are now being denied both welfare and EI support.

Bear in mind that most of this was happening in the decade with the highest unemployment rate and the poorest job-creation rate since the Great Depression.

In 2000, UNICEF measured the percentage of low-wage workers in fourteen "high development" countries. Canada had the second-highest percentage; only the U.S. had a worse record.

Do we need a national childcare program in Canada? Ask the almost two-thirds of all married women with children who are in the work force. Better still, ask the other third, who can't afford child care and can't even think about getting a job. Then perhaps we might ask the man who while in opposition said:

> How are these poor mothers going to get off social assistance? How are they going to be trained? How are they going to get jobs if they don't have an adequate day care system?

Better still, wouldn't it be great if some enterprising MP or member of the press gallery reminded Paul Martin of these questions that he asked almost ten years ago?

While most Canadians heard frequently from Jean Chrétien about Canada's number-one ranking from the United Nations, few know that the UN has twice strongly criticized Canada (1993 and 1998) for allowing so much poverty, so much homelessness, and so much hunger, and so little support for poor children and poor families – "the degree of homelessness and poverty in Canada is really quite shocking."

The number of working poor in Canada is also shocking. In 1998, some 94,000 families in Canada were poor even though the husband and wife worked for a combined total of 100 or more weeks during the year! In 1998, some six hundred thousand children were living in poor families where the parents had a minimum of a full year's work.

Even though Ontario and Alberta booted huge numbers of families off welfare, while in 1989 there were 625,000 Canadian children who relied on welfare, ten years later there were almost 800,000. Even in the provinces that didn't slash welfare payments and eligibility drastically, since no province provides for indexation, the value of welfare payments has eroded considerably.

My previous books have been full of quotations from Jean Chrétien and Paul Martin showing the gap between their words and actions in relation to poverty in Canada. Here are a few more recent examples. Here is Jean Chrétien at a Liberal fundraiser in Toronto soon after the last federal election:

> Giving money to the poor is far more productive than big tax breaks, particularity for the wealthy.
>
> There remain, unfortunately, serious social problems in the land. Too many children live in third world conditions. As a Liberal, I believe that the government has the responsibility to promote social justice.

And then here is the Speech from the Throne that followed and promised

> to ensure that no Canadian child suffers the debilitating effects of poverty. The elimination of child poverty will be a national objective.

What colossal hypocrites! Go back to the first paragraph of the Chrétien speech above and read it again. Now let's return to what Paul Martin did in his February 2000 budget and his October mini-budget just prior to the last federal election.

In every objective public opinion poll during the two years prior to the election, Canadians said that health care, education, social spending, and child poverty were higher priorities than tax cuts. Here's what Steve Kerstetter had to say about Martin's February 2000 budget:

> Martin turned his back on the poorest of the poor and rewarded his fellow millionaires down at the club instead.

And so he did. In the budget there were significant reductions in capital gains taxes and taxes on stock options. There were significant reductions in corporate taxes, plus elimination of high-income surtaxes and favourable changes in high-income tax bracket thresholds. Overall, there were new tax cuts amounting to $58 billion, most of it going to big corporations and higher-income Canadians.

There was no desperately needed national child care or national housing program. There were no steps to encourage the provinces to stop clawing back the child benefit from needy mothers (as urged by many, including the United Nations), and, as a direct result of Martin's budget, the already record gap between rich and poor in Canada would widen even further.

Even after this massive tax cut, forecasts still indicated a $64 billion surplus over the next six years. In his February speech Martin had said:

> We must work towards reducing the gap between rich and poor. . . . We have always said that as resources permit we would do more for low-income Canadians . . . the government has always understood that there are certain priorities that cannot be deferred.

And, try this:

> The choices we make will mirror our values as a society and our obligations to each other as citizens.

So, just exactly what did Paul Martin do in his subsequent mini-budget? In the words of *Toronto Star* columnist Thomas Walkom,

> Paul Martin's October mini-budget completes one of the most fundamental redistributions of income in recent history.

Usually, those who redistribute income take from the rich and give to the poor. The federal finance minister . . . has turned this on its head.

The war against the deficit . . . is being fought on the backs of the sick and the poor.

Once again, while reducing taxes by another $40 billion, Paul Martin gave wealthy Canadians and big corporations far greater tax relief than poor or middle-class taxpayers. And, incredibly, while again increasing the child benefit for poor children by a miserly few cents a day, Martin extended the benefit to families with incomes of $60,000, $70,000, $80,000, or even $90,000 a year.

Not to be outdone, Ontario premier Mike Harris announced: "Ontario's Promise is a call to action . . . whose goal is to leave no child behind." To help announce his new program with great fanfare, Harris brought in Colin Powell and actor Dan Aykroyd. And, what about the new program? It amounted to the grand total of $3.72 for each of the 537,000 children living in poverty in Ontario.

From 1988 to 1999, the number of two-parent families who turned up at Toronto emergency shelters increased by 500 per cent. Meanwhile, in an editorial, the *National Post* told its readers that "Genuine privation is rare in Canada."[*]

About the time this book is published, there will be another Speech from the Throne in Ottawa. And, as they did in the January 2001 Throne Speech, the Liberal government will yet again earnestly promise that they will do something significant about child poverty.

Given their pitiful record over the past nine years, it's hard to be optimistic.

The Long-Term Trend Towards Inequality

In September 2000, the *Financial Post* had a bold front-page headline: IT JUST KEEPS GETTING BETTER. The sub-headline read "Prosperity at a level not seen in a generation," and the first paragraph told readers:

---

[*] October 9, 1999.

Economists are exhausting their superlatives in trying to describe the Canadian economy as two separate reports from banks yesterday said the country is at a level of prosperity not seen in a generation.

The story would have been fine if the words "income of the economic elite" replaced the word "country." Let's look at what happened to income distribution in Canada after the FTA came into effect.

Between 1989 and 1998, the lowest 80 per cent of Canadians in terms of their income lost ground to the top 20 per cent.

If you were to add the total average incomes of the lowest 80 per cent of Canadians together, the combined income would not equal the average incomes of the top 20 per cent of Canadian families.

In 1989, the top 20 per cent of Canadian households earned $18 for every $1 earned by the bottom 20 per cent. By 1998 it was $27 for the rich for every $1 earned by the poor.

In 2000, Statistics Canada said that the gap between rich and poor in Canada had increased again and was greater than at any time since the agency began compiling distribution-of-income information thirty years earlier.

As an aside, over the past decade we have been inundated by newspaper editorials and columns that have told us that rising personal taxes were the most important drag on personal disposal income in the 1990s. This is simply not true. While personal taxes rose during the decade, over 80 per cent of the decline in family disposable income was the result of a loss in market income, essentially a loss in real wages.

In 1989, the lowest 20 per cent of Canadians had average incomes of $12,372, including all provincial and federal government transfers. Nine years later, in 1998, their total average income had dropped by almost $1,700 down to $10,688, or $891 a month. Now an income decline of $1,700 might not seem like a disaster to some, but to the poor it is a cataclysmic development resulting in increased hunger, poorer living conditions, poorer health, and a host of other serious ramifications.

Meanwhile, how did the *top* 20 per cent fare during the same period? Their income increased by $6,500 to $113,400.

Perhaps one of the most interesting comparisons in Canada is to look at how the lowest 40 per cent of Canadians fared in terms of market income in comparison with the top 40 per cent in 1998. The comparison is stark indeed. The bottom 40 per cent took home only 6.9 per cent of market income, the top 40 per cent took home 78.6 per cent.

How does Canada compare to other developed countries in terms of income distribution? In the period 1987 to 1998, fifteen countries have a better record. They are Norway, Sweden, Belgium, Netherlands, Finland, Germany, Denmark, Austria, Luxembourg, Italy, Spain, Slovenia, the Czech Republic, Slovakia, and Hungary.[*]

As the Canadian economy improved during the last part of the 1990s, income inequality grew even more rapidly. In 2001, economists Pierre Fortin, Andrew Sharpe, and Frances St.-Hilaire wrote:

> Reducing inequality can, in the medium-to-long run, foster economic growth.
>
> Harvard University's Philippe Aghion, one of the leaders in the new field of research on inequality and growth, has argued that inequality actually proves bad for growth . . . redistribution is growth-enhancing because it creates opportunities, improves . . . incentives and it reduces macroeconomic volatility.[†]

But, it shouldn't take four distinguished economists to figure out that by raising the standard of living of the poor and near-poor, the benefits to society will be most rewarding, far more so than if a small percentage of the population receives more and more of the share of income and wealth every year. There are many obvious reasons for this, but let me dwell on two.

Raising the standard of living of the dispossessed will result in more people working, more tax revenue for government, and smaller social assistance payouts.

Moreover, raising the incomes of the lowest 40 per cent of Canadians will mean more money injected into the Canadian economy to recirculate in a multiplier effect locally.

Raising the incomes of the already wealthy inevitably means more money invested outside of Canada, much of it in tax havens, more dollars spent in Florida, Arizona, California, Hawaii, and in the Caribbean, and more money spent on imported luxury goods.

---

[*] United Nations *Human Development Report*, 2000.

[†] *Globe and Mail*, January 25, 2001.

The Rich Getting Much Richer

Let's move from the distribution of annual income to consider wealth.

In March 2001, the Southam newspapers reported "Canadians' net worth rising. Assets minus debt means per-person wealth of $105,700." The story picked up on a new Statistics Canada publication[*] which showed that the national per capita net worth had risen from $83,200 in 1994 to $105,700 in 2000. The following year, per capita wealth increased to $112,800.

There's one small problem: Dividing national assets by population to measure average net worth is even more misleading than dividing total GDP by population to measure standard of living.

In 1984, Statistics Canada produced a long-awaited study of the distribution of wealth in Canada. The results shocked many Canadians. It was another seventeen-and-a-half years before an updated wealth study was published.[†]

Here are some of the results:

- The top 50 per cent of all Canadian families owned 94 per cent of net worth. The bottom 50 per cent owned 6 per cent.
- The top 10 per cent of Canadian families owned more than the combined assets of the bottom 80 per cent.
- Between 1984 and 1999, only the top 10 per cent of families increased their share of total wealth. The other 90 per cent saw their shares decrease.

Most interesting is the fact that the response rate for the survey was one of the worst ever for a major Statistics Canada study. Overall, it was an acceptable 75.7 per cent, but among those with high incomes it was only 59.9 per cent. The implication, of course, is that the polarization of wealth in Canada is even greater than the results shown above.

By the end of 2001, Canada's 100 wealthiest people were worth approximately $120 billion. That's about equal to the combined wealth of the bottom 5.4 million Canadian families.

---

[*] *The Daily*, March 27, 2001.
[†] *The Assets and Debts of Canadians*, 1999, Catalogue no. 13-595-XIE.

The Pressures for Social Policy Convergence

Free trade has been hugely beneficial economically,
and, therefore, socially in terms of funds available.
– Diane Francis[*]

L et's return briefly to the question of social spending in Canada, keeping in mind Canada's high poverty rates and the very high unemployment of the 1990s and the decade's truly miserable rate of job creation.

While the radical right constantly proclaims that "Canada spends generously on programs for the disadvantaged," and our "social safety net is incredibly generous," and the Fraser and C. D. Howe institutes, the *National Post*, and the Alliance Party all paint a picture of profligate government social spending, Canadian governments have reduced social spending, which was already well below the levels in most other developed countries.

For generations, we Canadians have been proud of our social programs. The polls show that even today, even after substantial federal and provincial cutbacks in social spending as a percentage of GDP, Canadians regard social programs as a fundamental keystone of our society.

The day that I began researching this chapter, December 21, 2000, the morning edition of the *National Post* produced an excellent example of one of the main themes in what follows. The *Post*'s story was headed: "Support for social programs waning, new report says." In the newspaper's story, we learned that a news release from the Conference Board of Canada "suggests Canadians are returning to a 1950s-style view of the social safety net as a safeguard of 'last resort.'"

The same day, the annual year-end edition of *Maclean's* magazine arrived in my mailbox. The year-end poll of 1,400 adult Canadians showed that, in Allan Gregg's words, "In 1996 we found 11 per cent of respondents mentioned social issues as their dominant, top-of-mind concern. Today, that number has grown to almost half the population, as social issues eclipse any other category by a ratio of more than 4:1." A rate double that of 1998.

---

[*] *Edmonton Journal*, July 3, 2001.

When asked what the most important issue facing Canada was, 45 per cent mentioned health, social services, and education, compared to 8 per cent who named taxes, 11 per cent, unemployment and the economy, and 7 per cent, government, government spending, and deficits.

Poll results showed strong support for increasing spending on social programs, support that was considerably higher than that for tax reduction or paying down the national debt. There was strong support for housing for the homeless (75 per cent) and for funding child care (70 per cent).

Now, how can you reconcile this with the *National Post* story?

The answer is that it can't be done.

For many years, public opinion polls have consistently shown that Canadians are not only very attached to Canada's social programs, but that they consider them to be a key aspect of our national identity. However, in a recent paper, two political scientists indicate

> those same polls and wider polls reflect an underlying anxiety that increasing economic integration with the United States is narrowing the scope for a distinctive social policy path on the northern part of the continent.[*]

The authors go on to suggest that as a result of NAFTA, "there are reasons to anticipate that social policy convergence might be strong . . . the overwhelming dominance of the American market and the deeply asymmetrical relationship between the two countries would seem to create especially potent pressures for convergence."

Already, dramatic changes to unemployment insurance and family support policies in Canada have brought us closer to the American models.

Where in the late 1980s well over 80 per cent of the unemployed in Canada received unemployment benefits, by 2000 that number was down to only 36 per cent. In the last few years the Employment Insurance surplus passed $36.5 billion and was headed for $44 billion at this writing and billions more next year.

In April 2001, the *Toronto Star* complained that "the government calls EI a mainstay of Canada's social safety net. But it has been cynically

---

[*] Gerard W. Boychuk and Keith G. Banting, *Converging and Diverging Paradoxes*, June 2001.

refashioned into a safety net for government."[*] Canada abandoned the universal family allowance program and moved to refundable tax credits and the Canada Child Tax Benefit while the U.S. moved in a similar direction.

This erosion in Canada's social programs has been happening despite all the public opinion polls. In a 2000 *Globe and Mail*/CTV/Angus Reid Poll, 55 per cent of Canadians said that medicare and health care "should receive the greatest attention from Canada's leaders," followed by education and schools at 23 per cent.

Later in the year, in *Maclean's* 2000 year-end poll, the growing worry about the decline of social services in Canada was remarkable. Here are the percentages of those polled who picked social services as their top concern:

1995	0
1996	11
1997	15
1998	22
1999	31
2000	45

One year later, in a 2001 Ekos poll, two-thirds of Canadians said that protecting Canada's social programs should be the number-one priority in negotiating trade agreements. Later in the year, in the 2001 year-end poll by *Maclean's* and the CBC, issues such as health, education, and unemployment continued to be of far greater concern than government spending and deficits.

Susan Riley, writing in the *Ottawa Citizen* ten years after the FTA came into effect, said:

> Pressure to "harmonize" our social programs, foreign policy and culture . . . is an ongoing fact of life. Still, it is disturbing to think that a process which could lead, logically, to the disappearance of our country, is most eagerly pursued by Canadians, not Americans.
>
> No wonder we don't know who to trust.[†]

---

[*] April 16, 2001.
[†] June 29, 1999.

The 2000 annual Hunger Report from the Canadian Association of Food Banks pinpointed major problems relating to Canada's social programs:

> In the past few years, we have witnessed radical shifts in the direction and focus of social assistance programs across Canada. While many people are aware of the role of provincial governments in cuts to social assistance rates and the proliferation of so-called "workfare" programs, the role of the federal government has been less recognized. Prior to April 1996, cost-sharing arrangements and transfer payments for social assistance, education, and health care were regulated through the Canada Assistance Plan (CAP) and the Established Program Financing Act (EPF). On April 1, 1996, the Canada Health and Social Transfer (CHST) replaced CAP and EPF. This change resulted in the introduction of block funding which removed provincial requirements to maintain funding levels for specific programs, leaving social assistance benefits vulnerable to cuts. The introduction of CHST also resulted in the loss of national standards for welfare, including measures established to ensure adequate social assistance rates and prohibit mandatory work-for-welfare programs. The loss of CAP created an environment that allowed provincial governments to make deep cuts to social assistance benefits and institute workfare programs. In addition, the federal government reduced transfer payments to the provinces, resulting in less money for social programs and providing a justification for social assistance cuts. Social assistance programs were particularly vulnerable as they may have appeared less relevant to middle class Canadians.

As we shall see, Ottawa's social spending as a percentage of GDP has dropped by tens of billions of dollars, while between 1995 and 2000, provincial and territorial expenditures on social services were down almost $450 million. Increased population and inflation made the real decreases even more severe.

How does Canada compare to other countries in social spending? An OECD study showed that in a list of twenty-six OECD members, nineteen spent a higher percentage of GDP on social programs than Canada. Contrary to all the nonsense from our radical right, social spending in Canada is *far* below the average for developed countries. All of the following countries have a higher rate of social spending than

Canada: Portugal, New Zealand, the Czech Republic, Ireland, Iceland, Spain, the United Kingdom, Italy, Switzerland, Luxembourg, Austria, Netherlands, Norway, Belgium, Germany, France, Finland, Denmark and Sweden. Mexico, Korea and Turkey have appallingly low levels of social spending, while, as indicated earlier, the United States's level was far below Canada's.

Leaving aside education and health spending, how do we do in terms of other social spending as a percentage of GDP? In a list of twenty developed countries, we're down in twelfth place. All the following countries spend more than we do: Denmark, Sweden, Finland, the Netherlands, Norway, France, Germany, Luxembourg, the Czech Republic, Ireland, and Britain.*

If Canada's social spending as a percentage of GDP were simply the *average* of all the other twenty-nine OECD members, we'd have absolutely no trouble properly funding health care, post-secondary education, a national child care program, low-income housing, a national pharmacare program, and effective programs to help lift the poor up out of poverty. If we were only average.

Instead, with the Americanization of Canada, we're heading in exactly the opposite direction.

Our History Is a Mystery

In the mid-1970s, after spending years travelling across Canada speaking at teachers' conventions and visiting elementary and high schools in every province, I became quite dismayed by how little the students leaving high school knew about Canada. Their lack of knowledge of our country was truly beyond comprehension.

Not only did the students know almost nothing about our history, our politics, our social problems, our geography, and other matters, but their libraries and classrooms were full of American books, magazines, and U.S. educational materials.

---

* UNICEF *Innocenti* vol. 1, 2000.

The major reason our students were so poorly informed about our country was that provincial curriculum people somehow had managed to forget that we lived in a separate country on the North American continent.

In my trips, I gathered hundreds of depressing examples. I will list only a handful:

- A text titled *How People Live in Canada* had a picture of Abraham Lincoln on the cover.
- A hockey novel called *Fury on Ice* ended with the dirty French-Canadian centre getting a penalty, which allowed the valiant American captain to score the winning goal.
- A class assignment about the Stars and Stripes was all about "our flag."
- Another class assignment said that Robert E. Lee was "one of our greatest generals."
- Another class assignment was about "our nation's birthday on the fourth of July."

I could fill a good-sized book with similar examples. Allow me to quote briefly from my memoir, *At Twilight in the Country*:

> In my travels across the country the question I asked over and over again was: "How can we expect to survive as a country if, in the face of massive inundation of American culture, we fail to teach our own kids about our own history, culture, traditions, heroes, accomplishments and values?"
>
> One day in 1974, after visiting a high school in Ottawa and once again being disappointed by the lack of Canadian content, I decided to see if I could somehow give the Canadian educational establishment a jolt.

And I did. After a great deal of planning and the help of many teachers, we surveyed students in every province and territory, in rich and poor areas, in villages, towns, and cities. Almost all the thousands of students surveyed were just finishing their final year of high school. Here are just a few of the results:

- 63 per cent were unable to name any three prime ministers who held office since the end of the Second World War.
- 61 per cent were unable to name the BNA Act as Canada's constitution.
- 66 per cent were unable to name the Canadian who was awarded the Nobel Peace Prize in 1957.
- 89 per cent could not identify Gabriel Dumont, 69 per cent René Lévesque, 96 per cent Emily Murphy, 92 per cent Norman Bethune.
- Given a list of authors, 69 per cent failed to select Margaret Atwood as a Canadian, 79 per cent Al Purdy, 70 per cent Margaret Laurence.

And on and on and on. A shocking 62 per cent got fewer than half the questions right. And most said that they were ashamed about how little they knew about Canada. One of the students wrote "Margaret Atwood, Margaret Laurence – never heard of them so they must be Canadian."*

The survey results were published prominently across the country. Many editorials, op-ed pages, and television and radio shows focused on the awful results. People across the country were furious. I was inundated with letters and phone calls expressing outrage. The premier of Ontario, John Robarts, was very angry and called to express his appreciation for the survey.

That was then, and this is now. Three separate national polls in 2001 showed that things are just as bad now, twenty-seven years later, and likely even worse. In polls done for the *Ottawa Citizen*, CTV, the Dominion Institute, the *Globe and Mail*, and by Angus Reid:

- Only 23 per cent of Canadians passed a simple quiz about our country.
- Only 51 per cent could name our first prime minister and only 19 per cent our first Francophone prime minister.
- Two-thirds couldn't identify 1867 as the date of Confederation.
- Only a quarter knew which Canadian won the Nobel Peace Prize.

In one of the surveys, 14 per cent couldn't answer a single question and another 14 per cent could answer only one, while only 17 per cent could answer six of ten elementary citizenship examination questions.

Through the last half of 2001 and the first months of 2002, the head-

---

* *At Twilight in the Country, Memoirs of a Canadian Nationalist*, Toronto, Stoddart, 1996.

lines and editorials read "National Amnesia," "Ignorance Shames Canadians," "Canadian Knowledge Pathetic," and "Disgrace!"

Historian Jack Granatstein said:

> This must be the only country in the world that does not teach its history to all its young people. . . . It is a national scandal.

In an editorial, the *Globe and Mail* wrote:

> A country without a history doesn't have a soul. A country without a soul is barely a country at all. A country that has lost touch with its history is essentially a faceless suburb, nice to live in but little more.[*]

In the words of Toronto lawyer Harvey Haber,

> Canadian history isn't even taught in our schools until Grade 7. . . . It's no wonder they don't get it. . . . I used to go around to schools talking about Sir John. I've asked kids who Canada's first prime minister was and been told "Ronald McDonald!"[†]

Most new immigrants to Canada know more about our history than most citizens who are Canadian-born.

Tom Symons, founding president of Trent University, chair of the 1972 Commission on Canadian Studies and author of *To Know Ourselves*, writes about Canadian studies in our universities: "there have been some surprising and often considerable losses" in the field in recent years. Canadian studies must continue "to fend off marginal status at many of the universities where it exists, and it is still not a recognized subject on the curriculum of most of the universities of Canada."

Both the University of Guelph and the University of Alberta have decided to close down their Canadian Studies programs.

> It was argued, with unconscious but delicious irony, that, if attention to Canadian content and context is still needed, it can be better found in a new framework of North American studies.

---

[*] June 30, 2001.
[†] *Toronto Star*, January 11, 2001.

McMaster and Concordia no longer have Canadian Studies programs. Another dozen programs "are in trouble and fading."

Mostly, the problem seems not to be lack of interest, but lack of money. Meanwhile, Ottawa pours many millions of dollars each year into subsidizing Canadian Studies at universities and colleges in other countries. This compares with the tiny $800,000 Ottawa pays to support Canadian Studies in Canada.

It would be unfair not to mention that several Canadian universities have excellent, well-funded programs. Yet, as Tom Symons writes,

> The evidence is pretty clear that Canadians are remarkably ignorant of even the principal characters and events in the Canadian experience. At one university, for example, 61 per cent could not name Sir. John A. Macdonald as Canada's first prime minister; only 17 per cent could identify Sir Wilfrid Laurier, 59 per cent could not name even one Canadian artist, and 62 per cent could not name even one Canadian author.

And these results are for university students! In high schools across the country,

> Canadian history itself is often not taught, being dumped instead into the soft-study mish mash called social studies or transmuted into half-baked courses in civics. The resulting Pablum is so feeble that it turns good minds away from the subject, sometimes for life.
>
> As Keith Spicer wrote in the *Report of the Task Force on Canadian Unity* in 1991, Canada is dying of ignorance. The country is facing all the great issues of economic change . . . while Americanization proceeds apace.
>
> At a conference some years ago, the question was put: do Canadian Studies have a future? I would put beside that a companion question: does Canada have a future?[*]

Is the problem that Canadian history is boring? Last year, 74 per cent of those polled said quite the contrary, that it was interesting. And so did the millions of Canadians who watched the CBC's *Canada: A People's History*.

---

[*] *Journal of Canadian Studies*, vol. 35, no. 1.

What an awful job our educational establishment is doing teaching young Canadians about our country. I know many teachers who do a superb job, but our ministers of education and their blind bureaucracies should be ashamed of their dismal performance and their failure to do justice to one of their most important responsibilities.

What about our school libraries? Author and national librarian of Canada, Roch Carrier, says: "The state of our nation's school libraries can only be described as desperate in almost every province." Jon Lorinc of *Quill & Quire* writes that Carrier's

> view is based on a growing body of evidence that indicated that Canada's approximately 15,000 school libraries are being sacrificed on the altar of cost-cutting drives imposed by provincial governments and school boards.
>
> In Ontario, only 18 per cent of schools now have a full-time teacher-librarian, while the number of librarians employed in Alberta is roughly half what it was in the late 1980s.[*]

"If You Think Education Is Expensive, Try Ignorance"[†]

Over and over and over again we hear that with globalization the world is becoming an increasingly competitive place. We hear that knowledge-based industries are the key to the future, and that our economic prospects and our standard of living will be closely tied to our innovative abilities.

Yet during the past decade, money-starved Canadian universities have been forced to decrease their number of faculty members, increase class sizes, drop courses, and curtail library purchases. Per capita student funding has dropped by an alarming 20 per cent over the past two decades.

According to *Maclean's*,

---

[*] *Quill & Quire*, February 2002.
[†] Former Harvard University president Derek Bok.

Not so long ago there were 532,000 university students enrolled in Canada, with 36,400 faculty to teach them. That was 1990. But in the fall of 2001 there are a further 93,000 students in the system, with 1,900 fewer faculty.[*]

Between the years 1992–93 to 1998–99, full-time enrolment at Canadian universities increased by almost 111,000. But during the same years, part-time enrolment fell by a huge 70,000 students, despite a large increase in the university-age student population.

There's little doubt that few students from high-income families were deterred from attending university because of rapidly rising tuition fees and other costs of attending university. But for students from low-income families, the costs become "a real inhibitor," as one university president told me, and "staggering" for a low-income family when a four-year program is factored into their financing. Another university president said that, given the weak job market of the 1990s, it's safe to say that students from the top 40 per cent of families, based on income, now make up an overwhelming majority of university students.

Henry Jacek, president of the Ontario Confederation of University Faculty Associations, writes:

> There is folly and danger . . . in the recent calls to deregulate tuition in undergraduate arts and science programs. Across the board tuition deregulation serves one purpose only and that is to place the province on the cusp of losing its public university system.

The impact of who gets to go to university is clear:

> For example, a study done by an organization of medical students at the University of Western Ontario last spring shows the average family income of first-year medical students at Western has increased from $80,000 in 1998 to $140,000 in 2000 after three years of deregulation. The number of medical students from low and middle-income families dropped from 36 per cent to 15 per cent in four years as annual tuition fees rose from $4,800 to $10,000. Qualified students from low-income families are bowing out due to the prohibitive costs.[†]

---

[*] November 19, 2001.
[†] *Toronto Star*, January 11, 2002.

Another factor discouraging students from low-income families has been provincial government cutbacks of grants and more stringent loan eligibility requirements in Ontario.

Without question, in recent years Canadian universities have been short of required funds and the resulting tuition increases have inhibited enrolment among students intimidated by large debt loads.

Economist Pierre Fortin writes about the importance of education:

> Canada has been able to earn the United Nations' top ranking because past generations of Canadian teachers and educational managers have succeeded in keeping a balance between access and quality.
>
> Broad access to a college education is the guarantor of society-wide increases in the standard of living . . . If the immediate cost of university education to students is very high and front loaded – with average tuition fees of, say, $12,000 instead of $3,000 in public institutions – a lot of young people will be discouraged from persevering to the postsecondary level.[*]

However, according to the *Toronto Star*,

> Between 1991 and 2001, the cost of attending university went up six times faster that the cost of living.
>
> The average Canadian family manages to set aside $3,000 per child for post-secondary education. That does not even pay one year's tuition, let alone athletic fees, student association fees, books, supplies, meals, clothing and shelter. Low-income parents have trouble setting aside anything at all.
>
> Canada urgently needs new teachers, doctors, nurses, engineers, scientists, and civic leaders. It is shortsighted to let tuition fees stand in the way.[†]

Short-sighted indeed. Over the past decade, university undergraduate fees have increased in some provinces by as much as 150 per cent. Some of the largest increases have come in Canada's two wealthiest provinces, Ontario and Alberta, the two provinces that in recent years made massive corporate and individual tax cuts.

---

[*] *The Canadian Standard of Living: Is There a Way Up?*
[†] September 1, 2001.

Across the country, more and more students and parents now fear and feel that rapidly escalating tuition fees will place a university education beyond their reach, and beyond the reach of all except the children of the wealthy, or those especially brilliant students who are able to win scholarships. Clearly, the trend is towards elite U.S.-type graduate schools, their high tuition fees, and American-style application practices.

So now we have the University of Toronto's Dean of Law proposing to raise annual student tuitions from $12,000 to $25,000. And Queen's University wants tuition caps removed, and British Columbia has already removed their tuition freeze. In the U.S., top universities have fees ranging to $35,000, and that's the direction some of our leading university administrators want us to move in.

In the early 1980s, the average undergraduate loan was about $6,000. Today, it's closer to $20,000. For students now beginning their university education, it's going to be significantly higher. While the prospect of a $20,000 or $30,000 or $40,000 loan may not seem daunting to some, young people from low- or even middle-income families find the prospect of such a heavy burden intimidating.

But what about the Chrétien government's much-advertised Millennium Scholarships? The Caledon Institute of Social Policy has this to say:

> The Millennium Scholarships are taxed as income. Students effectively are being taxed as though they actually receive these funds as cash. In fact, the monies are diverted to the provincial loan reduction program and are never received by the students at all.*

If we're not satisfied with the results we are getting from our universities, it's instructive to return to the words of noted American economist Lester Thurow:

> In both Canada and the United States, building and financing a stronger education system would have a much bigger payoff in the long run than simply cutting taxes. . . .
>
> Within the United States, the two states with the best new start-up high tech performances, California and Massachusetts, aren't known

---

* Caledon Institute of Social Policy, October 2000.

for low taxes. The race in a knowledge-based economy goes to those with the best skilled top-to-bottom workforce.*

There's another thing about today's Canadian universities that is disturbing. In other countries, the sellout of their industries and resources, the abandonment of long-standing standards and values, the progressive erosion of national sovereignty, the threat to traditional institutions, and the possible demise of their nation would see universities across the country the centre of strong, passionate, articulate opposition. Historians, political scientists, economists, sociologists, and other educators would be up in arms leading protests in the media and in the streets. Where are these people now when we need them so badly? True, there are some exceptions at every Canadian university, but, for the most part, our academic community seems to have slumbered into a deep pathetic silence.

How very sad.

Visiting a Brothel to Learn About Chastity

In spite of the voluminous amount of well-documented evidence published in both Canada and the United States that clearly shows the overall superiority of Canada's publicly supported and publicly managed medicare system, during the last few years there has been an almost daily barrage of attempts to discredit medicare. The Americanization of Canada represents a growing threat to the long-established fundamentals of health care in this country.

Where is the pressure to Americanize our health care system coming from? Try the big U.S. insurance companies for one, and the U.S. Health Maintenance Organizations, the pharmaceutical giants, and our own radical right, most of whom can well afford to buy their way to the head of any line.

And who else has been leading the privatization charge? Well, it's none other than the three far-right provincial governments in Ontario, Alberta, and British Columbia. Aside from their radical conservative

---

* *Globe and Mail*, June 5, 2000.

ideologies, these three governments have two other features in common. First, they claim that our present health care system is in crisis and is unsustainable because we can no longer afford medicare. Second, all three provinces have drastically cut taxes, while two are implementing large increases in their flat-tax health care premiums.

In fall 2001, a *National Post* headline reported "Senate argues for more private health care," and in the story we learned that the Canadian Chamber of Commerce says that "the private sector must be allowed to have a greater role in the provision of health care services."*

Add to the above privatization proponents the C. D. Howe, Atlantic, and Fraser institutes, the Aspers and their cross-Canada editorials, and the president of the B.C. Medical Association, among others.

We have a steady stream of health care misinformation in our newspapers, on TV and the radio, and in chamber-of-commerce speeches across the country. What we hear is that medicare costs are exploding and that privatization is inevitable and that it should be encouraged. User fees and delisting will have to be on the agenda. Far more costs will have to be shifted to "the consumer," or, if you will, "the customer."

For years now, the intention of the Alberta government has been clear: more overall private-sector involvement in health care, reduced services, increased premiums, private hospitals, and continuing challenges to the principles of the Canada Health Act.

Ralph Klein's hiring of former Mulroney deputy prime minister Don Mazankowski to produce a report on health care made it certain that the report would please the Alberta premier and his Calgary friends.† Incredibly, among Mazankowski's suggestions is that health authorities should consider selling public hospitals to private entrepreneurs. He said he could see no disadvantage in allowing private interests to own and manage hospitals. The fact that under such a scheme either costs would escalate rapidly or patient care would suffer seems to have escaped the former Tory cabinet minister. If he has ever read and understood the numerous studies relating to the high costs of private hospitals, there is no sign of it.**

---

* September 17, 2001.

† *A Framework for Reform*, Edmonton, Government of Alberta, 2002.

** In 1999, the *New England Journal of Medicine* published a Harvard study of 5,000 hospitals which showed non-profit U.S. hospitals were not only cheaper than private hospitals, but also produced lower death rates.

One thing we know already: when Don Mazankowski was Brian Mulroney's finance minister, he managed to help add $76 billion to the federal debt.

A week after the Mazankowski report came out, an editorial in the *Globe and Mail* put it this way:

> The promise of medicare is that the collective will take care of individuals through taxes, or, in a couple of provinces, premiums to look after their health. This system makes so much sense and has so much going for it that to dismantle it by promoting an alternative in which people must pay privately to get quick service would represent a colossal failure of imagination.[*]

Jamie Swift of Kingston, in a letter to the *Globe*, wrote:

> Here we have a former minister in the Mulroney government – notorious for its fiscal incompetence – telling us that health-care costs are out of control. What's more, the man is a director of a large insurance company. Such firms stand to make big money should the private sector gain further access to the public health-care system.[†]

About the same time, Ontario premier Mike Harris indicated that he had no qualms about foreign firms participating in Canada's health care system.

If Jean Chrétien and Allan Rock were widely regarded as terribly weak defending the basic principals of the Canada Health Act, what can we make of the new health minister, Anne McLellan, who says that she has no problem with private hospitals and other forms of for-profit health care delivery being planned in Ontario, British Columbia, and Alberta? Despite the fact that numerous experts have demonstrated that for-profit private hospitals are *much* more expensive than non-profit public hospitals, somehow the minister "has no problem."

It seems difficult, at least at this writing, to differentiate McLellan's health care philosophy from that of Ralph Klein, and that means the

---

[*] January 11, 2002.

[†] Letter to the *Globe and Mail*, January 10, 2002. Mazankowski is a board member of Great-West Life.

long-standing principles of the Canada Health Act will be increasingly ignored.

Soon after she was appointed to her new cabinet post, McLellan said "I don't think the Canada Health Act should be etched in stone." It's hard to imagine what she might want changed. Could it possibly be universal access? How about public funding? Or is it comprehensive coverage? Or portability? Or could it be public administration?

Surely it can't be universal access. That would mean that only some Canadians would be able to benefit from medicare.

And surely she can't be referring to portability, where if you move from one province to another the services you are entitled to might not be available to you, an outsider.

It can't possibly be public administration she was thinking about, since it's well known that this saves the system many billions of dollars every year.

Comprehensive coverage? Is she, like her neighbour Ralph Klein, thinking of delisting a bunch of services? Drop, for example, hip and knee replacements? Perhaps, but certainly not before the next election.

Let's see now, what does that leave? Public funding! Is McLellan suggesting that Ottawa and the provinces should encourage more privatization so more health care costs come out of citizen's pockets? Don't for a moment bet against it.

In Alberta, private clinics and a private hospital are already offering everything from MRIs to cataract surgery to hip and knee replacements and back and shoulder operations. And private clinics are open or opening in Ontario, Quebec, British Columbia, and Nova Scotia. With more to come. A steep, slippery slope is turning into an avalanche.

Suppose we agreed to even more privatization, allowing a two-tier health care system? And suppose doctors move to the private system as clinics and hospitals decide to work outside of medicare and charge their well-to-do patients much higher fees? Supposing queue-jumping becomes common? What would happen to the rest of the population? To the overall quality of health care? To waiting lists? Doctors and nurses can't be in two different places at the same time. And substantial evidence shows that overall there would be longer, not shorter, waiting lists, not to mention the inevitable higher fees for "special services."[*]

---

[*] See *Mythbusters*, Canadian Health Services Research Foundation, on the Web.

Now the privatizers are again telling us that there's "no choice," user fees are "inevitable." But more well-documented studies show that the elderly and the poor cut back their visits to the doctor because of user fees, and that the extra administration costs and subsequent health costs because of delayed treatment end up costing more in the long run than would have been the case had user fees not inhibited visits to the doctor. As well, in case it's of any concern, user fees increase the risk that people will die unnecessarily.

Too bad that Anne McLellan hasn't seen the excellent studies that show that hospital administration costs at for-profit hospitals in the U.S. are over twice as high as public hospital costs in Canada.

Until recently, Canada was the only country in the OECD "where there is no way to buy your way to the front of the line for medically-necessary medical and hospital services."* For the most part this is still true, but in some cases – laser cataract surgery, for example, or private MRI clinics or a new B.C. specialist clinic – this is changing.

While the fundamental principle of equal access remains intact, and Canadian Institute for Health Information (CIHI) studies confirm that contacts with physicians in Canada are "basically equal for all income levels," there are now growing, troubling erosions.

Two provinces, Alberta and British Columbia, charge health care premiums, a form of flat tax that discriminates against those with low or middle incomes who must pay the premiums. Charging a family earning $25,000 a year the same premiums as a family earning $2.5 million a year has nothing to do with fairness and a lot to do with favouring the well-to-do.

Aside from the horrendous administration costs in the U.S. health care system, there are several other important reasons why overall and family and individual health care costs are lower in Canada. One is early diagnosis resulting in early treatment. In the U.S., the tens of millions without health insurance or with inadequate insurance are, for the most part, men, women, and children who don't get to see a doctor very often. Even when they are ill or when symptoms of disease appear, many of these people don't go to a doctor, or put off going, because they don't have the money and adequate U.S. health programs to assist them. According to the widely respected *New England Journal of Medicine*,

---

* Terry Sullivan, *Canada Watch*, November 2000.

public administration of health care in Canada saves us at least $10 billion every year.

Phillip Berger, chief of the department of family and community medicine at St. Michael's Hospital in Toronto, writes:

> Compelling the affluent to participate with the poor in a national health care system guarantees for those without money a standard of care expected by those who would purchase that same standard of care in a private system. In a universal system, the wealthy will always ensure that the standards of health care are upheld for everyone else. They will have to if they, themselves, want to benefit from a publicly funded system.
>
> The authors of the Canada Health Act were prescient in adopting the five principles that have ensured that for most services health care is not a commodity. These principles have prevented the establishment of separate tiers where an affluent social class can purchase necessary services unaffordable to a poor social class.[*]

Some of our anti-medicare advocates like to emphasize that in Europe many countries with public health care systems also allow private for-profit health care, so why shouldn't we? But, about 27 per cent of health care spending in Canada is already in the form of private expenditures. Comparatively, in the U.K. it's less then 17 per cent, in Sweden it's about 16 per cent. So, those who urge us to move closer to the European models are actually asking that we sharply *reduce* private health spending in Canada.

In 1998, eighteen OECD countries provided a higher percentage of per capita health care costs from government revenues than Canada. Only the United States, Australia, Italy, Portugal, Greece, and Korea had a higher percentage of private spending. Far down at the bottom of the public spending list was the United States at 45 per cent, with only Korea as a rival at 46 per cent.

At the same time, total U.S. per capita health spending *far* exceeded that of every OECD country, and was more than *double* the costs in half the OECD countries.[†]

---

[*] *Toronto Star*, January 10, 2002.
[†] OECD Health Data for 1998.

Those who use Canada's total national health care costs as an indication that spending is out of control often do so with the intention of misleading. Simple total spending figures ignore population growth, inflation, new procedures, and expensive but invaluable new medical equipment and technologies.

A much better method of measuring costs is as a percentage of GDP, or on a per capita basis. By both these measurements, Canada has been doing well, especially, as shown earlier, in comparison with the U.S., but also compared to many other developed countries.

What about provinces, such as Alberta and Ontario, that perpetually complain that health care costs are consuming an increasing percentage of their revenues and expenditures? There are two answers.

First, without question, the federal government must increase its overall share of health care funding. A cash increase would be an enormous help to the provinces.[*]

But secondly, since both Alberta and Ontario have made substantial cuts in taxes, health care cost will automatically represent a higher percentage of revenue. If Alberta had anywhere near the same comparative revenue as Alaska and Norway from oil and natural gas sales, or if the province had the same average tax revenue as the other nine provinces as a percentage of the provincial economy, there would be zero problem properly funding health care in the province.

As Edward Greenspon of the *Globe and Mail* has pointed out,

> When you calculate health expenditures as a share of provincial revenues rather than program costs, the picture changes markedly. Suddenly, health care accounts for precisely the same proportion – 32.5 per cent as it did five years ago.[†]

Greenspon and many others have noted that provincial public health care spending in recent years, when measured as a percentage of GDP, has remained around 6 per cent, about what it was seven years ago.

---

[*] Ottawa's share in cash transfers and tax points now stands at just under 30 per cent of total public funding, far greater than claimed by the provinces, but still well below the 50–50 concept originally promised.

[†] *Globe and Mail*, February 6, 2002.

Those who talk about public health care spending in Canada exploding out of control either don't know what they are talking about or intentionally set out to deceive. The superb Canadian Institute for Health Information shows that total public health care spending in Canada as a percentage of GDP fell from a high of 7.4 per cent in 1992 down to 6.8 per cent in 2001. That's some explosion!

In 1999, private per capita health care spending in Canada was about $725 U.S. In the United States it was $2,420. (Most private health spending in Canada is for prescription drugs, dental, and vision care).

Sometimes I think the folks at the Canadian Chamber of Commerce aren't the sharpest knives in the drawer. Canada's medicare system represents a huge advantage to corporations in this country. One recent study showed U.S. manufacturers pay on average $2,500 more per employee for health insurance. The Canadian Labour Congress estimates that without medicare, employers of unionized workers would have to pay out $30 billion more in health insurance costs.

In 2000, according to the New York investment firm Morgan Stanley Dean Witter & Co., General Motors alone paid out $3.9 billion worth of health care insurance for their U.S. employees, their dependents, and the firm's retirees. That worked out to $932 for every vehicle GM produced in the States that year.[*] This represents a huge competitive advantage for Canadian-based automakers.

One former CEO of a major U.S. firm operating in Canada told me that if Canada ever moved to a private health care system, the whole automobile industry and the entire Ontario economy would be in huge trouble.

What about all the scary warnings about Canada's aging population? Three different studies have shown that the overall impact on costs will be smaller than many expect because the elderly are healthier now, hospitalization rates have fallen dramatically for over thirty years, and long-term institutionalization rates have been cut in half over the past two decades.

An excellent study by Marcel Mérette says that ignoring some positive impacts of aging, "leads to overly pessimistic scenarios about the economic and fiscal consequences of aging in Canada." And, with some reasonable adjustments "there is no need to dread the impact of the

---

[*] *Globe and Mail*, February 12, 2002.

aging of our population on Canadians' standard of living or on the public purse."[*]

How do Canadians feel about health care in Canada? In 1996, an Ekos poll showed that 91 per cent of Canadians thought that it was "very important" to have strong national medicare standards. In 1994/95, only 4 per cent of Canadians reported "unmet health care needs," mostly due to long waiting lists and unavailability of services when needed. By 2000/01, that figure had grown to 12.5 per cent; the main complaint was increased waiting times.[†] In 1998, in an Angus Reid poll, concerns about health care didn't even register. From 2000 to 2002, these concerns have invariably been at the top or near the top of every poll.

What about the quality of care received? An Ipsos-Reid poll in early 2002 showed that 26 per cent of those polled described Canada's health care system as excellent or very good, 64 per cent rated it good to fair, and 9 per cent poor or very poor.[**]

In 1997, the National Forum on Health produced an excellent report urging the creation of national home care and pharmacare programs. The vast majority of Canadians agree. Instead, we are moving in the opposite direction, planning to cut back and ration services.

By the way, doctors who graduate from Canada's medical schools receive an excellent education, largely at public expense. Why do we not require that they promise, after final graduation, to stay in Canada to practise for at least ten years? Or, if they do not choose to do so, they agree to pay their province back the full taxpayers' share of their education cost?

What are the solutions to increasing health care concerns? About the time this book is published, Roy Romanow will have his list of recommendations, which will undoubtedly be more logical and palatable than those found in the Mazankowski report.

Many thoughtful students of health care in Canada support expanded "storefront" primary care facilities, with doctors, nurses, and other health care experts working together in accessible twenty-four-hour walk-in family clinics.

---

[*] *Choices*, vol. 7, no. 6, IRPP, November 2001.
[†] Statistics Canada, *The Daily*, March 13, 2002.
[**] *Globe and Mail*, January 26, 2002.

Dr. Tom Noseworthy, professor of health policy and management at the University of Calgary, was a member of the National Forum on Health:

> As our politicians contemplate the future of health care in Canada, and we study our system again and again, let us not throw the baby out with the bath water. We should keep the fundamentals of medicare – a universal, publicly-funded, single-payer model, for services we choose to insure.[*]

Consider that total health care spending in Canada was about 10 per cent of GDP in 1992, and is now down to 9.3 per cent. In 2002 the difference amounts to well over $7 billion. Let's split the difference. An additional $3.5 billion a year from Ottawa devoted to health care would be a good start in increasing the federal government's share of the costs and would have an enormous beneficial impact. Ottawa's current promised health care spending increase is only a *partial* restoration of health care spending cutbacks. Increasing the CHST from $15 billion a year to $18.3 billion still leaves the new spending level below the $18.7 billion in 1993, the year Paul Martin and Jean Chrétien took over. And that doesn't begin to take into consideration inflation, and our increased population.

Dr. Peter Barrett, a past president of the Canadian Medical Association, writes that

> from about 1992 to 1999 the signal to physicians was that they were not wanted.
>
> As budgets were squeezed over the 1990s, the infrastructure that contributes to the provision of quality patient care has been neglected.

Moreover, somehow government health ministers decided to implement a 10-per-cent cut in first-year medical school enrolment in 1993. At about the same time, the Ontario government proposed major cuts to doctor's fees.

Against this backdrop one could scarcely wonder why the number of physicians leaving Canada doubled between 1989 and 1994. It has only

---

[*] *National Post*, November 2001.

been in the last few years, with the growing awareness of the emerging physicians shortage, that provincial/territorial governments have begun to acknowledge the need to treat the health workforce as a valuable resource.[*]

No one can argue with Dr. Barrett's conclusions. This said, it's interesting to note again that more and more doctors who left Canada are returning to this country every year. Nevertheless, in terms of doctors per hundred thousand people, we don't do that well. In a recent UN list, Canada is down in forty-fifth place, far behind most developed countries.[†]

According to the Canadian Nurses Association, by 2011 there will be a shortage of over one hundred thousand nurses in Canada.

As a result of provincial health care reforms throughout the 1990s, thousands of nursing positions were eliminated and thousands more were reduced to part-time or casual status. At the same time, the number of nursing graduates in Canada was reduced from 10,000 annually in the late 1980s to the current 5,000, about half the number this country needs if we are to avert a massive shortage of nursing professionals.

Shortages mean increased stress,

increased workloads, higher nurse/patient ratios, increased absenteeism and poorer patient health outcomes.

Without question, although we're slowly catching up, the availability of up-to-date medical technology is poor. Among OECD countries, we're 14th of 18 in computer tomography scanners, 14th of 17 in MRIs, 13th of 14 for lithotripters, and 6th of 20 countries in radiation-therapy equipment.[**]

Keith Banting makes an important point:

If the Canada Health Act is weakened, the health care that citizens are entitled to will depend even more on the region in which they live . . .

---

[*] *Choices*, vol.7, no. 6, IRPP, November 2001.
[†] United Nations *Human Development Report*, 2002.
[**] Southam News, September 24, 2001.

Canada would depart from the pattern of federal states in advanced democratic countries.*

And that's precisely what we're doing as Ottawa ignores provincial decisions to go their own way. The Chrétien government's concept of leadership has been to bury its head deep in the tundra.

A few words about prescription drugs. According to Senator Michael Kirby, his committee studying medicare was told by pharmacists about patients frequently coming into their stores to have prescriptions filled and then, when informed of the cost, leaving with the prescription unfilled.

Don Mazankowski and the Mulroney government took steps to change drug legislation to delay the introduction of less expensive generic drugs. In 1975, prescription drug costs were about 8.8 cents of every health care dollar. By 2001, they were up to 15.5 cents. Many millions of dollars could be saved every year by more quickly approving more low-cost generic drugs, and avoiding expensive new brand-name pharmaceuticals, which provide little or no improvement over existing medicines. By 1997, rising drug costs, increasing at well over twice the rate of inflation and twice the rate increases for other health care costs, overtook the costs of all spending on physicians in Canada, and since then the spread has been growing.

In 2001, the costs of drugs to the health care system amounted to $15.5 billion, and were still growing at twice the rate of the costs for the overall system, and three times the inflation rate. (One study of nine giant pharmaceutical firms showed that in the 1990s they had average profits of over 40 per cent). In the words of Theodore Marmor of the Yale School of Management and the Institute of Medicine:

> Turning to the United States for [health care] cost-control models would be like visiting a brothel to learn about chastity; we Americans spend more than 14 per cent of GDP on health care, compared to Canada's less than 10 per cent.
>
> Serious investigation of the U.S. health-care system would, I believe, lead most thoughtful Canadians to conclude that the ordinary

---

* *Toronto Star*, February 2, 2002.

financing and delivery of medical care south of the border does not provide many solutions for Canada's stress.

That level of understanding, however, is not apparent to this observer in the Canadian debate.[*]

Alas, how true. Yes, total health care spending in Canada has increased, but what about the results? Between 1971 and 1997, average life expectancy at birth in Canada increased from 73 years to almost 79 years. Six extra years!

A Canadian Medical Association public-opinion poll in the summer of 2001 is revealing. About half of those polled said that government should devote more money to health care, *even if it meant higher taxes.* And a 2002 Ekos poll showed that a strong majority of Canadians want the federal government to take primary responsibility for health care.

In the CMA poll, fewer than one in three supported the idea of more private-sector involvement, three of five said home-care costs and long-term institutional-care costs should be part of medicare, and, despite the fact that those polled were critical of both the federal and provincial governments, 58 per cent agreed that "Canada's health-care system is one of the best in the world."[†]

Canadians should note well the words of Dr. Arnold S. Relman, former editor-in-chief of the *New England Journal of Medicine*, who was asked to appear before the Standing Committee on Social Affairs, Science, and Technology in Ottawa in February 2002.

My conclusion, from over two decades of study, is that most of the current problems of the U.S. system – and they are numerous – result from the growing encroachment of private-for-profit ownership and competitive markets on a sector of our economy that properly belongs in the public domain.

No health care system in the industrialized world is as heavily commercialized as ours, and none is as expensive, inefficient, and inequitable – or as unpopular. Indeed, just about the only parts of U.S. society happy with our current market-driven health care system are the owners and investors in the for-profit industries now living off the system.

---

[*] *Globe and Mail*, February 12, 2002.
[†] *Globe and Mail*, August 13, 2001.

There is now much evidence that private businesses delivering health care for profit have greatly increased the total cost of health care and damaged – not helped – their public and private nonprofit competitors.

The U.S. experience has shown that private markets and commercial competition have made things worse, not better, for our health care system. Markets simply are not designed to deal effectively with the delivery of medical care – which is a social function that needs to be addressed in the public sector.

And, as for Canada, and the Senate Kirby report,[*]

I am surprised and disappointed in your Committee's Interim Report, which seems to favour policy options dependent on private market involvement in Canadian health care.

I suspect most Canadians understand why health care is special and why it needs to be insured by a public system like the one you now have. I would be surprised if they want the fundamental fairness of their medicare system to be changed by the introduction of market forces.

This is a wise, experienced man. And he is right about how most Canadians feel. But, once again, here's another example of the huge differences between the desires of our plutocracy, and the wishes of the vast majority of Canadians.

Senator Michael Kirby has been a director of a for-profit, long-term care firm, Extendicare, since 1985.

One more point about medicare. Those who value it had best pay careful attention to the General Agreement on Trade in Services, the GATS negotiations. Given the preliminary evidence, and there's lots of it, given the Chrétien government's abysmal record in defending Canadian sovereignty, and their inept trade negotiations history, we all could wake up one day to find that medicare has not only been on the table, but that its principles have been abandoned and Canada is wide open for American health care corporations. More about the GATS later.

---

[*] *The Health of Canadians – The Federal Role*, March 2001 and April 2002.

PART
6

The Best Country

No Thanks! We Don't Want to Become Americans. We Can Do Much Better

After spending good parts of four decades travelling across Canada and meeting Canadians from every walk of life in every province and territory, the same firm conviction remains with me. I'm convinced that Canada not only should be, but can be, the best country in the world. I'm also convinced that unless some very important changes are made soon, Canada is going to become no better than a totally dominated, weak colony of the United States.

One of the most serious problems Canada has is the quality of our corporate leaders, and their motivations. Lewis H. Lapham described "the American claim to an advanced state of economic and political enlightenment . . . the pillars of imperishable wisdom."

1. Big government is by inclination Marxist, by definition wasteful and incompetent, a conspiracy of fools indifferent to the welfare of the common man. The best government is no government. The agencies of big government stand as acronyms for overbearing bureaucracy, as synonyms for poverty, indolence, and disease.
2. Global capitalism is the eighth wonder of the world, a light unto the nations and the answer to everybody's prayers. Nothing must interfere with its sacred mysteries and omniscient judgement.

3. The art of politics (embarrassingly human and therefore corrupt) is subordinate to the science of economics (reassuringly abstract and therefore perfect). What need of political principle or philosophy when it is the money markets that set policy, pay the troops, distribute alms? What need of statesmen, much less politicians, when it isn't really necessary to know their names or remember what they say?[*]

Sound at all familiar? Although Lapham's words are written as caustic satire, isn't this exactly the same sort of thinking that we've heard and read more and more of from many of Canada's business leaders, politicians and right-wing journalists?

I can't imagine anyone who might want to argue that many of Canada's corporate leaders have shown concern for Canadian sovereignty and independence. Nor do I think many Canadians believe that corporate ethics, decency, morality, and public responsibility have done anything but deteriorate in recent years. Instead, what we've witnessed is increased arrogance, greed, self-serving well-financed lobbying, and, frequently, grossly unprincipled and even illegal conduct, all seemingly without conscience. We can do much better than continuing to let these people dominate our government and run our country.

In the past, we've built up one of the best countries in the world. We've welcomed immigrants from around the world; we have one of the best-educated populations anywhere; we have a relatively high standard of living; we're blessed with an abundance of natural resources including oil, natural gas, forests, and fresh water. In mineral production we're number two in the world in zinc and nickel, number three in aluminum, palladium, and platinum, number four in copper and gold, number five in lead and silver, and number nine in coal. In total energy production, we're number five.

Economists Lars Osberg and Andrew Sharpe have pointed out that when the World Bank estimates natural capital ("the entire environmental patrimony or a country," which includes pastureland, cropland, timber resources, protected areas, and sub-soil assets), on a per capita basis New Zealand is in first place, followed by Canada and then Australia, all well ahead of the sixteen other developed countries in the study, including the U.S.

---

[*] *Harper's Magazine*, December 2001.

In area, Canada is the second-largest country in the world, behind only Russia, bigger than China, the United States, or Brazil, and all the other countries you can think of.

In cereals production and wheat, we're the sixth-largest producers; in services output we're eighth; in total industrial output we're number ten, and in manufacturing number twelve.

In terms of the business environment, that is the attractiveness of the country as a place to invest, we're anywhere from number one to number four (depending on the survey). In total GDP, we're ninth, in per capita GDP we're seventh, and in market capitalization we're tenth.[*]

We have one of the highest university- and college-enrolment percentages of any country in the world, and one of the longest life expectancies for both men and women.

We're the eighth-most-favoured destinations for tourists from around the world.[†]

Given all these assets, and the excellent quality of life many Canadians still have despite the sad deterioration previously described, why should we let our corporate elite, our selfish plutocracy, our radical right, and our inept politicians continue to sell out our country?

We don't have to. And we should quickly stop them from doing so. We *can* be the best country in the world; there's not the faintest shadow of a doubt in my mind about this.

But, hasn't the United Nations *already* said that Canada has been the number-one country in the world for seven consecutive years, and is still number three (behind Norway and Sweden and just ahead of Belgium and Australia) in a list of 173 countries?

We have every reason to be proud of these high UN rankings. In the words of the Canadian Council on Social Development, "They reflect important investments in the public good, notably the development of universal health care and the expansion of public education."[**]

But aren't these two of the most important elements of Canadian life now under attack from our right-wing businessmen and governments?

There's a problem, though, with the UN's annual Human Development Index. Their rankings are based only on four indices: life expectancy

---

[*] United Nations *Human Development Report*, 2001 and 2002.
[†] Most of the above from *The Economist's Pocket World in Figures*, 2001.
[**] *The Canadian Fact Book on Poverty*, 2000.

at birth; school primary, secondary, and tertiary enrolment; adult literacy; and GDP per capita. It's an arbitrary selection of indices, and based on some misleading concepts. For example, as we've already discussed, GDP per capita, where income distribution is skewed, is no proper measure of overall living standards, and Canada's income distribution is one of the worst in the developed world.

As well, we're far down the UN's latest list when poverty among eighteen developed countries is considered. (The U.S. is in last place; Norway is in the number-one spot, with the lowest level of poverty. The corporate elite's tax mecca, Ireland, has the second-worst level of poverty on the list).

A large number of other factors are not included in the Human Development Index, such as pollution, hunger, and homelessness. Supposing the already high levels of poverty, hunger, and homelessness in Canada were to double next year? Our UN ranking wouldn't change one bit.

So the annual UN lists should be taken for what they're worth. They are a partial, but a very incomplete indication of the quality of life in different countries.

Before I go on to make some suggestions about how Canada *could* become the best country in the world, or at least one of the very best, it might be worthwhile quoting from an article about Norway in the *Los Angeles Times*:

> Imagine a world so shielded from modern dangers that children accept candy from strangers. Think about a place where lifelong financial security is guaranteed, no matter how many layoffs, stock market crashes or catastrophic illnesses come your way.
>
> Consider the psychological well-being of belonging to a country where no one is homeless or hungry, where women and men are equal, where a pristine environment is reverentially protected and where sharing the wealth with the world's less fortunate is a moral obligation.
>
> Norway is not utopia – after all, it does suffer the occasional incursions of the cruel outside world. But most Norwegians admit that in terms of uplifting ideals and earthly comforts, life in this country is as good as it gets.
>
> The UN's glowing report card has filled many Norwegians with

newfound pride and a sense of validation that sharing and caring aren't extinct.

And although there is much muttering over high taxes, many Norwegians contend they should be giving even more of their money to solve the rest of the world's problems.

"Our moral obligation to share the wealth increases with the amount of our wealth," says International Development Minister Anne Kristin. "We could easily give five times as much as we do in foreign assistance," argues Ingebrigt Steen Jensen, a media magnate who insists that most Norwegian entrepreneurs hold global welfare above personal enrichment. "We have this huge cake, but we can't eat it all, so isn't it better to share it with this room full of hungry people than to put it in the freezer for later?"

Can anyone remember any one of our current crop of corporate leaders or media magnates saying anything remotely similar? In fact, can anyone remember more than a small handful of them saying anything else except lower our taxes and stop spending so much money on social programs?

True, Canada isn't Norway; they have only 4.5 million people and substantial annual revenue from North Sea Oil. But, based on equivalent production levels, if Canada received as much in the way of royalties, tax revenue, and profits from oil and natural-gas sales as the state-owned petroleum industry in Norway does, we'd bring in almost $25 billion extra a year. Wouldn't that do wonders for our health care, housing, and education shortfalls?[*]

In Norway, the police are unarmed, people leave their homes unlocked, the public schools are high-quality, maternity leave is generous, as are paid vacations, and so is assistance for single mothers. The libraries and child care are excellent, and work hours flexible.

---

[*] Calculations by economist Mark Anielski, Anielski Management Inc., based on Alberta and Norway budget forecasts for 2002.

Selling Parliament Hill and Grandma

If Canada is to survive as a proud, independent country in charge of its own political social, economic, and cultural policies, four vitally important things must happen.

The first thing Canadians *must* do is put a stop to the growth of foreign ownership and foreign control in Canada. It's already at levels that would never be tolerated in other developed countries. As discussed earlier, it seriously harms Canada in many important ways. No self-respecting country would allow foreign corporations to control so many industries and so much of their economy. Canada cannot survive as an independent country if we continue to allow foreign ownership to grow.

There are a number of different ways we can accomplish this vitally important and essential policy change. We can widen our sectoral controls (many countries have these, including the U.S.). We can put into place tough limits for all forms of foreign direct investment involving takeovers. We can have strong rules relating to required benefits to Canada for new foreign direct investment in existing foreign corporations. We can institute a total ban on takeovers for, say, five to ten years. We can put a stop to Canadian banks funding foreign takeovers in Canada and insist that they make more Canadian capital available to Canadians for investment in this country.

No one is suggesting nationalizing foreign firms, or forcing them to sell existing assets. Over time, with the right policies in place, foreign ownership and foreign control will diminish as a percentage of the economy and become less of a problem.

Of course, our radical right will all scream blue murder. They should be ignored. They're the ones who got us into this mess in the first place. They would probably sell Parliament Hill and their grandmothers if they thought the price was right.

In 2001, a Vector poll showed that 75 per cent of Canadians believe that government should have the right to regulate foreign investors in the public interest, and 73 per cent believed that governments have the right to give preference to local suppliers over foreign multinational corporations.

The survival of Canada depends on stopping the growth of foreign ownership, but before we can do that, there is another essential thing we'll have to do first. I'll come back to that a bit later.

Improving and Expanding Medicare

A few final words about changes to medicare. In relation to drugs, we'll have to work hard with like-minded countries – and there are many who want patent terms shortened so that more cheaper generic drugs can be used. Worry not about the pharmaceutical giants; they're almost all making record profits and have been for years. Had the pro-free-traders not been so anxious to lock Canada into agreements which curtail our ability to develop and use generic drugs, billions of dollars in excessive costs would have been avoided, money that could have been diverted to other much-needed areas of health care.

Canada should be training more doctors and retraining more immigrant doctors who now are prohibited from practising in this country. We need to take steps to lure back doctors who have emigrated, something that is becoming less and less difficult as the now infamous HMOs and American health insurance companies have taken over the health care system in the U.S., controlling the lives of doctors, robbing them of their critical independence far beyond anything they might ever experience under medicare in Canada.

To be the best country in the world we need to have the best overall health care for all our citizens. We can achieve this not by destroying medicare, but by improving and expanding it. We can carefully plan and gradually put into place national home care, drug, and eyeglasses plans, and dental plans for children. We can't afford to do this on a universal basis for now, but we can afford to begin with national plans for low-income men, women, and children.

One thing we could do would be most effective – a national bulk-purchasing program for drugs that would reduce costs, bypass expensive drugs that provide little or no extra benefit, and favour the use of generic drugs where possible.

Where will all the additional money we're going to need come from? I'll discuss that shortly.

Higher Education – Death by a Thousand Cuts

The "We *must* cut taxes to be competitive" mantra from our corporate leaders directly conflicts with the widely accepted view that education is a key to the future in our increasingly competitive world. But in 1998 (the latest year for available comparative figures) Canada spent $14,579 per student in post-secondary education, while the U.S. spent $19,802.* The same year, 19 per cent of the population in Canada, ages twenty-five to sixty-four, attained type-A post-secondary education, compared to 27 per cent in the U.S.

How exactly are we going to be competitive? While it's clear that in most but not all respects we're doing a good job in our elementary and high schools, and there's little question that we have fine colleges and universities across the country, if we continue to underfund college and university education our ability to compete is going to be seriously compromised.

At the same time, an increasingly worrying trend is the commercialization of Canadian universities. In an important new book, Paul Axelrod, Dean of the Faculty of Education at York University, writes:

> Governments are increasingly excising the universities' ability to provide broad and balanced academic programs, and the space for liberal education is shrinking. Marketplace jargon now accompanies these restrictive policies. So-called clients and customers (students) expect service providers (faculty) to enhance their economic worth in the labour market. Subordinate to bureaucratic and political regulations designed to prepare students for the economy, universities may be losing the authority to fashion a future that includes liberal education.
>
> Much has changed with the sudden arrival of "globalization" and

---

* Equivalent U.S. dollars, converted using PPPs, *Education at a Glance*, 2001, OECD.

the unleashing of "market" forces on educational and other institutions. The impact of these changes has been profound.[*]

Increasingly, as in the U.S. the private sector in Canada is determined to play an active role in university and college affairs. Universities are expected to expand their partnerships with business. Axelrod continues:

> To turn higher learning into a mere market commodity is to betray the generations of students yet to be and to turn our backs on the past by privatizing valuable public enterprises.
>
> The erosion of public funding for higher education in Canada . . . has been extensive and consequential. Provincial expenditures on higher education, measured in constant dollars, fell 12 per cent between 1992–93 and 1999–2000. University revenues from government sources dropped from 74.5 per cent in 1978 to 55.6 per cent in 1998, and tuition fees rose 224 per cent between 1981 and 1998.
>
> The bleakest scenario suggests that in the years ahead humanities and social science programs are more likely to face death by a thousand cuts than by the guillotine.

So, increasingly, across the country, university autonomy is being compromised. Corporate rather than academic protocols are being followed, academic research is more and more dependent on corporate funding and priorities, autonomous intellectual practices and enquiry are being subverted. Perhaps even more worrisome is the potential for challenges by American private universities for government funding under NAFTA or future GATS agreements. This is not some vague, paranoid hypothetical danger, but a real and ominous possibility in the opinion of numerous international trade and higher education experts. In Axelrod's words,

> The greater the degree of privatization and commercialization [in educational institutions] the more vulnerable they are to challenge by foreign "competitors" seeking "fair" (i.e. similar) treatment.

---

[*] *Values in Conflict: The University, the Marketplace and the Trials of Liberal Education*, McGill-Queen's University Press, 2002.

Meaning that they can claim they *must* be eligible to receive comparative public funding for their private, for-profit colleges and universities.

> One final observation. Statistics Canada reports that "while the university participation rates for young people from low and middle SES [social-economic status] backgrounds were quite similar in 1986, by 1994 a wide gap has occurred between these two groups.

As tuition fees between 1990 and 2000 increased at six times the inflation rate "those from especially modest backgrounds were having greater difficulty in attending university."

In 1992/93 there were 771,300 undergraduate students enrolled in Canadian universities. By 1999/2000 that number had *fallen* by 51,400! Overall enrolment was down by 42,700 students despite a large increase in student-age population.

Statistics Canada reports that in 1998, "Young people from high-income families were more than twice as likely as those from low-income families to have participated in university education."* Is that the kind of post-secondary education system most Canadians want? I very much doubt it.

Axelrod points out that when the University of Western Ontario Medical School raised its tuition fees from $4,844 in 1998 to $10,000 in 2000, the average family income of the medical students climbed from $80,000 to $140,000!

As government funding has failed to meet demand, increasingly, according to Axelrod, there are

> Huge classes (taught primarily by teaching assistants and poorly-paid part-time faculty), diminishing library resources, minimal research funding and academic and research agendas driven increasingly by commercial interests.

All this will have to change, and change fast. As with medicare, Ottawa will have to inject additional dedicated funding into post-secondary education. And the provinces of Ontario, Alberta, and British Columbia are going to have to rescind some of their excessive corporate and high-

---

* Statistics Canada, *Perspectives*, Spring 2002.

income tax cuts so they can properly fund education in their provinces.

As I'm writing these words, the papers are full of headlines: "Law schools to more than double tuitions"; "U.B.C. fees going from $3,000 to $9,000"; "Tuition hikes of up to 321 per cent approved"; "Provinces ending tuition freezes."

In Sweden, Finland, Norway, the Netherlands, Denmark, Austria, and Greece, there are no tuition fees for nationals. In Ireland there are no fees for nationals who are full-time students. In Germany there are no tuition fees for either domestic or international students. In France there are no tuition fees at public universities for nationals, but there is a registration fee of about $80 (Canadian). Scotland and Wales have announced plans to scrap tuition fees. In England, if your family income is under £20,000, there are no tuition fees.

In Canada, once again, we're going in exactly the opposite direction, the American direction.

Harry Arthurs writes:

> Government grants are falling, tuition fees and student indebtedness are rising, private sector research partnerships are being encouraged, the state's monopoly on higher education is being questioned . . . These measures may further reduce the capacity, and ultimately the inclination of Canadian universities to resist globalization in its most importunate – American – manifestation.

One thing we Canadians must do is improve and expand our student loan system to give more students access to the loan programs. We need to raise the loan limits and extend the payback time after students leave university. We need to design repayment schemes so they better reflect earnings and do not create undue hardship. We need to keep interest costs on student loans low. We need to increase grant programs for low-income students.

If we're serious about being more competitive and more productive, and if we're serious about Canadians achieving a higher standard of living, it's imperative that we improve access to higher education and improve the quality of our universities.

Another thing we *must* do, beginning in high school and continuing into college and university, is teach students civic responsibility, how politics works, why it's important to be politically involved, the shortcomings and strengths of various electoral systems, how political parties operate, how leaders and candidates are chosen, how politics is financed, how provincial and federal politics could be democratized, and a whole host of other matters relating to how democracy is supposed to function, how it often fails us, and how it can and must be improved.

These courses should be mandatory; their whole purpose should be to interest students in the democratic political processes and to encourage active participation in them.

And, by the way, isn't it just great that you can get a Ph.D. in history at most Canadian universities without ever taking a single Canadian History course?

Lastly, isn't it disgraceful that our two wealthiest provinces (Ontario and Alberta) rank so poorly (tenth and eighth) compared to the other provinces in terms of their overall commitment to post-secondary education when equity, accessibility, accountability, and quality are measured?*

Progress, Civilization, and the Lottery of Birth

Canada can't even begin to pretend that we're one of the best countries in the world when we have such shameful levels of individual, child, and family poverty. When we compare our poverty rates with those of most European countries, it's difficult to understand how we could have allowed such misery and suffering to exist in our own relatively affluent country.

What can we do about poverty in Canada? In my last book I spelled out a long list of solutions. Is there a magic cure? The answer is no. Is the elimination of most poverty a difficult, complex thing to accomplish? Again, the answer is no. All we have to do is look at what so many European countries have done. No magic, but simple common sense.

There's no room here to repeat the list of suggestions in my last book, but I do want to make a few quick points. The United Nations says it clearly:

---

* March 2002 study on higher education by the Canadian Centre for Policy Alternatives.

The fact that a child depends completely on others underlines the importance of obligations. The needs of very young children cannot wait – whether for care, food and warmth or for loving stimulus, basic education and health.[*]

Isn't it utterly disgraceful that our hypocritical politicians have allowed so many Canadian children to live in poverty when so many less fortunate countries have reduced child poverty to rates that are but a small fraction of our own? Shouldn't we be ashamed of ourselves for allowing this to continue?

Here's some of the things we need to do. We need to stop the provincial clawbacks of the Canada Child Benefit. Five provinces – Newfoundland and Labrador; New Brunswick; Nova Scotia; Quebec; and Manitoba (for children under seven) – do not claw back the benefit. What does it say when such relatively low-income provinces allow the poor to keep this supplement to their incomes, while well-to-do provinces such as Alberta and Ontario do not?

In effect, the clawbacks have to a large extent frozen welfare payouts and the Child Benefit helps the provinces to avoid their responsibilities to the poor.

We need to reconfigure the Child Benefit so that more money goes to the poor, and much less to higher-income families. By 2004, over 90 per cent of all families in Canada will be receiving the Canada Child Benefit, including families with incomes of up to $90,000. In two years, of $9 billion in benefits, families that are not poor will receive $3 billion. This is absurd. The very poor and the poor need that money to pay the rent and feed their kids. It's preposterous that they are shortchanged when billions of political dollars go to those who are not impoverished.

Three billion dollars in extra funds for programs to assist Canada's poor children would make an enormous difference.

There are now more than three hundred thousand poor single-parent mothers with children in Canada, about one hundred thousand more than when we began our "war against child poverty" in 1989. The average total monthly income for these poor families who have to rely on welfare is about $1,100. Most of those who are on welfare can't afford to go to work because they can't afford child care, and provincial

---

[*] *Human Development Report,* 2000.

clawbacks produce little net benefit from minimum-wage employment income.

Despite the fact that child care in Canada has been a prominent public issue for over thirty years, only Quebec and British Columbia have had decent provincial child care, and Gordon Campbell's government is sharply curtailing the B.C. programs. Yet year after year after year there has been strong public support for a national child care program in public-opinion polls all across the country.

Canada is one of the few developed countries in the world without a national child care program; it's time we joined the many civilized countries that have one.

Canada is also one of a handful of developed countries with no national affordable-housing program.

In the winter of 2002 – thousands of Canadians will be turned away from packed shelters across the country; many of them will end up on the streets, in ravines, and under bridges. In every Canadian city there will be thousands of households waiting, to no avail, for low-income housing.

Apparently the Liberal government in Ottawa is unimpressed by tragedy and deprivation. Or perhaps they are relying on that noted authority, David Frum, who advised that "the whole phenomenon of homelessness is a con."*

As they say, it takes one to know one.

Today, as you are reading these words, all across Canada there are hungry children and hungry adults, including parents who give up their food so their children can have something to eat. Most of these hungry people are from low-wage working families. The biggest causes for so much hunger in Canada are escalating rents, inadequate and eroding minimum wages, and social policies which fail to ensure the well being of those in need.

Now consider the words of Canada's first ministers after their September 2000 meeting on early childhood services:

> every child should be valued and have the opportunities to develop his or her unique physical, emotional, intellectual, spiritual and creative potential.

---

* *National Post*, January 6, 2001.

A much better communiqué would have promised:

> every child will have enough good quality food, proper clothing and decent shelter.

It would have been much more meaningful. And it would have been much more meaningful if they had announced a badly needed national school-lunch program.

Why do other countries have such low poverty rates? First of all, they really care about the poor, about a fair, egalitarian society. Secondly, they have better tax, distribution of income, wage, housing, and child policies than we do.

A United Nations publication tells us that

> Countries with good unemployment benefits, family allowances and services, disability and sickness benefits, and other forms of social assistance have low poverty rates.
>
> ... clearly ... no country with a high rate of social expenditure has a high rate of child poverty.

For example, Norway cut their child poverty rate from 15.9 per cent to 3.9 per cent, Finland from 16.4 per cent to 4.3 per cent, Sweden from 23.4 per cent to 2.6 per cent, France from 28.7 per cent to 7.9 per cent, etc.

Canada desperately needs a new – and *this time*, a meaningful – commitment to a real and substantial reduction of poverty, beginning with measures that will alleviate the suffering of children. We can't possibly be the best country, or even one of the best, unless we make this a priority.

When the Bad Guys Become the Police

There's a long list of other things we can do to make Canada a better country. I'll touch on a few of them very briefly.

For our corporate plutocracy, bigger and bigger is better and better. But in many sectors of the Canadian economy, excessive corporate concentration is already a serious problem. When a few firms dominate the market, true free enterprise and competition become a myth. Canada needs much tougher anti-combines legislation. Compared to most other developed countries, we're hopelessly weak in our record of allowing oligopolies to dominate business activities.

Over ten years ago, James Gillies, who has served on the boards of more than thirty-five major companies, wrote:

> While anti-combines legislation to prevent the restraint of trade has been on the books in one form or another since the 1880s, the laws have never been seriously enforced. Unlike the United States where anti-trust legislation has usually been vigorously enforced, in Canada there have been few if any mergers turned down by government agencies because they might result in a restraint of trade.
>
> Approximately 80 per cent of all the companies in the Toronto Stock Exchange Composite Index have a controlling shareholder with the balance widely-held; in the United States it is almost exactly the reverse – about 80 per cent of the firms in the Standard and Poor's Index are widely held and only 20 per cent have a controlling shareholder.
>
> With a few exceptions, Canadian businessmen have never wanted or encouraged competition.*

The combination of excessive foreign ownership and excessive corporate concentration is lethal. The result is a relatively small number of large, powerful, dominant firms that are used to getting their way and only rarely fail to do so. These are also the firms that fund politics in Canada.

The degree of corporate concentration in the media in Canada is alarming. To allow such a small number of corporations (almost all owned by men to the far-right of the political spectrum) to control so many newspapers, magazines, television and radio stations, is to say in effect that Canadians are best served when heavily neo-conservative political, social, and economic philosophy is served up on a daily basis to the vast majority of our citizens. Instead, we need a healthy, balanced mix of left, right, and centre. We need to make sure that most Canadians do not find themselves in the ideological trap that results when the same owners control the daily newspaper and television stations in their communities.

---

* _Inside Guide_, June 1991.

And we need to have a *much* more effective new body to replace the CRTC as soon as possible.

Peter C. Newman, in his chapter "Taking Over the National Agenda" in his 1998 book *Titans: How the New Canadian Establishment Seized Power*, tells how Tom d'Aquino and the Business Council on National Issues took over the revamping of Ottawa's competition policy from a weak minister and a government with little desire for effective new legislation. The result?

> There were no provisions for class-action suits; conspiracies remained just about impossible to prove; and prosecutions were moved from criminal to civil courts. It was the only time in the history of capitalism that any country allowed its anti-monopoly legislation to be written by the very people it was meant to police.

Newman sums it up: "Whoever has the money has the power."

It *doesn't* have to be that way. It's certainly the way that both Canada and the U.S. are now run. But we can change that. Meanwhile, keep in mind when you hear how urgent and necessary it is to create even bigger corporations so that they can be competitive, you're inevitably hearing from the very same corporations that have already made Canada the country with the least competition anywhere.

The best country needs a broadly owned corporate sector with real competition, not just hollow, misleading slogans about the market and free enterprise.

"We Can Hardly Save the Country by Destroying It"

Year after year after year, Canadians hear and read the same sort of nonsense from some of our politicians, editorial writers, and columnists: "Canada is overcentralized . . . Ottawa has far too much power . . . the provinces are being shortchanged."

Whether it's a Lucien Bouchard, a Bernard Landry, a Ralph Klein, a Mike Harris, a Preston Manning, or a Stephen Harper, the story is always the same: there's far too much power in Ottawa and a long list of powers must be transferred to the provinces. (Interestingly enough, you never hear the provincial premiers talking about transferring some of *their* powers to the municipalities or to the cities that badly need them).

Is government in Canada over-centralized?

Beginning in the 1960s, and in every decade thereafter, the federal government's share of total government revenues and expenditures has been shrinking. Where Ottawa was at one time spending over 65 per cent of total government spending, today it's closer to 40 per cent, as provincial, territorial, and local governments have all increased their shares.

Canada's central government's 41.3 per cent share of the country's total government revenue is far below the OECD's average for federal governments (49.4 per cent). In the U.S., Washington accounts for 65.6 per cent of all government spending.

In a United Nations list of the top fifty "high development countries," thirty-three central governments have a greater share of total government revenue as a percentage of GDP than Canada.[*]

So, contrary to all the nonsense from our premiers and the Alliance Party and their journalistic supporters, Canada is already one of the most decentralized federal countries anywhere in the world.

Here's a quick look at Canadian government revenues as a percentage of GDP:

	Federal	Provincial and Local
1970	16.7	26.8
1980	15.7	29.9
1990	17.9	32.3
2000	16.9	30.6

You get the same sort of results if you compare expenditures, or if you subtract grants from one level of government to another.

By next year, Ottawa's share will likely be down to 15.5 per cent.[†]

Rather than being overcentralized, many informed observers believe that successive federal governments, particularly under Trudeau, Mulroney, and Chrétien, have transferred so much jurisdictional and

---

[*] United Nations *Human Development Report*, 2000.

[†] Budget 2000 and *Finances of the Nation*, 2001, Canadian Tax Foundation. The above figures include grants and transfers, hence there is some double-counting.

taxing power over to the provinces that the country is close to being ungovernable. Combined with the extensive emasculating powers of the FTA and NAFTA, the federal government is in a drastically weakened position.

Journalist Giles Gherson put it this way:

> No other federal government has constrained its own spending power in this fashion. Least of all Washington, which is forever fashioning legislation mandating states to fulfil specific requirements to access federal funding for everything from road building to welfare.

Gherson believes that the result of all the devolution of powers to the provinces

> will shift Canada from its post-war structure of being a relatively loose federal state – but a nation state nonetheless – towards a federation of sovereign states that operate through a weak central authority.[*]

Columnist Andrew Coyne is equally perceptive:

> Of all the ills that might be said to afflict Canada, the one thing we are *not* suffering from is an overly centralized system of government . . . if anything, the pendulum has swung too far in the direction of devolution already and if we were serious about reforming the federation we should find there was more need to strengthen federal powers than provincial.
>
> We can hardly save the country by destroying it, which I am afraid is what the devolution movement amounts to.

Coyne goes on to make another important point:

> In no other federation in the world has the First Ministers Conference or its equivalent become the sort of parallel government – unaccountable and unconstitutional – that it has become in Canada.

And *why* have successive governments in Canada abandoned so much power to the provinces?

---

[*] Southam News, April and August 1997.

Simple: it is to mask the devolution of powers to Quebec; to make the paying of ransom to nationalist blackmailers less odious.*

So Ottawa hands over labour-market training, immigration, social housing, environmental legislation, and tourism, and complete control over forestry and mining, to the provinces in successive sweeping retreats. Most of these powers were transferred in an effort to placate Quebec separatists, who will never be satisfied, no matter how much you ever give them.

Coyne made a further point after Ralph Klein's embarrassing performance in Moscow, disgracing himself and joining other premiers in "grabbing for the microphone like a gang of drunken exchange students on Karaoke night":

> When the President of the United States goes abroad, he does not pack all 50 governors on Air Force One with him. Neither does the Prime Minister of Australia, nor the Chancellor of Germany nor any other federal leader you can think of.†

Can anyone remember a U.S. president sitting down for a couple of days at a nationally televised conference with the fifty American governors to discuss power-sharing, or any other matter?

In the past, when Ottawa transferred money to the provinces, the payments were meant specifically for health care or education or social services. But, since the Liberals replaced the Canada Assistance Plan with the lump-sum Canada Health and Social Transfer (CHST), the provinces can now spend the money as they wish; it's a block grant with few strings attached. In the past, the provinces were required to maintain certain social-services standards. For the most part, these requirements have disappeared.

According to the Caledon Institute of Social Policy, as a result of Ottawa's 1999 Social Union Framework Agreement with the provinces, the federal government can no longer firmly attach pullable strings to its financial assistance. No new programs can be launched unless Ottawa

---

* *Policy Options*, IRPP, April 1997.
† *National Post*, February 18, 2002.

gets the agreement of at least six provinces, and even then the provinces can design their own programs.

Carol Goar of the *Toronto Star* writes:

> Slowly and painfully, it is beginning to dawn on social activists that there isn't going to be a national child care strategy, or a national drug plan or any new pan-Canadian program.

Why would that be?

> The Prime Minister has bargained away most of Ottawa's power to combat poverty, fix medicare, build a highly educated workforce and tackle inequities at birth.
>
> Canadians who once looked to their national government to solve societal problems must now ask Ottawa to transfer more money to the provinces, hoping the benefits will reach them.

And, it will be entirely up to the provinces how they use the money.

> There used to be a Liberal Party that stood for a Canada of shared values and collective social responsibility. Its leaders used to be willing to fight for national goals and national standards.[*]

What the ill-advised Social Framework Agreement did was tie Ottawa's hands in the future evolution of social policy. As in the case of medicare, a paralyzed federal government is unable to show strong leadership where strong leadership is desperately needed. So the premiers now say "We don't care about the federal government, we're going to call the shots on health care and we're going to act, whether Ottawa likes it or not."

Aside from the provincial premiers, some of our staunch provincial chauvinists, the Alliance Party, Quebec nationalists, and our major think tanks, who else has been pushing for a weaker national government? Who else but big business, formerly in the guise of the Business Council on National Issues? When the BCNI released a paper calling for even greater decentralization, Dalton Camp accurately described it in a sentence as

---

[*] September 23, 2000.

"laying waste to federalism to make it easier for transnational corporatism to do business after the dismantling of government."*

Big business doesn't like government and it hates a strong government. Give the provinces more and more power; weaken Ottawa, so corporations can play one province against the other. Lower your taxes or we'll move to Alberta. Get rid of those burdensome environmental laws or we're heading to Ontario. Give us bigger grants or we're off to Alabama.

Jack Mintz of the C. D. Howe Institute wants Ottawa to hand over to the provinces the taxing authority for the Canada Health and Social Transfer. So then the provinces would be completely in charge. There would be no "stifling" national standards in health care.

In the words of Howard Pawley, former premier of Manitoba, proposals by the BCNI for the further decentralization of federal powers would lead to the shredding of Canada's social fabric . . . an abandonment of our national sense of community. Such suggested restrictions of Ottawa's powers, had they

> been in effect 30 years ago, would have prevented the establishment of Canada's present health care system. Any chance of a future administration introducing a national child care program will be eliminated.
>
> Such an enfeeblement of the federal government would lead to a form of patchwork federalism in which individual Canadians would receive wildly disparate levels of service, depending on the province in which they happen to live.
>
> The proposed legislation changes would extinguish the very essence of Canada.

According to *Saturday Night* magazine, "Thomas Courchene is our most provocative and best policy thinker" and "the country's most influential policy thinker." "And he thinks the provinces should run the country."†
For Courchene, rather than thinking of Canada as a country,

> It is time to view Canada as a series of north-south, cross-border economies with quite distinct industrial structures. British Columbia is orientated towards the Pacific Rim and the U.S. Northwest; the

---

* *Toronto Star*, August 13, 1997.
† December 1996.

energy-based Alberta economy competes with the oil and gas producing regions of the Texas gulf; the breadbaskets of Saskatchewan and
Manitoba keep a competitive watch on the U.S. Midwest; the Great
Lakes economies of Ontario and Quebec are integrated with each other
and with their counterparts south of the border; and the fortunes of
Atlantic Canada likely will increasingly be linked to the Atlantic Rim
and the Boston/New York axis . . .

Here's more wisdom from Courchene:

the more Canadians do business with the world, the more they see the
central government as a hindrance rather than a help.

Andrew Coyne sums it up well:

The federal government is the only government of all Canadians. The
very existence of a federal government, as distinct from those of the
provinces, presupposes a Canadian nation, a single self-governing body
of citizens from which it derives its sovereignty and to which alone it
is answerable.[*]

The question for all Canadians is do we want to be a nation, or do we
want to just be a bunch of people living in fragmented provinces? We
can only be a nation if the federal government reasserts its authority and
demonstrates strong leadership and an ambitious vision in the future.

What a refreshing, long-overdue change that would be! Once again,
the polls show how different the wishes of the majority of Canadians
are from those of our radical-right plutocracy. Earlier this year an
Environics poll showed that not only did most Canadians oppose giving
more powers to the provinces, but they supported increasing the powers
of the federal government, including in areas such as health and education. "In the latest poll, Environics found support for decentralization
has substantially evaporated."[†]

Nevertheless, what was once a national community of dreams is
now more and more a loose federation of increasingly foreign-owned

---

[*] *Edmonton Journal*, June 5, 1997.
[†] Southam News, March 18, 2002.

fiefdoms, easy pickings for any aspect of manifest destiny that U.S. corporations or the American government may choose to pursue.

As already mentioned, Canada's provinces have far stronger and wider powers than U.S. states, but are also more powerful than the German *Länder*, the French *départements*, Australian states, or regional governments in England and Japan.

Enough is enough, or, more likely, it is far too much already. It's time to stop dismembering our country. With the abdication of federal authority comes the disappearance of national standards and a patchwork Canada, a slow but relentless unravelling of the fabric of the country. Despite the fact that Canadians overwhelmingly rejected both Meech Lake and the Charlottetown accord, they are now effectively getting the terms of those failed agreements by the back door. Polls continue to show Canadians strongly identify more with their national government then they do with local or regional governments. And Canadians understand and support "the unique role of the federal state in constructing a highly relevant source of national identity and belonging."[*] Canadians fully understand the importance of a strong central government, and, according to Ekos, "devolution and decentralization are codes for federal withdrawal and abandoning responsibilities."

And if we continue devolution in the future as we have in the past? University of Toronto political scientist David Cameron says of Canada:

> It'll become like the Holy Roman Empire. It will just fade away. There'll be no need for it. The dukes and the earls and sovereigns running the provinces will be what actually counts.[†]

And won't that be just great?

To be one of the best countries in the world, we need a strong national government with a clear vision of a truly great country for all of its citizens. What we don't need is the new Northern Balkan States.

---

[*] Ekos Research Associates, 2000.
[†] Southam Newspapers, no date.

Dancing to the Americans' Tune

The same gang of slick, well-financed hucksters who first talked Canadians into what they promised would be an "exclusive" free trade deal with the U.S. that would bring us vastly improved productivity; jobs, jobs, jobs; guaranteed access to the U.S. market; and a higher standard of living, soon announced that the FTA wasn't enough. We had to expand free trade into a NAFTA, with Mexico joining in. So much for exclusivity.

Now, exactly the same promoters say that the two "trade" agreements just aren't doing the job; Canada must go further, *much* further, into more formal "deep" integration with the U.S. The next urgent and "inevitable" (there's that word again) step must be a customs union, a "grand strategic bargain" in d'Aquino's words, since NAFTA is "a piece of unfinished business."

Former Liberal external affairs minister Mitchell Sharp warned way back in 1972 that free trade with the U.S. would tend "towards a full customs union and economic union as a matter of internal logic . . . Canada would be obliged to seek political union with its superpower neighbour."[*]

In 2001, Peter C. Newman wrote that "Measures to expand free trade will inevitably lead to the end of our dollar – and then our sovereignty."[†] Free trade will lead to a customs union and then a full economic union. The result "would mean nothing less than the disappearance of Canada as an effective, independent nation."

I asked Donald Macdonald for his opinion about a customs union. He is very strongly opposed. He said that most people who were proposing this step didn't understand the ominous ramifications; they thought a customs union simply meant that there would be no duty to pay at the border.[**]

Even the continentalist Macdonald Royal Commission, which was the launching pad for a "leap of faith" into free trade, was apprehensive:

---

[*] From Peter C. Newman's *The End of Canada? Maclean's*, January 8, 2001.
[†] Ibid.
[**] Telephone conversation, December 5, 2001.

For two major reasons this Commission rejects the common-market form of free trade as inappropriate in the North American context. A common market requires that a uniform set of trade and allied commercial policies be applied to all non-member countries. In the past, Canada has not always wished to follow U.S. initiatives on trade with the outside world: for instance Canada maintained trade relations with China and Cuba after the United States ceased to do so. If we Canadians are to preserve our autonomy in foreign political and economic policies, our government cannot accept a common market's legal restrictions on its capacity for independent action.[*]

During the great free trade debates between 1985 and 1989, I twice debated the number-one pro-free-trade guru, economist Richard Lipsey. The first debate was in front of a large crowd of diplomats from External Affairs in the auditorium of the Lester B. Pearson building on Sussex Drive in Ottawa. The second debate was sponsored by the *Kingston Whig-Standard*, and was televised across Canada by CTV.

During the debates, Richard Lipsey said that, while he was in favour of the FTA, he was opposed to going into a customs union, because it would likely mean the end of Canada.

This spring, I called Richard Lipsey at his home on Bowen Island and asked if he would like to give me a couple of paragraphs for this book. Here they are:

As a large superpower the United States often uses trade policy as an instrument of foreign policy – as when it has restricted trade with China, Vietnam, and Cuba for political reasons. As a superpower, the United States would dominate any "joint" decision on a common commercial policy. If NAFTA were a customs union, Canada and Mexico would, for example, now be joined with the United States in what many Canadians regard as its misguided restrictions on trade with Cuba. Canada wants to avoid becoming a U.S. puppet in foreign policy and desires to preserve its rights to do what it has done in the past: trade on terms not allowed to Americans with countries such as the former

---

[*] Report of the Royal Commission on the Economic Union and Development Prospects for Canada, 1985, vol. 1, p. 303.

U.S.S.R., China, Vietnam, and Cuba. For this reason, it is Canadian policy that the NAFTA should remain an FTA.[*]

I hasten to add that this certainly *was* Canadian policy and one with which I strongly agreed. If Canadian policy were to change and try and push NAFTA into a full customs union, or even to accept passively that this was to happen, it would entail a severe loss of Canadian independence in the sphere of foreign policy. We would then have to dance to the American's tune on what they call trade policy but which is really political foreign policy.

Well, that's all pretty clear, isn't it? Even some of the most vocal and passionate proponents of the FTA are dead set against a customs union.

But not today's avid, continentalist Americanizing zealots. Liberal MP Tony Valeri and supreme Liberal integrationalist Maurizio Bevilacqua, chair of the House of Commons Finance Committee, want that committee and the Commons Economic Development Committee to begin studying a customs union.

As is often the case, McGill economist and *National Post* columnist William Watson is front-and-centre in moves to integrate Canada into the U.S.:

> What's different nowadays is that even long-time proponents of economic liberalism seem to admit that free trade is not enough . . . we have to integrate our two economies much more than most of us thought necessary in the 1980s.[†]

And, how should this "deep" integration proceed? We should be

> entering into a customs union with the United States [even though] this would clearly reduce our sovereignty.[**]

And then? Well, of course – we'll need to adopt the U.S. dollar. If Watson can be relied upon to trample upon Canadian sovereignty on a regular

---

[*] *Western Hemisphere Trade Integration: A Canadian–Latin American Dialogue with Patricio Meller*, Hampshire, U.K.: Macmillan, 1997.

[†] *National Post*, August 18, 2001.

[**] *Financial Post*, September 29, 2001.

basis, Drew Fagan sometimes makes the Montreal economist look like an economic nationalist:

> What remains unspoken is the logical, if not inevitable end to this process: A Canada–U.S. customs union that would significantly deepen economic connections but also have significant sovereignty repercussions.[*]

There's that "inevitable" again. What *is* inevitable is that people like Watson, Fagan, Thomas Courchene, and the C. D. Howe Institute, and much of our corporate plutocracy, consistently promote policies which erode Canadian sovereignty.

Sovereignty is a synonym for self-determination and freedom.

What about the ramifications for Canadian foreign and defence policy that the Macdonald Commission, Richard Lipsey, and others have warned about?

Canadian historians Norman Hillmer and Jack Granatstein quote Canada's brilliant ambassador to Washington, Charles Ritchie, as calling Washington's interference in Canadian defence policy in 1963 "heavy-handed and overbearing," prompting "the very Canadian question, 'Who the hell do they think they are?'"[†] Can anyone, even in their wildest dreams, ever imagine two of our more recent ambassadors to the U.S., Allan Gotlieb or Raymond Chrétien, having the courage or convictions to say or even privately think anything even remotely similar?

So, what should a more independent Canada be doing in relation to foreign and defence policy?

In 2001, in a list of twenty-two OECD countries, Canada was eighteenth in official development assistance as a percentage of GNP. At .23 per cent, we were far behind the generosity of countries such as Denmark (1.06 per cent), the Netherlands, Sweden, and Norway. At the very bottom of the list was the world's wealthiest country, the United States, at .10 per cent (compared to .75 per cent in 1960). And, how do Americans feel about their foreign aid contributions? Fifty-three per cent say they're too high.[**]

---

[*] *Globe and Mail*, December 8, 2001.

[†] Charles Ritchie, *Storm Signals*, Toronto: McClelland & Stewart, 2001, p. 29, and *Diplomatic Passport*, Toronto: McClelland & Stewart, 2001, p. 166.

[**] *National Post*, March 23, 2002.

Canada's foreign-aid contributions in 2001 were at a thirty-year low. Even with the 8-per-cent increases promised by Jean Chrétien in March 2002, it will take us many years to return to the .45 level when the Liberals were elected in 1993. (Canada made a commitment to contribute at least .7 per cent to foreign aid in the 1960s and the Liberal's 1993 election Red Book promised more aid for poor countries. At the time, we were in fifth place in development assistance.)

Shouldn't Canada do more to help the world's impoverished developing countries? And doesn't it strike you as pathetic that after eight years of cutting foreign aid, Jean Chrétien now wants to increase it by 8 per cent a year, so that in about fourteen years from now we'll almost be up to the current level of the Nordic countries? Some journalists have actually suggested that Chrétien was thinking of foreign aid as "his legacy."

Let's stop and consider what defence spending should be all about. Isn't defence supposed to be about protecting our citizens, our freedom, our sovereignty? Shouldn't we, for example, concentrate on building up our armed forces so they can properly inspect and protect our three-ocean borders?

But, if our armed forces are subsumed in an American military organization, a "Northern Command," as many are now suggesting, won't we be abandoning our sovereignty and freedom that we are supposed to be defending?

For example, let's consider the Northwest Passage, which in a few years will be navigable for commercial or military vessels for most or all of the year. The U.S. considers this vitally important passageway to be international waters. They say they can use it without our permission. Of course that would mean anyone could use it without our permission. Anyone like terrorists, smugglers, drug or weapons dealers, boatloads of illegal immigrants.

Shouldn't establishing a good military presence in the Arctic be one of our top defence priorities? That means more than a small group of Inuit Arctic Rangers making periodic snowmobile excursions.

Yes, we absolutely must spend more on our armed forces. But we need to do so keeping our own priorities in mind. In a 2000 poll, *Maclean's* asked whether Canada should invest in a stronger and more up-to-date military or fund housing for all the homeless in Canada. While 19 per cent opted for a stronger military, 75 per cent chose housing for the homeless. More recently, in April 2002, a COMPAS Inc. poll showed that 65 per cent of Canadians said they would not favour increasing the military budget at the expense of health care and education.[*]

This said, we have to pay careful attention to what our own defence goals and priorities should be. Obviously, we need to replace the ancient Sea King helicopters, the sooner the better. We need to beef up our long-range air reconnaissance and transportation capabilities. We need a permanent military presence in the Arctic.

Above all, we have to plan our defence polices on the basis of probabilities, not possibilities. In other words, how much more should we spend, and for what purpose? Should we plan for invasion? Who then might invade us? Probable, not possible. Do we need more infantry? For what purpose? Shouldn't defence against terrorism be one of our top priorities? And won't Bush's destabilizing National Missile Defense Plan endanger rather than protect us?

And then there's perhaps what might well be our very best defence strategy. Wouldn't we be *much* better off, and wouldn't many people around the world be much better off, if we focused our activities on peacekeeping and humanitarian assistance? Wouldn't this be a wonderful way to help other people, a way which almost automatically will enhance our own security?

Shouldn't we be promoting multilateralism in the United Nations and in other world bodies, instead of attaching ourselves too closely to American unilateralism and aggression? Canada had a much-admired role as a middle power in the past; we should make our goal to re-establish ourselves as the middle power with no colonial baggage, no record of aggression, no long list of enemies, a country that promotes human rights and international agreements to promote disarmament and peace, helping the afflicted, and doing the best job we can to join with other countries to work towards the reduction of world poverty.

In the words of Richard Gwyn, "we are relevant internationally only to the extent that we are seen as the good guys." I completely agree. In the past we have been admired as "the good guys." We can be similarly regarded in the future by returning to our earlier policies and goals. There *is* a time to go to war. We recognized that with no hesitation in 1939; the U.S. did not. There *is* a time to fight for peace. Canadians should

---

[*] *National Post*, April 30, 2002.

demand of our government that world peace and disarmament should be the cornerstones of our foreign policy.

Military strategists are increasingly saying that, in the eyes of the U.S., the military power even of countries such as France and Germany is irrelevant. No matter how many more billions of dollars Canada spends for armaments, how relevant would it really be? Lewis Lapham quotes Yale historian Paul Kennedy, at the Manhattan 2002 World Economic Forum, who said:

> the grand amalgam of U.S. power is so colossal that only a madman would attack it [given the] mind-boggling and staggering supremacy of America's military and economic power. In military terms the United States is the only player on the field that counts and all its European allies amount to little more than minor appendages, ancillary and of no significance except in a smallish way.[*]

If European military power is deemed insignificant,[†] what should our own goals be for our own military?

George W. Bush has said "Those who are not with us are against us." This is nonsense and we need to tell him so. Canadians are, almost to a person, with the U.S. in wanting to help crush terrorism, in our desire to beef up continental security. But we will *not* be with the U.S. in aggressive military behaviour that cannot be justified. The U.S., as indicated earlier, will soon want us to join with them in their dangerous, nonsensical plans for a missile defence shield and the weaponizing of outer space. Canada should firmly reject participation. Last year the United Nations voted 156 – 0 against the weaponizing of outer space. Canada, Russia, and China were all enthusiastic backers of the resolution, but if we become part of the American Northern Command we'll have no choice but to support the U.S. Star Wars plan.

If the U.S. does proceed with their plans, there is a common-sense way in which we could contribute to our own defence and sovereignty. I can see no reason why *we* could not offer to develop and man early-warning

---

[*] *Harper's Magazine*, April 2002.

[†] James Travers writes that U.S. military expenditures are now greater than that of Britain, Russia, Japan, Germany, France, China, and the next eight countries combined. *Toronto Star*, July 6, 2002.

stations across the Arctic and on our east and west coasts. The Americans would have to pay for most of the costs of these installations and their maintenance by Canadians. However, before we would agree to this new warning system on Canadian soil, the U.S. would have to reciprocate by agreeing to an ironclad treaty acknowledging Canadian sovereignty in our Arctic waters. Joint Canada–U.S. surveillance makes sense, but under the right conditions. Participating in the weaponizing of outer space makes no sense.

Perhaps the Americans won't require the warning system. Good. But whatever we do, we must maintain an independent defence policy focused on Canadian priorities and Canadian sovereignty.

Any student of history will know that American and Canadian military and defence objectives have often been very different. That will most certainly frequently be the case in the future unless we foolishly follow the advice of our Americanizers and abandon our freedom to chose our own priorities.

We need to continue to work within the multilateral Conference on Disarmament for the negotiation of a Convention for the Non-Weaponization of Outer Space, whether the Americans like it or not. We need to strongly support the 187-nation Nuclear Non-Proliferation Treaty, the Anti-Ballistic Missile Treaty, and the Comprehensive Nuclear Test Ban Treaty, whether the Americans like it or not. And we should avoid like the plague any formal involvement in the American Northern Command. We will have more important priorities of our own for our scarce defence dollars and for our strengthened military.

Let's All Stop Breathing

Should we let the U.S. set our environmental policies? Of course, says the Canadian Manufacturers and Exporters Association, headed by former Mulroney cabinet minister Perrin Beatty. According to Alan Toulin of the *National Post*'s Ottawa bureau,

> The CME said it worried that Canada, by deviating from the policies of the United States, its major trading partner, will create additional

costs for Canadian industry, rendering it less competitive with its U.S. counterpart.[*]

The logic here is clear. If there are Canadian laws or policies designed to protect the environment or guard against contaminated food or that might hurt automobile sales or protect infants from insecticides, or you name it, we better forget about it and go with whatever standards the Americans use.

Forget about global warming, ditch the Kyoto Agreement; George W. Bush says he has a better idea. But experts now say that under the Bush plan U.S. greenhouse-gas emissions will increase by over 300 million tonnes within the next five years.

Joining Perrin Beatty and friends is the good old dependable Canadian Chamber of Commerce, and, of course, the patriotic Canadian petroleum industry and their buddy Ralph Klein.

Eric Reguly spells out the reliability of the anti-Kyoto crowd's assertions:

> The figures used . . . are as compelling as those found on Enron's financial statements. The Chamber of Commerce claimed that meeting the Kyoto requirements would lop $30 billion a year from GDP by 2010. Not to be outdone, the Canadian Manufacturers and Exporters throw out a figure of $40 billion, plus the loss of 450,000 manufacturing jobs. The Alberta government tossed in a cost range of $25 billion to $40 billion and as many as 70,000 jobs. Why stop there? Do we hear $100 billion and a million jobs? A lobby group could invent any figure and the media would dutifully report it as if it had some basis in reality.[†]

As Reguly points out, exactly the same sort of threats were made when we took steps towards curtailing the acid rain which was killing thousands of lakes in Eastern Canada. Jobs would be lost. Smelters would have to shut down. Towns would disappear.

It's too bad that the likes of the Chamber of Commerce haven't thought to examine what will happen if global warming continues apace. Perhaps none of the Chamber members have children or grandchildren.

---

[*] *National Post*, February 8, 2002.
[†] *Globe and Mail*, March 5, 2002.

And it's too bad none of the anti-Kyoto crowd seems to have tried to measure the positive impact of developing new technologies and improving existing technologies to cut down on noxious emissions.

A national public-opinion poll taken in 2001 shows that more than three-quarters of Canadians believe that the quality of the environment has declined.[*] And a study of OECD countries the same year said that Canada was the second-worst of twenty-nine OECD countries in its care for environment, better only than the United States.[†]

And, in some areas, U.S. environmental policies are better than ours. Several U.S. states are now well ahead of Canada in reducing greenhouse gases. In 1997, Canada was one of the worst producers of greenhouse gases in the world, behind only the United States and Australia in our carbon dioxide emissions measured in metric tons per person.[**]

In July 2001, as Mark Mackinnon of the *Globe* noted,

> Canada, its environmental sheen already dimmed by its controversial position in international climate-change negotiations, will join the United States in rejecting a new G8 report calling for countries to stop subsidizing fossil fuels and nuclear power.
>
> Critics lashed out at Canada's impending move, saying it shows the federal government placed a higher priority on maintaining export levels than it does on reducing the emissions of pollutants that cause global warming.[††]

In 1995, a large group of scientists from around the world warned of potential catastrophic results if significant steps weren't taken to reduce greenhouse gases caused by burning fossil fuels. That was seven long years ago. More recently Spain's Environment Minister Jaume Matas, who at this writing is also the European Union's president, warned: "Global warming is the greatest environmental problem facing humanity."[***]

Fear not, Ralph Klein has joined Ronald Reagan in the pantheon of environmental deep thinkers. According to Reagan, all that carbon

---

[*] Léger Marketing poll, August 2001.

[†] *Canada vs. the OECD, An Environmental Comparison*, David Boyd, University of Victoria.

[**] *World Bank Atlas*, 2001.

[††] *Globe and Mail*, July 13, 2001.

[***] *National Post*, March 5, 2002.

dioxide was caused by trees. According to Klein, the problem would be solved if we all stopped breathing.

An editorial in the *Toronto Star* points to the Liberal government's appalling lack of leadership:

> For two decades, Canadians have been told that if something isn't done, global warming could cause economic and political havoc throughout the world. Rising seas could destroy coastal cities, prime agricultural land could turn to wasteland – the risks were high enough to prompt the U.S. Energy Department to issue this warning in 1986: "Human effects on atmospheric composition may yet overwhelm the life-support system crafted in nature over billions of years."
>
> It is nothing short of a disgrace that Ottawa, the provinces and Canadian business are still debating the merits of the international agreement on global warming that Canada signed nearly five years ago.[*]

In 1993, the same Liberals promised action with respect to climate change far more ambitious than anything in the Kyoto accord, promising to cut carbon dioxide emissions by 20 per cent from 1988 levels by 2005. Instead, over the last decade, emissions have risen by almost 20 per cent.

David Suzuki writes:

> According to federal government statistics, as many as 16,000 Canadians die prematurely each year from air pollution.
>
> In many European nations, gasoline costs twice what it does here and the tax revenue generated is used to improve public transportation and encourage energy efficiency.
>
> Canada meanwhile, is the only country in the developed world that does not provide meaningful federal funding for public transportation.

So, what *should* we be doing? There's a whole long list:

- We should develop and deploy the world's most efficient wind turbines instead of importing turbines from Denmark, and we should locate wind farms in strategic locations across the country. Turbines

---

[*] March 3, 2002.

already are more efficient and cheaper than nuclear power and are competitive with coal and natural gas.

- We should be spending less money on fossil fuel incentives and more on solar power research and deployment, and in particular on the type of solar shingles that the Japanese have developed. Even the U.S. has good solar panel tax incentives. The cost and efficiency of solar energy has been improving rapidly.
- We should convert our coal-burning generators into natural-gas generators, even if that means we have to reduce exports for air conditioning and to heat swimming pools in the U.S.
- We should accelerate legislation requiring more fuel-efficient vehicles and increase taxes on big gas-guzzling SUVs and inefficient minivans, and we should make transportation fuels containing ethanol mandatory.
- We should step up fuel-cell, tidal, and biomass research and development. We should accelerate research into large, stationary fuel cells.
- We should expand the use of hydro power to the best of our ability.
- We should raise the price of gasoline closer to European levels, and invest the substantial new tax revenue in public transportation.
- We should provide tax incentives to help homeowners and businesses to renovate to achieve greater conservation and to convert to renewable energy.

According to David Boyd of the University of Victoria, we've spent $40 billion in fossil fuel research-and-development incentives and less than $1 billion on renewable energy. In the future, public money should go into aggressive renewable-energy and hydrogen-economy research.

Some last points. If we let the Americans determine our responses to greenhouse gas emissions and global warming, what's the use of even having a country? And, how can we possibly aspire to being the best country in the world, or even one of the best, if we have a poor environmental record? In April 2002, a Decima poll showed that 78 per cent of Canadians favoured ratifying the Kyoto protocol. I hope that by the time this book is published we'll have done so.

Let's End the Brain Waste

If we're going to be the best country, or one of the best, we're going to have to step up immigration. By now, most Canadians know that our declining birth rate means that within a decade immigrants will have to make up *all* of our net labour-force growth (already it's in the 70–75-per-cent range). Simply put, we're not going to have enough workers and already we have huge skills shortages in some areas of industry. As well, since our population is aging, we're going to need more workers to help support those no longer in the labour force.

Until fairly recently, we've done an excellent job of welcoming immigrants and melding them into our communities and workforce. But sadly, that has changed in recent years. Highly qualified professionals are driving cabs because they have been denied access to their professions. A study by professor Jeff Reitz of the University of Toronto says that "persistent employment discrimination" and the resulting under-utilization of the skills of immigrants is costing the Canadian economy $15 billion a year in "brain waste." Haroon Siddiqui, editorial-page editor emeritus of the *Toronto Star*, points out that in 2000, 58 per cent of working-age immigrants had post-secondary education, compared to 43 per cent of the Canadian population. But many of these educated immigrants have been denied access to appropriate employment.

According to the Canadian Council on Social Development, racism and failure to recognize education and skills have been factors. As well,

> The large gaps in earnings between recent visible minority immigrants and other Canadians cannot be explained by inferior levels of formal education.

Where not too long ago the proportion of immigrants to Canada who lived on low incomes was only about one-third, the percentage is now over one-half.

Keeping qualified scientists, engineers, teachers, doctors, and others out of their profession is unforgivable. Unfortunately, not only has the federal government failed to show leadership on this issue, but the bureaucrats in the Department of Immigration have drawn up new rules for immigrants that will very severely restrict the entry into Canada of talented, valuable men and women. All across Canada there are hundreds of thousands of prominent and successful Canadians, in every field of endeavour you can think of, who were immigrants to our country, but would not be admitted today under the Chrétien government's new rules, which slam the door on the kind of capable, hard-working people who have built this country. The new immigration rules make no sense and it's beyond comprehension that the cabinet approved them.

Canada is far from perfect when it comes to openness and respect for minorities. But in many ways we've been much better than most. Now is the time to step up improved retraining and internship programs and English-language training for immigrant adults and children. It's time to acknowledge more foreign credentials and welcome more qualified immigrants into the workforce. And we need to remember that, as much as we need more doctors, nurses, engineers, and other professionals, we're also going to need immigrants who start off as labourers, clerks, home-care workers, and service-station attendants.

In the past we've done a good job of welcoming individuals and families from all over the world. Immigrants have played an increasingly important role in science, industry, education, medicine, sports, you name it. Every important business, labour, education, and health group will recite statistics about how many new teachers, doctors, nurses, scientists, machinists, tool-and-die makers, and millwrights we need right now and how many more we're going to need in the future.

Canada should step up immigration to at least 325,000 a year. To be one of the best countries in the world we're going to have to increase immigration and do a better job of welcoming our new immigrants and helping them to contribute to our country to the best of their ability, while, at the same time, they have the opportunity for a freer, more prosperous future for themselves and their family.

We now have a backlog of hundreds of thousands of skilled workers and business immigrants and their families waiting for entry into Canada, and, at the same time, a shortage of at least three hundred thousand skilled workers who are "desperately needed," according to the Canadian Association of Management Consultants. We should scrap the Immigration Bill C-11 and get on with the job of building our country.

Innovation, Competitiveness, and Productivity: Why We Do So Poorly

In February 2002, Industry Minister Allan Rock announced plans for a doubling of government-funded research (which was budgeted at $7.4 billion in 2001–2). The objective was to move Canada into the top five countries in the world in terms of research and development by 2010.

This would be wonderful, but in their 1993 Red Book and in both elections since then, the Liberals also promised equally ambitious R&D objectives. If we have failed in the past when we have had among the very best tax and other r&d incentives in the world, can we be optimistic that Rock's announcement will be anything better than more of the same old?

Every year, year after year, decade after decade, when the annual international r&d comparisons are published, Canada ends up near the bottom of the list of developed countries. In the latest list, as a percentage of GDP, we're in fourteenth place, far behind countries such as Sweden and the U.S. As well, year after year, we see that business in Canada does much less of total R&D than in most developed countries. The only reason that Canada doesn't sink completely off the charts is the continued financing of research and development by the taxpayer.

The 2002 United Nations *Human Development Report* makes for depressing reading for any Canadian concerned with productivity, competitiveness, and our future standard of living. In the report, we find that in a list of patents granted to residents per million people, Canada was far behind other countries, in twenty-third place. For example, patents granted in Sweden were nine times those granted in Canada, the Netherlands and France six times as many, Norway three times as many, and even tiny New Zealand, with fewer than 4 million people, registered over three times as many patents. Japan recorded over thirty times as many. In March 2002, a study by a British think tank said that Canada's poor innovation performance could be "blamed on weak entrepreneurship and too much emphasis on trying to 'copy' the U.S. . . . instead of developing sectors where the country has a competitive advantage.

Canada needs to go back to the sectors where it is strong and develop its own indigenous policy."[*] Well said!

Why is it that despite all the generous incentives for scientific and industrial R&D, we continue to do so poorly? The answer is as plain and obvious as the big chin on Brian Mulroney's face. Manufacturing in Canada and other key sectors of our economy is foreign-dominated. Branch-plant economies do little R&D; why should they? They import their research-intensive products into Canada at high, non-arm's-length prices, making a nice profit back home, and reducing taxes in Canada. Industry Canada, forever out hustling more and more foreign investment, which invariably means more foreign ownership and control, scratches its head in bewildered denial, while soliciting research papers from American consulting firms in their attempts to identify the sources of our perpetually poor R&D showing.

Canada can't compete with large economies such as the U.S. in the total amount spent on R&D, but we certainly can compete in areas of our own special interests, ambitions, comparative advantages, and expertise. We've already shown what we can do in fuel cells, in medical research, aircraft, urban transportation, recreational vehicles, communications systems, oil sands technology, and the Imax system, to name a few. (And don't forget your zipper!)

To be one of the best countries in the world in the future, we need to step up our research and development. We need to ensure that only Canadian companies receive government funding for R&D, and that the benefits of university research go to companies that are owned and controlled in this country. If we fail to do these things, what we will be saying is that we're prepared to accept a standard of living far below our logical potential.

We have an abundance of talent and brilliance in Canada. It's time we gave them more support and more opportunity to go to work for themselves and for our country.

One caveat. It's no use pouring taxpayer R&D money into new Canadian companies and projects if, as soon as they are successful, they are sold off to foreign buyers eager to gobble up the new technology. Companies that accept public funds will have to agree that they cannot be sold to foreign buyers.

---

[*] *National Post*, March 23, 2002.

Robin Hood in Reverse

To be a better country, and to aspire to be the best country, we're going to have to spend more money on health care, education, social programs, defence, and innovation.

Where are we going to get the money? An educated guess is that we're going to need an additional $30 billion a year to solve our most pressing problems and to put us well on the road to a better society. In my last book I addressed in some detail the question of where we could get the money to do something important about poverty in Canada. In what follows, there are some updated figures and some other suggestions.

First, if Canada's total tax revenue as a percentage of GDP was *only the equivalent* of the European Union average, we'd have over $39 billion more to spend on our own priorities. That's a lot of money.

Secondly, as indicated earlier, if Canada's social spending was only the average of all the OECD countries, again as a percentage of GDP, we'd be spending as additional $47 billion on health care, education, job training, helping poor families, and other social programs.

But where are these tens of billions of dollars to come from? Much has been written about the "radical" 1969 tax plans of Pierre Trudeau's finance minister, Edgar Benson, who became Bay Street's most hated man. Benson's tax model was a watered-down version of Kenneth Carter's six-volume 1966 Royal Commission on Taxation report, which

> declared that fairness should be the foremost objective of the taxation system; the existing system was not only too complicated and inefficient, but under it the poor paid more that their fair share while the wealthy avoided taxes through various loopholes.[*]

What Carter recommended was that all income should be treated the same: "a buck is a buck." If implemented, almost half of all taxpayers would have paid less tax, only 10 per cent would have paid more, and the balance would have seen their taxes largely unchanged.

---

[*] Les MacDonald, *The Canadian Encyclopedia* (now available free and updated on the Internet).

Bay Street, business, and the oil industry produced such bitter and vocal opposition that most of Carter's proposals were abandoned.

Almost exactly the same thing happened when Benson produced his budget in November 1969. James Travers writes:

On the surface Benson's plan was a model of '60s Liberal thinking. Translating Trudeau's "just society" into tax policy, Benson proposed imposing Canada's first capital gains tax, integration of corporate and personal taxes, an exit levy on people leaving Canada.[*]

Benson also proposed some other changes designed to make the tax system fairer by broadening the tax base. Renewed hostility from Bay Street and others was so intense that the final 1971 tax bill contained only minor changes to the existing system and just over one year later Edgar Benson left politics. Today Canada taxes only half of capital gains, and our effective rates are actually lower than in the U.S.

For those concerned about our persistent income and wealth gaps, and with how poorly Canada does in terms of distribution of income compared to most other developed countries, a close look at our tax system is in order.

Should we be taxing the wages of workers much higher than we tax stock-market windfalls?

Why don't we, like most all other nations, have an inheritance tax (but one that only takes effect on estates over a million dollars)? Only a small percentage of Canadians would be affected, but the tax could bring in several billion dollars every year.

And what about RRSPs? They've been a wonderful savings mechanism for a great many Canadians, but they cost the federal government many billions of dollars every year, and provincial governments many more billions. In 2002, the drain on government treasuries will probably be in the order of $18 billion. This is, for example, much more than we spend on defence or welfare payments or employment insurance.

Economist Jim Stanford has shown that the top 10 per cent of tax-filers account for about half of all RRSP contributions, and because the tax relief is in the form of a tax deduction, the benefits are worth more for high-income taxpayers. According to Stanford, "a full two-thirds of

---

[*] *Toronto Star*, November 9, 1999.

the annual cost of the RRSP deductions is claimed by the highest-income 10 per cent of the population" while "the lowest-income 50 per cent of taxfilers pocket less than 5 per cent of the total RRSP subsidy. Talk about Robin Hood in reverse."[*]

What we should be doing is restructuring the RRSP rules to make it easier for low- and middle-income Canadians to take advantage of RRSPs, and at the same time lower the annual maximum eligibility limits for those who need the program the least. Overall, we should lower the total RRSP cost to governments by $5 billion a year.

Tax policy should be based on total income and on ability to pay. Flat taxes, like Alberta's, go with flat, greedy heads. Flat taxes polarize society, punish low- and middle-income families, and reduce government revenues (by over $1 billion in Alberta) so that social services are eroded. Aside from Alberta, Hong Kong, and Russia(!), plus a handful of U.S. states, I can't think of any place, anywhere that supports a flat tax, because it's so patently unfair. Ralph Klein and Stockwell Day do; both are strange birds. The Aspers' must-not-be-contradicted editorials support flat taxes. Poor enlightened editorial writers and columnists at their papers have to suffer in silence.

What we should be doing is raising the basic Personal-Amount tax credit for low-income Canadians and lowering it for high-income earners. It simply doesn't make any sense giving Ken Thomson and your minimum-wage convenience-store clerks the same basic credit of $7,400. The present exemptions will cost the federal government about $21 billion this year. We should plan to reduce that by $3 billion.

As Roger Martin has pointed out:

> poor taxpayers in Canada face extremely high marginal effective tax rates – higher than the richest Canadians – and thereby have the least encouragement in Canada to work, save, invest and grow out of poverty.[†]

Doesn't make much sense, does it?

Contrary to what you often read, measured on a per capita basis, seventeen OECD countries have higher total taxes than Canada, and

---

[*] *Facts from the Fringe*, May 24, 2000.
[†] *Globe and Mail*, October 18, 2001.

twelve have lower total taxes.[*] If we look at the OECD estimates for 2001, total government outlays to GDP for Canada come in at 39 per cent; for the OECD, 45.1 per cent. That's a difference of the equivalent of over $60 billion dollars!

So, then, why *can't* we spend as much on social programs as only the average of other developed countries? The answer, alas, is simple. Thanks to the huge deficits of the Trudeau and Mulroney governments, and the early years of the Chrétien government, the three administrations racked up a combined debt of an enormous $560 billion. (The Mulroney share was more than half, $297 billion.)

This year interest payments on our remaining debt will be in the range of $39 billion, or almost 23 cents of every dollar of federal-government revenue. Imagine what we could have done with that money if previous governments hadn't been so irresponsible in their monetary and tax policies, which combined to produce a quarter century of deficits until 1997–98.

One painful lesson I trust we've learned is that protracted periods of deficit spending must be avoided like anthrax. When we spend, we must make sure the necessary tax revenue is there. And we must avoid the absurd, harsh monetary policies that helped suppress the economy in the early 1990s at such heavy cost.

For years now we've had concerted attempts by the likes of the *National Post*, the Reform and Alliance parties, Conrad Black, the Business Council on National Issues (now the CCCE), the Fraser Institute, Jack Mintz of the C. D. Howe Institute, and big business in general, to induce tax rage in the general population in Canada. They failed. As shown earlier, their narrow, radical-conservative prescriptions for Canada don't mesh with the wishes of the vast majority of Canadians. Their "let's be more like the U.S." solutions to Canada's problems are far out-of-touch with the wishes and dreams of most Canadians.

If we look at Ottawa's total budgetary revenues, including employment-insurance premiums, excise taxes, and duties, in 2000–2001 they amounted to 16.9 per cent of GDP. They're now projected to be about 15.5 per cent next year, and Paul Martin's $100 billion in tax cuts will take that figure considerably lower. Combined with provincial tax cuts, the impact on total government spending has been substantial.

---

[*] Table 34, *Revenue Statistics*, OECD, 2001.

In 1984–85, Ottawa's program spending was 19.4 per cent of GDP. In 2000–2001 it was 11.3 per cent, the lowest level in over fifty years. The difference of 8.1 per cent works out today to a difference of a huge $89 billion. In 2001–2, program spending increased modestly, but the difference compared to earlier years could still be measured in many tens of billions of dollars.

Let's take a longer look and compare Ottawa's program spending since 1972, when all provinces and territories joined medicare:

1972–79	17.8 per cent of GDP
1980s	17.6 per cent of GDP
1990s	14.5 per cent of GDP

Today, Ottawa's program spending to GDP is far below pre-medicare days. How's that for downsizing?

When the Chrétien government cut cash transfers to the provinces in 1996, many provinces cut their social spending almost immediately. From the time Chrétien and Paul Martin took over to last year, Ottawa's total transfers to other governments and to persons have fallen by a huge $62 billion.

Over four years (1997–98 to 2000–2001), Ottawa racked up surpluses totalling almost $36 billion, and the provinces over $15 billion in 1999 and 2000, with the biggest combined surplus in history in 2000–2001, $25.7 billion. At this writing, it looks very much like Ottawa will have posted another large surplus, perhaps $7 billion for 2001–2, and will have another $8 billion surplus in 2002–3.

It's clear that the previously mentioned employment insurance surpluses have made up almost all of Paul Martin's surpluses. I doubt that very many Canadians believe that this is a fair way for Ottawa to solve its budgetary problems. But Jean Chrétien and Paul Martin remained unconcerned and John Manley will be no different.

Let's turn to the question of tax evasion. In the United States, the *New York Times* told its readers earlier this year that

> The IRS said yesterday that Americans in far greater numbers than it had once thought, were evading taxes by secretly depositing money in tax havens like the Cayman Islands, and withdrawing it using American Express, MasterCard and Visa cards.

The IRS said it estimates that one million to two million Americans might be using such accounts.

The Internal Revenue Service said that from records of purchases, it had already identified hundreds of income tax cheats, including executives of publicly traded companies, businessmen, doctors, lawyers and investment professionals.

Setting up such accounts has become a popular practice among a number of financial institutions that provide services to affluent individuals.[*]

And guess who the IRS identified in court papers as among those advertising secrecy for those interested – none other than our very own Royal Bank of Canada. Today as I am writing these words, there's news that the Royal Bank is planning to extend its activities in the well-known Channel Islands tax haven.

One month earlier, the following story appeared in the *Financial Post* under the heading "Offshore numbers surprise regulators":

Canadian securities regulators yesterday admitted they were surprised by the number of offshore accounts used as a base for stock trading.

A survey of investment dealers revealed that 13,000 client accounts have been opened in offshore money havens where the activities of their owners can escape regulatory scrutiny.

Why don't we ask the Canadian banks how many offshore accounts they have set up in tax havens for their customers, and which of their customers used their credit cards to pay for their expenses from these accounts? And, if the banks won't tell us, why don't we make them do so? And why don't we do exactly the same thing with our brokers and with other financial institutions operating in Canada? Can you imagine the many billions of dollars in lost tax revenue that we could recover to pay for more MRIS, more nurses, lower tuition fees, and so on, without raising tax rates?

It seems clear to me that many Canadian corporations (but certainly not all) are paying their fair share of the tax load, but many big foreign multinationals are not, escaping billions of dollars in taxes that should be paid in Canada every year.

---

[*] March 26, 2002.

Through overcharging their Canadian operations for parts, components, management fees, advertising fees and so on, through loading up their subsidiaries with excessive debt, and through a variety of other mechanisms, Canada's tax revenue from huge sectors of our economy is but a fraction of what it should be, and you're the one who has to help make up the difference.

Other countries, including the U.S., clamped down on such practices long ago. Why don't we hire hundreds of talented, well-paid accountants to better monitor the activities of foreign corporations in Canada? We could quickly regain the costs of the new staff many times over. I have little doubt that we could bring in a net *minimum* of $5 billion in new tax revenue (and fines!) in the first year.

Colin Freeze, who does an excellent job on this topic for the *Globe and Mail*'s investigations unit, reported last year that,

> In 1998, Canada's auditor-general looked at the nation's international tax directorate and was alarmed by what he saw as a lack of experienced staff.

Canada Customs and Revenue added staff and found more than $1 billion in "adjustments." Unfortunately, "the public is largely unaware of this. In Canada, audits are secret and so are any tax settlements that may result." We should change this. Foreign corporations caught evading Canadian taxes should be fined, charged heavy interest, and the details released to the media. Better still, corporate executives of foreign corporations whose Canadian operations are found to be guilty of evading taxes in Canada should also be heavily fined and jailed for any second offence.

Last year, federal capital-consumption allowances in Canada were about 13.2 per cent of GDP. In 1947, they were only 9 per cent of GDP. Supposing we reduced these allowances by 2 per cent. That would bring in additional tax revenue of over $2 billion, yet the allowances would still be higher than in earlier years.

Then here's something special for all our Americanizers who want us to adopt U.S. policies. The U.S. taxes gambling and lottery winnings. In Las Vegas, and elsewhere, tax money is withheld at the teller's window. If we had a similar tax in Canada, we'd bring in about $4 billion a year.

There is a long list of other tax changes we could make to ensure a fairer system. Since I discussed many of them in some detail in my last book, I won't repeat all of them here.

But one suggestion I do need to repeat. We badly need a new Royal Commission on Taxation composed of good people like David Perry of the Canadian Tax Foundation; Neil Brooks, York University's respected tax expert; a couple of CEOs from good Canadian corporations; and representatives from the federal government, unions, and social agencies. The Commission should be told only two things. First, you have exactly one year to report, no more. Second, your responsibility is to find an additional $30 billion a year in new tax revenue as fairly as possible, without raising taxes for average Canadians.

There's another important thing we can do. In 1998, the highest 20 per cent of Canadian families and unattached individuals received on average $4,258 in government transfer payments. Couldn't the $2.54 billion be better used? Why do we subsidize the already well-off? Or, if we must, why do we subsidize them by two-thirds as much as we give the poor? (The poorest 20 per cent of Canadians received on average only $6,260). Government transfers make up only 2 per cent of the total incomes of the well-to-do, but over half of the total incomes of our poorest 20 per cent. Couldn't we juggle things around to do a much better job of helping the poor who desperately need more help?

One last point about the terribly "punitive" tax rates paid by our high-income earners. We're constantly hearing about how the rich in Canada are assaulted every year with income-tax burdens in the range of 50 per cent or over. But, there's an enormous gulf between taxes *actually paid* and tax rates. It's the latter that are so prominently and persistently featured in our business press.

In 1998, despite what you've been told elsewhere, the top fifth of Canadian income-earners paid taxes at the rate of 24.5 per cent of their sizable taxable income. According to William Watson, in 1999, people making $250,000 or more paid 23.6 per cent.[*] You might want to compare that with your own effective tax rate.

Summing up, if we broaden our tax base, bring in an inheritance tax on large estates, reduce only the maximum limits on RRSP contributions, properly monitor offshore investment and banking accounts,

---

[*] *Financial Post*, May 1, 2002.

clamp down on multinational transfer pricing, modestly reduce capital consumption allowances, cut back on transfer payments to the well-to-do, and begin bringing in more revenue from our petroleum resources, we should easily be able to properly finance medicare, education, child care, and a host of other areas, which are our priorities.

And, if we did *all* of those things, our total tax revenue and social spending as a percentage of GDP *would still be below the* OECD *and* EU *averages,* and our total program spending to GDP *would still be well below the averages for the 1950s, the 1960s, the 1970s, the 1980s and the 1990s.*

Sure, our radical right, our Americanizers, our sellout plutocracy will scream to high heaven. Let them scream. Better still, let them move to the U.S. and join Conrad.

What's the bottom line? It's this. We *can* be the best country anywhere, or at least one of the very best, if we set our sights on being a normal developed country. We should stop comparing our tax and social spending levels with those of the U.S. We should spend much more time looking at the successful, far more civilized policies of the fifteen EU countries, and remembering the good country that we ourselves developed in the past.

We can easily bring in additional revenue to solve our medicare, education, housing, and other social problems through an intelligent mix of better tax monitoring, tax reform, cuts to subsidies for the affluent, and improve our society via measured spending closer to European levels.

Whatever we do, we should listen very closely to the abundant advice of our Americanizers, and then do exactly the opposite of what they suggest.

"Sucked into the U.S. Economy."

Free trade has been the best thing ever for Canada.
– Brian Mulroney

Today, fourteen years after the FTA came into effect, we know for certain some things that we only suspected during the great free trade debates of the last half of the 1980s. The Business Council on National

Issues took part in a series of private talks to discuss the possibility of new sectoral managed trade deals like the Auto Pact, but instead the U.S. wanted much more, a comprehensive binational deal that in dozens of ways would go well beyond anything anyone had previously contemplated.

However, led by U.S. Ambassador Paul Robinson, both sides recognized that a proposal for such an agreement would have to be seen as a Canadian initiative, even though it was the Americans who had proposed a totally unprecedented package which ended up going far, far beyond what most Canadians ever would have previously considered. I wrote about this covert manipulation of the facts in *The Betrayal of Canada* back in 1991.

Robinson told Peter C. Newman:

> Back in January of 1983, I asked my embassy staff to see what we could do to initiate a free trade deal with Canada. I realized, of course, the public initiative had to come from Canada because if it came from us, it would look as if we were trying to gobble up our neighbour.

So the Mulroney government and big business in Canada misrepresented the origins of the deal to Canadians. As far as the Canadian public knew, it was Canada that proposed a comprehensive free trade agreement, not the U.S.

To say that the Americans got pretty well everything they wanted by the time the FTA was signed in 1988 would be an understatement. Canada gave away item after item after item during the negotiations so we could have "guaranteed access" to the U.S. market. Time after time Canadian negotiators buckled under to U.S. pressure, making important concessions in areas never even thought about when the negotiations began.

Forgive me for repeating the telling words of U.S. Trade Representative Clayton Yeutter, who said:

> The Canadians don't understand what they signed. In twenty years, they will be sucked into the U.S. economy.*

Yeutter subsequently added:

---

* *Toronto Star*, October 22, 1987.

Free trade talks with Canada shouldn't be an end in themselves, but should ultimately lead to the creation of a North American common market. Free trade is just the first step in a process leading to the creation of a single North American economy.

Campaigning in advance of the 1988 "free trade election," Brian Mulroney said that an agreement with the U.S. was "absolutely essential to sustain economic growth and prosperity in Canada." The Conservatives embarked on a well-financed "selling job" but only after first trying an unsuccessful strategy of encouraging "benign neglect," while at all times hiding from the public the profound economic, political, social, and cultural changes in Canada that must inevitably follow what was now to clearly be much more than a trade agreement.

The Mulroney government promised Canadians improved productivity and competitiveness, a higher standard of living, greater prosperity for all, more factories from many different countries locating in Canada to serve the U.S. market, better wages, and a long list of other promises that were certain to materialize because of our newly-gained "guaranteed access."

As well, we were promised that our social programs would not be eroded and that our identity and values, which in many ways were so different from the U.S., would not be threatened. Those of us who warned about the consequences of abandoning so much of our precious sovereignty were denounced as "scaremongers."

Somehow, during the FTA negotiations, the Mulroney government thought it was acceptable to make unprecedented, vitally important concessions that had either little or nothing to do with previous international trade negotiations. Even now, so many years after the agreement came into effect, most Canadians still don't realize that Mulroney and friends agreed to terms that no self-respecting country would have tolerated. As bad as these were, the Chrétien government then accepted Mulroney-negotiated NAFTA terms that were even worse, and some that can only be described as astonishing. This was of course, the very same bunch of Liberals who so earnestly and enthusiastically promised in the 1993 federal election that they would negotiate away all the objectionable and damaging FTA and NAFTA provisions.

We now know how little "guaranteed access" we actually have, despite the two agreements, when you are dealing with a protectionist American government that somehow managed to retain the rights to apply contentious countervailing and anti-dumping duties under the terms of the agreement, and, remarkably, the ability to change its own trade laws virtually whenever and however it wishes.

A major American and BCNI objective in the negotiations was to effectively, permanently tie the hands of Canadian governments so that many well-established Canadian practices were no longer possible.

Let's quickly review just a few of the long list of provisions in the agreement that are detrimental to Canada.

In energy and in resources, Canada's ability to control its own supplies and prices has been drastically reduced. Canadian oil and natural gas prices are now set in the U.S. If the U.S. faces a severe shortage and their market dictates huge price increases, too bad, Canadians will face the same high prices. Canadian oil and gas can no longer be sold at lower prices in Canada than the prices we charge Americans.

Just as bad, and perhaps even worse, even if we begin to run short of oil and gas supplies in Canada, we must still continue to supply the U.S. on a pro rata basis, a truly astonishing concession no other country would have considered even for a moment. (Whatever happened to comparative advantage? Isn't the whole basis of free trade theory the idea that countries may be more efficient than others in producing a good or service and they can concentrate on such production for competitive advantage? One thing we know for certain is that Adam Smith and David Recardo would never have agreed to the absurd energy and resource provisions in the FTA and NAFTA).

While it might be argued that proper government guidelines can assure substantial domestic benefit from foreign investment, unfortunately, both the FTA and NAFTA prohibit regulations designed to encourage a long list of requirements that would guarantee a better performance by foreign corporations operating in Canada. Gone are the days when federal, provincial, or local governments could mandate performance standards affecting job creation, R&D, technology transfers, domestic content, or mandate local, regional, or domestic purchasing or hiring requirements.

Shovelling Money Out of the Country,
Then Complaining About Lack of Investment

The FTA, *and the subsequent* NAFTA *and* WTO, *provided a much
improved trade policy environment for investors in Canadian-
based production. . . . Bilateral freer trade has clearly met the
objectives and expectations of the U.S. and Canadian
governments and business interests.*
– Michael Hart (Simon Reisman Professor of Trade Policy, Carleton
University, and Senior Advisor to the Chief Trade Negotiator for
Canada, 1986)

If the following wasn't so truly sad, it could have been the basis for a
splendid comic opera starring Tom d'Aquino, Brian Mulroney (remember, he can sing), Wendy Dobson, and Sherry Cooper.

The same gang that talked Mulroney, and then many Canadians,
into backing the FTA on the basis that it would mean jobs, jobs, jobs, and
three chickens in every pot, did so by arguing that, with guaranteed
access to the U.S. market, Canada would become a great place to invest
and prosperity forever would be ensured for all.

Then, after the FTA came into effect, the very same bunch, led by our
big five banks (who else?), began to pump tens of billions of dollars out
of the country for investment in the U.S.

And then (how's this for chutzpah?) exactly the same group of patriots began a steadily increasing hue and cry that Canada wasn't getting
enough new investment, so we must sharply cut taxes and government
regulations in this country. Here's Jack Mintz in his recent C. D. Howe
book, *Most Favored Nation:*[*]

> Location thus matters to firms today . . . On pure economic terms, it is
> more natural for high-value-added businesses to locate in the larger
> U.S. market, rather than here.

---

[*] I asked Mintz why the foundation uses American spelling in all their publications. It
is because of "our long historical association with our U.S. counterparts."

In other words, exactly the opposite of what we were so often promised during the free trade debates of the 1980s.

Perhaps as bad as their never-ending campaign for ever lower taxes is the constant bellyaching by the same bunch about the low value of the Canadian dollar. But the money that they are pouring into the U.S. every week automatically results in downward pressure on the Canadian dollar, and they well understand this. Talk about a bunch of hypocrites!

Let's see what happened once the FTA was signed. Here's a quick look at direct investment originating in Canada, mostly going to the U.S.:

1970s	$17.0 billion
1980s	$68.4 billion
1990s	$181.4 billion

That's a *huge* difference. During the 1990s, new annual direct investment abroad records were set six times. Then, in 2000 and 2001, Canadian direct investment abroad set new records once again, totalling a staggering $114.5 billion for only the two years. Compare this to the figures above!

In 1997, for the first time in the history of Canada, direct investment abroad from Canada exceeded foreign direct investment in Canada.[*] By the end of 2001, Canadian direct investment abroad stood at $389.4 billion, a giant increase of almost $310 billion since the FTA came into effect. The same thing happened with Canadian portfolio investment abroad. This time, the increase was over $200 billion. So, together, there was a colossal increase of $510 billion in investment abroad, the overwhelming majority of which went to the U.S.

In a country where government has historically considered the nation to be hugely dependent on the inflow of foreign capital, somehow the geniuses who are on bended knee to attract even more foreign ownership and foreign control came up with the brilliant decision to raise the foreign-content limit for Canadian pension funds and registered retirement savings plans from 20 per cent to 30 per cent. The result probably means another outflow of at least $50 billion in equity capital.

---

[*] Statistics Canada, *Canada's International Investment Position*, Catalogue no. 67-202 XPB.

Clever. Seeing itself as heavily reliant on foreign capital, Ottawa allows more and more of our country to be sold to non-residents while Canadian savings pour out of the country. Bear in mind that the RRSP and pension-fund dollars represent billions of dollars in tax breaks designed to encourage Canadian savings. *No one suggests for a moment that average Canadians shouldn't be allowed to invest outside of Canada.* But *why* give people tax breaks to do so?

And now the same old, same old are suggesting that the 30-per-cent limit be raised again, or even wiped out entirely.

At the end of 2001, trusteed pension funds were worth over $615 billion. So now, the Ontario Teachers' Pension Plan places $500 million with a San Diego investment company, and the Caisse de dépôt et placement du Québec, with huge investments in New York already, announces that it plans much more in the future.

And how do our Canadian senators feel about pension-fund savings flowing out of the country? In 1998, a Senate report recommended the abolition of all limits on investing outside of Canada.

Meanwhile, as leaders of the Canadian business community continued to bad-mouth Canada as a poor place to invest, foreign direct investment and foreign takeovers of Canadian businesses were setting new records. While our politicians and newspapers were pleading for even more of the same, they were also endorsing increased investment of RRSP and pension funds abroad. And Canadian business continued to shovel money out of the country in record amounts.

As journalist Rod McQueen has written,

Free trade with the United States was supposed to bring the benefits of global product mandating to Canada. Multinationals would designate a factory in Canada as the worldwide source for a particular product.

Instead,

Every day, in every region, another firm disappears (as) foreign firms are busily scooping up Canadian assets, while our biggest firms consolidate and, too often, move away.[*]

---

[*] *National Post, Business* magazine, February 2001.

And, irony upon irony, as corporate Canada is hollowed out, supporters of more unrestricted foreign direct investment in Canada are now also complaining that,

> When Canadian pension funds and big Canadian institutions are looking to buy Canadian stocks, and they're looking for liquidity, it's difficult to find it.[*]

And Michael Wilson complains that the reduced options for investors increases the risk of investing in Canada.

Is this not all too amazing? And disgusting? Sell off your country, then complain that our big savings institutions have no place to invest in Canada.

Earlier, I made the point that much of so-called Canadian direct investment abroad was not really Canadian. Of the balance that is, our banks make up over half. And other big business in Canada makes up almost all of the rest. In other words, it's not the average Canadian who is responsible for the enormous increase in direct investment abroad. Nor is it, to any significant degree, small and medium-sized Canadian businesses. No, once again it's big business, the very guys who so earnestly promised us something else entirely.

Keep that in mind the next time they go to work to slickly sell you some deal, either directly or via the "think tanks" they fund and control.

As our big five banks continue to rapidly expand in the U.S., it's important to note the impact on business in Canada. Catherine Swift is the President and CEO of the Canadian Federation of Independent Business:

> The highly concentrated and ultra-conservative nature of the Canadian banking system has for many years constrained the ability of small- and medium-sized businesses to readily access financing on fair and flexible terms. During the recession of the 1990s, for instance, lending to large corporations dropped very little while loans to the small-business sector fell precipitously and unnecessarily delayed the economic recovery of small firms. As small businesses now represent about half of the

---

[*] *Financial Post*, May 22, 2002.

Canadian economy and about 80 per cent of net new job creation, this lack of adequate financing options for small firms represents a significant drag on overall Canadian economic potential.

It's both amusing and sad to juxtapose Catherine Swift's comments with those of Royal Bank President and CEO Gordon Nixon, who, in a Montreal Canadian Club speech said:

> [Canadian banks] need to improve our ability to grow our small and medium-sized enterprises, the backbone of our economy. We need to improve Canada's ability to grow our most promising small firms, not only to replace those that are disappearing, but also to ensure we remain a diversified, value-added economy with high-paying jobs.[*]

Now let's hear from Peter Currie, the bank's vice-chairman and Chief Financial Officer, who one month later said:

> Our first priority is to expand in personal and commercial banking, largely in the southeastern U.S.[†]

If there's anyone who wants to bet that the Royal Bank's loans to small and medium-sized businesses in Canada in the next few years will be greater than their new investment outside the country, please get in touch. I'm willing to give good odds.

---

[*] May 6, 2002.
[†] *Edmonton Journal*, June 13, 2002.

"Trade at the Expense of Everything Else," and a Corporate Bill of Rights

*I think we can conclude that NAFTA has been a good
thing for Canada, the United States and Mexico.*
– Paul Cellucci

By now many Canadians have begun to understand that the FTA and NAFTA were less about trade than about enhancing the rights and powers of corporations while constraining the actions of government. Canada's ability to act in an autonomous manner in the country's best interests has been severely curtailed, even within our own boundaries. But the rights of American corporations have been dramatically expanded.

NAFTA's now-notorious Chapter 11 allows private corporations to sue governments if potential profits are deemed to be diminished. U.S. corporations have already launched hundreds of millions of dollars in legal actions in response to Canadian environmental laws, our ban on bulk water exports, and even in relation to Canada Post's parcel-delivery service.

The terms of NAFTA give corporations enormous powers to challenge the actions of democratically elected government at every level across Canada. The potential for future U.S. corporate claims relating to health care, education, social services, municipal water delivery, federal and provincial resources and cultural policies, are real and ominous.

For example, when a Mexican municipality, citing environmental concerns, refused to allow an American company to operate a toxic-waste dump, the U.S. company, Metalclad, took Mexico to a closed-door NAFTA tribunal and won a $17 million award.

The United Parcel Services' $230 million Chapter 11 suit demanding compensation from the Canadian government because of "unfair competition" from Canada Post strikes at the heart of all public services in Canada in an action that could endanger scores of long-standing federal, provincial, and municipal government practices and programs.

As Linda McQuaig writes,

NAFTA has created a new international legal tribunal system. . . . If government regulation makes a corporation's investments less profitable, the corporation can argue that this is "tantamount to expropriation" – a concept that is considered grounds for compensation under the rules of NAFTA.

What's new about the trade deals today isn't that they promote trade. What's new is that they promote trade (and investment) – *at the expense of everything else.*

If you ever wanted a succinct, bottom-line explanation of what Canada got itself into when it so poorly negotiated the FTA and NAFTA, that last sentence is it. McQuaig continues:

> Under NAFTA, virtually any attempt by government to improve restrictions on corporations – in the interest of protecting the environment, preserving natural resources, defending public health, ensuring labour rights or culture – can now be defined as a trade barrier. And governments imposing such restrictions can find themselves subject to expensive legal challenges from corporations until they remove these so-called trade barriers.[*]

If you were to want an iron-clad big-business bill of rights, it would be difficult to improve on the principles enunciated in the above paragraphs.

In 1998, Sergio Marchi was Canada's Trade Minister. During negotiations for the Multilateral Agreement on Investment (MAI), Marchi told the press

> I will not sign on Canada's behalf an MAI that does not fully support key Canadian values and safeguard vital Canadian interests.

Moreover,

> The MAI must make it clear that any government legislation or regulation in the public interest should not require compensation, even if the rules hurt profits.[†]

---

[*] *All You Can Eat: Greed, Lust and the New Capitalism*, Penguin/Viking, 2001.
[†] *Globe and Mail*, February 14, 1998.

360 • THE VANISHING COUNTRY

One has to wonder if Marchi ever read the NAFTA agreement. Marchi has been Canada's Ambassador to the WTO since 1999. Keep that in mind when you read what follows about the General Agreement on Trade in Services.

Back to Chapter 11. In the mid-1990s, Environment Canada officials became very concerned about the fuel additive MMT, produced by the American Ethyl Corporation. Ottawa decided to ban the product from use in Canada, since it considered MMT to be a hazard to human health. But after the Ethyl Corporation filed a $350 million NAFTA legal action, Ottawa not only withdrew its ban, but also paid Ethyl $19 million.

More recently, there has been a steady stream of Chapter 11 legal suits launched by a Mexican drug company, a petroleum products firm, a company asking for $400 million because B.C. has banned bulk water exports, a hazardous-waste company, two investment corporations, and a lumber company. There are many more certain to come in the future.

Not only is United Parcel Service of America Inc. suing Ottawa in relation to Canada Post, but Dallas-based Trammell Crow Co. has joined the party, seeking U.S. $32 million in supposed lost profits because Canada Post didn't give Trammell a fair chance to manage its real-estate holdings.

Even Brian Mulroney's former deputy prime minister, Don Mazankowski, is upset at the United Parcel Services action. After all,

> Crown corporations have operated as legitimate businesses in Canada since Confederation . . . and the post office has been delivering parcels for more than 120 years.

By any measure, Canada has treated UPS with an even hand:

- UPS is not denied access to the Canadian courier market.
- The company is subject to the same competition laws as every other company in the courier and parcel business – including Canada Post.
- Like privately owned companies, Canada Post has been a taxable entity since 1994 and has not received taxpayer support for more than a decade.

Ironically, UPS cannot use the investor-state provisions against the U.S. Postal Service, because NAFTA's Chapter 11 does not allow a company to sue its own government.[*]

All this said, what can possibly be wrong with Canadians deciding that they want to keep the parcel-delivery business in Canadian hands so that decisions about its operations, the key jobs, and the profits remain in Canada?

It's important to emphasize that Canadian corporations cannot sue Canadian governments for compensation for lost profits if new legislation is passed. But, remarkably, U.S. companies can, have, and will do so often in the future. If that isn't bizarre, I don't know what is.

I cannot imagine any Canadian who understands NAFTA's Chapter 11 having the slightest modicum of confidence in the ability of our trade negotiators, or their political masters.

A further aspect of NAFTA is that tribunal hearings are secret and documents and decisions are made public only after the fact.

Moreover, according to press reports, a tribunal ruling earlier this year

> ruled Canada must defy its access-to-information law and withhold documents requested by the public concerning a U.S. forest company's bid for compensation from Ottawa.
>
> Critics say the decision is another worrisome sign of how tribunals can override Canadian law.

One of the worst aspects of the FTA and NAFTA is the inability of future governments to change course should they so desire. For example, if Ontario Hydro is privatized, and if U.S. corporations enter the power business in the province, and if privatization and deregulation turns out to be a terrible disaster for the people of Ontario, not only would the provincial government have to reimburse U.S. investors for their assets if public ownership were to be reintroduced, but the government also would have to pay enormous punitive potential-profit compensation. Essentially, it would be impossible to reintroduce public ownership.

The same principle would apply to scores of other government activities. In short, the FTA and NAFTA both tie the hands of future

---

[*] *Globe and Mail*, February 8, 2001.

democratically elected governments, producing a policy freeze that will never thaw as long as the agreements are in force.

"It's Going to Be a Bloodbath"

It's impossible to discuss the FTA and NAFTA without considering Mexico. Canadians were promised that the FTA would be an exclusive deal, giving Canadians special access to the U.S. market. But that all changed in 1993 with NAFTA. Now we're being told by the same FTA hucksters who promised us exclusivity that unless we reduce taxes to U.S. levels, or preferably below U.S. levels, and unless we change our policies to conform to U.S. policies, we're going to be out of luck. "Mexico may take Canada's spot as top U.S. trade partner,"[*] warns the Bank of Nova Scotia. Mexico will attract more foreign investment. Mexico has millions of low-wage workers. Taxes are very low in Mexico.

It's not difficult to see how successful the U.S. game plan has been. Sign a "trade" deal with Canada allowing American corporations the right to buy up the country and guaranteeing the U.S. virtually unrestricted access to the Canadian resources the U.S. desperately needs. Then, sign a deal with Mexico guaranteeing the U.S. access to dirt-cheap Mexican labour.

So, what has been the result? As but one example, Canada was for decades the largest supplier of auto parts to the U.S., now Mexico is. "Certainly lower wages are driving these big gains," says the Bank of Nova Scotia's auto-industry economist.[†]

Canadian vehicle production is down 800,000 units since NAFTA came into effect, and Mexico production is up 750,000 units. More Canadian plants are scheduled to close and new Mexican plants are being planned. Auto-assembly and parts jobs in Canada are down by 13,000 since 1999. One industry spokesman said, "It's going to be a bloodbath!"[**]

But, overall, has NAFTA been good for Mexico? Hardly. Mexican per

---

[*] *Edmonton Journal*, March 5, 2002.

[†] *Financial Post*, December 1, 2001.

[**] *Globe and Mail*, April 15, 2002.

capita income growth and real wages are far below pre-NAFTA levels. After eight years of NAFTA, both the real minimum wage and manufacturing wages in Mexico are down by over 20 per cent, and the minimum wage has lost close to half its purchasing power. Labour conditions have deteriorated, while real incomes for all but the top 10 per cent have fallen.

The average pay in Mexican assembly plants is now about $2 an hour. Living conditions in the 3,700 U.S. border *maquilladora* plants are abysmal. Ciudad Juárez, with 1.3 million people, has enormous slums lacking both sewage and running water. High school drop-out rates are over 90 per cent. In the early 1980s, about half of all Mexicans lived in poverty; today, it's almost three of every four.

In 2001, the Economic Policy Institute produced an excellent study on the impact of NAFTA.[*] In the Introduction, economist Jeff Faux writes:

Each year since the implementation of the North American Free Trade Agreement (NAFTA) on January 1, 1994, officials in Canada, Mexico, and the United States have regularly declared the agreement to be an unqualified success. . . .

For *some* people, NAFTA clearly has been a success. This should not be a surprise inasmuch as it was designed to bring extraordinary government protections to a specific set of interests – investors and financiers in all three countries who search for cheaper labor and production costs. . . .

But most citizens of North America do not support themselves on their investments. They work for a living. . . . NAFTA, while extending protection for investors, explicitly excluded any protections for working people in the form of labor standards, worker rights, and the maintenance of social investments. . . .

In the United States. . . . As manufacturing jobs disappeared, workers were downscaled to lower-paying, less-secure services jobs. Within manufacturing, the threat of employers to move production to Mexico proved a powerful weapon for undercutting workers' bargaining power. . . .

While production jobs did move to Mexico, they primarily moved to *maquiladora* areas just across the border. . . . in which wages,

[†] *Nafta at Seven: Its Impact on Workers in All Three Nations*, Washington, D.C., EPI, April 2001.

benefits, and workers' rights are deliberately suppressed. . . . It is therefore no surprise that compensation and working conditions for most Mexican workers have deteriorated. The share of stable, full-time jobs has shrunk.

Faux goes on to describe a

> continent-wide pattern of stagnant worker incomes, increased insecurity, and rising inequality . . .
>
> The experience suggests that any wider free trade agreement extended to the hemisphere that does not give as much priority to labor and social development as it gives protection to investors and financiers is not viable.

The impact of NAFTA on Mexico has been dramatic. Mexico's imports from abroad are now higher than exports to the U.S. Low-wage jobs have increased and benefits for workers have fallen. Overall, according to Mexican economist Carlos Salas,[*] by 1998, the incomes of salaried workers had fallen 25 per cent, while those of the self-employed had declined 40 per cent.

Last year, Dalton Camp wrote:

> Many of us didn't read the NAFTA because we took somebody else's word for it – the media, the politicians, the bureaucrats, the establishment – that is was all about free trade, which, like lemonade, was just plain good for everyone.

But, in fact, it was something else entirely:

> Nothing has done greater damage to the environment, potable water and to public health, than the devastating combination of new industrial border towns and dirt cheap Mexican labour. Globalization's apologists say this is about "development." There is overwhelming evidence it is really about exploitation of the poor and the powerless.

---

[*] *The Impact of NAFTA on Wages and Incomes in Mexico*, Washington, D.C., EPI, April 2001.

A Look at the "Great Success" of the FTA and NAFTA

Free trade is demonstrably the best
public policy ever adopted in Canada.
— Diane Francis

In the millions of words that have poured forth about the economic impact of free trade, one thing is consistent – a remarkable lack of facts about what happened to the Canadian economy since the Free Trade Agreement went into effect in 1989. Here are some numbers and results from Statistics Canada that can't be ignored, no matter how much Brian Mulroney and Tom d'Aquino would like them to be.

In the decade before the FTA, employment in Canada increased by just over 2.3 million jobs. During the first decade of the FTA, employment in Canada increased by only 1.5 million jobs. That's a huge decline.

The 1990s not only saw the worst average employment growth rate since the Great Depression, but also the highest average unemployment rates. Moreover, average GDP growth during the decade was also the worst since the 1930s.

How's that for a success story?

According to Trade Minister Pierre Pettigrew, in his *Second Annual State of Trade Report*,[*] as a result of the FTA and NAFTA, in 2000, "we registered the ninth consecutive year of record growth." There are several other nonsensical statements in the minister's Report, but they all have one thing in common: they aren't true.

Let's look at Canada's GDP growth records.

According to Pierre Fortin,

During the 1990s, Canada's aggregate economic performance has been the worst since the Great Depression, and very nearly the worst among all industrial countries.[†]

---

[*] International Trade, Ottawa, May 1, 2001.
[†] Industry Canada, *Micro*, vol. 7, no. 2, Summer 2000.

Just how bad was Canada's economic performance during the first decade of the FTA? The following table shows our average annual GDP growth rate during the past four decades.

1960s	5.11 per cent
1970s	4.43 per cent
1980s	2.95 per cent
1990s	2.28 per cent

Some great success story!

Joe Martin, Adjunct Professor of Strategy at the Rotman School of Management has shown that in nine of the thirteen decades since Canada became a nation, we outperformed the U.S. in our GDP growth rate. But, since the FTA, Canada's rate of growth has been below the U.S. rate in eight of thirteen years.

> From 1939 to 1989, Canada made extraordinary progress compared with the United States. In 1939, our GDP per capita was less than 70% that of the United States. In 1989 it was 90%. Then, the wheels came off . . . our snails-pace growth resulted in our sinking to 80% of the United States by 1999, a precipitous decline in only 10 years.[*]

So, overall, how did Canada do in the 1990s compared to other countries?

In terms of the average annual per capita growth of GNP, seventy-nine countries had a better performance than Canada.[†]

In the decade before the FTA, Canada's GDP growth rate outperformed the averages of the G7, the OECD, and the European Union countries. In the first FTA decade, we fell behind all of them.

Pierre Fortin has shown that during the first ten years of the FTA, when GDP per capita growth in twenty-five OECD countries is measured, Canada ended up near the very bottom of the pack, in twenty-fourth place! For the right-wingers who invariably blame tax policy for dismal economic performance, eleven of the countries that finished ahead of

---

[*] *National Post*, December 1, 2001.
[†] *The State of the World's Children, 2001*, United Nations Children's Fund.

Canada had higher tax-to-GDP ratios than Canada during these years, and only nine had lower tax ratios.[*]

The United Nations *Human Development Report* measures annual growth rates. Between 1990 and 2001, Canada ranked sixty-fifth in the GDP per capita annual growth rates. All told, growth in Canada since the FTA went into effect has been terrible. If population growth and inflation are considered, real GDP per person increases averaged an awful 1.1 per cent per year.

According to Andrew Sharpe in a Centre for the Study of Living Standards report, in 1988 our GDP per capita was 87.5 per cent of that in the U.S. But in 2001, after thirteen years of free trade, it had fallen to 79.5 per cent. Meanwhile, Canada's productivity fell from 86 per cent of the American level down to 79 per cent.

Please go back to the beginning of this chapter and read the quote from Diane Francis again.

And then consider Tom d'Aquino's comments in *Time* magazine late last year:

> Free trade created immense benefits for Canadians.[†]

Jobs! Jobs! Jobs! And Other Baloney

> *The widespread belief that the quality and security of jobs declined during the 1990s is a myth.*
> – *National Post*, editorial, August 29, 2000

Another important way of looking at what happened to the Canadian economy during the first full decade of free trade is to measure the unemployment and employment rates. Once again, the comparisons are remarkable and not exactly anything you're likely to ever find in a Canadian Council of Chief Executives newsletter. Here are the

---

[*] Comparative figures for five countries were not available.

[†] December 17, 2001.

average annual Canadian unemployment rates for the last half of the twentieth century:

1950s	4.2 per cent
1960s	5.0 per cent
1970s	6.7 per cent
1980s	9.3 per cent
1990s	9.5 per cent

Once again, the 1990s were the worst decade since the Great Depression.

When the Free Trade Agreement came into effect, the labour-force participation rate was 67.2 per cent. During the 1990s, it dropped to an annual average of only 65.5 per cent. The difference of 1.7 per cent may not seem large, but it works out to loss of some 272,000 jobs in the year 2000 alone. If the people who dropped out of the labour force were added to the unemployment rate in the 1990s, the results would have been even worse than the already dismal figures.

During the 1990s, the quality of the jobs that were created also deteriorated. There were fewer new full-time jobs created, while part-time jobs jumped by over half a million and the self-employed increased by 618,000. If one subtracts the large increase in the self-employed from the total number of jobs created during the 1990s, the results for the first decade of free trade can only be described as appalling.

Altogether, self-employed, temporary, and part-time jobs included, the private sector in Canada produced a pathetic average annual increase of only 88,300 new jobs during the 1990s, compared to an average of 153,200 new jobs in the 1980s.

So much for Jobs! Jobs! Jobs!

Pierre Fortin has shown that

90 per cent of the deterioration in Canada's economic performance in the 1990s relative to the 1980s reflects the setback in the growth of the employment rate, and only 10 per cent the small slowdown in productivity. The Canadian employment rate caught up with the U.S. rate in the 1970s, increased as rapidly as the U.S. rate in the 1980s, but then fell sharply in absolute and relative terms.

Fortin says "There is no question that Canada's poor employment performance has been the major event of the 1990s."

Today, twenty OECD countries have a smaller percentage of part-time workers than Canada, and eighteen have a higher percentage of employed youth, while almost all have a smaller percentage of low-wage workers.

Returning to self-employment, most of the self-employed wanted but could not find payroll jobs. These self-employed accounted for almost 60 per cent of the increase in total employment in the 1990s, compared with only 6 per cent in the U.S. In 1989, an average self-employed person in Canada earned $20,700. By 1998, they were down to $15,200.

Perhaps the most startling figures of all are the facts that in the 1980s, full-time jobs accounted for 58 per cent of all new jobs created, but in the 1990s they made up a pathetic 18 per cent of new job creation. In the 1990s, 653,000 fewer full-time jobs were created in Canada than during the 1980s.

How's that for another great free trade success story?

But hasn't Canada's unemployment rate fallen in recent years? A Statistics Canada study, published in the fall of 2000, suggested that while the official unemployment rate in 1997 was 9.1 per cent, the actual unemployment rate experienced by families was 15.2 per cent, while the unemployment rate for individuals was 17.3 per cent. Moreover, for the past eleven years, the labour-force participation rate has been lower than it was in 1988.

It's true that Canada's economy has been looking good in 2002 and job creation is up. But after thirteen years of free trade there were over 124,000 more unemployed in Canada. And one or two good years does not a decade make. In 2001, Canada had the worst employment increase in five years and the worst GDP increase in nine years.

In what follows, we'll see what has happened in the free trade years to average Canadians.

The Well-Being of Workers and Their Bosses

The massive growth in exports to the United States "gives you an idea as to how our well-being . . . is tied to free trade with the U.S."
— Brian Mulroney, June 2001

If the FTA and NAFTA weren't supposed to improve the well-being of average Canadians, what *was* the objective supposed to be? Let's have a look at how personal income in Canada fared and compare the result with previous years. Here are the average annual increases in personal income for the past four decades:

1960s	8.3 per cent
1970s	13.4 per cent
1980s	9.7 per cent
1990s	3.2 per cent

So, you can clearly see "how our well-being is tied to free trade with the U.S." Let's look at what happened to workers' wages by measuring average annual labour-income increases by decade. Here the results are most revealing:

1940s	6.9 per cent
1950s	8.4 per cent
1960s	9.1 per cent
1970s	13.0 per cent
1980s	8.9 per cent
1990s	3.3 per cent

During the 1990s, workers' wage increases in Canada were well below the level of the averages of the EU and OECD countries.

In terms of negotiated wage settlements, during the 1980s they averaged 6.3 per cent for all industries in Canada. But during our first free trade decade, they fell all the way down to 2.2 per cent, below the 2.5 per cent average of consumer price increases. So much for the bottom line of how working men and women made out during the first free trade decade.

More than a few political economists and other observers have suggested that one of the principal reasons big business so strongly pushed the FTA was their desire to put labour in its place. Whether or not this was a prime objective of the agreement, and of NAFTA a few years later, the results clearly speak for themselves.

So much for the fate of Canadian workers. What about the bosses? The headlines say it clearly: "Canadian CEOs salaries soar," "Big increases for bank heads," "Corporate elite take home big pay raises."

In 2000, private-sector employees increased their base wages by 2.4 per cent, again below the consumer price increase of 2.8 per cent. The same year,

> The chief executives of Canada's top companies scored a stunning 42.9% median pay increase . . . John Roth, Nortel Corp's president and CEO, led the way with total direct compensation of $70.8 million – a 91% increase over his 1999 pay.[*]

Even though profits were down in 2001, Canadian CEOs' compensation increased another enormous 54 per cent. David O'Brien's package added up to $84.6 million. Meanwhile, workers' wage settlements were up 3.2 per cent.

While Canadian workers saw their income changes remain just below or just above inflation, CEO compensation exploded to levels far exceeding anything imagined previously. Meanwhile, Ontario Premier Mike Harris announced that though provincial politicians would see their base salaries increase by $30,000, there would be no increase in the province's minimum wage, which remained frozen at $6.85 an hour since 1985.

And more recently, Jack Mintz, the ubiquitous radical-right representative of the C. D. Howe Institute, warned that,

> if workers demand wages much greater than those paid in other localities, parts of the production process can be easily moved elsewhere without significantly affecting its efficiency.[†]

---

[*] *Financial Post*, May 22, 2001.
[†] *Most Favored Nation*, C. D. Howe Institute, 2001.

Get the picture? It's okay if senior executive remuneration rockets through the roof into outer space, but if workers demand more they had better watch out – they could lose their jobs.

Surely, though, there must be some logical explanation for all of this. Maybe Canadian workers aren't productive enough? Baloney. From 1989 to 1996, worker output per hour rose by 9.4 per cent while real average weekly earnings increased by only 2.8 per cent.

> *During the 1988 free trade debate, economists often argued that it would take time to see the effects of free trade in the data. Free trade did exactly what it was supposed to do.*
> – William Watson

Pardon? Given the disastrous results for average Canadians, how can Watson say such a thing?

Easy.

Here's a look at corporate profits in Canada:

1967–77	$152.1 billion
1978–88	$458.4 billion
1989–99	$694.6 billion

But for average Canadians, in all the following categories, the results for the 1990s were dismal compared to the 1980s:

- personal and family income;
- personal disposable income;
- increases in employment;
- full-time jobs.

Housing starts in the 1990s were far below the levels for previous decades, including the 1960s, when the population was smaller by 12 million people. At the end of the 1990s, average personal savings were the lowest since Statistics Canada first began keeping track of the savings rate. At the same time, average annual increases in consumer spending were well below that of previous decades.

Osberg and Sharpe sum it up: "The overall index of economic

well-being for Canada . . . rose in the 1980s to a peak . . . and has fallen continually in the 1990s."

But wait a minute, didn't *anything* in Canada besides corporate profits and CEO wages and benefits increase in the 1990s compared to the decade before free trade? Here's a little list:

- Personal debt escalated to modern highs.
- Child, family, and individual poverty increased.
- Personal bankruptcies skyrocketed.
- The dollar amount of business bankruptcies more than doubled.
- The income and wealth gaps between rich and poor reached all-time record levels.

Stark "Unexpected and Worrisome" "Contradictions to Predictions"

We have failed to keep pace with the Americans on job growth and productivity over the period as a whole, which starkly contradicts the predictions of those of us who fought for free trade.
– William Thorsell, *Globe and Mail*, May 14, 2001

Indeed it does. Thorsell, when he was editor of the *Globe and Mail*, was one of the leading and most enthusiastic free trade cheerleaders. The column from which the above quote is taken was titled "Second thoughts on free trade."

One of the oft-repeated promises made by proponents of the FTA was that it would have a major impact on improving Canada's productivity and competitiveness, and hence the Canadian standard of living. Today, the same people are complaining about Canada's productivity.

Instead of the promised improvements due to increased exports, an Industry Canada document shows that

Exports today have a much higher import content of intermediate inputs than in the past.

There has been almost no growth in labour productivity in export sectors.[*]

In another paper, prepared by three employees of the Micro-Economic Analysis division of Industry Canada, we learn that,

Despite the growing economic linkages, Canada's productivity and real economic performance lagged far behind the US in the 1990s and the Canada–U.S. productivity and real income level gaps widened significantly, exactly opposite of the expectations.[†]

When I asked Industry Canada why they thought this had happened, the answer was that it was "Mainly because Canadian firms were not investing in R&D and new machinery and equipment and as a result there was poorer innovation."

Could they, by any chance, be referring to the 150 big firms who make up the Canadian Council of Chief Executives?

The productivity gap between Canada and the United States has widened. This trend is

quite unexpected and worrisome, especially in view of the dramatic increase in Canada's outward orientation, partly due to FTA/NAFTA, and the implementation of a number of structural reforms.[**]

These results, noted by two Industry Canada economists, would be worthy of satire if they were not so pathetic. One reason for the poor productivity performance that the economists mention is "the large negative impact of the slowdown of machinery and equipment investment in Canada."

In the second half of the 1990s, labour productivity in U.S. manufacturing increased at more than three times the Canadian rate. The two economists show that investment in machinery and equipment in

---

[*] Peter Dungan and Steve Murphy, *The Challenging Industry and Skills Mix of Canada's International Trade*, Industry Canada, April 1999.

[†] Acharya, Sharma, and Rao, *Canada's Trade and Foreign Direct Investment Patterns with the United States*, June 2001.

[**] Someshwar Rao and Jianmin Tang, Industry Canada.

Canada in the period 1989–95 "increased by a meager 0.7 per cent per year, compared to 9.3 per cent in the United States."

Those who are puzzled by Canada's comparatively poor productivity performance need look no further than the above paragraph for a large part of the explanation. As for the future,

> Canada's labour productivity growth is expected to remain modest in the first half of this decade.

During the 1990s, in a list of twenty-six OECD countries, Canada was twentieth in trend growth of labour productivity.[*]

Through the thirty-year period prior to the FTA, Canada's real GDP per capita gap with the U.S. had been narrowing. In the 1990s, it began to widen.

In 2001, Canadian productivity growth was the worst in four years. In the same year, the Canadian Manufacturers and Exporters released a report that claimed that for the second year in a row Canada is last among G7 countries in terms of competitiveness.

Only during one year since the FTA came into effect has the industrial capacity utilization rate reached the pre-free-trade level. And, again, what about the eternal complaint that taxes are the problem? In recent years, Germany has easily outperformed the U.S. in productivity, but German taxes are among the highest in the OECD, while U.S. taxes are among the lowest.

Economist Myron Gordon points out that the percentage of managerial and professional jobs in Canada which at one time was higher than in the U.S. had been falling. By 1996 it was only about 33 per cent of production employment, while the U.S. rate had climbed to over 53 per cent. Gordon says that the most important reason for this change has been the rise in foreign ownership. He goes on to show how foreign ownership is a key factor in Canada's disappointing productivity showing. For Gordon, the bottom line is clear: "participation in the Canadian market by large multinational corporations should be related to the level and quality of their production and employment here."[†]

---

[*] Dirk Pilat, "Productivity Growth in the OECD Area," *International Productivity Monitor* no. 3, fall 2001, Centre for the Study of Living Standards.

[†] *Policy Options*, May 2000.

Sounds like a good idea, but, because of the FTA and NAFTA, we can insist on no such thing.

One of the key reasons Canadian productivity has fallen behind is the performance of the manufacturing sector (over 50 per cent foreign-owned). Note that the year before the FTA was implemented, manufacturing productivity in Canada was about 83 per cent of the U.S. level. By 2000, it had dropped all the way down to 65 per cent.

So much for all those lavish productivity promises.

To top off this rosy picture, recent reports indicate that Canada's international competitive position has fallen from sixth place all the way down to eleventh.[*]

Before we turn to softwood lumber and increasing U.S. protectionism, I must repeat one point. Labour productivity has little to do with how hard workers work. It has everything to do with big business failing to invest, failing to do R&D, and failing to develop innovative competitive strategies.

Being Trampled with Impunity

> The free trade agreement was far more successful than
> I would have contemplated. It really was dramatic.
> – Donald Macdonald

Canada getting "guaranteed access" to the U.S. market was supposed to relieve all those worries about trade barriers and American "trade remedy" harassment. Of course we now know that this was yet another false promise and that those who made such false promises either knew better or should have known better.

Not only is U.S. action relating to softwood lumber and other exports destroying huge numbers of jobs in Canada and threatening to bankrupt scores of firms, but other American protectionist and politically motivated actions, such as agricultural and natural gas subsidies, will prove terribly damaging to Canadian producers.

---

[*] World Economic Forum *Global Competitiveness Reports*, October 2001.

The reality is that the U.S. practises and preaches free trade only when it's going to be to their advantage. And the American version of fair trade is directly tied to what is happening in U.S. congressional elections. And, if you think we've already seen blatant politically motivated protectionism since the election of George W. Bush, just wait until the presidential election in 2004.

Of course it's not only Canada that is suffering from renewed American protectionism. The EU, Asian, and developing countries are all heaping scorn on American steel duties, agriculture subsidies, and other U.S. mid-term actions. Drew Fagan, commenting on the softwood lumber mess, writes,

> The most interesting thing [is] there's virtually no outrage.
>
> Where are the opponents of free trade, who could stand up now and say "we told you so" with justification?*

No outrage? Try B.C.'s forestry minister, who calls the Americans a "hostile foreign power." Try the anti-American letters to the editor in newspapers across Canada. But, according to Fagan, "there's not much that activists such as the Ragin' Grannies can do about it."

But there *is* something that can be done. Here's a letter from a Stratford, Ontario, former free trade supporter:

> I do not make my living by lumber, and never likely shall. Yet the central issue concerning softwood lumber "fairness" wholly escapes W. J. (Rusty) Wood, chairman of the so-called Coalition for Fair Lumber Imports in the United States.
>
> There exist international trade agreements through the World Trade Organization. The WTO has determined three times that Canadian lumber practices are both wholly legitimate and wholly fair.
>
> If the new world order is an American one, administered by U.S. judges, I want to get off the train – now. Moreover, if the North American Free Trade Agreement is to become an assault on all Canadian practices that are distinct from American ones yet legitimate under international

---

* *Globe and Mail*, December 19, 2001.

trading arrangements, then I want to reverse my 1988 vote in favour of NAFTA.[*]

L.W. Naylor

Even continentalist Diane Francis is incensed:

> I think we need an amendment to the Free Trade Agreement so that these protectionist games stop. Short of that, they will never stop. It's obvious that whatever compromise that we come up with never amounts to a permanent fix.[†]

The American action on softwood lumber makes a mockery of the FTA and NAFTA. For the Americans, protectionism is a dirty word unless it's protectionism to protect U.S. jobs. Then it's okay to ignore bilateral or multilateral trade rules using a whole panoply of barriers based on phony charges or suggestions that Canadian practices don't conform to practices in the U.S.

In Paul Krugman's words, recent U.S. protectionism "demonstrates an unprecedented contempt for international rules."[**] The editor of *Foreign Policy* magazine says that no important country is less committed to globalization than the U.S. under George W. Bush, and *The Economist* describes America's commitment to freer trade as "laughable."[††]

Bruce Little, the always temperate, even-handed, and perceptive *Globe and Mail* economics columnist, comments on the egregious U.S. softwood lumber actions:

> The Americans are not our best friends and probably not our friends at all; they are simply our neighbours. You might even say that the Americans have no real friends. Rather they have interests – entirely domestic – that must be appeased.
>
> A level playing field is one on which Americans win, because as every American knows in his bones, Americans always win a fair fight.

---

[*] *Globe and Mail*, April 4, 2002.

[†] *National Post*, September 11, 2001.

[**] *New York Times*, May 24, 2002.

[††] May 11, 2002.

If they lose, the fight is by definition unfair. And if the competitors are foreigners who don't vote in U.S. elections, so much the better. They can be trampled with impunity.[*]

Most likely Canada will eventually win the softwood lumber dispute (for the fourth time!) at the WTO, but it will probably take years. By June 2002, thousands of jobs had been lost, with the toll expected to reach at least 30,000 by the end of the year. Mills have closed down and many more will close; lumber companies will go bankrupt. Meanwhile, the B.C. government has allowed an increased number of raw logs to be shipped to the U.S. Mill jobs will be shifted to Oregon and Washington. Tough luck for workers and their families in communities across B.C.

And, of course, after the mills close down, more of the industry will be sold off to Americans for rock-bottom prices. According to Frank Dottori, Tenbec Inc. CEO,

> If we go by history, the only time we ever had an agreement is when Canada surrendered.

And Rick Doman, president of Doman Industries, points out:

> U.S. rules unfairly allow the U.S. industry to win twice. Canadian companies are effectively fined, then those fines are handed to U.S. companies that are Canadian competitors. The funds provide a financial was chest for the U.S. industry to continue and increase its actions against the Canadian industry.[†]

Is Canadian softwood lumber subsidized? Nonsense. As Bob Rae has pointed out,

> It is the U.S. industry that is subsidized. Governments in the United States build and maintain the roads, plan the harvest, reforest, pay for protection against forest fires. In Canada, the private companies pay for all of that.

---

[*] *Globe and Mail*, March 28, 2002.
[†] The Canadian Press, January 29, 2002.

> This dispute is all about a relatively inefficient and decidedly less productive U.S. industry using its political clout to keep out products that will keep prices in the United States low.[*]

The U.S. lumber lobby in Washington has been harassing Canadian producers for twenty years. Any Canadian federal government with any kind of backbone would long ago have told the Americans that their actions clearly are unacceptable to Canadians. And, unless the U.S. takes prompt action to remove duties on softwood, Canada will place equivalent duties on oil, natural gas, and electricity exports to the U.S. Do you think that might get some attention in Washington?

Alas, Jean Chrétien, Paul Martin, John Manley, and Allan Rock are terrified of doing anything that might irritate the U.S. and their own Canadian petroleum industry financial backers.

Cowards they've been, cowards they are, and cowards they will remain.

Does anyone really expect that the spineless wimps in Ottawa will do *anything* to prevent future unfair trade harassment? Won't Canada simply roll over yet once again and won't Ottawa continue to tremble every time Cellucci gives a threatening speech?

So, after we buckle under again, what will be next? You can bet it will be more punitive American actions against Canadian wheat exports; the Canadian Wheat Board; the hog, beef, dairy, and poultry industries; pulse crops; and other industries that are competitive in American states that might go Democrat in 2004.

If Canada fails to take strong action in response to U.S. protectionism, the bully will strike again and again every time a U.S. industry mounts a lobby in Washington. Every time Ottawa fails to respond with decisive action, it simply invites yet more of the same.

And is there any chance that the U.S. might ignore another WTO softwood decision in Canada's favour? If the polls for the 2004 presidential election are close, take it as a given. The U.S. has already ignored a WTO decision that tax-related American export subsidies are illegal, despite the fact the European Union is threatening $4 billion (U.S.) in retaliation on exports from the U.S.

Earlier this year, former U.S. diplomat Goodwin Cooke, who served

---

[*] *Financial Post*, May 18, 2002.

in the U.S. embassy in Ottawa and is now a well-regarded lecturer on American foreign policy, had this to say about George W. Bush:

> He's likely thinking "I'm going to get re-elected and I'm going to try to get a Congress that agrees with me ... I'm going to pursue the protection of the homeland and who cares what Canada thinks? Twenty-five or 30 million Canadians carping away in the frozen north, to hell with it."[*]

Now for Some More Bad News and Then Finally Some Good News

The General Agreement on Trade in Services (GATS) came into effect the same year as NAFTA. (Services in Canada represent about two-thirds of our economy). The new World Trade Organization GATS negotiations, scheduled for completion in 2005, are *very* worrisome. The U.S. coalition of Service Industries is suggesting that "public ownership of health care has made it difficult for U.S. private sector health care providers to market in foreign countries."

Numerous federal, provincial, and municipal agencies and practices could be extremely vulnerable to American aspirations. While public higher education in Canada is already threatened by NAFTA provisions, the GATS agreement now under discussion could present much more serious problems. Banking and other financial services might be opened up to foreign buyers. So, too, might telecommunications and cultural industries.

Most Canadians have never heard of GATS, and most that have aren't aware of the likely ramifications. Incredibly, yet once again, just as was the case with the MAI, it's our own federal government that is one of the most enthusiastic behind-the-scenes backers of an agreement that could very well prove fatal for Canada's survival. While the Department of Foreign Affairs and International Trade is one of the leading culprits, the bottom line is that Jean Chrétien, Paul Martin, John Manley, and Allan

---

[*] *National Post*, June 4, 2002.

Rock are all either blissfully unaware of the GATS dangers, or, more likely, entirely behind our negotiators' positions at the behest of their corporate backers.

It's important to understand that GATS talks are held behind closed doors and Ottawa has been highly circumspect in its public announcements with respect to both Canada's position, and the progress of negotiations.

Without question, the current WTO GATS discussions are potentially ruinous. The present GATS objective is to further expand trade rules into standards and services, intellectual property, and almost all areas subject to government regulation.

There is a huge pro-corporate and anti-government bias behind the closed-door negotiations. At the same time, there is an appalling lack of information available to the public, as well as a plethora of conflicting reports and misleading half-truths. At the heart of the proposed agreement is entry into areas that should be none of the WTO's business – intrusion into democratic decision-making by elected legislatures endangering the rights of all levels of government in favour of newly established rights of foreign corporations. Rather than regulatory chill, GATS represents a permanent deep freeze on government actions.

Scott Sinclair, Senior Research Fellow at the Canadian Centre for Policy Alternatives (CCPA), is one of the leading experts on the GATS. Here are a few quotations from his paper presented last November to a Royal Society of Canada symposium on the WTO:

> GATS changes qualitatively transform not only the GATT regime, but the entire multilateral system. Taken together, they amount to a constitutional shift, a fundamental reworking of the basic legal precepts of the multilateral trading regime and of its role in the international system. Multilateral rule-making, and especially enforcement, to protect commercial trading interests surged ahead of international rule-making in other vital areas such as environmental protection, human rights, public health, and cultural diversity. These changes, are now proving both controversial and destabilizing.
>
> GATS critics and proponents agree on at least one critical point. The scope of GATS is very broad: far broader than traditional rules governing trade in goods. Indeed, the subject matter of the GATS – services – is immense. These range from birth (midwifery) to death (burial); the

trivial (shoe-shining) to the critical (heart surgery); the personal (hair-cutting) to the social (primary education); low-tech (household help) to high-tech (satellite communications); and from our wants (retail sales of toys) to our needs (water distribution).

Many governments restrict the private delivery of certain social services such as childcare to non-profit agencies. Many also confine certain basic services such as rail transportation, water distribution, or energy transmission to private, not-for-profit providers. These have never before been subject to binding international treaty obligations. They are now exposed to GATS challenge.

Postal services, the distribution and sale of alcoholic beverages, electrical generation and transmission, rail transportation, health insurance, water distribution, and waste disposal and exclusive supplier arrangements in post-secondary education, health care and other social services [would be vulnerable to] an extraordinary intrusion into democratic policy-making.

In his excellent book *Facing the Facts: A Guide to the GATS Debate*,[*] Sinclair quotes former United States Trade Representative Jeffrey Lang:

> Virtually every normative provision of the GATS is interesting and even novel. Some of these provisions are so obviously problematic that they cry out for substantive renegotiation. So little is known about their origin and intention that it may be years before we discover the impact of these provisions.

In Scott Sinclair's words,

> The GATS restrict the ability of future governments to restore, revitalize, or expand public services.
>
> The GATS is, by design, a formidable instrument [which] is, at root, hostile to public services. It treats them, at best, as unfair competition or barriers to entry for foreign services and suppliers.

Lori Wallach of Global Trade Watch in Washington, D.C., calls the GATS "NAFTA on steroids," with planned intrusion into intellectual property,

---

[*] CCPA, 2002.

information technology, investment, environmental regulations, competition policy, and labour standards, as well as the areas already mentioned.

Canada has until March of next year to lay out its GATS position. By then we'll be able to see if the Liberals are bent on national suicide.

Why might you think Canada is yet once again backing such awful deals? It's really not difficult to understand. The Canadian Council of Chief Executives and, in particular, the big five banks are there behind the scenes twisting arms and stuffing bank accounts. The banks have many billions of dollars invested in Mexico and South America and the banks, despite the disaster that happened to them in Argentina, want to invest even more. A GATS or FTAA with a Chapter 11 might let them sleep better.

Too bad they couldn't have figured out a way to apply something like Chapter 11 to their billions of dollars in loans to Enron, WorldCom, Adelphia, XO Communications, Tyco, and their other disastrous U.S. adventures.

So, if there's going to be a Free Trade Area of the Americas (FTAA), George W. Bush's pet project, would the U.S. then agree to abandon its trade-remedy actions, such as countervail and anti-dumping legislation, and its other, often phony protectionist measures? There's about as much chance of that happening as there is of Texas abolishing the death penalty or of Elvis showing up at a G8 conference.

Putting Plutonium in Children's Food

As if the current WTO round of GATS negotiations are not in themselves worrying enough, the American-led proposed Free Trade Area of the Americas is being negotiated, yet again, behind closed doors. Peter C. Newman says that the FTAA agenda will

Threaten this country's future in dramatic ways. The agreement would in reality become the modern version of the Monroe Doctrine of 1823 . . . a bald attempt to define the Americas as an exclusive sphere of U.S. influence. That imperialistic impulse was aimed at giving Washington economic and political sway over anything that moved between Alert at the frozen edge of Ellesmere Island in the Canadian Arctic to Cape

Horn, the wind-swept tip of South America. This treaty, despite its multinational roots, will have a similar effect.*

From what we have been able to learn about the American FTAA objectives, the proposed agreement represents a massive assault on national sovereignty intruding into all the GATS areas already mentioned. In short, all rules, procedures, administrative provisions or other government practices for all levels of government would be covered. Once again what is being considered is an extremely broad-based corporate bill of rights that squashes the authority of democratically-elected legislative bodies.

Among the principal and powerful behind-the-scenes FTAA backers are U.S. health care and insurance companies. And, the U.S. wants provisions similar to NAFTA's Chapter 11 included. In the words of trade lawyer Barry Appleton, "They could be putting liquid plutonium in children's food; if you ban it and the company making it is an American company, you have to pay compensation."

Knowledgeable Ottawa trade lawyer Steven Shrybman says that between 95 and 98 per cent of NAFTA's language on foreign investment is included in a leaked preliminary FTAA text obtained in 2001, and there are suggestions that some parts of the leaked text are actually worse than NAFTA. Where does the Canadian government stand? Here is how Canada's minister of foreign affairs, Bill Graham, feels:

> Mr. Graham said he is personally interested in expanding the North American integration beyond trade and tariffs into social policy . . . NAFTA could be expanded to cover social, environmental, justice and other issues, Mr. Graham said.†

Can you believe it?

And listening to the earnest reassurances about the FTAA from Pierre Pettigrew resurrects a spooky feeling of déjà vu to the days when nearly identical streams of assurances flowed from Brian Mulroney, Derek Burney, John Crosbie, Pat Carney, and Simon Reisman to the effect that the FTA talks were progressing well and the world was unfolding as it should.

---

* *Maclean's*, January 8, 2001.
† *National Post*, January 17, 2002.

The Good News, with
Special Thanks to George W. Bush

David Crane, writing from the OECD in Paris earlier this year, quoted an official of the organization to the effect that "The United States has become the new leader of the anti-globalization movement."* Recent American actions motivated by George W. Bush's concerns about U.S. mid-term elections, his own narrow victory in the 2000 presidential election, plus the memory of his father's defeat after one term as president, have inflamed anti-American sentiments around the world because of unfair and illegal protectionist measures.

Barrie McKenna, the *Globe and Mail*'s Washington correspondent, spells out the results:

> Against huge odds, the 141 members of the World Trade Organization had finally agreed that there was just enough common ground to push ahead with a new round of trade-liberalizing negotiations.
>
> The object was to get a trade deal by 2005 that would dramatically expand free trade in areas such as agriculture and services.
>
> Forget that. Any lingering goodwill is gone and you can blame the United States.
>
> There isn't a WTO member on the planet – Canada among them – that isn't steamed by a rising tide of U.S. protectionism.†

As if recent Fortress America actions relating to steel, agricultural subsidies, and softwood lumber weren't bad enough, the U.S. Senate, also looking ahead to upcoming elections, passed a new trade bill that will be certain to discourage scores of countries from getting involved in bilateral or multilateral trade talks with the U.S. in the future. The Senate's action gave the Senators the power to veto any sections of any future negotiated deal. A bill opponent, Senator Phil Gramm, said

---

* *Toronto Star*, May 16, 2002.
† *Globe and Mail*, May 17, 2002.

I'd like to ask what country in the world is going to be foolish enough to negotiate with us when they know that there's going to be a separate vote on the parts of the agreement that we like least.[*]

McKenna has it right:

The Senate amendment is a virtual death sentence for Doha [the WTO meeting place in 2001], the Free Trade Area of the Americas and any other trade deal involving the United States.

As Senator Gramm put it,

We would never negotiate with another country under circumstances when their legislative body could take out the parts of the negotiations they did not like, but leave in the parts we did not like.

In the words of the Royal Bank's Washington, D.C.–based David Kohl, the Bush administration's new $190 billion, ten-year farm subsidy program

sets back American agriculture ten years. It basically says we farm the mailbox for cheques instead of finding unique strategies to keep our agriculture globally competitive.[†]

U.S. subsidies are not going to be the only agricultural trade actions that will bring great pain to Canadian producers. Recent U.S. country-of-origin labelling legislation will have a terrible impact on Canada's $3.2 billion a year beef export industry. And the new farm subsidy bill will cause enormous damage to Canadian and other agricultural producers around the world. Even our normally cautious government Public Works Minister Ralph Goodale called the new subsidies legislation "a foul and insidious piece of legislation that we must fight by every means at our disposal."[**]

---

[*] Ibid.

[†] *Edmonton Journal,* May 18, 2002.

[**] Canadian Press, May 3, 2002.

In the summer of 2001, a *Globe and Mail* editorial had it right. The biggest WTO division is the same as it was in Seattle:

> The thorniest issue is the propensity of the world's richest countries to subsidize their farmers to the hilt, making it impossible for food producers in poor countries to compete. This is a crucial, life-and-death issue in the Third World where agriculture remains the primary industry in many countries. Rich countries spend a whopping $300 billion a year on farm subsidies, more than the entire gross domestic product of sub-Saharan Africa. Continuing such policies amounts to condemning millions to lasting poverty.
>
> The WTO is an organization on the run. After the debacle in Seattle, the group had to scour the planet to find a city willing to host its next meeting. It settled on Qatar primarily because it was willing and able to minimize public displays of dissent.[*]

Bear in mind that all this was before George Bush announced his new $190 billion in agricultural subsidies.

Another priority for developing countries has been the curbing of countervailing and anti-dumping legislation which has frequently been used to discriminate against poor countries (not to mention poor Canada). Where the vast majority of WTO members were upset by these actions in the past, American protectionist actions since Qatar have incensed not only Third World countries, but the EU fifteen, Japan, China, and many other major developed trading nations. At this writing, Japan, South Korea, China, and the European Union are all planning retaliatory action against the U.S., as is Brazil, while other countries are certain to join in. The man who is likely to be next Brazilian President, Jose Serra, says of the proposed FTAA:

> America talks constantly about free trade, but when it comes to practice, it is protectionist.

During the past few years, there has been growing anger in the developing world where scores of countries are feeling shut out from many promised benefits from the Uruguay round of GATT negotiations.

---

[*] August 7, 2001.

Developing countries made minor progress in gaining access to the affluent markets of the wealthy G7 and other countries, while multi-national corporations based in the wealthy countries obtained the rights to establish themselves around the world.

There's now growing evidence that as more information about the WTO, the GATS, and the FTAA becomes available, there will be growing opposition from citizens, from civil society groups, and from governments. Already many developing countries are opposed to many aspects of the proposed new agreements. There's increasing reason to believe that the forces of dissent and opposition that stopped the MAI and blocked talks progress in Seattle will be able to coalesce to prevent democracy-damaging agreements from proceeding. Scott Sinclair sums up nicely at the end of his book:

> If there is one lesson that proponents [of the new agreement] should have learned from the Seattle debacle and the failed MAI, it is that, no matter how emphatic or strident their voices, they cannot simply shut down or control the debate. With modest effort, non-governmental organizations, elected officials and ordinary citizens are more than capable of sorting out the issues, of separating GATS fact from fiction. And when they do, they are likely to react with shocked disapproval at how far, and in what direction the proverbial bicycle has been driven. Then the main questions will be how quickly citizens mobilize and how effectively they bring their considerable influence to bear on their respective governments – both in changing the nature of GATS negotiations that are now underway in Geneva, and in charting a more balanced future.

How seriously does the world view the trade policies of the Bush Government? The normally reserved and moderate *The Economist* calls the recent U.S. protectionist actions "poisonous," the steel tariffs "outrageous," and the farm-subsidy bill "monstrous."[*]

The new U.S. subsidies for corn, wheat, soybean, peanut, lentil, chickpea, honey, wool, and dairy farms will be at levels that are as much as four times European subsidies and two to three times higher than those in Canada.

---

[*] May 11, 2002.

Even prior to the recent spate of U.S. protectionism, more and more developing countries were growing hostile to further liberalization, especially where it was little related to trade.

Dalton Camp rightly called the WTO "the most powerful, influential, and feared unelected body in the universe since Tomás de Torquemada headed up the Spanish Inquisition."[*]

Canada can and should lead a campaign to reform the WTO so that it is more concerned about fair trade, about world poverty and environmental issues, and less focussed on promoting the rights of corporations in place of the rights of democratically elected governments. The next WTO ministerial meeting is in 2003. Before Canada puts its services bargaining position on the WTO table, Canadians had better join in the campaign against yet another sellout and capitulation before it's too late.

Fortunately, with friends like George W. Bush, our chances of stopping more trade sellouts are better now than they were before the current GATS talks got underway. As far as the FTAA is concerned, it's hard to imagine any country in the Americas which now will not show anything but deep apprehension towards a proposed deal.

Dependency, Vulnerability, and Mythology

> Today, trade represents 45 per cent of the Canadian economy,
> 85 per cent of which is with the United States. This trend
> has enhanced Canadian growth and employment.
> – Sherry Cooper, December 2001

An absence of facts to back their ideology has never bothered our pro-free-trade Americanizers. Canadians have been constantly bombarded with statements to the effect that our exports now account for between 40 and 50 per cent of our GDP. We hear and read this so often from so many supposedly reputable sources that it seems that it must be true. And, if true, that means our lives are utterly dependent on exports, and we better not forget that.

---

[*] *Toronto Star*, April 22, 2001.

Even bright women and good Canadians such as Anne Golden ("In Canada, one in three jobs depends on exports") and Naomi Klein ("With almost half of our economy now directly dependent on an open border, it's difficult to see how Canada can stand up to U.S. pressure") are convinced of our dependency and vulnerability.

Economist Jim Stanford presents a different picture:

> It is commonly claimed that foreign trade now accounts for almost all of Canada's economy. It's true that the total gross value of exports and imports exceeds 80% of our GDP. But these trade figures double-count and triple-count the value of many manufactured products which now flow back and forth across the Canada–U.S. border in the course of their final processing.
>
> In reality, the relative importance of the traded and non-traded portions of our economy is actually the opposite: over 80 per cent of our total economic output is produced in Canada, and consumed in Canada by Canadians, for Canadians, never crossing a national boundary.[*]

Philip Cross, Chief of Current Analysis at Statistics Canada, explains further that if double- and triple-counting is removed, the real value-added contribution of exports is much smaller. Madeline Drohan, writing about Cross's research, puts it in perspective. As to our exports,

> If you put it in terms of the total economy's exposure to the United States, it ends up being about 20 per cent of the economy. All of a sudden we're not looking quite so vulnerable.
>
> The bottom line on all of this is that exports are not as large a share of our economy as people think and that means we are less dependant on the United States than is commonly thought.[†]

Trade is good. Exports are important. But neither are supposed to be the *raison d'être* of our existence as a nation. And those who purposely exaggerate their importance are doing Canada a great disservice by exaggerating our dependency and vulnerability.

---

[*] CCPA *Monitor*, June 2001.
[†] *Globe and Mail*, January 13, 2001.

A further point needs to be made here. Much of what we have been exporting to the U.S. in increasing quantities represents things that Americans need and in many cases need badly.* This applies not only to oil and natural gas and electricity, and other resources, but to other exports. Our long-term automotive trade surplus with the U.S. will inevitably fall somewhat, but U.S. auto producers are highly cognizant of their own huge exports to Canada and the growing competition from offshore auto producers. Where we are vulnerable now in auto trade is in the shift of production to Mexico because of NAFTA. It's no exaggeration to say that NAFTA spells a potential disaster for auto production in Canada.

The given – that Canada is so dependent on the United States because over 85 per cent of our exports go to the U.S. and because these exports supposedly represent 46 or 47 per cent of our GDP – limits consideration of the full spectrum of our public policy options.

But the "obvious truism" of our dependency can largely be ascribed to our elites' colonial mentality and their timidity. They live in constant terror of somehow annoying the U.S. and thereby damaging our economy and (always unsaid) their own growing investment in the U.S.

Allan Gotlieb, who now heads the Canadian branch of the right-wing American Donner Foundation, is a good example of our dependency and vulnerability mentality:

> As a society depending on the U.S. for some 40 per cent of its national annual economic income, Canada needs the White House and administration on its side.

Moreover, Gotlieb says "It's important for Canada to be sympathetic to the U.S. conception of the special role it plays in the world." And why not, so long as such needs do not produce supplicant and mendicant behaviour.

But, the truth is that we're not even remotely near being 40 per cent dependent on the U.S. for our income. Gotlieb should know and probably does know better.

---

* In May 2002, a conference of international petroleum experts predicted that world supplies of crude oil will peak as early as 2010, and then start to decline with inevitable soaring prices and economic instability. In particular, the U.S. will be the most vulnerable and the hardest hit.

Should our ability to shape policies in our own best interests be straitjacketed? I think not. On the contrary, there is no reason why we cannot deal with the U.S. from a position of strength, or, at the very least, on an equal, level playing-field basis.

Let's look at what it is that we export to the U.S. Let's start with resources. Is there anyone who seriously believes that an upset American government would take steps to curtail Canadian oil and natural gas exports? Instead, as every year goes by as far as we can see into the future, the U.S. will become even more dependent on our oil and natural gas. Canada is already the number-one energy supplier to the U.S., and that ranking will do nothing but strengthen in the years ahead.

What about forest products? An extraordinarily weak-spined Canadian government has allowed the U.S. to once again curtail our softwood lumber sales. Without question, the EU would have long ago told the Americans that if they wish to behave in such an outrageous manner then the EU would have no choice but to reciprocate. Canada has numerous alternatives starting with cutting back on oil, natural gas and electricity exports to the U.S. or, as mentioned earlier, adding billions of dollars in export taxes.

Had we not been such consummate cowards, imagine what the response would be from energy- and power-hungry U.S. states and communities. The uproar against the lumber lobby in Congress would have been unprecedented. The same Congressmen who so unreservedly backed the lobby would be facing outraged constituents, including most of the large corporations that finance their election campaigns.

In yet another example of blatant intimidation, Paul Cellucci has warned Canada not to retaliate against U.S. protectionist policies. The warning came after several Canadians suggested taking retaliatory action relating to Canada's energy exports to the U.S. (The day I am writing these words Cellucci earnestly proclaimed that the U.S. wants to "promote freer and fairer trade"). Cellucci should be ignored. How dumb does he think Canadians are?

Motor vehicles are among our key exports to the U.S. But most of these cars, vans, and trucks are assembled in this country by very profitable U.S. auto companies, and much of the content of these exports are parts and components already imported from the U.S. Bear in mind that almost 70 per cent of the cross-border trade of foreign corporations is with their parent firms at non-arms-length prices. The parts and components sold to assembly plants in Canada create many jobs in the U.S., while the large profits from the U.S.-dominated motor vehicle sector in Canada increasingly show up in the U.S.

Because it's so important, I asked economist Jim Stanford to further explain why the exaggerated trade dependency is so misleading:

It is commonly suggested that Canada's economy has become almost completely dependent on foreign trade. A misleading statistic that is often used to support this claim, is the fact that the value of Canada's total exports now equal almost half of the value of our entire economy (measured by GDP). For example, in 2000 Canada's total exports equaled $480 billion (about 85 per cent of which went to the U.S.) This amount equals 45 per cent of our GDP for that same year. But it is wrong to therefore conclude that 45 per cent of our economic output is exported. The problem with this interpretation is that it compares apples to oranges: the measure of exports reports *gross* export sales, while the measure of GDP reports the *value added* at all the different stages of Canadian production. If exports were also reported on a value-added basis, they would be much smaller – since much of the value of things we export reflects the cost of imported inputs which were used in producing those exports.

Indeed, sometimes the same item could show up in our export figures two, three, or even more times. Suppose a Canadian plant manufactures a basic auto part, using steel that was produced in the U.S. from Canadian iron ore. The part is then exported to a U.S. facility which uses it in the production of a more complex sub-assembly. It then comes back to Canada for installation in a passenger car, which is then exported back to the U.S. The final value of the entire car, plus the basic auto part, plus the iron ore, is all counted in our gross export sales – triple counting Canadian content, and vastly overstating the true economic importance of the export business.

Foreign trade is very important to our resource and manufacturing industries, but together they account for less than one-quarter of our economy. In other sectors (especially services), trade is much less important – often insignificant. On a weighted average basis only about 15 per cent of the actual *value-added* output of our economy is exported. The vast majority of what we churn out in our economy, is done by

Canadians, and for Canadians. The claim that foreign trade is the dominant force in our economy is clearly wrong.

A well-known senior Canadian chief economist with a very large pro-free-trade organization asked me not to quote him by name but told me:

> I cringe every time I hear someone say exports are 45 per cent of GDP. In reality, it's value-added that has to be compared to GDP. In the end, it's really only 17 to 18 per cent.

Of course exports create lots of jobs. But the increased imports that have resulted from our two "trade" agreements have *cost* jobs.

Every time you hear Brian Mulroney or Tom d'Aquino or anyone else trumpet that exports are 46 or 47 per cent of GDP, remember that they almost certainly *know* this is a highly misleading use of statistics. Unfortunately, our newspapers usually cite such numbers without questioning their accuracy or relevance.

Let's dwell for a moment on Canadian imports. Here are our imports of goods and services measured as a percentage of GDP compared to those of other G7 countries:[*]

Canada	41 per cent
Germany	28 per cent
United Kingdom	27 per cent
France	24 per cent
Italy	24 per cent
United States	13 per cent
Japan	9 per cent

Think of all the jobs, retained profits, and overall increased economic activity if Canada was only an average trading country.

Since, for decades, from Richard Nixon to George W. Bush, American presidents never seem to have any idea that Canada is their largest trading partner, and since most Americans think it is Japan, Mexico, or the U.K. wouldn't it be a good idea to provide them with some information?

---

[*] United Nations *Human Development Report*, 2001.

In 2000, U.S. exports of goods and services to Canada, plus their income from investments, exceeded their sales to, and investment receipts from, any other country by a huge $177 billion. Their exports of goods to Canada (in U.S.$) were $68 billion higher than to Mexico and $115 billion higher than to Japan.

From 1946 to 2001, in every single year, the U.S. sold more goods to Canada than to any other country.

All told, in 2000, Canada bought about one-quarter of all U.S. exported goods, more than Japan, the United Kingdom, and Germany put together! Canada bought more U.S. goods than all fifteen EU countries combined and more than all Latin American and Caribbean countries combined.

Boy, are we vulnerable!

Supporters of the FTA base its supposed great success on our increase in exports. (They always somehow manage to ignore the increased imports).

Okay, let's look at the rate of growth of Canadian exports. In the first eleven years of the FTA our exports grew at an average annual rate of just under 9 per cent. However, during the eleven years prior to the FTA, our exports grew at an average annual rate of 11.5 per cent.

Now let's look at how the growth of our merchandise trade balances compared. During the first eleven years of free trade, our trade balances increased at an average annual rate of 8.7 per cent. But, during the previous eleven years before free trade, they increased at an annual average rate of 11.6 per cent. And in the 1970s they increased as the rate of 14 per cent.

There's a great deal of accumulated evidence that without making the many punitive FTA and NAFTA concessions, our exports to the U.S. would have been at the very least 90 to 95 per cent of current levels, and our job-creation record significantly better than it has been since 1989.

University of Toronto economist Peter Dungan emphasized how misleading it is to look only at exports in measuring the economic impact of the trade agreements. If increased imports are considered, the net impact on our economy is much, much smaller than widely claimed.

Dungan's colleague Dan Trefler shows that while the agreements did create jobs there were "huge job losses" as a result of increased imports from the U.S. And a 2001 Industry Canada study showed that the FTA and NAFTA accounted for only about 9 per cent of our increased exports to the U.S., while our low dollar and an expanding U.S. economy were mainly responsible for the balance. While it is now clear that most of our increased exports to the U.S. came as a result of our dollar decreasing in value in relation to the U.S. dollar (from well over 85¢ to as low as 63¢), it's interesting to note that those who brag so enthusiastically about our exports to the U.S. are invariably the very same people who complain so stridently about the low value of our dollar.

Well, despite all of this, surely with our burgeoning exports, our share of world trade has been increasing? Wrong. During the 1980s it averaged 4.2 per cent annually. During the 1990s, it fell to 3.9 per cent. Another broken promise.

Okay then, surely with our increased exports, our share of the U.S. market has increased because of free trade? Wrong, again. Mexico, China, and other Asian countries increased their U.S. market share, while Canada's share declined.

This, once again, is exactly opposite to what we were promised, the theory being that foreign manufacturers would flock to Canada because of our "guaranteed access" to the U.S. market, and use Canada as "an export platform" for shipments to the U.S.

The economist Richard Harris has told us that "free trade has been even more successful than one would normally predict." Obviously, Harris's normal measurements of success are difficult to predict. Perhaps the following addition to my previous comparisons of the years before the FTA with the FTA years will be of interest to Harris and other neo-con continentalist economists.

From December 1988, the month before the FTA was implemented, to the end of April of this year, during the entire 13¼ years, Canada created a pathetic total of less than 1,381,000 full-time payroll jobs. In the 13¼ years *before* the FTA, we created over 3 million full-time payroll jobs, and that was when our population was *much* smaller, and so were our exports. And, lastly with respect to GDP and exports, while during the 1990s our annual export increases averaged 9.7 per cent, our average annual GDP increases were a poor 2.28 per cent.

A thousand apologies for all these numbers, but they're important, and it's most unlikely that you've encountered many of them elsewhere.

So much for all the baloney about "40 per cent of our income" and all the rest of the constant stream of nonsense that we get from our radical conservative Americanizers.

Abrogation or Assimilation: Take Your Choice

Canada has always been a trading nation. While there is ample evidence that we have become over-reliant on both exports and imports and would have been considerably better off with trade levels closer to those in other G7 countries while concentrating more on serving our own domestic market, we will continue to be a major trading nation for as far as we can see into the future.

I have yet to meet a single Canadian nationalist who is opposed to trade, or one who is opposed to fair trade and fair international-trading rules. Nor do I know more than a tiny handful who are opposed to most of the trade policies that evolved after many years and several international rounds of GATT negotiations.

For as long as I can remember, Ottawa well understood that Canada would always be better off if we did our best to conduct our external affairs on a multinational basis. As Jeffrey Simpson has noted:

> Canada likes to get the U.S. inside multinational tents, where, with other like-minded countries, it can influence U.S. thinking before U.S. policy becomes carved in stone.
>
> A rules-based system of international affairs – with treaties and institutions and an important role for the United Nations – has always been in Canada's interests, and it's been an important system for engaging Americans.*

The Mulroney pursuit of the FTA changed all that, and NAFTA made it worse. Then, the U.S. capture of the WTO and GATS agendas made the multinational approach infinitely more difficult.

This said, while the WTO remains problematic for Canada, the FTA and NAFTA are certain to prove deadly for our survival as a country.

Four things have to happen if Canada is to survive as a prosperous, independent country in charge of its own future, instead of a dependent and weak American colony.

---

* *Globe and Mail*, April 6, 2002.

The first thing that must be done is to bring a halt to the growing foreign ownership and foreign control, mostly American, of our country.

But I've also indicated that under the terms of the FTA and NAFTA, Americans can continue buying up our country, even if (as the polls demonstrate) most of us are opposed. Both agreements have six-month abrogation clauses. Notice of abrogation can be given and six months later the agreements are no longer in effect. The clauses were inserted in the agreements for a good reason. Both Canada and the U.S. wanted them in case either was unhappy with the results.

Some might argue that a better course of action than abrogation would be to renegotiate the agreements, but this view is naive. After so adamantly promising the electorate in 1993 that they would renegotiate the two agreements once they were in office, the Chrétien government soon realized that renegotiation would be impossible; the Americans made that emphatically clear. Today, the Americans position would be even more opposed and intransigent. After all, why would the U.S. want to renegotiate agreements that brought them pretty well everything they wanted and that have been so beneficial for them?

What would be the difference if we operated under WTO rules instead of under the FTA and NAFTA? *The difference would be enormous.* In dozens of extremely important ways, the FTA and NAFTA tie our hands and leave us vulnerable. Our obligations under the WTO are much less onerous.

For example, gone would be the notorious NAFTA Chapter 11, which allows American corporations to sue Canadian governments. Gone would be the investment provisions allowing Americans to come into Canada and buy up the country. Current WTO investment obligations are very limited and certainly a pale imitation of those in NAFTA. Gone would be the onerous resource-sharing agreements which will certainly leave Canada terribly vulnerable in the near future. And if my optimism about GATS is accurate, gone would be much of our vulnerability in providing U.S. companies with access to health care, education and other public services. Gone too would be our inability to manage trade to our advantage by way of a whole list of options including export taxes. And, gone would be the necessity of charging Americans only what we charge Canadians for our resources. Gone too would be some of the national treatment provisions relating to services; instead we would be entitled to simply list our desired services exemptions. Gone would be our capitulation to American unilateralism and our excessive built-in vulnerability to U.S. dumping and countervailing legislation. Gone too would be the quirky NAFTA panels. Instead disputes would be settled by more balanced WTO panels where we would stand a much better chance of fair treatment. Barrie McKenna points out that Richard Braudo and Michael Trebilock from the University of Toronto law school say that NAFTA dispute panels are "institutionally incapable of resolving disputes as fundamental, complex and economically significant as that of softwood lumber" and Canada should abandon its NAFTA challenge and go with the WTO.*

Most of all, U.S. authority in our domestic affairs would be sharply diminished. Our ability to nurture and protect our assets, corporate and natural, would be substantially enhanced. Getting rid of all those grotesque FTA and NAFTA chapters and clauses that have little or nothing to do with trade would make us freer to chose our own priorities and our own destiny. Canada's trade strategy in the future would be to work with like-minded WTO countries concerned not only with fair trade, but with protecting their national integrity. Canada should lead the way in fighting off U.S. plans to entrench new WTO services rules, and any new investment rules. We need to become WTO activists, instead of NAFTA supplicants. We can work with the many WTO countries that now have serious reservations about the direction the WTO has taken in recent years. A huge split has developed between rich and poor countries; about three-quarters of WTO members are developing countries. Others, such as France and China, for example, want to guard their sovereignty carefully. Remember, it was France that killed the terrible MAI. There are many countries Canada could work with to realign the WTO back to where it should be, an international organization designed to promote international trade in goods and an organization that keeps its nose out of domestic policies, and especially services that are for the most part not involved in trade.

Canada's goal should be to work with EU countries that share many of our social values, and developing countries that view with enormous apprehension current American trade and other U.S. international policies. We can work with the Nordic countries, France, Brazil, China, and India to push for fundamental WTO reform and the

---

* *Globe and Mail*, May 31, 2002.

rebalancing of rules so they protect the best interests of citizens rather than corporations. And bear in mind that the increasingly powerful European community nations have long-established social, labour, regional and public service policies much closer to our own than those of the U.S.

And we must remind the self-inflated WTO bureaucracy that the organization was never intended to be omnipotent and no elected assembly anywhere ever told voters that the WTO was to be a new world government.

In both the FTA and NAFTA we're locked into an asymmetrical relationship with a dominant superpower that regards Canada with a mixture of indifference, apathy and scorn. In the WTO we could work to be a leader in international reform and return to our long-standing multilateral approach to our international relations.

Of course, the major problem we face is the continentalist, colonial bent of our Liberal government, and I'll return to that in the final chapters that follow.

But before that, a word about our Department of Foreign Affairs and International Trade. I asked one of Canada's leading trade lawyers how it was possible for our Ottawa bureaucrats to have performed so poorly in past trade negotiations and how is it that in the current GATS negotiations it already appears as if they're prepared to give away so much. Here's what he said:

> Over at the Department they have their thick ideological blinders on so tight they've cut off circulation to their brains. Now all that's left is institutional myopia where only the desires of transnational corporations are important.

No doubt the Canadian political, corporate and media establishment will respond with horror to my suggestion that we walk away from the FTA and NAFTA. Many of the same people who brought us these dreadful agreements and who are now planning more of the same, and worse, have a vested interest in preserving the governmental servitude they have helped produce.

At this writing, the C. D. Howe Institute is working on fifteen studies on continental integration, the IRPP is planning ten additional papers, and Yves Poisson of Public Policy Forum says:

Many people think NAFTA has reached its limits. Options are being examined for how to move beyond it.[*]

Tom Walkom, writing about the softwood lumber dispute had this to say:

> I don't understand why everyone gets so miffed with the Americans. Surely Washington is doing what a national government is supposed to do – protect its own economic interests. Maybe Ottawa should quit whining and take a lesson.
>
> Canada should rethink the whole idea of international trade. Trade is not new to this country; neither is globalization.
>
> But we've been most successful when we haven't given ourselves up completely to the vicissitude of the international marketplace, when we've maintained some level of autonomy and self-sufficiency.[†]

And when we've maintained our national self-respect and integrity.

Abrogation or assimilation.

Take your choice.

Is It Too Late to Save Canada?

It doesn't look good.

But there's still a chance.

Canada is too good a country to abandon without a damn good fight. It's time for a fight.

There's a long list of reasons why our country is disappearing. But, there still remains one potentially indomitable force that could stop the sellout of Canada.

The combination of negatives is almost overwhelming. Those who care about the survival of Canada face a disastrous accumulation of factors that together are likely to prove fatal:

---

[*] *Globe and Mail*, April 11, 2002.
[†] *Toronto Star*, August 14, 2001.

- excessive foreign ownership and foreign control
- excessive corporate concentration
- a powerful business elite determined to merge our country into the U.S.
- a compliant, bumbling political elite no longer concerned with Canadian independence and sovereignty
- a political system that has become increasingly dependant on big money from big business and wealthy individuals.
- a media mostly controlled by right wing continentalists
- so-called "think tanks," funded by big business, whose works are religiously reported in most of our media as gospel
- a federal government severely constrained by straitjacketing clauses in the FTA and NAFTA
- a federal government, blind and oblivious, that plans to enter into future agreements that will make things even worse
- a federal government so weakened by repeated transfers of power to the provinces that it considers itself unable to provide national leadership in a host of vital policy areas
- an increasing North-South commercial intercourse and the declining importance of East-West connections.

How ironic it is when ideas such as those found in this book are put forward, they are called nationalism, with many nasty negative adjectives attached. Meanwhile, in the U.S. self-determination and national pride are proudly called patriotism.

Richard Gwyn has called Canadian nationalism "a played-out political force."

> It seems that a conviction of inevitability has replaced passion about country, and has even displaced concern that the way things are going, not much will soon be left in Canada that's distinctively Canadian.[*]

Gwyn is partially right, but people are wrong if they believe that a visceral passion for this country doesn't still exist. It obviously doesn't exist in our corporate boardrooms, but who among us wasn't thrilled by the

---

[*] *Toronto Star*, July 2, 1999.

explosive, exuberant emotion displayed during the Salt Lake City Olympics? Across Canada if you can believe it, we became a nation of proud flag-wavers!

After Salt Lake, Charles Gordon wrote:

> Would you have predicted . . . that the country would erupt in a frenzy of nationalistic joy over the Olympics, and particularly Olympic hockey?
>
> Not many people would have. But it makes sense when you think about it. Canadians have always wanted to be proud of their country, but it has become unfashionable in recent years to do so.
>
> The prevailing mood, heightened by the wannabe-Americans in our news media, has been one of scorn for Canadian institutions, for Canadian accomplishments.
>
> Canadians disagreed. They were proud of their country and looking for a reason to shout it out. [*]

And what about the passionate display of deep cross-Canada sadness, emotion, and pride of country shown upon the death of Pierre Trudeau and the death of Peter Gzowski?

Canadians love their country, and don't want to see it disappear. The disgusting goal of the "deep integration" gang is not what the vast majority of Canadians want.

Dyane Adams, Canada's Commissioner of Official Languages, expressed this view well:

> A country is not a business and it's not just about the economy. It is a social contract and it's about people deciding to live together according to a series of shared principles, guidelines and values. [†]

Canadians don't want to become Americans. This doesn't make most of them anti-Americans. It means most of us believe in freedom – the freedom to decide our own future. Are Canadians unique in their attitudes towards the U.S.? Hardly. In 2001, a poll in France showed that 12 per cent of respondents said they admired the United States while 46 per cent were either critical of the U.S. or worried by it, and 75 per

---

[*] *Ottawa Citizen*, March 1, 2002.
[†] Letter to the *National Post*, March 13, 2002.

cent wanted less American economic and financial influence.[*] And the French have nowhere near the degree of American ownership, control, and cultural presence that we do.

If we must stop the growth of foreign ownership and foreign control and if we must step away from the FTA and NAFTA, if Canada is to survive, then the obvious question must be: Just *who* is going to do these things? The current Liberal government or any future Liberal government we can imagine?

Jean Chrétien's Liberals are the most continentalist and conservative Liberal Party in Canadian history, and in more than a few respects they so strongly resemble Brian Mulroney and friends that it's impossible to tell the difference. Both governments have one fundamental thing in common. They both have been almost totally dominated by the agendas of big business.

Jean Chrétien became prime minister of Canada in 1993 because Brian Mulroney had become the most unpopular prime minister in Canadian history[†] and, at least partially, because Chrétien promised to renegotiate NAFTA so that the agreement would be more favourable for Canada. Probably an even more important factor was that many Canadians perceived the Mulroney government as sleazy, dishonest, and corrupt, and Chrétien earnestly promised to reform the way politics was practised in Ottawa.

Is it any wonder that, after the scandals in the Mulroney government, Canadians are now fed up, disillusioned, and cynical after nine more years of Liberal pork barrel, patronage, sleazy contracts, mismanagement of public funds, allegations of kickbacks, hidden contracts, and, to boot, a large amount of arrogant indifference?

For most governments, such a history would sound a death knell. And the Grand Mère hotel should have been the final toll. But for the Liberals, even with 45 per cent of Canadians saying that the government is corrupt,[**] what's to worry, given the relative weakness and lack of appeal of the opposition? At least that was the case before Paul Martin's departure from cabinet.

---

[*] *The Economist*, August 4, 2001.

[†] In the 1993 federal election, the Progressive Conservatives were almost annihilated, losing all but two seats in the House of Commons.

[**] Pollara poll, *National Post*, May 17, 2002.

Lawrence Martin, long before the advertising contracts and the Gagliano, Boudria, and Eggleton messes became public, had this to say:

> A strong indictment of the Chrétien years has been the concentration and abuse of power. The Somalia inquiry was shut down, protesters were muzzled at APEC, grants and loans were politicized and mismanaged at the Human Resources Canada department, attempts to open up the system through parliamentary reform were stifled, allegations of conflict of interest and feathering friends' nests beat at the Prime Minister's door on the Shawinigate file.
>
> If there was an incriminating moment for the government party that encapsulated it all, it came early this year when the Liberals rose red-faced to vote down their own promise to create an independent ethics counsellor.[*]

An overbearing concentration of power has always been present in majority governments in modern Canada. But, under Jean Chrétien, this centralized domination has reached unprecedented levels. The brutal way in which the Prime Minister and his arrogant staff quashed dissent and freedom of expression in the party, is without parallel. This, combined with the most complacent, acquiescent, timid government backbenchers in the history of the House of Commons, makes a mockery of the way democracy is supposed to operate.

All things considered, who's really in charge? Last summer, Thomas Walkom wrote:

> What Chrétien has done, even more than his predecessor Brian Mulroney, is hand back full direction of the Canadian economy to business.
>
> Under Chrétien, the federal government has quietly set about to reverse about 60 years of Canadian history.
>
> It's not only taking the government out of the economy; it's taking the government out of government.[†]

More recently, Jeffrey Simpson characterized the Chrétien government as:

---

[*] *Globe and Mail*, October 23, 2001.
[†] *Toronto Star*, August 28, 2001.

A swirling mass of latent animus infects a vacillating government led by a leader without an agenda, except a highly personal and increasingly petty one.[*]

And, at this writing, just before the manuscript goes off to the publisher:

One Liberal MP, who asked not to be identified, said many Liberal MPs are glad the summer break is coming because there has been nothing for them to do.

"Caucus is just this side of irrelevant at the moment. There is no sign it is going to change. There is no debate in our caucus now.

"People are really tired, really fatigued with the Prime Minister, with the lack of agenda."[†]

Susan Riley sums it up succinctly:

It is very difficult to find an example of the Chrétien government acting firmly in the public interest.

So much for democracy in Canada.

In his reply to the Speech from the Throne on January 31, 2001, Jean Chrétien said:

When we formed the government more than seven years ago, we came with a vision of the country we wanted to build. Of the values and principles that would guide our actions. A distinct Canadian way. A distinct Canadian model. Our vision and our purpose has not changed.

A distinct Canadian way? A distinct Canadian model? No wonder Canadians are now so cynical about politics and politicians. No wonder voter turnout in the last election was the lowest in almost seventy years. And if Chrétien goes, will things be any better?

When he was in opposition, Paul Martin was supposedly concerned about the level of foreign ownership in Canada. He told the Council of Canadians about his experience working for an American company: "I

---

[*] *Globe and Mail*, May 4, 2002.
[†] *National Post*, May 15, 2002.

swore to myself that my children and grandchildren would never have to go to a foreign company (head office) and be treated like puppets who have to jump when somebody else pulls the strings."* Too bad Martin has such a poor memory.

For Martin now, eliminating the border "is overwhelmingly a commercial issue, not a sovereignty issue."† And how does he and his former Department of Finance feel about the growth of foreign ownership and control in Canada? The answer is straightforward: please give us more of the same, much more. Come on in, buy up and take over the country. The last two Speeches from the Throne waxed eloquently about the warm reception foreign investors could expect.

Mind you, neither Ottawa or any provincial government *ever* mentions the words "foreign ownership" or "foreign control." It's always "foreign investment." Too bad neither Paul Martin or anyone else in the Chrétien government has been unable to find the time to look at the disheartening monthly reports from the Investment Review Division of Industry Canada detailing the dimensions of the sellout of our country.

Is there even a tiny doubt how Martin and the Liberals feel about the growing foreign ownership and control of our country? Not an iota. A headline in the *Globe and Mail* while he was still finance minister told us "Martin to pitch to U.S. investors" in a major speech in New York. The story went on to report that "More than ever, Canada needs to maintain the flow of direct and indirect investment from the United States, analysts say."**

There probably would be one change relating to foreign ownership and foreign control and our melding into the American Empire if and when Martin becomes prime minister. It will probably proceed even faster than under Brian Mulroney and Jean Chrétien.

It's worth noting also that Martin supported the terribly decentralizing Meech Lake accord which would have weakened the national government even further.

Then there's "Governor" Manley. *Time* magazine describes Manley as

Ottawa's most assertive and pro-American figure.

---

* Southam Newspapers, August 8, 1998.
† *National Post*, November 16, 2001.
** January 15, 2001.

As far as Manley is concerned,

> On the economic side, integration is irreversible. I don't think we should get hung up on twentieth-century notions of sovereignty.[*]

Well, that's pretty clear, isn't it? Want to know all you need to know about John Manley? Read the above quote again. When Manley was minister of industry, his department listed as among the reasons for foreigners to come into Canada was "local financing . . . the ease of financing in Canada" and "the availability of subsidies."

There you have it. Come on in and we'll help you to buy up the country. We'll put up the money and we'll give you cash subsidies to boot. Anyway, there's nothing to worry about. Manley refers to concerns about the growing foreign ownership in Canada as "flashbacks to the sixties. It's so foolish."[†]

From the time he joined the cabinet, Manley has made it plain that he's prepared to sell off the country. One of the most blatant misrepresentations relating to foreign direct investment in Canada was an Industry Canada paper which wildly exaggerated the impact of foreign investment on job creation and other aspects of the Canadian economy. The paper raved about the positive contribution of foreign participation but considered none of the vitally important downsides. The widely circulated study was produced for Mr. Manley at the direction of his senior officials and was extensively and prominently quoted in newspapers across Canada. Clearly the intention of the "study" was to show how beneficial FDI is to Canada, but any first-year economics student could easily have picked it apart in a brief essay.

One part of the document, "Why Invest in Canada," was most revealing. Foreign investors invest in this country because "we have skilled labour, favourable regulations, subsidies, local financing, ease of financing, resource availability, managerial skills, and available technology."

Sounds to me like a darn good place for Canadians to start to regain control of their own country. You might think some intelligent government would see that all those subsidies and financing went to Canadian companies. With the understanding, of course, that no company receiving

---

[*] *Time*, January 7, 2002.
[†] *National Post*, March 31, 1999.

a penny of government subsidies, financing, or loan guarantees could be sold to foreigners.

One other thing. When John Manley hired an economic consulting firm to praise the benefits of foreign investment in Canada, he chose an American consulting firm to do the study.

Maybe being "Governor Manley" is what he really aspires to.

Maurizio Bevilacqua was the Liberal chair of the House of Commons Finance Committee and is now junior finance minister. Here's how David Crane describes him:

> Bevilacqua has become an all-out enthusiast for far-reaching integration with the United States, advocating not just harmonization of immigration policies but suggesting common competition policies, energy policies and environmental policies, for example. Canadians, he contends, should think of themselves as being part of a continental unit rather than a distinct nation.[*]

Please, heaven forbid, *not* a distinct nation!

With the Liberals in power, is there anything that isn't up for grabs? Water exports? American nuclear missiles based in Canada? The five principles of medicare? Wait until you see the long list that the Liberals have already decided to put on the GATS negotiations table. The Liberals are selling out our country. If they stay in power much longer, it will forever be too late to save Canada. And, if there's a single living soul who thinks the Liberals are going to change for the better in any significant way, I know of a friend's Enron shares I'd like to sell them.

For Eric Kierans, former Trudeau cabinet minister, the Liberals have abandoned all the best attributes and become simply "just another piece of political machinery in the service of corporatism."[†]

Wouldn't it be interesting to ask Jean Chrétien, Paul Martin, John Manley, and Allan Rock just how much of Canada they are prepared to see foreign owned? Would it be 40 per cent? Fifty? Sixty? More? Why doesn't some brave member of the press gallery or the House of Commons ask these questions? "And tell me, Mr. Martin, if foreign ownership becomes too high, what exactly would you do about it?" And you Mr. Manley?

---

[*] *Toronto Star*, November 7, 2001.
[†] *Remembering*, Stoddart, 2001.

And what of the Official Opposition, the party backed by anti-abortion, anti-gun-control, anti-Kyoto, anti-immigration, pro-private-health-care, and even greater decentralization enthusiasts?

For Stephen Harper, Canada must have even closer relations with the U.S.:

> It doesn't make sense to have anything but ideal relations and non-partisan relations with the President of the United States.[*]

Whatever that means.

From the early days of the Reform Party, the Americanization of Canada has been clearly on the agenda. Not satisfied with transferring even more power over our decision-making to the U.S., the Alliance is also a strong proponent of even more decentralization. Those Canadians who want a weaker national government will be right at home with Mr. Harper, the man who wanted to "firewall" Alberta to keep out the Canada Pension Plan, the RCMP, and Ottawa's involvement in health care.

Bob Rae described Mr. Harper and his party this way:

> Reform and now the Canadian Alliance have certainly affected the location of the centre, but they have been singularly unsuccessful at capturing it. They have been too simplistic, too narrow, too ideological and too deliberately regional. They are in a box of their own making. They owe their success in the West to an unapologetic appeal to local identity and grievance.

And, a party that has long promoted resentment of Central Canada

> should hardly be surprised that these millions of alleged oppressors do not rush to embrace them. A party cannot hope to govern without Ontario and Quebec. That's not a conspiracy; it's called democracy.[†]

In York University political science professor Jim Laxer's words, Stephen Harper's vision of Canada

---

[*] *National Post*, May 20, 2002.
[†] *Globe and Mail*, April 23, 2002.

Is so decentralist that it is not unfair to compare his ideas to those of the Bloc Québécois.

Those who value the Tory nation-building tradition should be extremely alarmed at the prospect of Stephen Harper becoming prime minister of Canada. Both Mr. Harper and Stockwell Day, his predecessor as Alliance Leader, are far more comfortable with American ideas about the state and the economy than they are with Tory ideas.[*]

For a view of Harper and the Alliance from the other side of the political spectrum, here's Robert Fulford:

> Mr. Harper has sometimes yearned in public for the chance to emulate the politics of Margaret Thatcher or Ronald Reagan.
>
> When Mr. Manning retired recently, even those who disagreed with his policies felt called upon to praise his integrity and leadership. In their eagerness to salute him, they failed to notice the major accomplishment of his political life: He made himself Jean Chrétien's and the Liberal Party's best friend by destroying the Progressive Conservatives. He replaced our frail alternative national party with no alternative party at all.[†]

Harper as prime minister? He is the man who, when leader of the extreme-right-wing and secretive National Citizens' Coalition, wrote:

> It is time to look at Quebec . . . and to learn. What Albertans should take from this example is to become *maîtres chez nous*.
>
> Such a strategy across a range of policy areas will quickly put Alberta on the cutting edge of a world where the region, the continent and the globe are becoming more important than the nation state.

In his first major speech in the House of Commons since becoming leader of the Alliance, Harper presented the most pro-American agenda since Brian Mulroney, from whom we have "much to learn." For Harper, if you can possibly imagine, the Chrétien government has been "anti-

---

[*] *Globe and Mail*, April 9, 2002.
[†] *National Post*, March 21, 2002.

American" and we now need to cozy up to the U.S. It boggles the mind.[*]

I'll leave the last word on Stephen Harper and the Alliance to an immigrant from the U.S. now living in Ottawa:

> I came to Canada because of its strong commitment to gun control, the rule of law, healthcare, a woman's right to choose and because of its abolition of the death penalty. These positions aren't unique in Canada, but they're unique in North America.
>
> The more that people like Canadian Alliance leader Stephen Harper would have Canada emulate the United States, the less attractive the country would seem to people like me. I've already lived his vision, and it's no vision at all.[†]

A distinctive hallmark of the Canadian Conservative Party has been its respect for tradition combined with a love of country. That all changed with the election of Brian Mulroney in 1984. Tradition was abandoned and love of country was subjugated to love of corporate control. Of all the off-the-wall claims made about free trade, it would be difficult to top Mulroney's assertion that "the free trade agreement has been a strong instrument of Canadianization" which has strengthened our sovereignty.[**]

For John Crosbie, the Mulroney minister who somehow helped negotiated the Free Trade Agreement but admitted that he never read it, economic union with the U.S. is now inevitable. And political union might very well follow.

The Conservatives, who established the CBC, subsidized the construction of the Canadian Pacific Railway, developed the publicly owned Ontario Hydro, and produced numerous nation-building policies from the days of John A. Macdonald through to the early Diefenbaker years, are now but a pale shadow of the old party.

In the very best of the long-term Tory tradition was Dalton Camp. Camp was a rare combination of a brilliant analytical mind, a lifetime of

---

[*] A May 2002 Ekos poll showed that only 12 per cent of Canadians wanted Canada to become more like the United States, but almost twice as many Alliance supporters agreed.

[†] Letter to the *Globe and Mail*, April 11, 2002, from V. Guihan.

[**] *National Post*, May 29, 1999.

hands-on political experience, a man with an excellent grasp of history, a wealth of knowledge from decades of remarkably eclectic reading, and, perhaps best of all, he was a truly marvellous writer, a superb, witty stylist. In a long obituary piece, Andrew Duffy nicely evoked the extraordinary Dalton Camp by using a quote from Camp's own 1995 book *Whose Country Is This Anyway?*

> It seems to me a mistake to call neo-conservatism anything other than the enemy of the society those of my generation built over the years since the war. As a Tory Canadian, neo-conservatism is as alien to me as Marxism or fascism or dadaism. It rejects the idea of Canada and the ideals that have, for so long, been the inspiration for the kind of society that has become a political wonder of the world.

The Progressive Conservative Party of today has no chance of returning to power for as far as we can see into the future. And one of the main reasons is that it has abandoned the traditions of Canada that so strongly appealed to so many millions of Canadians for so many generations. As for Joe Clark, according to columnist Bill Johnson,

> Mr. Clark still repudiates the Clarity Act that sets conditions for Quebec's secession. He still pursues a Faustian bargain with Quebec nationalists such as the one that made, then unmade Mr. Mulroney.*

Surely the Conservatives, if they hope to do better in the future, must find themselves a new leader who will guide the party back to its longtime principles instead of someone who wants to make another political deal with separatists.

And what of the NDP, fallen from as a much as one-fifth share of the votes in the 1980s down to half of that or less in recent elections, and now barely clinging to official party status in the House of Commons?

Founded in 1961, the NDP has had an important role to play in Canadian politics, forming provincial governments in British Columbia,

---

* *Globe and Mail*, December 27, 2001. For a more complete description of how Joe Clark is so far out of touch with the goals of the vast majority of Canadians, see Johnson's excellent column in the *Globe and Mail*, July 11, 2002.

Saskatchewan, Manitoba, Ontario, and in the Yukon, as well as being part of a Liberal minority government in Ottawa. Tommy Douglas, probably the most eloquent public speaker in modern Canadian politics, after a successful career as Saskatchewan premier and a crucial role in the evolution of medicare, became the NDP's first leader and held the post until 1971.

Perhaps the best days for the federal NDP were when, led by David Lewis, they were part of the Trudeau minority government of 1972–74, and were influential in pushing the Liberals into enacting or promising old age pension increases, the Foreign Investment Review Agency, and important steps towards electoral reform that for the first time began to shed some light on political financing.

But their prospects for the future? The misadventures of the party when in government in B.C., their abrupt defeat in Ontario, the terrible disappointment of Ed Broadbent's leadership during the crucial 1988 free trade election, and disappointing leadership in recent years, not to mention the antics of Svend Robinson, have all served to disillusion many long-time supporters and have turned off potential new ones.

While the NDP searches for a replacement for Alexa McDonough, activists on the left of the party are promoting a "New Politics Initiative" that will take the party in a more radical direction. The NPI has no constitution, no constituency organizations, no candidates, and no plans to contest the next federal election in 2004 or 2005.

Some good friends in the NDP suggest that with a new leader (Bill Blaikie? Jack Layton?), the last thing the party needs will be a far-left breakaway group to split the vote. Others say that if Svend Robinson continues to play a prominent role, they'll have no part of the NPI. Still others say that the NDP's traditional trade union financial support will be split between the two competing groups. As for trade-union voting support, outside of Quebec, more than twice as many unionists voted for the Alliance as for the NDP.

I'll leave the last words on the NPI to James Laxer, a former power in the NDP:

> Unfortunately, beyond its insistence on participatory democracy, the NPI vision is a murky one . . . without the necessary coherence . . . to fashion a political party.

The NPI is obsessed with decentralization. The enthusiasm ... for localism is eerily similar to the distaste for strong government that is so much in evidence among neo-liberals and the reactionary chic.

The further dismantling of the Canadian state and the enhancement of localism opens the way for real power to be exercised by global corporations and the United States. This is precisely what the left should oppose.

The NPI vision statement is so tepid on the issue of the American domination of Canada that half of the members of the Liberal caucus in Ottawa could easily sign off on it.

The NDP needs to put itself through a process of fundamental change that may lead to the launching of a new party. The New Politics Initiative should be welcomed as contributing to the debate. Unfortunately, the NPI does not provide a road map to guide the left through the difficult terrain that lies ahead.*

I have great respect for some of those involved in the NPI, Jim Stanford and Duncan Cameron in particular, but unless they and others quickly assume greater leadership in the organization, I am very sceptical about its potential impact on the future of our country.

The Third Thing That Must Happen If Canada Is to Survive

So, in view of all of this, what are we left with? Who is it that is going to be standing on guard for Canada? Perhaps there are other viable solutions. I wish there were, but I know of only one.

In a Canadian Club speech in January, 2001, Frank Graves said:

Despite clear dissatisfaction with the *status quo* there is no consensus for movement on the "new right." The "new" right is in fact seen as neither new nor particularly attractive as a mainstream vision for the future of Canada. Minimal government, social conservatism and moralistic government simply aren't selling.

---

* *Globe and Mail*, July 26, 2001.

That said, if the current perception of sleaze in the Liberal government persists, won't support for the Alliance improve?

An Alliance government wouldn't be the last nail in the Canadian coffin, it would be the final shovel of earth filling in the grave. Let's hope Stephen Harper continues to make stupid speeches offending the Atlantic provinces, Quebec, and the Prairies, as he did in May shortly after he returned to the House of Commons.

Ekos has also shown, "the plurality of the Canadian public pick 'neither' when asked to choose between small 'l' liberal or small 'c' conservatives." However,

> The declining affiliation with political ideologies is not shared by Canada's decision-making elites who are decidedly more ideological than the public.

And *decidedly* more right-wing. As we've also seen, in poll after poll most Canadians reject the radical right Americanizing policies of our decision-making elites.

So, let's see. If voters are turned off and view politicians with disdain or contempt, and more and more of them say in poll after poll "none of the above," what then? If voters are fed up with political sleaze and corruption, where will they be able to turn in the two crucial federal elections in this pivotal decade that will surely determine if there is to be a future of our country?

And, if the polls also show most Canadians are strongly opposed to the continuing sellout of our country,[*] where can the majority of Canadians turn if they love their country and want to see it survive? In Peter C. Newman's words:

> By year's end, it is clear that the Canadian debate of 2002 and the election that will follow two years later, will be the stark choice between total economic and eventually, political integration with the United States, or holding on to what remains of our political independence – and fighting for more.

---

[*] A 2000 Ipsos-Reid poll showed that three in five Canadians say that they are "angry that the federal government is not doing more to stop U.S. and other foreign corporations from buying up Canadian-owned companies."

Let us hope that this choice will be available. But, the vital question that must follow is exactly *who* will be doing the debating, and what choice will voters who want Canada to survive have?

The third thing that has to happen if Canada is going to survive is the formation of a new political party dedicated to Canadian independence and to true democracy.

In the next chapters I'll describe the one thing that could capture the huge undercurrent of potential political energy that exists across the country, and make the new party a success. First, several points.

A new party could be successful because a huge political vacuum exists now in Canada.

It could be a success because most Canadians who love their country don't know where to turn.

It could be successful not by trying to attract its membership from existing parties, but by turning on to politics the overwhelming majority of Canadians who have no political affiliation.[*]

What are the chances of a new political party forming the federal government in the near future?

They are none.

What are the chances of a new political party holding the balance of power in a minority government similar to the situation in the House of Commons thirty years ago?

It's a possibility, but the chances must be considered slim.

So, what's the use of forming a new political party? The answer is that there is no other alternative, and with a truly democratic platform, it could be successful before the country is doomed forever.

Even if the chances for success appear remote today, it must be worth a try. Look, for example, at the meteoric rise in the popularity in Quebec of Mario Dumont's Action Démocratique, mostly because of the dissatisfaction with the other parties that have long ruled the province.

Is it going to be difficult to start a new party?

Terribly.

Is all the effort that's going to be necessary likely to fail?

Quite possibly.

---

[*] A 2002 study by Mount Allison University political scientist William Corss showed that 98 per cent of eligible voters in Canada did not belong to any federal party.

Far too many Canadians, including far too many Canadian nationalists, say it's already too late. I say to heck with that. Even if the chances are slim, a new party is worth the try. And nothing else should be more important. It's the single most essential thing that must happen if Canada is to survive as an independent country.

I view with a mixture of sadness and disdain those Canadians who say it's too late to save our country and I view with even more dismay the activists who don't understand that politics and power are intrinsically linked. The cross-Canada effort devoted today to civil society groups, properly politically organized, could overthrow a government in a federal election.

No doubt some will think I am suggesting a new party as a personal political vehicle for myself. Wrong. A new party will need new young leaders. If I am asked, I will certainly help to the best of my ability, but the leadership for a new party will have to come from elsewhere. I will be happy to tell them about the many good things that happened in the National Party, and the crucial mistakes that must be avoided. To begin with, a democratic, bottom-up constitution will be essential, as will be tough limits on financial contributions.

Michael Valpy has put it well:

> We need to hear words, visions, concepts of why it remains important – if it does – to hold together this society on the northern half of a continent.
>
> The country and its needs have tumbled beyond the prime minister's intellectual and rhetorical grasp.[*]

And, after eighteen years of Mulroney and Chrétien governments, beyond the grasp of the country's current political leadership.

---

[*] *Globe and Mail*, December 29, 2001.

Making a Mockery of Democracy

Aside from regaining Canada's ability to manage its own affairs, what should a new political party stand for?

The answer can be summed up in two words – true democracy. Political reform should be at the top of the party policy list, reform at all levels of politics.

Here are some of the things a new party should campaign for:

- Total transparency at *all* levels of political financing: party, constituency, candidate, leadership, trust funds, election and non-election funding. Every penny of every donation must be reported and made public on a monthly basis. There is no reason why this cannot be done. Reporting political donations well after the fact is simply not good enough.
- Donations from corporations and trade unions should be banned. Corporations and trade unions can't vote, why should they be allowed to play such a dominant role in our electoral process? Many countries plus Quebec and Manitoba have banned corporate and union donations. All Canadian governments should do the same.
- Donations from non-Canadians, direct or indirect, should be banned.
- All government contracts should be put out to tender and awarded on the basis of merit. An appointed all-party citizens committee should be charged with assisting the Auditor General's scrutiny of government contracts.
- Additional funds should be allocated to the offices of the Auditor General so that they can better perform their responsibilities.
- Strict limits should be placed on political donations at all levels. The limits should apply to the total amounts that can be donated and to the total amounts that can be spent. The limits should allow for voter support to be properly reflected in the electoral process, but not so excessive spending can distort elections.

Why was the voter turnout so terribly low in the last federal election?

Between 1945 and 1988, over 75 per cent of those who were eligible voted. In 1988, 75.3 per cent cast their ballot. In 2000, it was down to just over 63 per cent, the lowest turnout in almost 70 years.[*] Only 39 per cent of eighteen-to-twenty-four-year-old eligible voters bothered to vote.

A Centre for Research and Information on Canada study says that among the reasons that voter turnout fell so sharply in 2000 was that 37 per cent of those surveyed said they didn't vote either because the election didn't matter or they felt they had no one to vote for.

> The problem lies with the way the political system is working. The point here is not that citizens have changed, but that the political system is perceived to be less and less responsive to people's concerns.[†]

What does that say about democracy in Canada?

In a United Nations list of 179 countries, when voter turnout as a percentage of eligible voters is measured, in the most recent federal election Canada is down in 93rd place. (The U.S. is number 134).

Is it any wonder that voter turnout was so low in 2000? In a Léger Marketing Poll, when asked which occupation people trusted, politicians were at the very bottom behind car salespeople and a long list of other professions. Fewer than one in five Canadians said that they trusted politicians. In another poll, 70 per cent said they felt disconnected from government. When asked why they didn't vote, many responded "My vote doesn't really matter" or "There is no political party that I agree with." In another poll, 73 per cent said that government in Canada has lost sight of the needs of average Canadians.[**]

Frank Graves and Ekos have shown that, whereas in 1960, 80 per cent of Canadians surveyed said that they trusted government to "do the right thing," in the most recent poll that number has plunged to only 30 per cent.

In *Maclean's* 2000 year-end poll, when asked "In the past year, has your opinion of Canadian politicians improved or decreased?" 50 per cent said that it had decreased and only 8 per cent said that it had improved.

Without question, the patronage and scandals of the Mulroney government helped turn many Canadians against politicians. The

---

[*] This updated figure is correct. Previous reports of somewhat smaller percentages are incorrect. The highest voter turnout in the U.S. in the past 72 years was 62.8 per cent in the Kennedy vs. Nixon 1961 election.

[†] *Edmonton Journal*, January 2, 2002.

[**] Ekos, 2000.

dismal ethics of the Chrétien government have made matters worse. In the most recent poll, 70 per cent said that they believed that politicians are corrupt.[*]

People say voters are cynical about politics and politicians and that's why they don't vote. But, why shouldn't people be cynical given the long list of broken promises, the political slush funds, the colossal waste of taxpayers' money, the prevalent perception that big money from big business calls the shots, the pork and patronage, and the lack of transparency?

Were there ever better Canadian examples of the old maxim that power corrupts than the eighteen years of Mulroney and Chrétien government?

In his 1983 leadership campaign, Brian Mulroney promised that he would oppose free trade. Ten years later, Jean Chrétien promised he would renegotiate NAFTA and if that was impossible he would walk away from the agreement. Both Mulroney and Chrétien made numerous other promises that they quickly forgot. Chrétien, for example, promised an independent ethics commissioner who would report directly to Parliament, an ethical renaissance in government, and swore to increase foreign aid for poor countries. Paul Martin, for over ten years, has repeatedly promised that he would take steps to significantly reduce child poverty. Allan Gregg describes what has happened. There has been

> a wholesale loss of faith in politicians and the political process. Where once prime ministers and members of parliament were venerated, they became the source of jokes or disdain. Where once the electorate looked to government as the arbitrator and often the main provider of the public good, it now associates the state with waste, inefficiency and ineffectiveness.

Most Canadians would agree with this analysis, yet

> The fact is that, no matter how some may try to persuade us otherwise, the state has power. Only through the state can we allocate society's scarce resources. The state and government are not "them," they are "us." When we lose sight of or chose to ignore this fundamental tenet,

---

[*] Léger Marketing, 2002.

we lose our capacity towards the ultimate ethical goal – namely, generating the largest good for the greatest number. We lose, in effect, a free and democratic society.[*]

Unfortunately, far too many Canadians don't seem to understand this, including some of our most prominent "civil society" activists.

Democracy in Canada today is a travesty of what it is intended to be. Voters are turned-off and cynical, revolted by political sleaze, pork barrel, patronage, the stench and scandals of corruption and taxpayer money being squandered by arrogant, inept politicians.

Common-sense rules and ethics that should apply to leadership selection, party financing, and government transparency are either non-existent or close to meaningless. The Liberal government ignores the excellent reports of Jean-Pierre Kingsley, the Chief Electoral Officer and tells him that some of his most important recommendations for reform are none of his business. Meanwhile, Liberal leadership candidates and their staff gather funds from big business donors, who already have or can anticipate large contracts from the government.

Canada badly needs a new, well-balanced Royal Commission on democracy. Here are some of the things the Commission should consider:

- Should Canada move to a system of proportional representation? There are only three major Western democracies that still employ the first-past-post electoral system, and two of them (the U.S. and the U.K.) are either two-party countries or close to being one. Over 70 countries now employ some form of proportional representation.
- In 1993, the Conservative Party captured more votes than the Bloc Québécois and close to as many as the Reform Party, but the Bloc won 54 seats, the Reform 52 and the Conservatives only two. Do we want to continue under such a distorting electoral system?
- In a proportional representation system, should it be a mixed-member system so that half of the MPs are elected by constituency and the other half on the basis of the national percentage of the vote the party receives? Should we look at the idea that each constituency has two MPs, one elected via the existing system, the other appointed on the basis of the national vote percentages?

---

[*] *Maclean's*, April 8, 2002.

- Canada is 14th in the world in terms of the number of females in our legislatures (24 per cent). Should we not encourage more equal representation of women? If so, how? At the extreme, should we have two MPs elected from each constituency; in one contest it would be all male, in the other all female? Alternately, in any list of those to be selected based on proportional representation, parties could see that half of those on their lists are women whose names are alternated on the list with men's names.[*]

- What about fixed terms for parliament? The Australian system of elections every three years is popular. Should Canada opt for every three years or perhaps every four years? Quebec is now considering fixed terms and proportional representation.

- Instead of proportional representation, would a preferential ballot system work better, where voters ranked their preferences in order and if no candidate received over fifty per cent then second and if necessary other choices would be added until a majority is achieved?

- In any new proportional representation system, should there be a required voter threshold? In some countries, parties with only 1.5 per cent of the vote get representation. In others it's 4 or 5 per cent.

- Should voting in federal elections be compulsory? In their most recent elections, over 95 per cent of Australians and over 90 per cent of Belgians voted. Both countries have statutory obligations to vote, and penalties. There are few complaints. 18 other democracies have compulsory voting. Australia's goes back to 1924.

- Should we get rid of the Senate and replace it with more elected MPs? Among other things, this would help us resolve the parliamentary imbalance that badly detracts from the principles of one voter/one vote and allow us far more equitable representation based on regional population.

- Admittedly this would require major constitutional amendments, but it definitely deserves consideration in our attempts to improve our democracy.

- Shouldn't we have a good national debate about the Senate and then

---

[*] Sweden has such a "zipper list" and about 45 per cent women in their national legislature. In France's relatively recent parity system, one-half of all candidates must be women, otherwise financial penalties are applied to state financing of the parties. In the last French municipal elections, 47.5 per cent of those elected were women, up from 28 per cent.

put the question of abolition to Canadians in a referendum to be held in conjunction with a federal election?

- More MPs would make a mixed-member proportional voting system easier to implement.
- Should we have a political system where it takes millions of dollars to run for party leadership? And where every year it takes more and more money? Shouldn't all leadership candidates have to disclose every donation received, on a weekly basis in advance of the leadership election?
- At the present time, no law exists to compel leadership candidates to disclose the sources of their donations or relating to the timing of the disclosure. Should federal legislation cover leadership finance rules, including all aspects of funding? The current system invites rule-breaking which has become the norm. In 1984 Brian Mulroney ousted Joe Clark with the help of unreported German money which was used to send Quebec delegates to the convention in Winnipeg, even though such funding broke Canadian laws.
- If we ban corporate and union donations, should we take some of the money that has gone for donation tax write offs and make some of it available for candidate advertising during election campaigns?

Money buys access. It buys influence. It buys involvement in the decision-making process. It buys homage from politicians and their senior civil servants. Most of all, it buys power. And frequently it buys money flowing back from the public purse, favourable government decisions and large government contracts.[*]

---

[*] When I was a member of the Liberal Party from 1967 to 1973, we spent at least half of our closed-door meetings talking about which law firm should be given government mortgage contracts, which architects should get which new government buildings, which engineering firms would get assignments, which car dealers would be able to sell cars to the RCMP, which accounting firms should be added to the patronage list, etc. and etc. and etc. If anything, the situation during the Mulroney years was worse, and under Chrétien probably worse still. Merit had little to do with the awarding of most contracts; deep pockets had a lot. And the deeper the pockets, the quicker they were filled with taxpayer money from Ottawa. In today's papers, a headline about law firms reads "Big donors win big contracts."

Call it kickbacks or patronage or sleaze, whatever you like, the system smells to high heaven and corrupts the democratic process. Both Brian Mulroney and Jean Chrétien, campaigning to become prime minister, promised to reform patronage. And they reformed it by increasing it and cementing in its practice.

- Should legislation set limits on political contributions? Canada's Chief Electoral Officer has suggested that no voter be allowed to donate more than $50,000 in a year to a single party, and no more than $7,500 to all riding associations of a party. Is $50,000 too high a figure? Is $10,000 likely to be fairer?[*] According to Michael Adams of Environics, "There are many reasons for the decline in voter participation, but the major one is that money has replaced votes as the most important political currency."
- Should we outlaw all anonymous political donations? And donations from associations such as American-style PACS (political action committees) which are set up to get around election laws?
- If we don't decide to end corporate donations, should we rule out donations from numbered companies? In recent years the Liberals, Conservatives and the Alliance have all received and receipted for tax purposes six-figure donations from numbered companies.
- Should it be an offence to make a political financial donation where no record is kept of the donation and no official receipt is issued?
- Should "third party" participation in federal elections be allowed, but limited to avoid the sort of big-business, big dollar intervention that occurred in the 1988 "free trade" election?
- To compensate for stricter election spending limits, shouldn't we make it mandatory for television and radio to supply more free time to candidates during a federal election?
- And why not have the Chief Electoral Officer begin plans for local internet sites where the candidates and parties could set out their views and update them as required during an election campaign?
- Should we also ask newspapers to guarantee local candidates a certain amount of free or low cost space during a campaign?
- Don't we badly need more detailed and precise conflict of interest and ethical behaviour rules which should apply to the prime minister, the cabinet, all members of parliament, and all parliamentary staff and civil servants? In many other countries a prime minister or president would never have survived something as sleazy as Shawinigate.
- Should we not make it an offence for cabinet ministers' staff to work

---

[*] Manitoba limits individual donations to $3,000, but provincial campaigns cost much less than federal campaigns.

on leadership or constituency campaigns while they are on the federal payroll? (See Allan Rock as but one example.)

- Should we forbid persons who have business contracts with government from acting as fundraisers for cabinet ministers? (See, among others, Sheila Copps and Paul Martin).
- What's the best way to strengthen our legislation regarding lobbying and lobbyists? Should we be concerned that BCE and Bell Canada, for example, have fifteen well-paid lobbyists registered in Ottawa, ten of them lobbying the PMO? Is it possible that they're only trying to sell their shares in Teleglobe, or might they have other corporate goals in mind?
- Should we allow situations whereby lobbyists such as the Earnscliffe Group receive millions of dollars in government contracts and then work on the leadership campaigns of the minister whose department doled out the contracts? (See Paul Martin and John Manley, among others.)
- Should we require cabinet ministers and public officials to report weekly the details of any contacts with lobbyists and prohibit lobbyists from obtaining government contracts for themselves or for their firms?
- Should we eliminate corporate tax deductions for lobbying expenses?

A Canadian prime minister heading a majority government, even if the party won less than 40 per cent of the vote, as Chrétien did in 1997, becomes all-powerful, more powerful than the elected head of any other democracy, and *far* more powerful than most. The present overwhelming dominance of the prime minister and the PMO makes a mockery of democracy.

- How can we take steps to ensure more free votes in the House of Commons and in parliamentary committees? What can we do to loosen the iron-bound party discipline and the squashing of dissent that has been prevalent during the Chrétien years? And, how can we see that private members' bills receive better consideration?

    Back in 1993, the Liberals promised more free votes and more authority for parliamentary committees. More broken promises. A 2001 Public Policy Forum survey of senior corporation executives and top federal bureaucrats showed that only 12 per cent believed that members of Parliament have a significant to moderate influence on decision making, compared to 60 per cent who felt that the Prime Minister's staff were influential. Shouldn't Commons committee chairs be chosen by secret ballot?

- Shouldn't all-party committees of the House of Commons be given the authority to examine, approve or reject key federal appointments including the heads of crown corporations, the CBC, the CRTC, the RCMP, the Bank of Canada, and ambassadorial appointments where the government wishes to make such appointments outside the professional ranks of the diplomatic service? Do we need more appointments like Gagliano and Marchi?

- What about the long-established corrupt business of busing in "instant members" to nominating and other political meetings? Should voters at such meetings be required to be party members for at least thirty days before they are eligible to vote? Should it be illegal to pay for someone else's party membership?

- Shouldn't a minimum voting age of eighteen apply to not only federal elections but to constituency candidate selection and party leadership votes?

- Shouldn't only Canadian citizens be allowed to participate in constituency candidate selection, party leadership votes as well as federal election voting?

- Would we be better off returning to door-to-door enumeration before a federal election, rather than relying on a permanent voters list?

- Don't we badly need an independent ethics commissioner who reports only to the House of Commons and who is selected by an all-party committee of the House?

- Shouldn't federal government advertising be restricted and closely monitored by the ethics commissioner and the auditor general?

- Don't we badly need vastly improved freedom of information legislation?

Obviously I have sketched out these proposals with little detail. But the intent of every one of them is to make Canada a far more democratic country and to help restore voter confidence in politics, our politicians and the political system.

Successive federal governments blatantly ignored the many excellent recommendations in the 1991 Lortie Royal Commission on Electoral

Reform and Party Financing. We urgently need a new Royal Commission and a new political party 100-per-cent dedicated to genuine democratic reform.

I have my own strong opinions on all of these points, but each and every one is debatable. I doubt, for example, that the NDP would ever support banning trade-union donations or that Stephen Harper and the Alliance would ever support limiting donations or third-party participation in election campaigns. Despite requests to do so, Harper has refused to disclose the donors to his own leadership campaign and his National Citizen's Coalition has always refused to disclose their funders. What we need is a first-class reincarnation of the Lortie Commission, extensive public hearings across the country, and a government firmly committed to democratic reform. Let the political parties battle it out once the Royal Commission publishes its report.

And the new political party that I am suggesting should be at the forefront of the debate on political reform. Then let's see who the public would support.

The saddest reflections of what has happened to our political system and to democracy in Canada can be found in the following:

- Over 80 per cent of adult Canadians have never belonged to any political party.
- In the last federal election, only 1.9 per cent of electors made a donation to any political party.
- In an average year, only about 2 per cent of adult Canadians are active in any political party.

The fourth thing that must happen if Canada is to survive is a radical reform of our political system to make it *much* more democratic.

Perhaps a new party might be able to convince Canadians that they should try to not only regain economic and social control of our country, but that an essential step in doing so would be to substantially strengthen our withering democracy. I cannot see why a well-organized campaign for democratic reform could fail. In the face of all the overwhelming odds against our survival as an independent country, true democracy is the one indomitable force that could stop the sellout.

A very worried Jean Chrétien will introduce some political reforms in his fall 2002 Throne Speech. If these new suggested reforms are similar to the half-measure, full of loophole changes that he introduced in June, the results will be as deficient and as relatively meaningless. Paul Martin is now making speeches about political reform. Where has he been on this important issue for the last nine years, and why has he been so reluctant to disclose his own political funding sources?

Let's Take Back Our Country

In November of 1988, the American actor Martin Sheen had this to say in Vancouver:

> I come from a land of lunatics. When I come to Canada, I see a country that represents the way it is possible to live. We've been tied together as nations for a long time on a long, loose rope. You shorten the rope by the free trade deal and we can hang you with it . . . you aren't our equal partner and never will be.
>
> We are an empire. And we are an aggressive nation. America doesn't want Canada as an equal partner. America wants to control you.
>
> Everything you are as a Canadian, you will lose to Americanism. If I was a Canadian citizen with a heart and a mind of my own, I would reject the free trade deal.[*]

With much more integration, the much proclaimed "inevitable" will indeed become inevitable. As more and more decisions about Canadian standards, procedures and social and economic policies are levelled to American standards and policies, then the next certain step will be a campaign by our Americanizers for political representation in Washington. You can already anticipate what they will be saying: "After all, if so many of the key decisions about our future are being made in the U.S., wouldn't we be a lot better off if we had some Canadians in the House of Representatives and in the U.S. Senate?"

But the salesmen of our nation who brought us the FTA and NAFTA, and who are already thinking of political union are hopelessly naive.

---

[*] *Vancouver Sun*, November 5, 1998.

Why would the American Republican Party want over 20 million adult Canadians, most of whom would likely vote Democrat? Better, they will say, Canada should be a northern Puerto Rico, a servile, non-represented, non-voting colony. And anyway, they will say, we're already well on our way to owning the whole country. Ekos research Associates put it well:

> The overall forces and patterns point to a closing window of opportunity to avoid or forestall North-American integration. There is a growing acceptance and recognition of this conclusion, but most Canadians have avoided an explicit consideration of the real issues.

Most Canadians better not avoid such consideration any longer or they will soon find that it's too late for them to have a choice in the matter. At the end of my 1996 memoir, I wrote:

> Perhaps Canada will not disappear. Perhaps there will still be maps with a different colour on the top half of the North American continent. There could even still be a Maple Leaf flag. But the nation we are now in the process of becoming will be a nation essentially in name only – an economic, social, political and cultural colony, a place not a country, a feeble remnant of a once proud nation.

Are we going to allow this to happen?

I fully recognize that in places this is a harsh and angry book. But, if now, as our country is being sold out and our national soul is being squashed, is not a time for harsh words and anger, when will it be? Is our strategy for national survival to conduct a polite academic discussion with those who are trying to stampede us towards obliteration?

Is the best we Canadians can aspire to a vassal state? Or do we care enough to want to reclaim Canada for Canadians? For our children and for our grandchildren.

The *National Post*'s astute columnist Roy MacGregor commented on the quickly forgotten Spicer Commission, the Citizen's Forum on Canada's Future:

> People, it turned out, felt helpless. They felt they had no say whatsoever, that they were outside the loop and were never going to be allowed in.

They had come to the conclusion, correctly, that Canada was in the grasp of an elite that believed that they alone knew what was best for ordinary Canadians.

The media howled with laughter at the presumptuousness of the ordinary Canadians . . . The media, of course, was every much a part of that elite.[*]

And the media will surely howl with laughter at the idea of abrogating the FTA and NAFTA and at the idea of a new political party.

Pay no attention. We have an important advantage.

We've already seen many times in this book how Canadians feel about our eroding sovereignty. In November, 2001, a Canadian Council on National Unity poll showed that two-thirds of Canadians felt that maintaining the sovereignty of Canada is the most important challenge now facing our country.

Since most Canadians feel this way, might there then be enough of them prepared to go to work to reclaim our country before its too late?

Earlier, I wrote about an "indomitable force" that could potentially stop the sellout of Canada, and also "a flood of determination" and "a collective national purpose." Democracy can be an indomitable force. Poll after poll after poll, year after year after year, shows that most Canadians, by far, oppose the policies of our sellouts. Our collective national purpose should be taking back our own country. A flood of determination can swamp the radical right, who are abandoning our country for their own personal gain.

What's the big advantage we have? It's the fact that there are many, many millions more proud Canadians who love their country than there are Americanizers who couldn't care less if Canada survives.

It's pretty hard to top Dalton Camp when it comes to summing up what has gone wrong in politics in Canada:

> I cannot remember a time – since the last war – when the political community has been so out of touch with the public that elects them and pays their keep. This estrangement is the most ominous when it becomes clear the politicians have abandoned their constituents to seek the indulgence of the rich and famous. It does seem to me, listening to

---

[*] *National Post*, January 19, 2002.

the Tories and the Liberals and the Reformists, that they are really working for the Business Council on National Issues by day and selling subscriptions to the Wall Street Journal by night.

We seem to have lost the spirit and meaning of representative democracy.[*]

Most of our politicians have indeed been out of touch with the wishes of most Canadians. It's time for a new political party to unite the population with a campaign stressing the marvellous benefits of true democracy and all the bountiful opportunities that the freedom to make our own decisions about our own future will bring.

In the introduction to this book, I said that ultimately there are only two questions. Do you or do you not care about the survival of Canada? And if you do care, what *are* you going to do about the fact that our country is vanishing so rapidly? Is the best you aspire to being a tenant in what should have been your own country, a squatter, or are you willing to get involved to help save your country? In other countries around the world crowds would be filling the streets and storming Parliament if their country was being sold out the way Canada is.

In this book I am not suggesting storming Parliament, except in a democratic way. Let's fill the streets and meeting halls with well-organized voters who love their country and care deeply about its future. Let's never, never give in to those who are selling out Canada.

Perhaps we will fail. But an ever greater failure will be if we don't even try. What a terrible tragedy that would be.

Mel Hurtig
Edmonton
June 2002
mhurtig@telusplanet.net

---

[*] *Toronto Star*, October 3, 1999.